**Chapter 10 Correlation**

$$r = \frac{N(\Sigma XY) - (\Sigma X)(\Sigma Y)}{\sqrt{[N(\Sigma X^2) - (\Sigma X)^2][N(\Sigma Y^2) - (\Sigma Y)^2]}}$$

$$df = N - 2$$

Proportion of variance accounted for $= r^2$

**Chapter 11 One-Way ANOVA**

$$SS_{\text{tot}} = \Sigma X^2_{\text{tot}} - \left(\frac{(\Sigma X_{\text{tot}})^2}{N}\right)$$

$$SS_{\text{bn}} = \Sigma\left(\frac{(\Sigma X \text{ in column})^2}{n \text{ in column}}\right) - \left(\frac{(\Sigma X_{\text{tot}})^2}{N}\right)$$

$$SS_{\text{wn}} = SS_{\text{tot}} - SS_{\text{bn}}$$

$$df_{\text{bn}} = k - 1$$

$$df_{\text{wn}} = N - k$$

$$MS_{\text{bn}} = \frac{SS_{\text{bn}}}{df_{\text{bn}}}$$

$$MS_{\text{wn}} = \frac{SS_{\text{wn}}}{df_{\text{wn}}}$$

$$F_{\text{obt}} = \frac{MS_{\text{bn}}}{MS_{\text{wn}}}$$

$$HSD = (q_k)\left(\sqrt{\frac{MS_{\text{wn}}}{n}}\right)$$

$$\eta^2 = \frac{SS_{\text{bn}}}{SS_{\text{tot}}}$$

**Chapter 13 Nonparametric Tests**

$$\chi^2_{\text{obt}} = \Sigma\left(\frac{(f_o - f_e)^2}{f_e}\right)$$

$$f_e = \frac{N}{k}$$

$$df = k - 1$$

or

$$f_e = \frac{(\text{Cell's row total } f_o)(\text{Cell's column total } f_o)}{N}$$

$$df = (\text{Number of rows} - 1)(\text{Number of columns} - 1)$$

$$\phi = \sqrt{\frac{\chi^2_{\text{obt}}}{N}}$$

$$C = \sqrt{\frac{\chi^2_{\text{obt}}}{N + \chi^2_{\text{obt}}}}$$

# List of Symbols

## Chapter 2

| | |
|---|---|
| $N$ | number of scores in the data |
| $f$ | frequency |

## Chapter 3

| | |
|---|---|
| $\Sigma X$ | sum of $X$ |
| Mdn | median |
| $\overline{X}$ | sample mean of $X$s |
| $X - \overline{X}$ | deviation |
| $\mu$ | mu; population mean |
| $\Sigma(X - \overline{X})$ | sum of deviations around the mean |

## Chapter 4

| | |
|---|---|
| $\Sigma X^2$ | sum of squared $X$s |
| $(\Sigma X)^2$ | squared sum of $X$s |
| $S_X$ | sample standard deviation |
| $S_X^2$ | sample variance |
| $\sigma_X$ | population standard deviation |
| $\sigma_X^2$ | population variance |
| $s_X$ | estimated population standard deviation |
| $s_X^2$ | estimated population variance |

## Chapter 5

| | |
|---|---|
| $\pm$ | plus or minus |
| $z$ | $z$-score |
| $\sigma_{\overline{X}}$ | standard error of the mean |

## Chapter 6

| | |
|---|---|
| $p$ | probability |

## Chapter 7

| | |
|---|---|
| $>$ | greater than |
| $<$ | less than |
| $\geq$ | greater than or equal to |
| $\leq$ | less than or equal to |
| $\neq$ | not equal to |
| $H_a$ | alternative hypothesis |
| $H_0$ | null hypothesis |
| $z_{obt}$ | obtained value of $z$-test |
| $z_{crit}$ | critical value of $z$-test |
| $\alpha$ | alpha; theoretical probability of a Type I error |

## Chapter 8

| | |
|---|---|
| $t_{obt}$ | obtained value in $t$-test |
| $t_{crit}$ | critical value of $t$-test |
| $s_{\overline{X}}$ | estimated standard error of the mean |
| $df$ | degrees of freedom |

## Chapter 9

| | |
|---|---|
| $n$ | number of scores in each sample |
| $s^2_{pool}$ | pooled variance |
| $s_{\overline{X}_1 - \overline{X}_2}$ | standard error of the difference |
| $\overline{D}$ | mean of difference scores |
| $\mu_D$ | mean of population of difference scores |
| $s_D^2$ | estimated variance of population of difference scores |
| $s_{\overline{D}}$ | standard error of the mean difference |
| $r^2_{pb}$ | effect size in a two-sample experiment |

# ESSENTIAL STATISTICS FOR THE BEHAVIORAL SCIENCES

Gary W. Heiman

**Buffalo State College**

**HOUGHTON MIFFLIN COMPANY  Boston  New York**

**For my wife, Karen, a beauty and a joy forever.**

Publisher: Charles Hartford
Senior Sponsoring Editor: Kerry T. Baruth
Senior Developmental Editor: Sharon Geary
Senior Project Editor: Margaret Park Bridges
Senior Manufacturing Coordinator: Priscilla Bailey
Senior Marketing Manager: Katherine Greig
Marketing Associate: Anne Tousey

Cover image: © Getty Images



Printed in the U.S.A.

Library of Congress Control Number: 2002109473

Student Text ISBN: 0-618-25200-2

23456789-QUV-10-09-08-07

# Contents

## 11

## Hypothesis Testing Using the One-Way Analysis of Variance 201

## 12

## A Brief Introduction to the Logic of the Two-Way Analysis of Variance 223



## 13

## Chi Square and Nonparametric Procedures 239

# Preface

Many statistics instructors share the problem of too much material to cover in too little time. However, the more that the textbook prepares students, the more that instructors can accomplish. Therefore, this text has two purposes: (1) to present the statistics that undergraduates need for reading the research literature or conducting their own research, and (2) to do so using an understandable approach that can be completed in minimal time. I want my students to be able to *use* and *understand* the common basic statistical procedures, even if they have a weak mathematics background, so I wrote this text to address this need.

Many textbooks include too much material to cover adequately in one semester, especially if the semester is brief or if the course requirements include software or Web-based materials. Statistics are typically presented with a healthy dose of research methods, which transforms the textbook into a reference book of the various statistics that students *might* someday use. (In fact, I'm guilty of writing one of those texts myself.) These more comprehensive texts have their place, but they cater to a different student audience. In this text, however, the discussion is limited to the types of basic statistics that students *do* use. At every step the word "essential" was my guide, to present only the material that is essential for a first course in statistics. Therefore:

- Only the necessary statistical procedures are discussed.
- A minimum of statistical theory and formula manipulation is presented.
- A minimum of research design is presented.

On the other hand, brief texts are often too brief, in that they do not adequately explain or provide proper practice and integration of the material. They seem to dangle a concept before students that we instructors know there is little hope of understanding. In contrast, this text strives to actively *teach* the material. I explain concepts and procedures and integrate them with previous material. Whenever possible, difficult concepts are presented in small chunks, which are then built into a foundation and later elaborated upon. To make the text readable and engaging, I use humor, address students directly, point out potential mistakes, and provide tips on how to get through the course. Many mnemonics and analogies are included to help promote retention and understanding and to provide students with simplified ways to think about statistics.

Of course, no group of instructors will agree on what constitutes the "essential" topics in this course. To allow some flexibility, I have included at the end of some chapters a brief description of additional procedures in sections titled "A Word About. . . ." The goal was to minimize computations, but still allow students to recognize and understand the basic concept when encountered in the literature. However, these discussions are self-contained and can be skipped without affecting later chapters. In addition, I have gone out on a limb by including a nonmathematical discussion of the two-way ANOVA. This is a brief chapter that does not discuss computations (formulas are in the Appendix), but the concepts of collapsing, main effects, and interactions are presented. Multifactor designs are too common to be ignored, and I have found that undergraduates can understand them. Finally, I have placed confidence intervals for two-sample *t*-tests in the Appendix. Although common in most statistics texts, they are not common in the literature.

## FEATURES

The approach of the text is that statistics are used to make sense out of data. Each procedure is introduced using a simple study with readily understandable goals. Examples contain small numbers of scores and require no background in content or research design. I focus on research as examining the relationships between variables with the purpose of statistics being to describe and infer relationships. The text's early examples involve simple variables and research questions, so that students have an intuitive feel for the meaning of the scores and relationships discussed. In later chapters, along with students' developing statistical thinking, examples become more representative of real research. Virtually all examples and study questions involve specific variables and research questions instead of generic data.

I have done everything I can to present the mathematical computations in an understandable, nonthreatening manner. To offset the weaker math skills of some students, I present each procedure using a verbal, nontheoretical approach that focuses on the logic behind the procedure and how researchers use it to draw conclusions about their data. To reduce the apparent complexity of statistics, I stress the similarities among different procedures, showing how, despite slight variations in computations, they have similar components and answer similar questions. Formulas are introduced in terms of what they accomplish, and only one version of each formula is presented. An example of each is then fully explained and worked through in literally a step-by-step manner. In fact, at first glance it may seem that I have oversimplified the computations, until one remembers that the goal is for students to view the calculations as simple.

The more reviews and practice that students receive, the more successful they will be (and the easier the instructor's task). To this end, periodic review sections occur within each chapter. Titled "A Quick Review," each contains a brief review of the previous concepts, more examples, which are worked through, and a few simple review questions. These sections will add to students' understanding and/or point out when they do not understand a topic before proceeding to the next. For the instructor such reviews mean that less class time is needed for covering basic material.

To provide further practice, approximately 20 conceptual and procedural questions are provided at the end of each chapter. The questions are divided into "Review Questions," which require students to define terms and outline procedures, and "Application Questions," which require students to perform procedures, interpret results, and critique the procedures of others. The answers to odd-numbered questions, with intermediate steps, are in Appendix C. The answers to even-numbered questions are in the Instructor's Resource Manual and on a password-protected website.

In addition, the following pedagogic features are included in each chapter:

- Each chapter begins with a list of previously discussed concepts that students should review, the learning goals for the chapter and an overview of the contents of the chapter.
- The opening section in each chapter emphasizes understanding the general concepts and procedures in the chapter and conveys why and how researchers use each procedure.
- Throughout each chapter, important points are emphasized by a "REMEMBER" summary reminder set off from the text.
- Summary tables and sections appear regularly and help organize and integrate the separate steps discussed in previous sections.
- Formulas are highlighted in color.
- Key terms are highlighted in bold, reviewed in the chapter summary, and listed in a "Key Terms" section at the end of the chapter. A glossary is also included.
- Graphs and diagrams are explained in captions and fully integrated into the discussion.
- Each "Chapter Summary" provides a substantive review of the material, not merely a list of the topics covered.
- A "Summary of Formulas" is provided at the end of each chapter.
- A list of all formulas is presented inside the front cover, and a list of symbols is presented inside the back cover.

## CHAPTER ORGANIZATION

Chapter 1 introduces the terminology and logic of behavioral research, relationships, experiments, and the four measurement scales.

Descriptive statistics begin in Chapter 2 with simple frequency tables and graphs, relative frequency, and percentiles. The proportion of the area under the normal curve is introduced here so that it can be applied in the subsequent chapters that deal with central tendency, variability, and $z$-scores.

Chapter 3 introduces measures of central tendency, presenting the mode and median, but focusing on means and how they are used to summarize the results of experiments.

Chapter 4 presents measures of variability (the range, variance, and standard deviation) and how they are used to describe data. Computing formulas are presented (as well as defining formulas), so that students are familiar with the summation symbols used in later formulas.

Chapter 5 presents $z$-scores and their use with the standard normal curve. Sampling distributions and computing $z$-scores for sample means are also included so that later, inferential statistics can be "painlessly" introduced as essentially involving $z$-scores.

Inferential statistics begin in Chapter 6 with the discussion of probability as it is used with the normal curve. The focus is how to make decisions about the representativeness of sample means, without the confusing terminology and details of hypothesis testing.

Chapter 7 formally presents hypothesis testing using the $z$-test, including the terminology and symbols that are used, showing how significant and nonsignificant results are interpreted, and describing Type I and Type II errors and power.

Chapter 8 presents the one-sample $t$-test and the confidence interval for a population mean.

Chapter 9 covers the independent- and the related-samples $t$-tests. "A Word About Effect Size" is included.

Chapter 10 introduces the logic and interpretation of correlation coefficients and scatterplots, and presents the computation of the Pearson coefficient and its procedures for hypothesis testing. "A Word About Linear Regression" and "A Word About $r^2$" are also included.

Chapter 11 presents the one-way, between-subjects ANOVA. The Tukey *HSD* post hoc test for equal *n*s is also presented. "A Word About Eta$^2$" is included.

Chapter 12 presents the purpose and logic of the two-way ANOVA but without the formulas. The chapter shows what main effects and interaction effects are, and briefly presents the logic of unconfounded post hoc comparisons, how to graph interactions, and the general interpretation of a two-way design.

Chapter 13 distinguishes parametric and nonparametric procedures, and covers the one-way and two-way chi square in depth. "A Word About Nonparametric Procedures for Ranks" provides a nonmathematical discussion of the uses of the Spearman correlation and the Mann–Whitney, Wilcoxon, Kruskal–Wallis, and Friedman tests.

## SUPPLEMENTARY MATERIALS

The following supplementary materials are available with *Essential Statistics for the Behavioral Sciences.* Contact your local Houghton Mifflin representative for more information.

### For Instructors:

**Instructor's Resource Manual with Test Questions** This instructor resource contains test items and problems, as well as suggestions for classroom activities, discussion, and use of statistical software. It also includes answers to the even-numbered end-of-chapter questions from this book for use in assigning homework or enhancing classroom tests. A computerized test bank is also available.

**Instructor's Website** An array of useful and innovative teaching resources can be found at the text's website, including PowerPoint presentations, Chapter Outlines, Lecture Aids, and the Answers to the even-numbered end-of-chapter questions from the text.

### For Students:

**Student Workbook and Study Guide** Additional Review Questions are available in the Student Workbook and Study Guide. Each chapter contains a review of objectives, terms, and formulas, a programmed review, conceptual and computational problems (with answers), and a set of multiple choice questions similar to those in the Instructor's Resource Manual. A final chapter, titled "Getting Ready for the Final Exam," facilitates student integration of the entire course. The workbook is available separately, or it can be packaged with the textbook.

**Using SPSS for Windows** This 50-page supplement, by Dr. Charles Stangor, helps teach SPSS to beginning students. It is compatible with this textbook, is easily understood, and comes complete with data sets on CD-ROM. The supplement is available separately, or it can be packaged with the textbook.

**Student Website** Students can enhance their classroom experience by visiting the text's website to try out the "ACE" practice quizzes that accompany the text. These tests were written specifically for the text and provide immediate feedback on test results along with explanations of answer selections. In addition, text learning objectives and key terms are available on the website for further study and testing.

## ACKNOWLEDGMENTS

I gratefully acknowledge the help and support of the many professionals associated with Houghton Mifflin Company. In particular, I want to thank Senior Sponsoring Editor, Kerry Baruth; Senior Development Editor, Sharon Geary; Senior Project Editor, Margaret Park Bridges; and Editorial Assistant, Nirmal Trivedi for their work on this textbook.

I am also grateful to the following reviewers who provided valuable feedback.

Khanh Van T. Bui, Pepperdine University

Maria Czyzewska, Southwest Texas State University

Jane Halpert, DePaul University

Scott Hershberger, California State University, Long Beach

Mark B. Johnson, University of Maryland, College Park

Jerwen Jou, University of Texas Pan American, Edinburg

Joseph G. Marrone, Siena College

Ben Newkirk, Grossmont College

Laura R. Novick, Vanderbilt University

Deborah Oh, California State University, Los Angeles

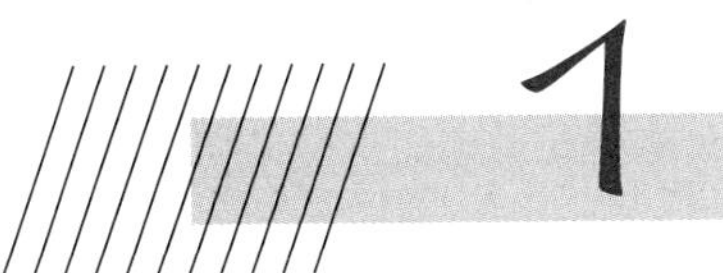

# 1 Introduction to Statistics and Research

**CHAPTER ESSENTIALS**

**Your goals in this chapter are to learn**

- The logic of research and the purpose of statistical procedures
- How to recognize a *relationship* between scores
- When and why *descriptive* and *inferential* statistical procedures are used
- What the difference is between an experiment and a correlational study, and what the independent variable, the conditions, and the dependent variable are
- What the four scales of measurement are

Okay, so you're taking a course in statistics. First of all, we all know that statistics involve math, and that may make you a little nervous. Well, relax. Statistics are not incomprehensible, they do not require you to be a math wizard, and you need to know only how to add, subtract, multiply, and divide—and use a calculator. Also, statisticians have already developed the statistical procedures you'll be learning about, so you won't be solving simultaneous equations, performing proofs, or doing other mystery math.

You are taking this course because statistics are an integral part of behavioral research. Therefore, the first step is for you to understand the basics of research so that you can see how statistics fit in. This chapter discusses (1) the logic of research and the purpose of statistical procedures, (2) the two major types of studies that researchers conduct, and (3) the four ways that researchers measure behaviors.

## WHY IS IT IMPORTANT TO LEARN ABOUT STATISTICS? (AND HOW DO YOU DO THAT?)

Statistics are important because people involved in the behavioral sciences use statistics and statistical concepts every day. Therefore, understanding statistics will allow you to understand behavioral research in your other courses and in your career. What are statistics? The term *statistics* is sometimes shorthand for *statistical procedures,* which are essentially formulas used to analyze the results of behavioral research. Also, the answers obtained from some procedures are called *statistics.*

Even if you're not interested in conducting research yourself, statistics are necessary for comprehending other people's research. First, you must speak the language, and the symbols and terminology you'll learn are part of the shorthand "code" used to describe statistical analyses and to communicate and interpret research results. A major part of learning statistics is merely learning this code. Once you speak the language, much of the mystery surrounding statistics and research evaporates. Second, you must understand how researchers *use* statistics. Behavioral research involves measuring one or more behaviors. This usually results in a large batch of scores—called the *data*—that must be made meaningful. **The purpose of statistical procedures is to make sense of data by *organizing, summarizing, communicating* and *interpreting* scores.** However, there are not many different procedures to learn, and these fancy-sounding "procedures" include such simple things as computing an average (which is a way to summarize scores) or drawing a graph (which is a way to organize them.)

Prepare yourself for the fact that to learn statistics you must *do* statistics. Each new discussion builds on previous procedures, so review a topic whenever necessary. Likewise, some of the formulas may *appear* difficult, but that's because they're written in code. They simply require a little practice. As we discuss each formula, we'll review the math involved, and throughout each chapter you can review and test yourself in the sections called **A QUICK REVIEW.** Also, at the end of a chapter you'll find additional practice problems. By getting practice at solving problems, the rest of the mystery surrounding statistics will evaporate.

Do not, however, get so carried away with the calculations that you forget that statistics are used to make sense of data. Statistics are a *tool* used in research that you must learn to *apply*. Therefore, your goal is to learn *when* and *why* to use each procedure and how to *interpret* its answer.

Now on to statistics and research.

## THE LOGIC OF RESEARCH

The goal of behavioral research is to understand the "laws of nature" that pertain to the behaviors of living organisms. That is, researchers assume that specific influences govern every behavior of all members of a particular group. Although any single study is a small step in this process, our goal is to understand every factor that influences the behavior. Thus, when researchers study such things as the mating behavior of sea lions or social interactions between humans, they are ultimately studying the laws of nature.

The reason a study is a small step is because nature is very complex, and so research involves a series of translations that simplify things so that we can examine a specific influence on a specific behavior in a specific situation. Then, using our findings, we *generalize* back to the broader behaviors and laws we began with. For example, here's an idea for a simple study. Say that we think a law of nature is that people must study information in order to learn it. We translate this into the more specific *hypothesis* that "the more you study statistics, the better you'll learn them." Next, we will translate the hypothesis into a situation where we can observe and measure specific people who study specific material in different amounts, to see if they *do* learn differently. Based on what we observe, we have evidence for working back to the general law regarding studying and learning.

Part of this translation process involves samples and populations.

### Samples and Populations

When researchers talk of a behavior occurring in nature, they say it occurs in the population. A **population** is the entire group of individuals to which a law of nature applies (whether all humans, all men, all four-year-old English-speaking children, etc.). For our example, the population might be all college students taking statistics. Notice, however, that although researchers ultimately discuss the population of individuals, in statistics we sometimes talk of the population of *scores,* as if we have already measured the behavior of everyone in the population in a particular situation.

The population contains all possible members of the group, so we usually consider it to be infinitely large. But, to measure an infinitely large population would take roughly forever! Instead, we measure a sample from the population. A **sample** is a relatively small subset of a population that is intended to represent, or stand in for, the population. Thus, we might study the students in your statistics class as a sample representing the population of all college students studying statistics. The individuals measured in a sample are called the **participants** or **subjects,** and it is the scores from the sample(s) that constitute our data. However, as with a population, sometimes we discuss a sample of *scores* as if we have already measured the participants in a particular situation. Thus, a population is the complete group of scores that would be found for everyone in a particular situation, and a sample is a subset of those scores that we actually measure in that situation.

The logic behind samples and populations is this: We use the scores in a sample to *infer*—to estimate—the scores we would expect to find in the population, if we could measure it. Then by translating the scores in the sample back into the behaviors they reflect, we can infer the behavior of the population. By describing the behavior of the population, we *are* describing how nature works, because the population *is* the entire group to which the law of nature applies. Thus, if we observe that greater studying leads to better learning for the sample of students in your statistics class, we will infer that similar scores and behaviors would be found in the population of all statistics students. This provides evidence that, in nature, more studying does lead to better learning.

> ***REMEMBER*** The *population* is the entire group of individuals—and scores— to which our conclusions apply, based on our observation of a *sample,* which is a subset of the population.

Notice that the above assumes that a sample is *representative* of the population. We discuss this issue in later chapters, but put simply, a representative sample *accurately* reflects the individuals that are found in the population. Then our inferences about the scores and behaviors found in the population will also be accurate. Thus, if your class is representative of all college students, then the scores the class obtains are a good example of the scores that everyone in the population would obtain. The problem is, however, that any sample can be *unrepresentative* and then it *inaccurately* reflects the population. (Maybe your class contains very strange, atypical students who do not behave at all like the population of students.) Therefore, as you'll see, researchers always consider the possibility that a conclusion about the population—about nature—might be incorrect because it might be based on an unrepresentative sample.

Researchers study samples by measuring specific *variables.*

## Understanding Variables

In research the specific factors that we measure that influence behaviors, as well as aspects of the behaviors themselves, are called variables. A **variable** is anything that can produce two or more different scores. A few of the variables in behavioral research include your age, race, gender, intelligence, and personality type; your salary or the type of job you have; how aggressive you are; and how accurately you can recall an event.

Notice that some variables indicate an amount or quantity: Your height, for example, indicates the *amount* of height you have. Other variables, however, do not indicate an amount, but rather indicate a quality or category. For example, a person's gender is a qualitative variable.

For our research on studying and learning statistics, say that to measure "studying" we select the variable of the number of hours that students spent studying for a particular statistics test. To measure "learning," we select the variable of their performance on the test. After measuring participants' scores on these variables, we examine the *relationship* between them.

## Understanding Relationships

If nature relates those mental activities we call studying to those mental activities we call learning, then different amounts of learning should occur with different amounts of studying. In other words, there should be a *relationship* between studying and learning. A **relationship** is a pattern in which specific scores on one variable are paired with specific scores on another variable so that, as the scores on one variable change, the scores on the other variable change in a consistent manner. In our example we predict the relationship in which the longer you study, the higher your test grade will be.

Say that we asked some students how long they studied for a test and their subsequent grades on the test. We might obtain the data in Table 1.1. To see the relationship, first look at those people who studied for 1 hour and see their grade. Then look at those who studied 2 hours, and see that they had a different grade from those studying 1 hour. And so on. These scores form a relationship because, as the study time scores change (increase), the test grades also change in a consistent fashion (also increase).[1] Further, when study time scores do not change (for example, Jane and Bob both studied for 1 hour), their grades also do not change (they both received Fs). We often use the term *association* when talking about relationships: Here, low study times are associated with low test grades and high study times are associated with high test grades.

> ***REMEMBER*** In a *relationship,* as the scores on one variable change, the scores on the other variable change in a consistent manner.

Because we see a relationship in these sample data, we have evidence that in nature, studying and learning do operate as we think: The amount someone studies does seem to make a difference in test grades. In the same way, whenever a law of nature ties

***TABLE 1.1***
Scores Showing a Relationship Between the Variables of Study Time and Test Grades

| *Student* | *Study Time in Hours* | *Test Grades* |
|---|---|---|
| Jane | 1 | F |
| Bob | 1 | F |
| Sue | 2 | D |
| Tony | 3 | C |
| Sidney | 3 | C |
| Ann | 4 | B |
| Rose | 4 | B |
| Lou | 5 | A |

[1]The data presented in this book are a work of fiction. Any resemblance to real data is purely a coincidence.

behaviors or events together, then we'll see that particular scores from one variable—call it *X*—are associated with particular scores from another variable—call it *Y*—so that a relationship is formed. Therefore, most research is designed to investigate relationships, because relationships are the tell-tale signs of a law at work.

> ***REMEMBER*** The purpose of most research is to study the relationships between variables.

A major use of statistical procedures is to examine the scores in a relationship and the pattern they form. The simplest relationships fit one of two patterns. Sometimes we see the pattern "the more you *X,* the more you *Y,*" with higher *X* scores paired with higher *Y* scores. Thus, the old saying "the bigger they are, the harder they fall" describes such a relationship. Other relationships like this include: taller people tend to weigh more, and the more often you speed, the more traffic tickets you accumulate.

At other times we see the pattern "the more you *X,* the *less* you *Y,*" with higher *X* scores paired with lower *Y* scores. Thus, that old saying "the more you practice statistics, the less difficult they are" describes a relationship. Other relationships of this sort include: the more alcohol you consume, the less coordinated you are, and the more often people "cut" classes, the lower their grades.

Relationships may also form more complicated patterns where, for example, more *X* at first leads to more *Y,* but beyond a certain point even more *X* leads to *less Y.* For example, the more you exercise, the better you feel, but beyond a certain point more exercise leads to feeling less well, as pain and exhaustion set in.

Although the above examples involve quantitative variables, relationships can also involve qualitative variables. For example, men typically are taller than women. If you think of male and female as "scores" on the variable of gender, then this is a relationship, because as gender scores change (going from male to female), height scores decrease. We can study any combination of qualitative and quantitative variables in a relationship.

**The Consistency of a Relationship** Table 1.1 showed a perfectly consistent association between hours of study time and test grades: All those who studied the same amount received the same grade. In a perfectly consistent relationship, a score on one variable is always paired with one and only one score on the other variable. In the real world, however, not everyone who studies for the same time will receive the same test grade. (Life is not fair.) A relationship can be present, though, even if there is only some *degree* of consistency, so that as the scores on one variable change, the scores on the other variable *tend* to change in a consistent fashion. For example, Table 1.2 presents a less consistent relationship between the number of hours studied and the number of *errors* made on the test. Here, not everyone who studies for a particular time receives the same error score, (e.g., 12, 13, and 14 errors are all paired with 1 hour.) Also, sometimes a particular error score is paired with *different* studying scores (e.g. 11 errors occur with both 1 and 2 hours of study.). Nonetheless, we still see the pattern where more studying *tends* to be associated with lower error scores, so a relationship is present. Essentially, one batch of error scores occurs at one study-time score, but a *different* batch of error scores tends to occur at the next study-time score.

> ***REMEMBER*** A relationship is present (though not perfectly consistent) if there tends to be a different group of scores on one variable associated with each score on the other variable.

***TABLE 1.2***

Scores Showing a Relationship Between Study Time and Number of Errors on Test

| *Student* | *Hours of Study* | *Errors on Test* |
|---|---|---|
| Amy | 1 | 12 |
| Karen | 1 | 13 |
| Joe | 1 | 11 |
| Cleo | 2 | 11 |
| Jack | 2 | 10 |
| Maria | 2 | 9 |
| Terry | 3 | 9 |
| Manny | 3 | 10 |
| Chris | 4 | 9 |
| Sam | 4 | 8 |
| Gary | 5 | 7 |

**When No Relationship Is Present** At the other extreme, sometimes the scores from two variables do not form a relationship. For example, say that we had obtained the data shown in Table 1.3.

Here, no relationship is present because the error scores paired with 1 hour are essentially the same as the error scores paired with 2 hours, and so on. Thus, virtually the same (but not identical) batch of error scores shows up at each study time, so no pattern of increasing or decreasing errors is present. These data show that how long people study does not make a consistent difference in their error scores, so that nature does not seem to tie these variables together. Therefore, this result would not provide evidence that in nature, studying and learning operate as we think.

> ***REMEMBER*** A relationship is not present when virtually the same batch of scores from one variable are paired with every score on the other variable.

A particular study can produce results that are anywhere between a perfectly consistent relationship and no relationship. In later chapters we'll discuss relationships and their consistency in detail. (You'll see then that the consistency of a relationship is also called the *strength* of the relationship, with less consistent relationships called *weaker* relationships.)

***TABLE 1.3***

Scores Showing No Relationship Between Hours of Study Time and Number of Errors on Test

| *Student* | *Hours of Study* | *Errors on Test* |
|---|---|---|
| Amy | 1 | 12 |
| Karen | 1 | 10 |
| Joe | 1 | 8 |
| Cleo | 2 | 11 |
| Jack | 2 | 10 |
| Maria | 2 | 9 |
| Terry | 3 | 12 |
| Manny | 3 | 9 |
| Chris | 3 | 10 |
| Sam | 4 | 11 |
| Jane | 4 | 10 |
| Gary | 4 | 8 |

## A QUICK REVIEW

- A relationship is present when, as the scores on one variable change, the scores on another variable tend to change in a consistent fashion.

### MORE EXAMPLES

Below, Sample A shows a perfect relationship: One *Y* score occurs at only one *X*. Sample B shows a more inconsistent relationship: Sometimes different *Y*s occur at a particular *X*, and the same *Y* occurs with different *X*s. Sample C shows no relationship: The same *Y*s show up at every *X*.

| A | | B | | C | |
|---|---|---|---|---|---|
| *X* | *Y* | *X* | *Y* | *X* | *Y* |
| 1 | 20 | 1 | 12 | 1 | 12 |
| 1 | 20 | 1 | 15 | 1 | 15 |
| 1 | 20 | 1 | 20 | 1 | 20 |
| 2 | 25 | 2 | 20 | 2 | 20 |
| 2 | 25 | 2 | 30 | 2 | 12 |
| 2 | 25 | 2 | 40 | 2 | 15 |
| 3 | 30 | 3 | 40 | 3 | 20 |
| 3 | 30 | 3 | 40 | 3 | 15 |
| 3 | 30 | 3 | 50 | 3 | 12 |

***For Practice:***

Which samples show a perfect, inconsistent, or no relationship?

| A | | B | | C | | D | |
|---|---|---|---|---|---|---|---|
| *X* | *Y* | *X* | *Y* | *X* | *Y* | *X* | *Y* |
| 2 | 4 | 80 | 80 | 33 | 28 | 40 | 60 |
| 2 | 4 | 80 | 79 | 33 | 20 | 40 | 60 |
| 3 | 6 | 85 | 76 | 43 | 27 | 45 | 60 |
| 3 | 6 | 85 | 75 | 43 | 20 | 45 | 60 |
| 4 | 8 | 90 | 71 | 53 | 20 | 50 | 60 |
| 4 | 8 | 90 | 70 | 53 | 28 | 50 | 60 |

**Answers**

A: perfect relationship; B: inconsistent relationship; C and D: no relationship

## APPLYING DESCRIPTIVE AND INFERENTIAL STATISTICS

Statistics help us make sense out of data, and now you can see that "making sense" means to understand the scores and the relationship they form. But, because we are always talking about samples and populations, we separate statistical procedures into those that apply to samples and those that apply to populations.

**Descriptive statistics** are procedures for organizing and summarizing *sample* data. The answers from such procedures are often a single number that *describes* important information about the scores. (When you see *descriptive,* think *describe.*) A sample's average, for example, is an important descriptive statistic, because in one number we summarize all scores in the sample. Descriptive statistics are also used to describe the relationship in sample data. For our study-time research, for example, we'd want to know whether a relationship is present, how consistently test errors decrease with increased study-time, and so on. (We'll discuss the common descriptive procedures in the next few chapters.)

After describing the sample, we want to use that information to estimate or *infer* the data we would find if we could measure the entire population in our study. However, we cannot automatically assume that what we see in the sample is what we would see in the population: Remember, the sample might be unrepresentative, so that it misleads us about the population. Therefore, we apply additional statistical procedures. **Inferential statistics** are procedures for drawing inferences about the scores and relationship that would be found in the population. Essentially, inferential procedures help us to decide whether to believe that our sample accurately represents the population. If it does, then, for example, we would use the class average as an estimate of the average score we'd find in the population of students. Or, we would use the relationship in our sample to estimate that, for everyone, greater learning tends to occur with greater studying. (We discuss inferential procedures in the second half of this book.)

> **REMEMBER** *Descriptive statistics* are for summarizing sample data. *Inferential statistics* are for estimating the scores and relationship found in the population.

After performing the appropriate descriptive and inferential procedures, we stop being a "statistician," and return to being a behavioral scientist: We interpret the results in terms of the underlying behaviors, psychological principles, sociological influences, and so on, that they reflect. This completes the circle, because then we *are* describing how nature operates.

### Statistics versus Parameters

Researchers use the following system so that we know when we are describing a sample and when we are describing a population. A number that is the answer from a descriptive procedure (describing a sample) is called a **statistic.** Different statistics describe different aspects of sample data, and the symbols for them are letters from the English alphabet. On the other hand, a number that describes an aspect of the population of scores is called a **parameter.** The symbols for different parameters are letters from the Greek alphabet.

Thus, for example, the average in your statistics class is a sample average, a descriptive *statistic* that is symbolized by a letter from the English alphabet. If we then estimate the average in the population, we are estimating a *parameter,* and the symbol for a population average is a letter from the Greek alphabet.

> **REMEMBER** *Descriptive procedures* result in *statistics,* which describe sample data and are symbolized using the English alphabet. *Inferential procedures* are for estimating *parameters,* which describe a population of scores and are symbolized using the Greek alphabet.

## UNDERSTANDING EXPERIMENTS AND CORRELATIONAL STUDIES

Researchers have a variety of ways to create a study to demonstrate a relationship. Part of your learning *when* to use different statistical procedures is to learn in what kind of study a procedure is applied. In other words, pay attention to a study's *design.* The **design** is the way the study is laid out, how many samples are tested, how participants are selected, and so on. Different designs require different statistical procedures. To begin, all research can be broken into two types of designs because we have two general ways of demonstrating a relationship: using experiments or using correlational studies.

## Experiments

In an **experiment** the researcher actively changes or manipulates one variable and then measures participants' scores on another variable to see if a relationship is *produced*. For example, say that we study amount of study time and test errors in an experiment. We decide to compare 1, 2, 3, and 4 hours of study time, so we select four samples of students. We have one sample study for 1 hour, administer the statistics test, and count the number of errors each participant makes. We have another sample study for 2 hours, administer the test, and count their errors, and so on. Then we look to see if we have produced the relationship where, as we increase study time, error scores tend to decrease.

You must understand the components of an experiment and learn their names.

**The Independent Variable** An **independent variable** is the variable that is changed or manipulated by the experimenter. In our studying experiment we manipulate study time so amount of study time is our independent variable. You can remember the independent variable as the variable that occurs *independently* of the participants' wishes (we'll have some participants study for 4 hours whether they want to or not).

Technically, a true independent variable is manipulated by doing something *to* participants. However, there are many variables that an experimenter cannot manipulate in this way. For example, we might hypothesize that growing older causes a change in some behavior, but we can't *make* some people be 20 years old and make others be 40 years old. Instead we would manipulate the variable by selecting one sample of 20-year-olds and one sample of 40-year-olds. We will also call this type of variable an independent variable, and statistically, we treat all independent variables the same.

Thus, the experimenter is always in control of the independent variable, either by determining what is done to each sample or by determining a characteristic of the individuals in each sample. Therefore, a participant's "score" on the independent variable is determined by the experimenter: Above, students in the sample that studied 1 hour have a score of 1 on the study-time variable, and people in the 20-year-old sample have a score of 20 on the age variable.

**Conditions of the Independent Variable** An independent variable is the *overall* variable a researcher examines, that is potentially composed of many different amounts or categories. From these the researcher selects the *conditions* of the independent variable. A **condition** is the specific amount or category of the independent variable that creates the specific situation under which participants are studied. Thus, although our independent variable is amount of study time—which could be any amount—our conditions involve 1, 2, 3, or 4 hours of study. Likewise, if we compare 20-year-olds to 40-year-olds, then 20 and 40 are each a condition of the independent variable of age.

**The Dependent Variable** The **dependent variable** is the variable that is measured under each condition of the independent variable. Scores on the dependent variable measure a behavior or attribute that presumably *depends* on the condition of the independent variable. In our studying experiment, the number of errors on the test is the dependent variable because we believe that errors depend on the amount of study. Or, if we measured how physically active 20- and 40-year-olds are, then activity level is the dependent variable. (*Note:* Because we measure participants' scores on the dependent variable, it is also called the "dependent measure" and we obtain "dependent scores.")

> *REMEMBER* In an experiment the researcher manipulates the *conditions* of the *independent variable* and, under each, measures participants' scores on the *dependent variable.*

## Drawing Conclusions from an Experiment

The purpose of an experiment is to produce a relationship in which, as we change the conditions of the independent variable, participants' scores on the dependent variable also change in a consistent fashion. To see this, a useful way to diagram an experiment is shown in Table 1.4. Each column in the diagram is a condition of the independent variable (here amount of study time) under which we tested some participants. Each number in a column is a participant's score on the dependent variable (here number of test errors).

Remember that a condition determines participants' scores on the independent variable. Thus, participants in the column labeled "1 hour" all had a score of 1 on the independent variable, and they scored either 13, 12, or 11 on the dependent variable. Those in the next column scored "2" on the independent variable, while scoring 9, 8, or 7 on the dependent variable. And so on. Thus, you can see a relationship here because as participants' scores on the amount of study time increase, their test errors tend to decrease. Essentially, participants in the 1-hour study condition produce one batch of error scores, those in the 2-hour condition produce a different, lower batch of error scores, and so on.

You'll see that we have specific *descriptive* statistical procedures for summarizing the sample's scores and the relationship found in such an experiment. Then, to infer that we'd see a similar relationship if we tested the entire population, we have specific *inferential* statistical procedures for experiments. Finally, we would translate the relationship back to the original hypothesis about studying and learning that we began with, so that we could add to our understanding of nature.

## Correlational Studies

Not all research is an experiment. Sometimes we do not manipulate or change either variable and instead conduct a correlational study. In a **correlational study** the researcher measures participants' scores on two variables and then determines whether a relationship is present. Thus, in an experiment the researcher attempts to *make* a relationship happen, while in a correlational study the researcher is a passive observer who looks to see if a

***TABLE 1.4***

Diagram of an Experiment Involving the Independent Variable of Number of Hours Spent Studying and the Dependent Variable of Number of Errors Made on a Statistics Test

*Each column contains participants' dependent scores measured under one condition of the independent variable.*

| | *Independent Variable: Number of Hours Spent Studying* | | | |
|---|---|---|---|---|
| | *Condition 1: 1 Hour* | *Condition 2: 2 Hours* | *Condition 3: 3 Hours* | *Condition 4: 4 Hours* |
| ***Dependent Variable: Number of Errors Made on a Statistics Test*** → | 13<br>12<br>11 | 9<br>8<br>7 | 7<br>6<br>5 | 5<br>3<br>2 |

relationship *exists*. For example, we used a correlational approach back in Table 1.1 when we simply asked some students how long they studied for a test and what their test grade was. Or, we would have a correlational design if we asked people their career choices and measured their personality, asking "Is career choice related to personality type?" (As we'll see, correlational studies examine the "correlation" between variables, which is another way of saying they examine the relationship.)

> ***REMEMBER*** In a correlational study, the researcher simply measures participants' scores on two variables to determine if a relationship exists.

As usual, we want to first describe and understand the relationship we've observed in the sample, and correlational designs have their own descriptive statistical procedures for doing this. Then, to describe the relationship we would find if we could measure the entire population in our study, we have specific correlational inferential procedures. Then, as with an experiment, we would translate the relationship back to the original hypothesis about studying and learning that we began with, so that we can add to our understanding of nature.

## A QUICK REVIEW

- In an experiment the researcher changes the conditions of the independent variable, and then measures participants' behavior using the dependent variable.
- In a correlational design the researcher measures participants on two variables.

### More Examples

In a study, participants' relaxation scores are measured after they've been presented music at either soft, medium, or loud volume. Because the researcher controls and manipulates the volume, this is an experiment. The independent variable is volume; the conditions are soft, medium, and loud; and the dependent variable is relaxation.

A survey measures participants' patriotism and also asks how often they've voted. This is a correlational design, because the researcher passively measures both variables.

### *For Practice:*

1. In an experiment the ____ is changed by the researcher to see if it produces a change in participants' scores on the ____.
2. To see if drinking influences one's ability to drive, participants' level of coordination is measured after drinking 1, 2, or 3 ounces of alcohol. The independent variable is ____, the conditions are ____, and the dependent variable is ____.
3. In an experiment the ____ variable reflects participants' behavior or attributes.
4. We measure the age and income of fifty people to see if older people tend to make more money. What type of design is this?

**Answers**

1. Independent variable; dependent variable
2. Amount of alcohol; 1, 2, or 3 ounces; level of coordination
3. Dependent
4. Correlational

## THE CHARACTERISTICS OF THE SCORES

We have one more issue to consider when deciding on the particular descriptive or inferential procedure to use in an experiment or a correlational study. Although we always measure one or more variables, the numbers that comprise the scores can have different underlying mathematical characteristics. The particular mathematical characteristics of the scores determine which particular descriptive or inferential procedure to use. Therefore, always pay attention to two important characteristics of the variables: the type of *measurement scale* involved and whether the scale is *continuous* or *discrete.*

### The Four Types of Measurement Scales

Numbers mean different things in different contexts. The meaning of the number 1 on a license plate is different from the meaning of the number 1 in a race, which is different still from the meaning of the number 1 in a hockey score. The kind of information that scores convey depends on the *scale of measurement* that is used in measuring the variable. There are four types of measurement scales: *nominal, ordinal, interval,* and *ratio.*

With a **nominal scale,** each score does not actually indicate an amount; rather, it is used for identification. (When you see *nominal,* think *name.*) License plate numbers and the numbers on football uniforms reflect a nominal scale. The key here is that nominal scores indicate only that one individual is qualitatively different from another. In research, nominal scales classify or categorize individuals. For example, in a correlational study, we might measure the political affiliation of participants using a nominal scale by assigning a 5 to democrats, a 10 to republicans, and so on (or we could use any other numbers). Then we might also measure participants' income, to determine whether as party affiliation "scores" change, income scores also change. Or, if an experiment compares the conditions of male and female, then the independent variable involves a nominal scale.

A different approach is to use an **ordinal scale.** Here the scores indicate rank order—anything that is akin to 1st, 2nd, 3rd . . . is ordinal. (*Ordinal* sounds like *ordered.*) In our studying example, we'd have an ordinal scale if we assigned a 1 to students who scored best on the test, a 2 to those in second place, and so on. Then we'd ask, "As study times change, do students' ranks also tend to change?" Or, if an experiment compares the conditions of 1st graders to 2nd graders, then this independent variable involves an ordinal scale. The key here is that ordinal scores indicate only a relative amount—identifying who scored relatively high or low. Also, there is no zero in ranks, and the same amount does not separate every pair of adjacent scores: 1st may be only slightly ahead of 2nd, but 2nd may be miles ahead of 3rd.

A third approach is use of an **interval scale.** Here each score indicates an actual quantity, and an equal amount separates any adjacent scores. (For interval scores remember *equal* intervals between them.) However, although interval scales do include the number 0, it is not a *true zero*—it does not mean *none* of the variable is present. Therefore, the key is that you can have less than zero, so an interval scale allows negative numbers. For example, temperature (in Celsius or Fahrenheit) involves an interval scale: because 0° does not mean that zero heat is present, you can have even less heat at −1°. In research, interval scales are common with intelligence or personality tests: A score of zero does not mean zero intelligence or zero personality. Or, in our studying research we might determine the average test score and then assign students a zero if they are average, a +1, +2, etc., for the amount they are above average, and a −1, −2, etc., for the amount they are below average. Then we'd see if more positive scores tend to occur with higher study times. Or, if we create conditions based on whether participants are in a positive, negative, or neutral mood, then this independent variable reflects an interval scale.

The final approach is to use a **ratio scale.** Here, each score measures an actual quantity, an equal amount separates adjacent scores, and 0 truly means that none of the variable is present. Therefore, the key is that you cannot have negative numbers, because you cannot have less than nothing. Also, only with a true zero can we make "ratio" statements, such as "4 is twice as much as 2." (So for *ratio,* think *ratio!*) We used ratio scales in our previous examples when measuring the number of errors and the number of hours studied. Likewise, in an experiment, if we compare the conditions of having people on diets consisting of either 1000, 1500, or 2000 calories a day, then this independent variable involves a ratio scale.

We can study relationships that involve any combination of the above scales.

> ***REMEMBER*** The *scale of measurement* reflected by scores may be *nominal, ordinal, interval,* or *ratio.*

## Continuous versus Discrete Scales

In addition, any measurement scale may be either continuous or discrete. A **continuous scale** allows for fractional amounts; it "continues" between the whole-number amounts, and so decimals make sense. The variable of age is continuous because it is perfectly intelligent to say that someone is 19.6879 years old. On the other hand, some variables involve a **discrete scale,** which can be measured only in whole-number amounts. Here, decimals do not make sense. For example, being male or female, or being in 1st grade versus 2nd grade are discrete variables, because you can be in one group or you can be in the other group, but you can't be in-between.

Usually researchers assume that nominal or ordinal variables are discrete, and that interval or ratio variables are at least *theoretically* continuous. For example, intelligence tests are designed to produce whole-number scores, so you cannot have an IQ of 95.6. But theoretically an IQ of 95.6 makes sense, so intelligence is a theoretically continuous (interval) variable. Likewise, it sounds strange if the government reports that the average family has 2.4 children, because this is a discrete (ratio) variable and no one has .4 of a child. However, it makes sense to treat this as theoretically continuous, because we can interpret what it means if the average is 2.4 versus 2.8.

> ***REMEMBER*** Whether a variable is *continuous* or *discrete* and whether it is measured using a *nominal, ordinal, interval,* or *ratio* scale are factors that determine which statistical procedure to apply.

## A QUICK REVIEW

- *Nominal* scales identify categories and *ordinal* scales reflect rank order. Both *interval* and *ratio* scales measure actual quantities, but negative numbers can occur with interval scales and not with ratio scales.
- *Interval* and *ratio* scales are assumed to be continuous scales, which include fractional amounts; *nominal* and *ordinal* scales are assumed to be discrete scales, which do not include fractional amounts.

### More Examples

If your grade on an essay exam is based on the number of correct statements you include, then a ratio scale is involved; if it is based on how much your essay is better or worse than what the professor expected, an interval scale is involved; if it indicates that yours was relatively one of the best or worst essays in the class, this is an ordinal scale (as is pass/fail); if it is based on the last digit of your ID number, then a nominal scale is involved. If you can receive one grade or another, but nothing in-between, it involves a discrete scale; if fractions are possible, it involves a continuous scale.

### *For Practice:*

1. Whether you are ahead or behind when gambling involves a(n) ____ scale.
2. The number of hours you slept last night involves a(n) ____ scale.
3. Your blood type involves a(n) ____ scale.
4. Whether you are a lieutenant or major in the army involves a(n) ____ scale.
5. A(n) ____ scale allows fractional scores; a(n) ____ scale allows only whole-number scores.

**Answers**

1. interval
2. ratio
3. nominal
4. ordinal
5. continuous; discrete

## CHAPTER SUMMARY

1. The group of all individuals to which a conclusion applies is the *population.* The subset of the population that is actually measured is the *sample,* and the individuals in a sample are the *participants* or *subjects.*
2. A *variable* is anything that, when measured, can produce two or more different values.
3. A *relationship* occurs when a change in scores on one variable is consistently associated with a change in scores on another variable.
4. *Descriptive statistics* organize, summarize, and describe sample data. *Inferential statistics* are for drawing inferences about the scores and relationship found in the population.
5. A *statistic* describes a characteristic of a sample of scores, symbolized by a letter from the English alphabet. A statistic is used to infer the corresponding *parameter* that describes a characteristic of a population of scores, symbolized by a letter from the Greek alphabet.
6. A *study's design* is the particular way in which the study is laid out.

7. In an *experiment* the researcher manipulates the *independent variable* and then measures participants' scores on the *dependent variable.* Each specific amount or category of the independent variable is a *condition.*
8. In a *correlational study* neither variable is actively manipulated. Scores on both variables are simply measured and then the relationship is described.
9. The four *scales of measurement* are (1) *nominal,* in which numbers identify a category; (2) *ordinal,* in which numbers indicate rank order; (3) *interval,* in which numbers measure a specific amount, but with no true zero; and (4) *ratio,* in which numbers measure a specific amount and 0 indicates truly zero amount.
10. A *continuous* variable can be measured in fractional amounts. A *discrete* variable is measured only in whole-number amounts.

## KEY TERMS: Can You Define The Following?

condition *9*
continuous scale *13*
correlational study *10*
dependent variable *9*
descriptive statistics *7*
design *8*
discrete scale *13*
experiment *9*
independent variable *9*
inferential statistics *8*
interval scale *12*
nominal scale *12*
ordinal scale *12*
parameter *8*
participants *3*
population *2*
ratio scale *13*
relationship *4*
sample *3*
statistic *8*
subjects *3*
variable *3*

## REVIEW QUESTIONS

(Answers for odd-numbered problems are in Appendix C.)

1. Why is it important for students of behavioral research to understand statistics?
2. (a) What is a population? (b) What is a sample? (c) How are samples used to make conclusions about populations?
3. What do you see when a relationship exists between two variables?
4. What is the general purpose of experiments and correlational studies?
5. What are the two aspects of a study to consider when selecting the descriptive or inferential statistics that you should employ?
6. What is the difference between an experiment and a correlational study?
7. What is the difference between the independent variable and the conditions of the independent variable?

*8.* In an experiment what is the dependent variable?
*9.* What are descriptive statistics used for?
*10.* What are inferential statistics used for?
*11.* (a) What is the difference between a statistic and a parameter? (b) What types of symbols are used for statistics and parameters?
*12.* (a) Define the four scales of measurement. (b) What are continuous and discrete variables? (c) Which scales are usually assumed to be discrete, and which are assumed to be continuous?

## APPLICATION QUESTIONS

*13.* A student, Poindexter, gives participants various amounts of alcohol and then observes any decrease in their ability to walk. Another student, Foofy, notes the various amounts of alcohol that participants drink at a party, and then observes any decrease in their ability to walk. Which study is an experiment, and which is a correlational study? Why?
*14.* In each of the following experiments, identify the independent variable, the conditions of the independent variable, and the dependent variable: (a) Studying whether scores on a final exam are influenced by whether background music is soft, loud, or absent. (b) Comparing freshmen, sophomores, juniors, and seniors with respect to how much fun they have while attending college. (c) Studying whether being first-born, second-born, or third-born is related to intelligence. (d) Examining whether length of daily exposure to a sun lamp (15 minutes versus 60 minutes) accounts for differences in self-reported depression. (e) Studying whether being in a room with blue walls, green walls, red walls, or beige walls influences aggressive behavior in a group of adolescents.
*15.* What is the general pattern found in (a) a perfectly consistent relationship? (b) an inconsistent relationship? (c) no relationship?
*16.* Using the words "statistic" and "parameter," how do we describe a relationship in a population?
*17.* Which of the following data sets show a relationship?

| *Sample A* | | *Sample B* | | *Sample C* | | *Sample D* | |
|---|---|---|---|---|---|---|---|
| *X* | *Y* | *X* | *Y* | *X* | *Y* | *X* | *Y* |
| 1 | 10 | 20 | 40 | 13 | 20 | 92 | 71 |
| 1 | 10 | 20 | 42 | 13 | 19 | 93 | 77 |
| 1 | 10 | 22 | 40 | 13 | 18 | 93 | 77 |
| 2 | 20 | 22 | 41 | 13 | 17 | 95 | 79 |
| 2 | 20 | 23 | 40 | 13 | 15 | 96 | 74 |
| 3 | 30 | 24 | 40 | 13 | 14 | 97 | 71 |
| 3 | 30 | 24 | 42 | 13 | 13 | 98 | 69 |

*18.* Which sample in problem 17 shows the most consistent relationship? How do you know?

*19.* In the chart below, identify the characteristics of each variable.

| *Variable* | *Qualitative or Quantitative* | *Continuous or Discrete* | *Type of Measurement Scale* |
|---|---|---|---|
| Gender | ________ | ________ | ________ |
| Academic major | ________ | ________ | ________ |
| Number of minutes before and after an event | ________ | ________ | ________ |
| Restaurant ratings (best, next best, etc.) | ________ | ________ | ________ |
| Speed (miles per hr) | ________ | ________ | ________ |
| Number of dollars in your pocket | ________ | ________ | ________ |
| Position when standing in a line | ________ | ________ | ________ |
| Change in weight (in lbs.) | ________ | ________ | ________ |

*20.* Using the terms *sample, population, variable, statistic,* and *parameter,* summarize the steps a researcher follows, starting with a hypothesis and ending with a conclusion about a nature.

# 2 Creating and Using Frequency Distributions

**CHAPTER ESSENTIALS**

**Before getting started, be sure you understand**

- That descriptive statistics are used to describe and summarize the characteristics of data
- What nominal, ordinal, interval and ratio scales of measurement are, and what continuous and discrete mean

**Your goals in this chapter are to learn**

- What *frequency* is and how a *frequency distribution* is created
- When to graph frequency distributions using a *bar graph, histogram,* or *polygon*
- What *normal, skewed,* and *bimodal* distributions are
- What *relative frequency* and *percentile* are and how we use the *area under the normal curve* to compute them

So we're off into the world of descriptive statistics. Recall that the goal is to make sense of the scores by organizing and summarizing them. One important procedure for doing this is to create tables and graphs, because they show the scores you've obtained and they make it easier to see the relationship between two variables that's hidden in the data. Before we examine the relationship between two variables, however, we first summarize the scores on *each* variable alone. Therefore, this chapter will discuss the common ways to describe scores from *one* variable by using a *frequency distribution.* You'll see (1) how to show a frequency distribution in a table or graph, (2) the common patterns found in frequency distributions, and (3) how to use a frequency distribution to compute additional information about scores.

## SOME NEW SYMBOLS AND TERMINOLOGY

The scores we initially measure in a study are called the **raw scores.** Descriptive statistics help us boil down raw scores into an interpretable, "digestible" form. There are several ways to do this, but the starting point is to count the number of times each score occurred. The number of times a score occurs in a set of data is the score's **frequency.**

If we examine the frequencies of every score in the data, we create a *frequency distribution*. The term *distribution* is the general name researchers have for any organized set of data. In a **frequency distribution** the scores are organized based on each score's frequency. (Actually researchers have several ways to describe frequency, so technically, when we *simply* count the frequency of each score, we create a *simple frequency distribution*.)

The symbol for a score's frequency is the lowercase $f$. To find $f$ for a score, count how many times that score occurs. If three participants scored 66, then 66 occurred three times, so the frequency of 66 (its $f$) is 3. Creating a frequency distribution involves counting the frequency of every score in the data.

In most statistical procedures, we also count the total number of scores we have. The symbol for the total number of scores in a set of data is the uppercase $N$. Thus, $N = 43$ means that we have 43 scores. Note that $N$ is not the number of *different* scores, so even if all 43 scores in a sample are the same score, $N$ still equals 43.

***REMEMBER*** The *frequency* of a score is symbolized by $f$. The total *number* of scores in the data is symbolized by $N$.

## UNDERSTANDING FREQUENCY DISTRIBUTIONS

The first step when trying to understand any set of scores is to ask the most obvious question, "What are the scores that were obtained?" In fact, buried in any data are two important things to know: What scores were obtained, and how often did each occur? These questions are answered simultaneously by looking at the frequency of each score. Thus, frequency distributions are important because they provide a simple and clear way to show the scores in a set of data. Because of this, they are always the first step when beginning to understand the scores from a study. Further, they are also a core aspect of up-coming statistical procedures.

One way to see a frequency distribution is in a table.

### Presenting Frequency in a Table

Let's begin with the following raw scores. (They might measure one of the variables from a correlational study, or they might be dependent scores from an experiment.)

| | | | | | | | | |
|---|---|---|---|---|---|---|---|---|
| 14 | 14 | 13 | 15 | 11 | 15 | 13 | 10 | 12 |
| 13 | 14 | 13 | 14 | 15 | 17 | 14 | 14 | 15 |

In this disorganized arrangement it is difficult to make sense of these scores. Watch what happens, though, when we arrange them into the frequency table in Table 2.1.

Researchers have several rules for making a frequency table, and so the table consists of a score column and an $f$ column. The score column has the highest score in the data at the *top* of the column. Below that are all *possible* whole-number scores in decreasing order, down to the lowest score that occurred. Thus, the highest score above is 17, the lowest score is 10, and although no one obtained a score of 16, we still include it. Opposite each score in the $f$ column is the score's frequency: In the sample there are one 17, zero 16s, four 15s, and so on.

**TABLE 2.1**
Simple Frequency Distribution Table
*The left-hand column identifies each score, and the right-hand column contains the frequency with which the score occurred.*

| *Score* | *f* |
|---|---|
| 17 | 1 |
| 16 | 0 |
| 15 | 4 |
| 14 | 6 |
| 13 | 4 |
| 12 | 1 |
| 11 | 1 |
| 10 | 1 |
| | Total: 18 = $N$ |

Not only can we see the frequency of each score, we can also determine the combined frequency of several scores by adding together their individual $f$s. For example, the score of 13 has an $f$ of 4 and the score of 14 has an $f$ of 6, so their combined frequency is 10.

Notice that, although 8 scores are in the score column, $N$ is *not* 8. We had 18 scores in the original sample, so $N$ is 18. You can see this by adding together all of the individual frequencies in the $f$ column: The 1 person scoring 17 plus the 4 people scoring 15 and so on adds up to the 18 people in the sample. In a frequency distribution, the sum of the frequencies always equals $N$.

**REMEMBER** The sum of all individual frequencies in a sample equals $N$.

That's how to create a table showing a frequency distribution.

## A QUICK REVIEW

- A frequency distribution shows the frequency of each score from one variable.

### More Examples

The scores 15, 16, 13, 16, 15, 17, 16, 15, 17, and 15, contain one 13, no 14s, four 15s, and so on, producing the following frequency table:

| Scores | $f$ |
|---|---|
| 17 | 2 |
| 16 | 3 |
| 15 | 4 |
| 14 | 0 |
| 13 | 1 |

***For Practice:***

1. What is the difference between $f$ and $N$?
2. Create a frequency table for these scores: 7, 9, 6, 6, 9, 7, 7, 6, 6.
3. What is the $N$ here?
4. What is the frequency of 6 and 7 together?

**Answers**

1. $f$ is the number of times a score occurs; $N$ is the total number of scores in the data.
2. Scores and $f$:

| Scores | $f$ |
|---|---|
| 9 | 2 |
| 8 | 0 |
| 7 | 3 |
| 6 | 4 |

3. $N = 9$
4. $f = 3 + 4 = 7$

## Graphing a Frequency Distribution

Often when researchers talk of a frequency distribution, they imply a *graph* that shows the frequencies of each score. To produce the graph we place the scores on the *X* axis and frequency on the *Y* axis.

> ***REMEMBER*** A graph of a frequency distribution always shows the scores on the *X* axis and their frequency on the *Y* axis.

We have several ways to draw the graph of a frequency distribution, depending on the *scale of measurement* that was used when measuring the raw scores. We may create a *bar graph,* a *histogram,* or a *polygon.*

**Creating Bar Graphs** Recall that with *nominal* data each score is a name for a category, and with *ordinal* data each score indicates rank order. We graph a frequency distribution of nominal or ordinal scores by creating a bar graph. A **bar graph** has a vertical bar at each score on the *X* axis, the height of the bar corresponds to the score's frequency, and *adjacent bars do not touch.*

For example, say that a survey measures the nominal variable of participants' political party affiliation, producing the table in the upper portion of Figure 2.1. In the graph of these data on the right, the *Y* axis is labeled frequency or *f,* and the *X* axis is labeled using the "scores" of political party. (This is a nominal variable, so they can be arranged in any order.) Then for the 6 republicans, we draw a bar at a height (frequency) of 6, and so on.

In the lower portion of Figure 2.1 are the results of a survey measuring the ordinal variable of military ranks. Here the *X* axis is labeled from left to right, corresponding with low to high rank. Again the height of each bar corresponds to the score's frequency.

> ***REMEMBER*** Create a bar graph to show the frequency distribution of nominal or ordinal scores.

The reason we create bar graphs with nominal and ordinal scales is that both are *discrete* scales: You can be in one group or the next, but not in-between. The space between the bars in a bar graph also indicates this. On the other hand, recall that interval and ratio scales measure actual quantities and they are usually assumed to be at least theoretically *continuous:* They allow fractional amounts that continue between the whole numbers. To communicate this, these scales are graphed using continuous figures.

**Creating Histograms** Create a histogram when you have only a few different interval or ratio scores, so that a small number of scores (labels) are on the *X* axis. A **histogram** is similar to a bar graph except that *in a histogram adjacent bars touch.* For example, say that we measured the ratio variable of number of parking tickets that participants received, obtaining the data in Figure 2.2. Again the height of each bar indicates the corresponding score's frequency.

> ***REMEMBER*** In a *histogram* the adjacent bars touch; in a *bar graph* they do not.

**FIGURE 2.1**
Frequency bar graphs for nominal and ordinal data
*The height of each bar indicates the frequency of the corresponding score on the X axis.*

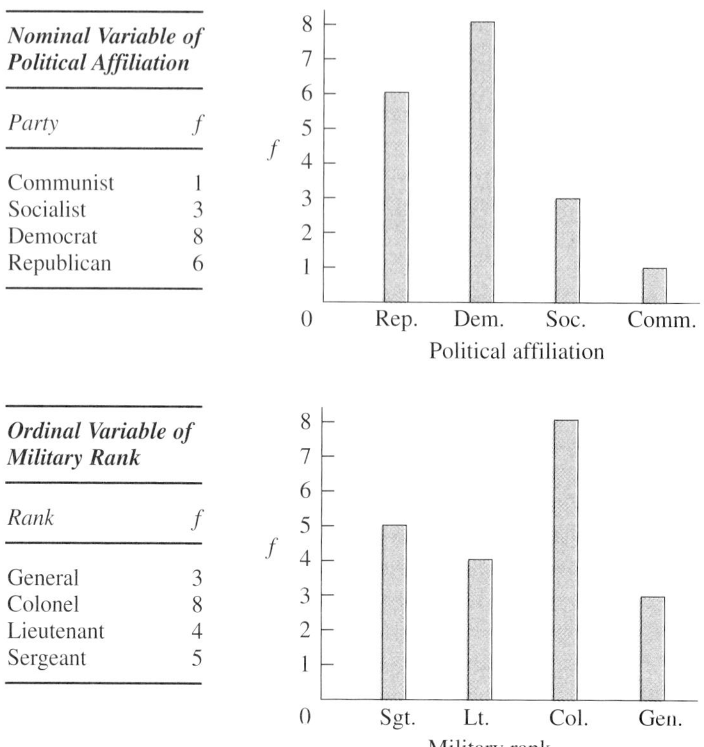

***Nominal Variable of Political Affiliation***

| *Party* | *f* |
|---|---|
| Communist | 1 |
| Socialist | 3 |
| Democrat | 8 |
| Republican | 6 |

***Ordinal Variable of Military Rank***

| *Rank* | *f* |
|---|---|
| General | 3 |
| Colonel | 8 |
| Lieutenant | 4 |
| Sergeant | 5 |



Do not create a histogram for a large number of different scores (say if our participants had from 1 to 50 parking tickets). The 50 bars would need to be very skinny, so the graph would be difficult to read. We have no rule for when the number of scores is too large for a histogram, so use your judgment. But, when a histogram is unworkable, instead create a *frequency polygon.*

**FIGURE 2.2**
Histogram showing the frequency of parking tickets in a sample

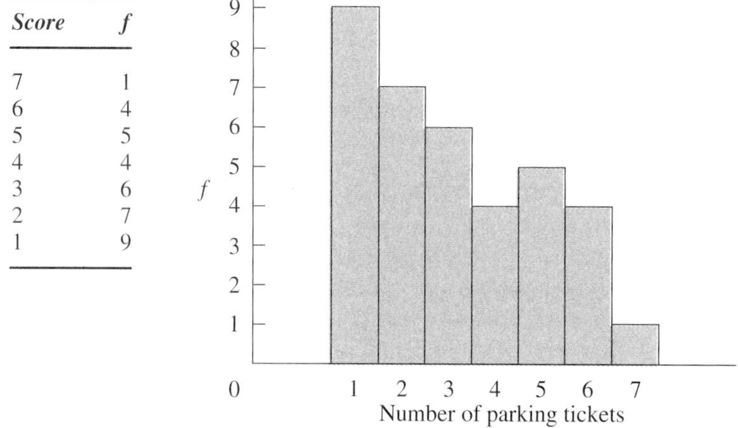

| *Score* | *f* |
|---|---|
| 7 | 1 |
| 6 | 4 |
| 5 | 5 |
| 4 | 4 |
| 3 | 6 |
| 2 | 7 |
| 1 | 9 |

**Creating Frequency Polygons** Create a frequency polygon when you have interval or ratio scores, but you have a wide range of different interval or ratio scores. In a **frequency polygon,** a "dot" is placed above each *X* score at the height on the *Y* axis corresponding to the appropriate frequency, and then the dots are connected using straight lines. Figure 2.3 (on the next page) shows the previous parking ticket data plotted as a frequency polygon.

Note: In any kind of graph, the "dot" plotted at the *Y* score paired with an *X* score is called a **data point.** So, for example, we placed a data point above an *X* of 4 parking tickets at the height on *Y* for a frequency of 4.

> ***REMEMBER*** A *data point* is the dot plotted on a graph to represent a pair of *X* and *Y* scores.

Notice that a frequency polygon also includes on the *X* axis the next score above the highest score in the data and the next score below the lowest score (in Figure 2.3, scores of 0 and 8 are included). These added scores have a frequency of 0, so the polygon touches the *X* axis. In this way we create a complete geometric figure—a "polygon"—with the *X* axis as its base.

## *A QUICK REVIEW*

- Create a *bar graph* with nominal or ordinal scores, a *histogram* with a few interval/ratio scores, and a *polygon* with many different interval/ratio scores.

### More Examples

After a survey, to graph (1) the frequency of males versus females (a nominal variable), create a bar graph; (2) the number of people who are first-born, second-born, etc. (an ordinal variable), create a bar graph; (3) the frequency of participants falling into each of five salary ranges (a few ratio scores), create a histogram; (4) the frequency for each individual salary reported (many ratio scores), create a polygon.

### *For Practice:*

1. A ____ has a separate, discrete bar above each score, a ____ contains bars that touch, and a ____ has dots connected with straight lines.
2. A "dot" plotted on a graph is called a ____.
3. To show the number of freshmen, sophomores, and juniors who are members of a fraternity plot a ____.
4. To show the frequency of people who are above average weight by either 0, 5, 10, or 15 pounds plot a ____.
5. To show the number of people preferring chocolate or vanilla ice cream in a sample plot a ____.
6. To show the number of people who are above average weight by each amount between 0 and 100 pounds plot a ____.

**Answers**

1. bar graph; histogram; polygon
2. data point
3. bar graph
4. histogram
5. bar graph
6. polygon

**FIGURE 2.3**
Frequency polygon showing the frequency of parking tickets in a sample

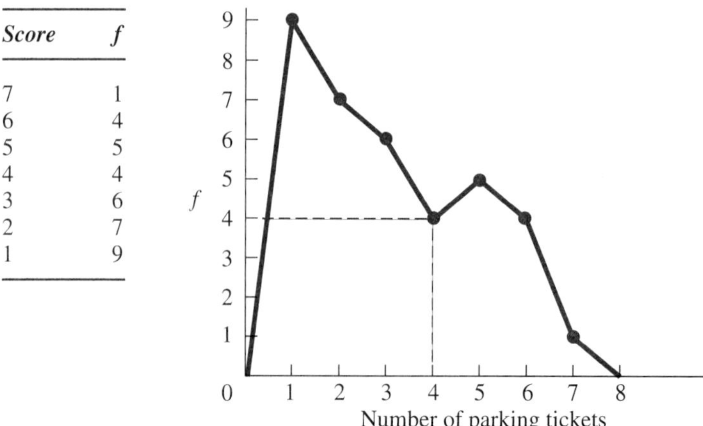

| *Score* | *f* |
|---|---|
| 7 | 1 |
| 6 | 4 |
| 5 | 5 |
| 4 | 4 |
| 3 | 6 |
| 2 | 7 |
| 1 | 9 |



## TYPES OF FREQUENCY DISTRIBUTIONS

Researchers often encounter polygons that have the same particular shape, so we have names for the most common ones. Each shape comes from an idealized distribution of a population. By far the most important frequency distribution is the *normal distribution*. (This is the big one, folks.)

### The Normal Distribution

Figure 2.4 shows the polygon of the ideal normal distribution. (Let's say these are test scores from a population.) Although specific mathematical properties define this polygon, in general it is a bell-shaped curve. But don't call it a bell curve (that's so pedestrian!). Call it a **normal curve** or a **normal distribution,** or say that the scores are *normally distributed.*

To help you interpret the normal curve (or any polygon for that matter), imagine that your view is from a helicopter flying over a parking lot. The *X* and *Y* axes are laid out on the ground, and those people who received a particular score stand in line in front of the marker for their score. The lines of people are packed so tightly together that, from the air, all you see is a dark mass formed by their heads. If you painted a line that went behind the last person in line at each score, you would have the outline of the normal curve. This "parking lot" view is shown in Figure 2.5.

**FIGURE 2.4**
The ideal normal curve
*Scores farther above and below the middle scores occur with progressively lower frequencies.*

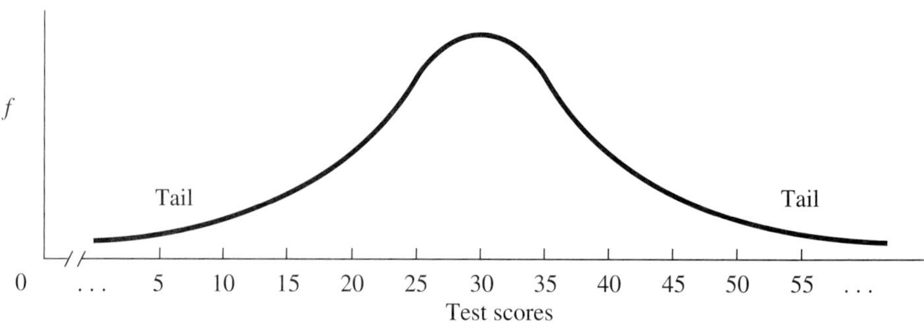

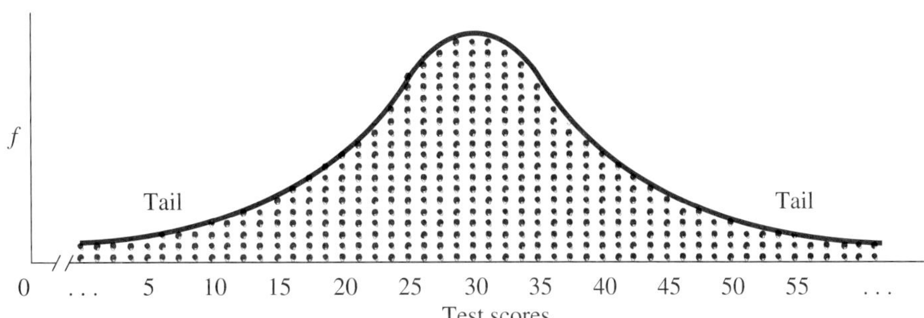


***FIGURE 2.5***
Parking lot view of the ideal normal curve
*The height of the curve above any score reflects the number of people standing at that score.*

Thus, think of the normal curve as representing a geometric figure made up of all of the participants and their scores. When we move vertically up from any score to the height of the curve and then read off the corresponding frequency on the $Y$ axis, it is the same as counting the number of people in line at that score. Likewise, we might, for example, read off the frequencies for each score between 30 and 35 and, by adding them together, obtain the combined frequency of these scores. We'd get the same answer if we counted the people in line above each score and added them together. And adding the frequencies for all scores would give the total number of scores ($N$). This is the same as counting the total number of people in the parking lot.

As you can see from Figures 2.4 and 2.5, the normal distribution has the following characteristics. The score with the highest frequency is the middle score between the highest and lowest scores. (In this example the longest line in the parking lot is at the score of 30.) The normal curve is *symmetrical,* meaning that the left half below the middle score is a mirror image of the right half above the middle score. As you proceed away from the middle score toward the higher or lower scores, the frequencies decrease with the highest and lowest scores having relatively very low frequency.

*Note:* In the language of statistics, the far left and right portions of a normal curve containing the relatively low-frequency, extreme high or low scores are each called the **tail of the distribution.** In Figures 2.4 and 2.5 the tails are roughly below the score of 15 and above the score of 45.

The reason the normal distribution is important is because it is a very common distribution in behavioral research and statistics: On most variables most individuals score close to the middle score, with progressively fewer individuals scoring at more extreme, higher and lower scores. However, because the ideal normal curve represents a theoretical infinite population of scores, it has several characteristics that are not found with real data. First, with an infinite number of scores we cannot label the $Y$ axis with specific values of $f$. Simply remember that the higher the curve above a score, the higher its frequency. Second, this polygon is a smooth curved line. With so many different scores, the individual data points fill in the curved line. Finally, regardless of how extreme a score might be, theoretically it will sometimes occur. Therefore, in the tails of the distribution, the frequencies approach—but never reach—zero, so the curve approaches but never actually touches the $X$ axis.

Before you proceed, be sure that you can read the normal curve. Can you see in Figure 2.4 that the most frequent scores are between 25 and 35? Do you see that a score of 15 has a relatively low frequency and a score of 45 has the same low frequency? Do you see that there are relatively few scores in the tail above 50 or in the tail below 10? And you should be able to see this in your sleep:

> ***REMEMBER*** On a normal distribution, the farther into a tail a score is, the less frequently the score occurs.

## Skewed Distributions

Not all variables form normal distributions. One of the most common *nonnormal* distributions is a skewed distribution. A skewed distribution is similar to a normal distribution except that it is not symmetrical and has only *one* pronounced tail. As shown in Figure 2.6, a distribution may be either *negatively skewed* or *positively skewed,* and the skew is where the tail is.

A **negatively skewed distribution** contains extreme low scores that have a low frequency, but does not contain low-frequency, extreme high scores. The left-hand polygon in Figure 2.6 shows an idealized negatively skewed distribution. This pattern might be found, for example, by measuring the running speed of professional football players. Most would tend to run at higher speeds, but a relatively few linemen lumber in at the slower speeds. (To remember *negatively skewed,* remember that the pronounced tail is over the lower scores, sloping toward zero and where the *negative* scores would be.)

On the other hand, a **positively skewed distribution** contains extreme high scores that have low frequency, but does not contain low-frequency, extreme low scores. The right-hand polygon in Figure 2.6 shows a positively skewed distribution. This pattern is often found, for example, when measuring participants' "reaction time" to a stimulus. Usually, scores will tend to be rather low (fast), but every once in a while a person will "fall asleep at the switch," requiring a large amount of time that produces a high score. (To remember *positively skewed,* remember that the tail slopes away from zero, toward where the higher, *positive* scores are located.)

> ***REMEMBER*** Whether a *skewed* distribution is *negative* or *positive* corresponds to whether the distinct tail slopes toward or away from zero.

## Bimodal Distributions

An idealized bimodal distribution is shown in Figure 2.7. A **bimodal distribution** is a symmetrical distribution containing two distinct humps, each reflecting relatively high-

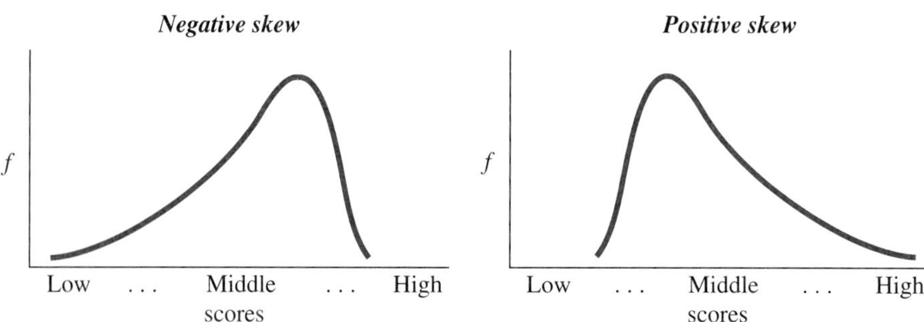


***FIGURE 2.6***
Idealized skewed distributions
*The direction in which the distinctive tail slopes indicates whether the skew is positive or negative.*

frequency scores. At the center of each hump is one score that occurs more frequently than the surrounding scores, and technically the center scores have the same frequency. Such a distribution would occur with test scores, for example, if most students scored at 60 or 80, with fewer students failing or scoring in the 70s or 90s.

## How to Label Distributions

You need to know the names of the previous ideal distributions because descriptive statistics describe the important characteristics of data, and one very important characteristic is the shape of the frequency distribution. Thus, although I might have data containing many different scores, if, for example, I tell you they form a normal distribution, you can mentally envision such a distribution, and so quickly and easily understand what the scores are like. Therefore, the first step when examining any data is to identify the shape of the frequency distribution that is present.

> ***REMEMBER*** The shape of the frequency distribution that scores form is an important characteristic of the data.

Data in the real world, however, never form the perfect curves we've discussed. Instead, the scores will form a bumpy, rough approximation to the ideal distribution. For example, data never form the perfect normal curve, and at best only come close to that shape. However, rather than drawing a different, approximately normal curve in every study, we simplify the task by using the ideal normal curve as our one "model" of any distribution that generally has this shape. This gives us one reasonably accurate way of envisioning the various, approximately normal distributions that researchers encounter. The same is true for the other shapes we've seen.

Thus, we apply the names of the previous distributions to samples as a way of summarizing and communicating their general shape. Figure 2.8 shows several examples, as well as the corresponding labels we might use. (Notice that we even apply these names to histograms or bar graphs.) We assume that the sample represents a population that more closely fits the corresponding ideal polygon: If we measured the population, the additional scores and their frequencies would "fill in" the sample curve, smoothing it out to be closer to the ideal curve.

***FIGURE 2.7***
Idealized bimodal distribution

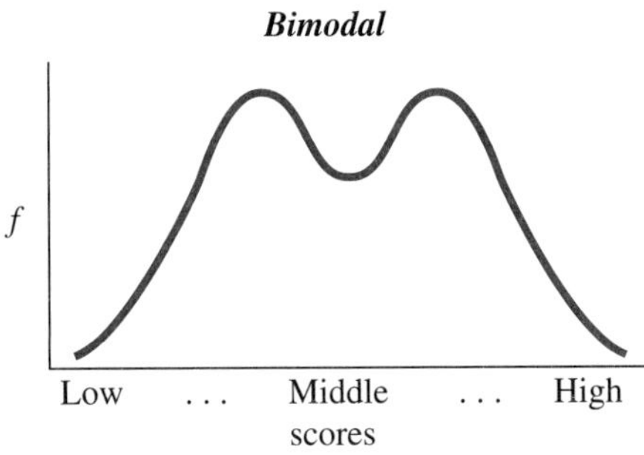

**FIGURE 2.8**
Simple frequency distributions of sample data with appropriate labels

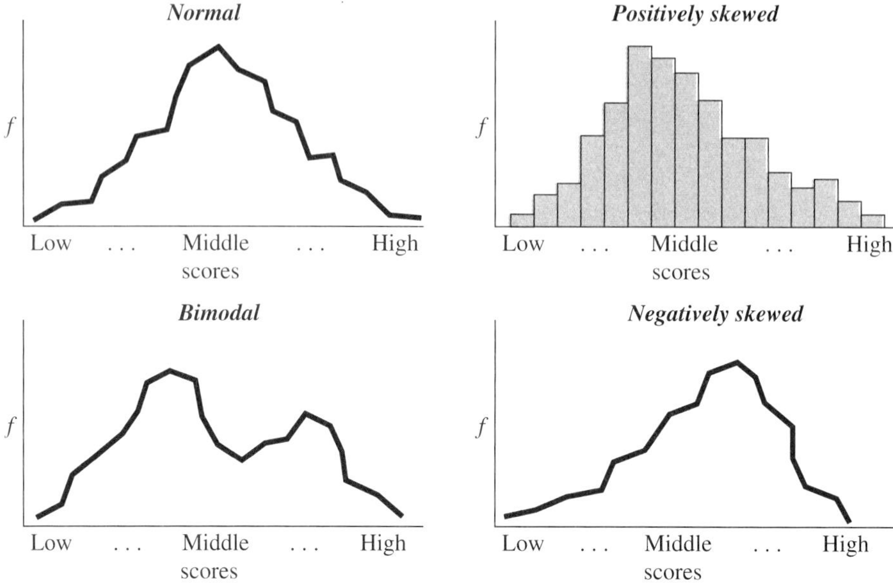


## A QUICK REVIEW

- The most common frequency distributions are *normal distributions, negatively* or *positively skewed distributions,* and *bimodal distributions.*

### More Examples

The variable of intelligence (IQ) usually forms a normal distribution: The most common scores are in the middle, with higher or lower IQs occurring progressively less often. If IQ was positively skewed, there would be only a few high scores, but frequent low scores. If IQ was negatively skewed, there would be only a few low scores, but frequent high scores. If IQ formed a bimodal distribution, there would be two distinct parts of the curve containing the highest-frequency scores.

### *For Practice:*

1. Arrange the scores below from most frequent to least frequent.

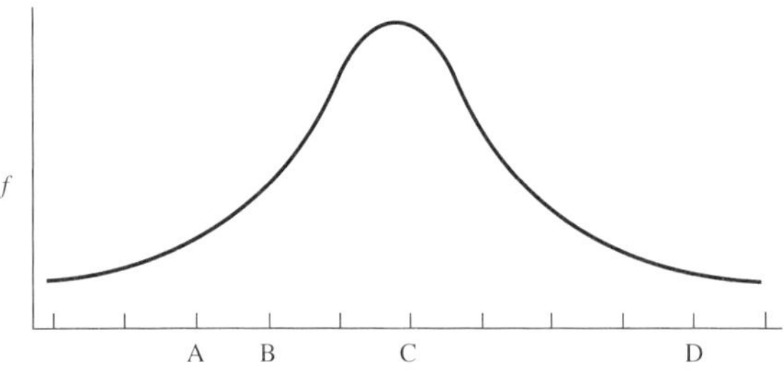


2. What label should be given to each of the following?

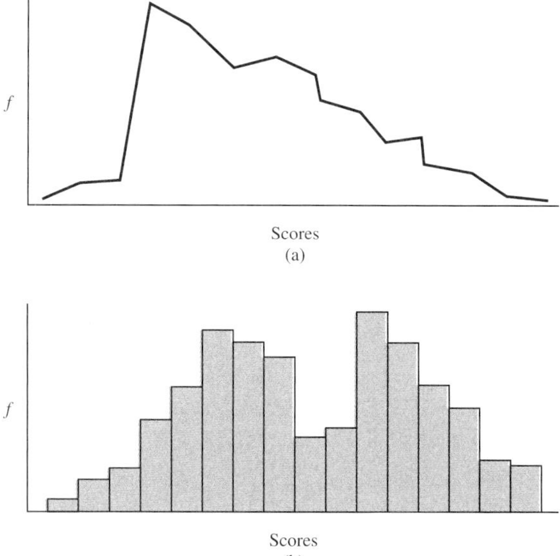

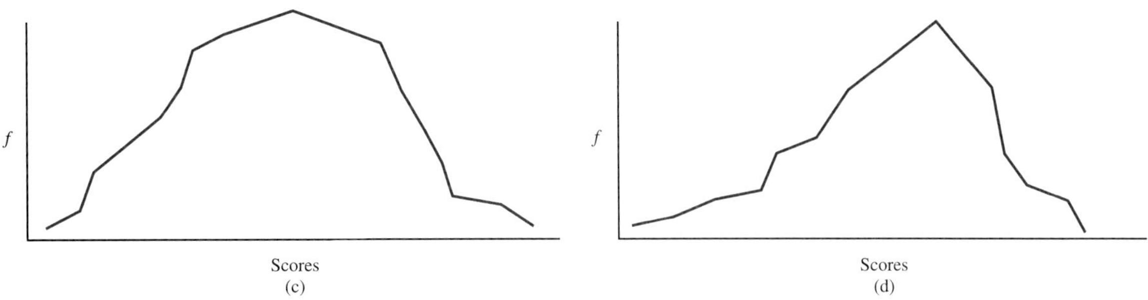


**Answers**

1. C, B, A, D
2. a. positively skewed; b. bimodal; c. normal;
   d. negatively skewed

## RELATIVE FREQUENCY AND THE NORMAL CURVE

We will return to frequency distributions—especially the normal curve—throughout the remainder of this course. However, counting the frequency of scores is not the only thing we do. You'll see that an important procedure is to describe scores based on another type of information called *relative frequency*.

### Understanding Relative Frequency

**Relative frequency** is the proportion of the time that a score occurs in a sample. A *proportion* is a decimal number between 0 and 1 that indicates a fraction of the total. Thus, we use relative frequency to indicate what fraction of the sample is made up by the times that a particular score occurs. In other words, we determine the proportion of $N$ that is made up by the $f$ of a score.

So that you understand relative frequency, let's first calculate it using a formula, although later we'll use a different approach.

*THE FORMULA FOR COMPUTING A SCORE'S RELATIVE FREQUENCY IS*

$$\textit{Relative frequency} = \frac{f}{N}$$

This says that to compute a score's relative frequency, divide its frequency ($f$) by the total number of scores ($N$). For example, if a score occurred 5 times in a sample of 10 scores, then

$$\text{Relative frequency} = \frac{f}{N} = \frac{5}{10} = .50$$

The score has a relative frequency of .50, meaning that the score occurred .50 of the time in this sample. Or, say that a score occurred 6 times out of an $N$ of 9. Then its relative frequency is 6/9, which is .666. *Note:* We usually "round off" relative frequency to two decimals, so .666 becomes .67. Finally, we might find that several scores have a combined frequency of 10 in a sample of 30 scores: 10/30 equals .33, so these scores together have a relative frequency of .33—they make up .33 of this sample.

> ***REMEMBER*** *Relative frequency* indicates the proportion of time (out of $N$) that a score occurred.

You may find it easier to work with relative frequency if you transform it to a percentage. (Remember that officially relative frequency is a proportion.) Converting relative frequency to percent gives the percent of time a score occurs. *To transform relative frequency to a percent, multiply the proportion times 100.* Thus, if a score's relative frequency is .50, then, using parentheses to indicate multiplication, we have (.50)(100) = 50%: This score occurred 50% of the time in this sample. *To transform a percent back into relative frequency, divide the percent by 100:* The score that is 50% of the sample has a relative frequency of 50%/100 = .50.

When reading research, you may encounter frequency tables that also show relative frequency and/or percentages. These are arranged in the same way as the simple frequency table that we saw earlier.

You should know what relative frequency is, but we will not emphasize the above formula. (You're welcome.) Instead, it is important to understand how we use the normal curve to determine a score's relative frequency. This is a core element in later descriptive and inferential statistics.

## Finding Relative Frequency Using the Normal Curve

When data are normally distributed, we can use the idealized normal curve to determine relative frequency. To understand this, realize that the reason for visualizing the normal curve as people in a parking lot is so that you think of the normal curve as a picture of something solid: The space *under the curve* has *area* that represents individuals and their scores. Figure 2.9 shows this parking lot view. The entire curve corresponds to everyone in the sample and 100% of the scores. Therefore, any portion of the parking lot—any portion of the space under the curve—corresponds to that portion of the

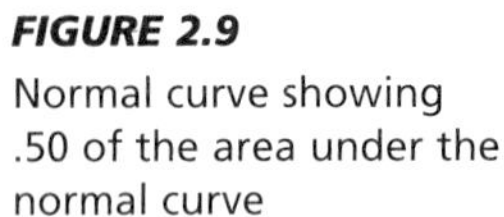

***FIGURE 2.9***
Normal curve showing .50 of the area under the normal curve

*The vertical line is through the middle score, so 50% of the distribution is to the left of the line and 50% is to the right of the line.*

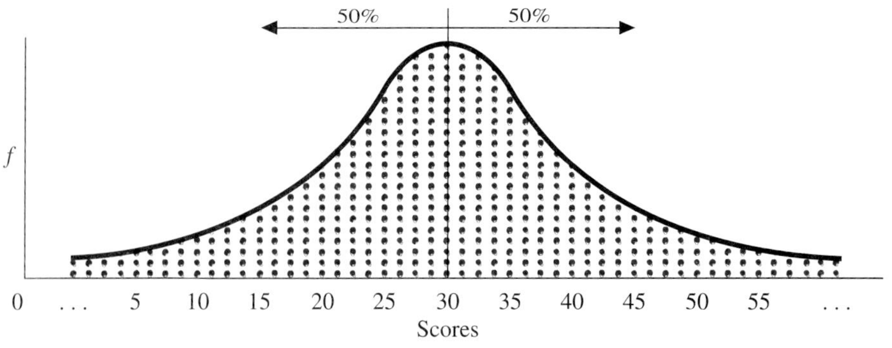

sample. For example, a vertical line is drawn through the middle score of 30, and so .50 of the parking lot is to the left of the line. Because the complete parking lot contains all participants, a part that is .50 of it contains 50% of the participants. (We can ignore those relatively few people who are straddling the line.) Participants are standing in the left-hand part of the lot because they received scores of 29, 28, and so on. So in total, 50% of the people obtained scores below 30. Thus, scores below 30 occurred 50% of the time, so the scores below 30 have a combined relative frequency of .50.

We can use the same procedure in any part of the curve. In statistical terms, the total space occupied by people in the parking lot is *the total area under the normal curve.* We take a vertical "slice" of the polygon above certain scores, and the area of this portion of the curve is the space occupied by the people having those scores. We then compare this area to the total area to determine the **proportion of the area under the curve.** Then

> **The proportion of the area under the normal curve at certain scores corresponds to the relative frequency of those scores.**

Of course, statisticians don't fly around in helicopters, eyeballing parking lots, so here's another example: Say that by using a ruler and protractor, we determine that in Figure 2.10 the entire polygon occupies an area of 6 square inches on the page. This total area corresponds to all scores in the sample. Say that the area under the curve between the scores of 30 and 35 covers 2 square inches. This area is due to the number of times these scores occur. Therefore, the scores between 30 and 35 occupy 2 out of the 6 square inches created by all scores, so these scores constitute 2/6 or .33, of the entire distribution. Thus, the scores between 30 and 35 constitute .33 of our sample, so they have a relative frequency of .33.

The above technique is especially useful because in Chapter 5 you'll see that statisticians have created a system for easily finding the area under any part of the normal curve, so we can easily determine the relative frequency of the scores there. (No, you won't need a ruler and a protractor.) Until then,

> ***REMEMBER*** The area under the normal curve corresponds to the times that all scores occur, so a proportion of this area above some of the scores is the proportion of time those scores occur, which is their relative frequency.

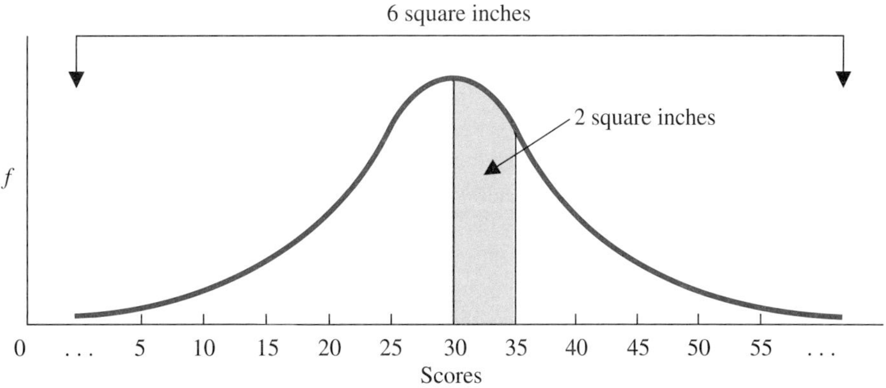


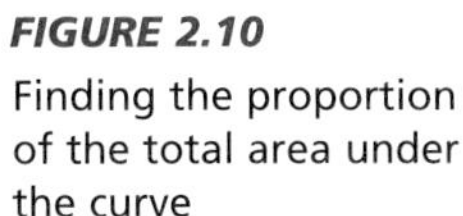

***FIGURE 2.10***
Finding the proportion of the total area under the curve

*The complete curve occupies 6 square inches, with scores between 30 and 35 occupying 2 square inches.*

## A QUICK REVIEW

- Relative frequency is the proportion of time that a score occurs.
- The area under the normal curve corresponds to 100% of a sample, so a proportion of the curve will contain that proportion of the scores, which is their relative frequency.

### More Examples

Below, the shaded area is .15 of the total curve (so 15% in the parking lot are standing at these scores). Thus, scores between 55 and 60 occur .15 of the time, so their combined relative frequency is .15. Above 70 is .50 of the curve, so scores above 70 have a combined relative frequency of .50.

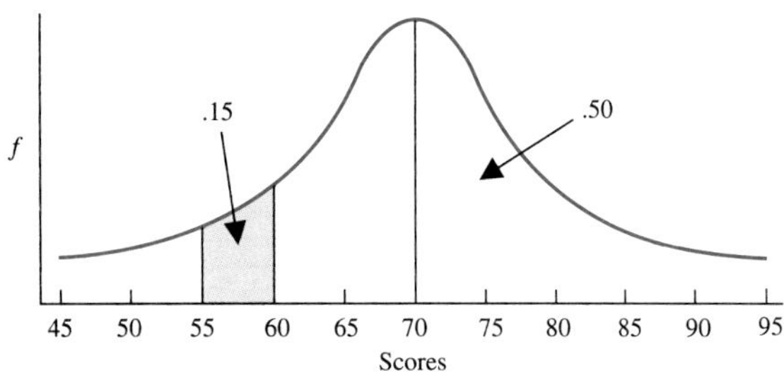


### *For Practice:*

1. If a score occurs 23% of the time its relative frequency is ____?
2. If a score's relative frequency is .34, it occurs ____ percent of the time.
3. Scores that occupy .20 of the area under the curve have a relative frequency of ____.
4. The scores between 15 and 20 have a relative frequency of .40, so they make up ____ of the area under the curve.

**Answers**

1. 23%/100 5 .23
2. (.34)(100) 5 34%
3. .20
4. .40

## UNDERSTANDING PERCENTILE

One other way to summarize scores is to compute their percentile. Usually a **percentile** is defined as the percent of all scores in the data that are *below* a particular score. (Technically a percentile is the percent of the scores that are *at* or below a score, but usually we ignore the relatively few that are at the score.) Thus, if the score of 40 is at the 50th percentile, we interpret this as indicating that about 50% of the scores are below 40 and 50% of the scores are above 40. Or, if you scored at the 75th percentile, then 75% of the group scored lower than you. If you scored at the 100th percentile, you have the highest raw score in the data.

A simple method for determining a score's percentile is to again use the area under the normal curve. Percentile describes the scores that are *lower* than a particular score, and on the normal curve, lower scores are to the *left*. Therefore, the percentile for a score corresponds to the percent of the area under the curve that is to the *left* of the score. For example, Figure 2.11 shows that .50 of the curve is to the left of the score of 30. Because scores to the left of 30 are below it, 50% of the distribution is below 30 (in the parking lot, 50% of the people are standing to the left of the line and all of their

*FIGURE 2.11*
Normal distribution showing the area under the curve to the left of selected scores

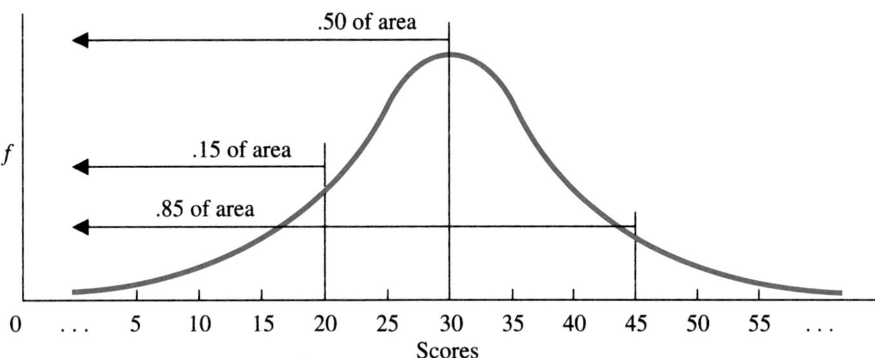


scores are less than 30). Thus, the score of 30 is at the 50th percentile. Likewise, say that we find that 15% of the distribution is to the left of the score of 20; 20 is at the 15th percentile.

We can also work the other way to find the score at a given percentile. Say that we seek the score at the 85th percentile. We would measure over to the right until 85% of the area under the curve is to the left of a certain point. If, as in Figure 2.11, the score of 45 is at that point, then 45 is at the 85th percentile.

> REMEMBER A score's *percentile* is the percent of the scores below it, equal to the percent of the normal curve to the left of the score.

## CHAPTER SUMMARY

1. The number of scores in a sample is symbolized by *N*.
2. A *frequency distribution* shows the frequency of each score. The symbol for simple frequency is *f*.
3. Graph a frequency distribution using a *bar graph* for nominal or ordinal scores, a *histogram* for a few different interval/ratio scores, and a *polygon* for many different interval/ratio scores.
4. A dot plotted on a graph is called a *data point.*
5. In a *normal distribution* forming *a normal curve,* the *tails* contain infrequent, extreme high and low scores, while scores closer to the middle score occur more frequently.
6. A *negatively skewed distribution* has a pronounced tail over the extreme low scores; a *positively skewed distribution* has a pronounced tail over the extreme high scores. A *bimodal distribution* is symmetrical, containing two areas with high-frequency scores.
7. *Relative frequency* is the proportion of the time that a score occurs in a set of data. On the normal curve the relative frequency of scores equals the proportion of the total area under the curve that they occupy.
8. *Percentile* is the percent of all scores in the data that are *below* a particular score. On the normal curve the percentile of a score equals the percent of the curve to the left of the score.

## KEY TERMS: Can You Define the Following?

*N* *19* *f* *19*
bar graph *21*
bimodal distribution *26*
data point *23*
frequency *19*
frequency distribution *19*
frequency polygon *23*
histogram *21*
negatively skewed distribution *26*
normal curve *24*
normal distribution *24*
percentile *32*
positively skewed distribution *26*
proportion of the area under the curve *31*
raw scores *18*
relative frequency *29*
tail of the distribution *25*

## REVIEW QUESTIONS

(Answers for odd-numbered problems are in Appendix C.)

*1.* What do the symbols *N* and *f* mean?

*2.* Why is it important to understand the frequency distribution produced by a set of data?

*3.* (a) What is the difference between a bar graph and a histogram? (b) With what kind of data is each used? (c) What is the difference between a histogram and a polygon? (d) With what kind of data is each used?

*4.* (a) What is the difference between a score's simple frequency and its relative frequency? (b) What is a score's percentile?

*5.* What is a dot plotted on a graph called?

*6.* (a) What is the difference between a skewed distribution and a normal distribution? (b) What is the difference between a bimodal distribution and a normal distribution?

*7.* What is the difference between a positively skewed distribution and a negatively skewed distribution?

*8.* What does it mean when a score is in a tail of a normal distribution?

*9.* What is the difference between a score in the left-hand tail of a normal curve and a score in the right-hand tail?

*10.* (a) What is a proportion? (b) How do you transform a proportion to a percentage? (c) How do you transform a percentage to a proportion?

## APPLICATION QUESTIONS

*11.* In reading psychological research you encounter the following statements. Interpret each one. (a) "The IQ scores were approximately normally distributed." (b) "A bimodal distribution of physical agility scores was observed." (c) "The distribution of the patients' memory scores was severely negatively skewed."

*12.* From the data 1, 4, 5, 3, 2, 5, 7, 3, 4, 5, Poindexter created the following frequency table. What three things did he do wrong?

| *Score* | *f* |
|---|---|
| 1 | 1 |
| 2 | 1 |
| 3 | 2 |
| 4 | 2 |
| 5 | 3 |
| 7 | 1 |
| | $N = 6$ |

*13.* The distribution of scores on your next statistics test is positively skewed. What does this indicate about the difficulty of the test?

*14.* (a) On a normally distributed set of exam scores, Poindexter scored at the 10th percentile, so he claims that he outperformed 90% of his class. Why is he correct or incorrect? (b) Because Foofy's score had a relative frequency of .02, she claims she had one of the highest scores on the exam. Why is she correct or incorrect?

*15.* What type of frequency graph is appropriate when counting the number of (a) blondes, brunettes, redheads, or "other" attending a college; (b) people having each body weight reported in a state-wide survey; (c) children in each grade at an elementary school; (d) car owners reporting above average, average, or below average problems with their car.

*16.* Why are adjacent bars in a bar graph separate, but the adjacent bars in a histogram and the data points in a polygon are connected?

*17.* Interpret each of the following: (a) You scored at the 35th percentile; (b) Your score has a relative frequency of .40; (c) Your score is in the upper tail of the normal curve; (d) Your score is in the left-hand tail of the normal curve; (e) From the normal curve your score is at the 60th percentile.

*18.* The grades on a test form a bimodal distribution. What does this indicate about performance on the test?

*19.* The following shows the distribution of final exam scores in a class. The proportion of the total area under the curve is given for three segments.

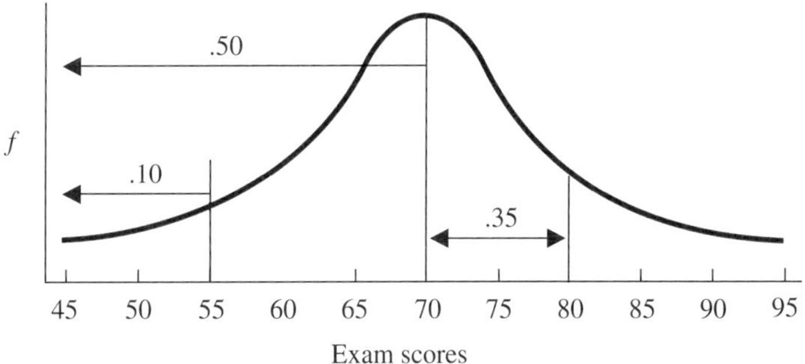


(a) Order the scores 45, 60, 70, 72, and 85 from most frequent to least frequent. (b) What is the percentile of a score of 55? (c) What proportion of the sample scored below 70? (d) What is the relative frequency of scores between 55 and 70? (e) What is the percentile of the score of 80?

*20.* On a normal curve identify the approximate location of the following scores: (a) You have the most frequent score; (b) You have a low-frequency score, but the score is higher than most; (c) You have one of the lower scores, but it has a relatively high frequency; (d) Your score seldom occurred.

*21.* Organize the ratio scores below in a table to show their simple frequency and relative frequency.

| | | | | | | | | |
|---|---|---|---|---|---|---|---|---|
| 49 | 52 | 47 | 52 | 52 | 47 | 49 | 47 | 50 |
| 51 | 50 | 49 | 50 | 50 | 50 | 53 | 51 | 49 |

*22.* Draw a frequency polygon using the data in problem 21.

*23.* Organize the nominal scores below in a table to show their simple frequency and relative frequency.

| | | | | | | | | |
|---|---|---|---|---|---|---|---|---|
| 16 | 11 | 13 | 12 | 11 | 16 | 12 | 16 | 15 |
| 16 | 11 | 13 | 16 | 12 | 11 | | | |

*24.* Using the data in problem 23, draw the appropriate graph showing simple frequency.

## SUMMARY OF FORMULAS

1. *Relative frequency* $= \dfrac{f}{N}$

2. *Percent* = (*Relative frequency*)(*100*)

3. *Relative frequency* = *Percent/100*

# 3 Summarizing Scores with Measures of Central Tendency

**CHAPTER ESSENTIALS**

**Before getting started, be sure you understand**

- From Chapter 1, the logic of statistics and parameters
- From Chapter 1, what independent and dependent variables are and how experiments show a relationship
- From Chapter 2, what normal, skewed, and bimodal distributions are
- From Chapter 2, how percentile is computed using the area under the curve

**Your goals in this chapter are to learn**

- How measures of *central tendency* describe data
- What the *mean, median,* or *mode* indicate and when each is appropriate
- What is meant by "deviations around the mean"
- How a sample mean is used to describe individual scores and the population
- How to interpret and graph the results of an experiment

The frequency distributions discussed in Chapter 2 are important because the shape of the distribution is always an important characteristic of data for us to know. However, graphs and tables are not the most efficient way to summarize a distribution. Instead, we compute individual numbers—statistics—that each provide information about the scores. This chapter discusses statistics that describe the important characteristic of data called *central tendency.* The following sections present (1) the concept of central tendency, (2) the three ways to compute central tendency, and (3) a detailed discussion of the uses of one of them—the mean. But first, here are some symbols and terms.

## SOME NEW SYMBOLS AND TERMINOLOGY

Formulas are written to be applied to any set of scores. Usually we use $X$ as the generic symbol for a score. When a formula says to do something to $X$, it means to do it to all of the scores you are calling $X$ in the sample.

A new symbol you'll see is $\Sigma$, the Greek capital letter *S,* called sigma. Sigma is used in conjunction with a symbol for scores, especially $\Sigma X$. In words, $\Sigma X$ is pronounced **"sum of *X*"** and literally means to find the sum of the *X* scores. Thus, $\Sigma X$ for the scores 5, 6, and 9 is $5 + 6 + 9$, which is 20, so $\Sigma X = 20$. Notice that we do not care whether each *X* is a different score. If the scores are 4, 4, and 4, then $\Sigma X = 12$.

*REMEMBER* The symbol $\Sigma X$ indicates to sum the *X* scores.

Finally, often a calculation will produce an answer with a string of decimal numbers, so we need to "round it off." The rule is simple: *The final answer after rounding should have two more decimal places than were in the original raw scores.* Usually, we have whole-number scores and then the final answer contains two decimal places. When needed, add zeroes to the right of the decimal point to show the rounding: If the answer is 5, it becomes 5.00.

*REMEMBER* A final answer should contain two more decimal places than the original raw scores.

Now on to *central tendency.*

## WHAT IS CENTRAL TENDENCY?

Statistics that are "measures of central tendency" are important because they answer a basic question about data: Are the scores generally high scores or generally low scores? For example, after you've taken a test in some class, your first question is how did you do, but your second question is how did the class as a whole do? Did everyone generally score high, low, or what? You need this information to understand both how the class performed and how you performed relative to everyone else. But it is difficult to do this by looking at the individual scores, or even at a frequency distribution. Instead, it is better if you know something like the class average. Likewise, in all research, the first step is to shrink the data into one summary score, called a *measure of central tendency,* that describes the sample as a whole.

To understand central tendency, first begin thinking of a score as indicating a *location* on a variable. For example, if I am 70 inches tall, don't think of my score as indicating that I have 70 inches of height. Instead, think of me as located on the variable of height at the point marked 70 inches. Think of any variable as an infinite continuum—a straight line—and a score as indicating a location on that line. Thus, as in Figure 3.1, my score is at the "address" labeled 70 inches. If my brother is 60 inches tall, then he is located at 60. The idea is not so much that he is 10 inches shorter than I am, but rather that we are separated by a *distance* of 10 inches. Thus, scores are locations, and the difference between any two scores is the distance between them.

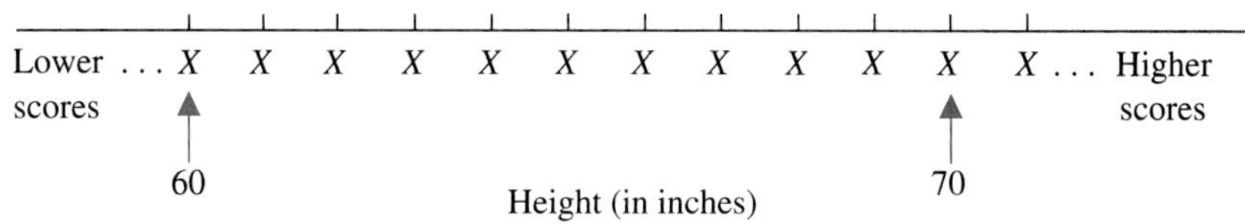


*FIGURE 3.1*
Locations of individual scores on the variable of height

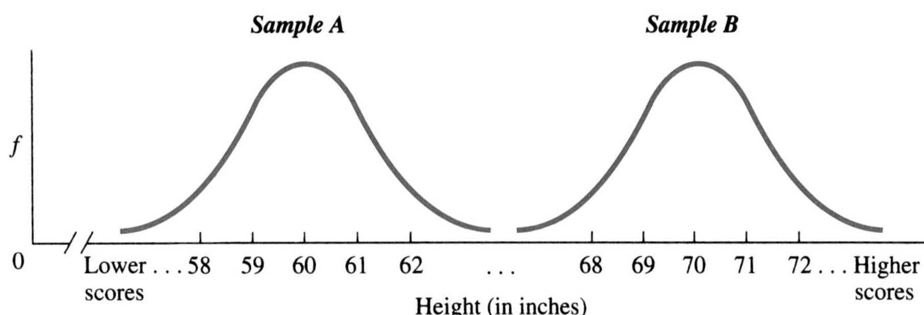


*FIGURE 3.2*
Two sample polygons on the variable of height
*Each polygon indicates the locations of the scores and their frequencies.*

From this perspective a frequency polygon shows the location of all scores in a distribution. For example, Figure 3.2 shows the height scores from two samples. In the parking lot view of a normal curve, participants' scores determine *where* they stand. A high score puts them on the right side of the lot, a low score puts them on the left, and a middle score puts them in the crowd in the middle. Further, if we have two distributions containing different scores, then the *distributions* have different locations on the variable.

So when we ask, "Are the scores generally high scores or generally low scores?" we are actually asking, "*Where* on the variable is the distribution located?" A **measure of central tendency** is a statistic that summarizes the location of a distribution on a variable. Listen to its name: It indicates where the *center* of the distribution *tends* to be located. Thus, it is the point on the variable *around* where most of the scores are and provides an "address" for the distribution as a whole. Thus, in Sample A in Figure 3.2 most of the scores are in the neighborhood of 59, 60, and 61 inches, so a measure of central tendency will indicate that the distribution is located *around* 60 inches. In Sample B the distribution is centered at 70 inches. You'll see other statistics that add to our understanding of a distribution, but measures of central tendency are at the core of summarizing data.

> *REMEMBER* The first step in summarizing any set of data is to compute a *measure of central tendency.*

In the following sections we consider the three common ways to measure central tendency: the *mode,* the *median,* and the *mean.* Then we'll see how to use them to interpret experiments.

## The Mode

The **mode** is a score that has the highest frequency in the data. For example, say that we have these scores: 2, 3, 3, 4, 4, 4, 4, 5, 5, 6. The score of 4 is the mode. (There is no conventional symbol for the mode.) The frequency distribution on the left in Figure 3.3 shows that the mode does summarize this distribution because the scores *are* located around 4. Notice that this polygon is roughly a normal curve, with the highest point over the mode. When a polygon has one hump, such as on the normal curve, the distribution is called **unimodal,** indicating that one score qualifies as the mode.

We may not always have only one mode. Consider the scores 2, 3, 4, 5, 5, 5, 6, 7, 8, 9, 9, 9, 10, 11, 12. Here, two scores, 5 and 9, are tied for the most frequent score. This

***FIGURE 3.3***
A unimodal distribution (a) and a bimodal distribution (b).
*Each vertical line marks a highest point on the distribution, thus indicating a most frequent score, which is the mode.*

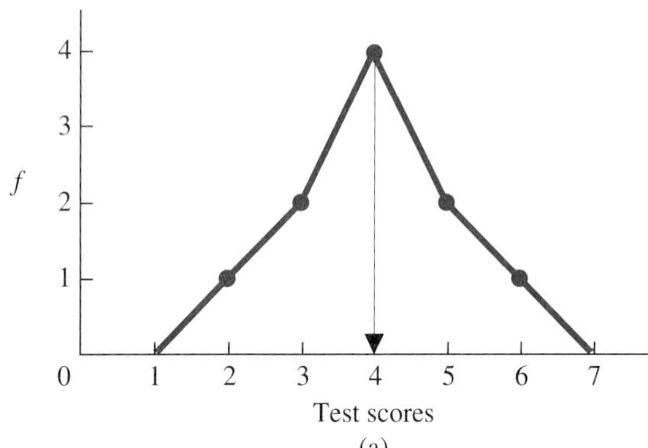


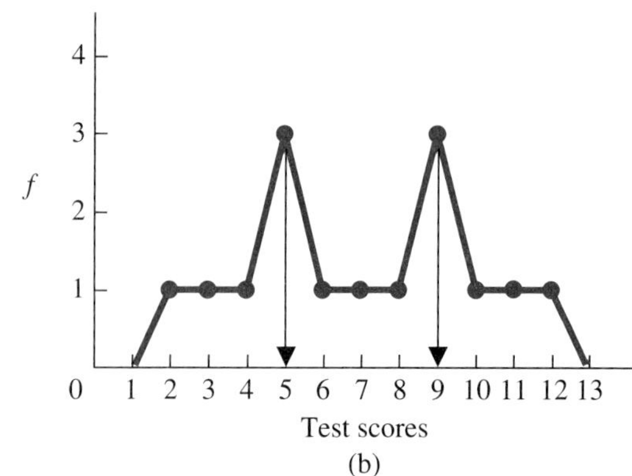


sample is plotted on the right in Figure 3.3. In Chapter 2 such a distribution was called **bimodal** because it has two modes. Identifying the two modes does summarize this distribution, because most of the scores are either around 5 or around 9.

The mode is typically used with scores that reflect a nominal scale of measurement (when participants are categorized using a qualitative variable). For example, say that we asked some people their favorite flavor of ice cream, counting the number of people choosing each category. Reporting that the mode was "Goopy Chocolate" does summarize the results, indicating that more people chose this flavor than any other.

> ***REMEMBER*** The *mode* is the most frequently occurring score in the data, and is usually used to summarize nominal scores.

There are, however, two potential limitations of the mode. First, the distribution may contain many scores that all have the same highest frequency, and then the mode does not summarize the data. In the most extreme case we might obtain scores such as 4, 4, 5, 5, 6, 6, 7, 7. Here there is no mode.

A second problem is that the mode does not take into account any scores other than the most frequent score(s), so it ignores much of the information in the data. This can produce a misleading summary. For example, in the skewed distribution containing 7, 7, 7, 20, 20, 21, 22, 22, 23, and 24, the mode is 7. However, most scores are not around 7, but instead are in the low 20s. Thus, the mode may not accurately summarize where *most* scores in a distribution are located.

Because of these problems, for ordinal, interval, or ratio scores, we can usually compute a better measure of central tendency, such as the median.

## The Median

The **median** is simply another name for the score at the 50th percentile. Recall that a percentile indicates the percent of the scores below a score, so 50% of a distribution is below the median. Thus, if the median is 10, then 50% of the sample scored below 10.

The median is typically a better measure of central tendency than the mode, because (1) only one score can be the median, and (2) the median will usually be around where most of the distribution is located. The symbol for the median is Mdn.

As you saw in Chapter 2, a score's percentile equals the *proportion of the area under the curve* that is to the left of the score, so the median separates the lower 50% of the distribution from the upper 50%. For example, look at the normal curve in graph (a) in Figure 3.4. Because 50% of the curve is to the left of the line, the score at the line is the 50th percentile, so that score is the median. In fact, the median is the score below which 50% of *any* polygon is located. Thus, in the skewed distribution in graph (b) of Figure 3.4, 50% of the curve is to the left of the vertical line, so the score at the line is the median.

There are several ways to calculate the median. First, when scores form a perfect normal distribution as in graph (a), the median is also the most frequent score, so it is the same score as the mode. When scores are approximately normally distributed, the median will be close to the mode. When data are not normally distributed, however, there is no easy way to determine the median. You can, however, *estimate* the median using the following system. Arrange the scores in order from lowest to highest. With an odd number of scores, the score in the middle position is the approximate median. For example, for the nine scores 1, 2, 3, 3, 4, 7, 9, 10, 11, the score in the middle position is the fifth score, so the median is the score of 4. On the other hand, if $N$ is an even number, the average of the two scores in the middle is the approximate median. For example, for the ten scores 3, 8, 11, 11, 12, 13, 24, 35, 46, 48, the middle scores counting from the lowest are at position 5 (the score of 12) and position 6 (the score of 13). The average of 12 and 13 is 12.5, so the median is approximately 12.5. (To precisely calculate the median, consult an advanced text for the appropriate formula. Most computer programs employ this formula, providing the easiest solution.)

The median is the preferred measure of central tendency with ordinal (rank-ordered) scores. For example, say that a group of students ranked how well a college professor teaches. Reporting that the professor's median ranking was 3 communicates that 50% of the students rated the professor as number 1, 2, or 3. Also, as you'll see, the median is appropriate when interval or ratio scores form a very skewed distribution.

> ***REMEMBER*** The *median* (Mdn) is the score at the 50th percentile, and is used to summarize ordinal or highly skewed interval or ratio scores.

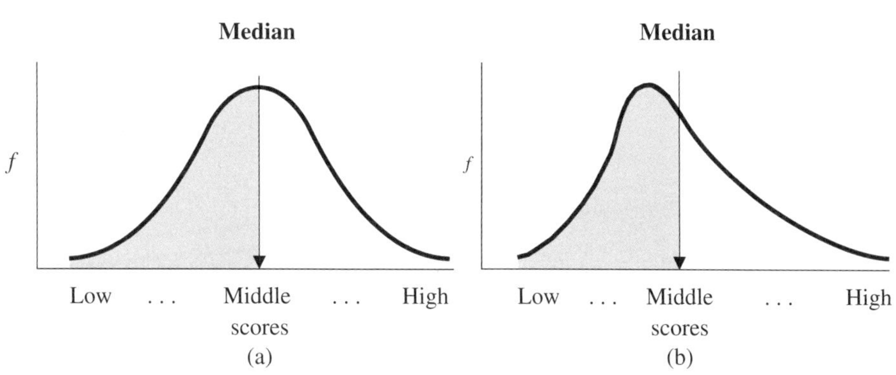


***FIGURE 3.4***

Location of the median in a normal distribution (a) and in a skewed distribution (b)

*The vertical line indicates the location of the median, with one-half of the distribution on each side of it.*

## A QUICK REVIEW

- The mode is the most frequent score in the data.
- The median is the score at the 50th percentile. If $N$ is an odd number, the median is the middle score. If $N$ is even, the median is the average of the middle scores.

### MORE EXAMPLES

For the scores 1, 4, 2, 3, 5, 3, the mode (the most frequent score) is 3. The median is found in two steps. First, order the scores: 1, 2, 3, 3, 4, 5. Then, $N$ is even, so the median is the average of the scores in the 3rd and 4th positions: The average of 3 and 3 is 3. However, for the scores 3, 4, 7, 9, 10, $N = 5$, so the median is at the middle position, which is 7. There is no mode here.

***For Practice:***

1. What is the mode in 4, 6, 8, 6, 3, 6, 8, 7, 9, 8?
2. What is the median in the above scores?
3. With what types of scores is the mode used?
4. With what types of scores is the median used?

**Answers**

1. In this bimodal data, both 6 and 8 are modes.
2. $N = 10$; the median is the average of 6 and 7, which is 6.50.
3. With nominal scores
4. With ordinal or skewed interval/ratio scores

## The Mean

The median ignores some information in the data because it reflects only scores in the lower 50% of a distribution without considering their size, and it ignores the upper 50% of the distribution. Therefore, the median is not used with most distributions of interval or ratio scores. Instead, the measure of central tendency that does not ignore any information in the data is the mean. The **mean** is another name for the "average," which technically is the score located at the *mathematical center* of a distribution.

Let's first compute the mean in a sample. The symbol for a *sample* mean is $\overline{X}$. Compute the mean in the same way you compute an average: Add all of the scores together and then divide by the number of scores you added. The symbol meaning "add the scores" is $\Sigma X$, and the symbol for the number of scores is $N$, so

*THE FORMULA FOR COMPUTING A SAMPLE MEAN IS*

$$\overline{X} = \frac{\Sigma X}{N}$$

For example, in the scores 4, 3, 7, 6:

**Step 1:** *Compute* $\Sigma X$. Add the scores together. Here, $\Sigma X = 4 + 3 + 7 + 6 = 20$
**Step 2:** *Determine* $N$: Here, $N = 4$
**Step 3:** *Divide* $\Sigma X$ *by* $N$. Here, $\overline{X} = 20/4 = 5$

Saying that the mean of these scores is 5.00 indicates that the center of this distribution is located at the score of 5.

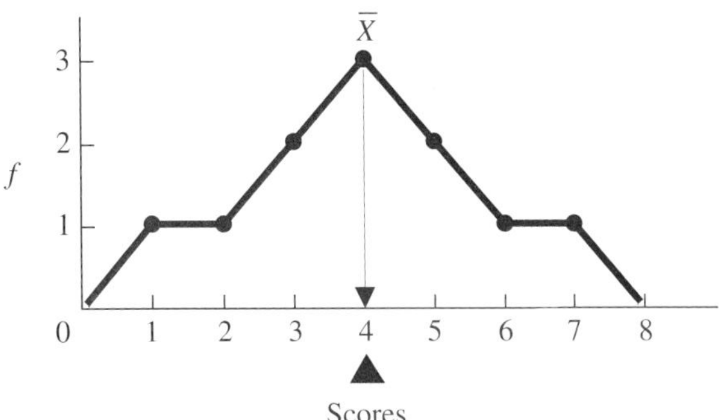


***FIGURE 3.5***

Location of the mean on a symmetrical, normal distribution.

*The vertical line indicates the location of the mean score, which is the center of the distribution.*

What is the mathematical center of a distribution? Think of the center as the distribution's *balance point.* Thus, on the left of the figure below the mean of 5 is the point that balances the symmetrical distribution of 3, 4, 6, and 7. On the right the mean is the balance point even when the distribution is not symmetrical. Here, the mean of 4 balances the distribution.

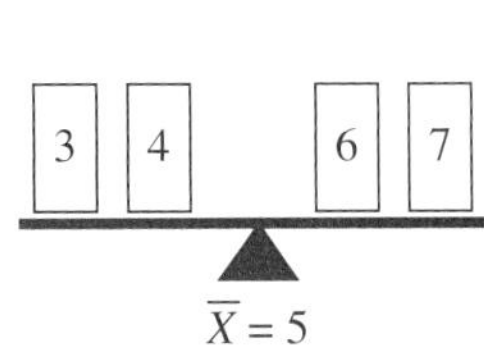


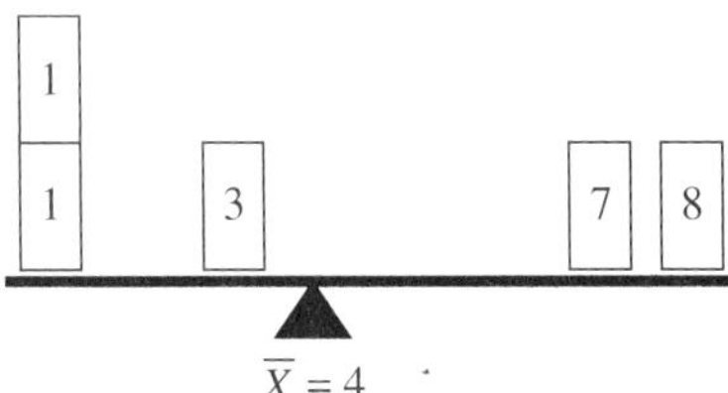


The mean is appropriate with interval or ratio data (scores that measure actual amounts and include zero). But, in addition, the distribution should be *symmetrical and unimodal.* In particular, the mean is appropriate with a normal distribution. For example, say we have the scores 1, 2, 3, 3, 4, 4, 4, 5, 5, 6, 7, which form the roughly normal distribution shown in Figure 3.5. Here, $\Sigma X = 40$ and $N = 10$, so the mean score—the center—is 4. Notice that the reason we use the mean with such data is because the mean is always the mathematical center of any distribution: On a normal distribution the center *is* the point around where most of the scores are located, so the mean is an accurate summary and provides an accurate address for the distribution.

## A QUICK REVIEW

- The mean is the average score, located at the mathematical center of the distribution.
- The mean is appropriate for a normal or symmetrical distribution of interval or ratio scores.

### MORE EXAMPLES

To find the mean of the scores 3, 4, 6, 8, 7, 3, 5:

1: $\Sigma X = 3 + 4 + 6 + 8 + 7 + 3 + 5 = 36$

2: $N = 7$

3: Dividing gives $\overline{X} = 36/7 = 5.1428$; this rounds to 5.14.

### *For Practice:*

1. What is the symbol for the sample mean?
2. What is the mean of 7, 6, 1, 4, 5, 2?
3. With what data is the Xw appropriate?
4. How is a mean interpreted?

**Answers**

1. $\overline{X}$
2. $\Sigma X = 25$, $N = 6$, $\overline{X} = 4.1666$, rounding to 4.17.
3. With normally distributed or symmetrical distributions of interval or ratio scores.
4. It is the center or balance point of the distribution.

## Comparing the Mean, Median, and Mode

In a perfect normal distribution, all three measures of central tendency are located at the same score. For example, back in Figure 3.5 the mean of 4 also splits the curve in half, so 4 is the median. Also, the mean of 4 has the highest frequency, so 4 is the mode. If a distribution is only roughly normal, then the mean, median, and mode will be close to the same score. However, the mean uses all information in the data, and most of the *inferential* procedures we'll see involve the mean. Therefore, the rule is that the mean is the preferred statistic to use with interval or ratio data unless it clearly provides an inaccurate description of the distribution.

The mean will inaccurately describe a highly skewed (nonsymmetrical) distribution. This is because, to balance the distribution, the mean is pulled toward the extreme tail of a skewed distribution, so that the mean does not describe where *most* of the scores are located. You can see this starting with the symmetrical distribution containing the scores 1, 2, 2, 2, 3. The mean is 2 and this accurately describes most scores. However, including the score of 20 would skew the sample, giving 1, 2, 2, 2, 3, 20. Now the mean is pulled up to 5. But! Most of these scores are not at or near 5. As this illustrates, the mean is at the *mathematical* center, but in a skewed distribution that center is not where most of the scores are located.

The solution is to use the median to summarize a very skewed distribution. Figure 3.6 shows the relative positions of the mean, median, and mode in skewed distributions. In both graphs the mean is pulled toward the extreme tail and is not where most scores are located. The mode is toward the side away from the extreme tail and so the distribution is not centered here either. Thus, of the three measures, the median most accurately reflects the central tendency of a skewed distribution.

> ***REMEMBER*** With interval or ratio scores the mean is used to summarize normal distributions; the median is used to summarize skewed distributions.

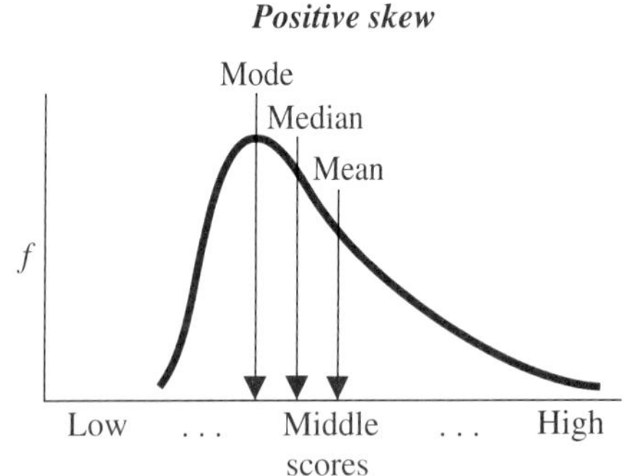


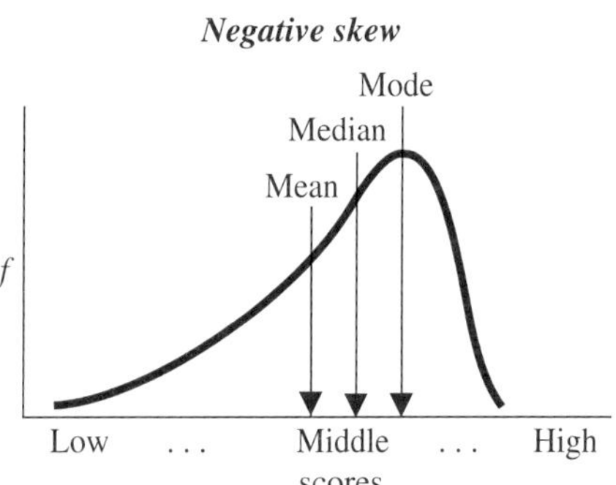


***FIGURE 3.6***

Measures of central tendency for skewed distributions

*The vertical lines show the relative positions of the mean, median, and mode.*

It is for the above reasons that the government uses the median to summarize such skewed distributions as that of yearly income or the price of houses. For example, the median income in the United States is around $38,000 a year. But there is a relatively small number of corporate executives, movie stars, professional athletes, and the like who make millions! Averaging in these high incomes would produce a much higher mean. However, because most incomes are not located there, the median is a better summary of this distribution.

Believe it or not, we've now covered the basic measures of central tendency. In sum, the first step in summarizing data is to compute a measure of central tendency to describe the score *around* which the distribution tends to be located.

- Compute the mode with nominal data or with a distinctly bimodal distribution of any type of scores.
- Compute the median with ordinal scores or with a very skewed distribution of interval/ratio scores.
- Compute the mean with a symmetrical, unimodal distribution of interval or ratio scores.

## APPLYING THE MEAN TO RESEARCH

Most often the data in behavioral research are summarized using the mean. This is because most often we measure variables using interval or ratio scores that, simply because of how nature works, form a roughly normal distribution. Because the mean is used so extensively, we will delve further into its characteristics and uses in the following sections.

### Deviations Around the Mean

First, you need to understand why the mean is at the center of a distribution. The answer is because the mean is just as far from the scores above it as it is from the scores below it. That is, the *total distance* that some scores are above the mean equals the *total distance* that the other scores are below the mean.

The distance separating a score from the mean is called the score's **deviation,** indicating the amount the score "deviates" from the mean. A score's deviation is equal to the score minus the mean, or in symbols, to $X - \overline{X}$. Thus, if the sample mean is 47, a score of 50 deviates by $+3$ because $50 - 47$ is $+3$. A score of 40 deviates from the mean of 47 by $-7$ because $40 - 47 = -7$.

***REMEMBER*** Always subtract the mean *from* the raw score when computing a score's *deviation.*

Notice that a deviation consists of a number and a sign. A positive deviation indicates that the score is greater than the mean, and a negative deviation indicates that the score is less than the mean. The size of the deviation (regardless of its sign) indicates the distance the score lies from the mean: the *larger* the deviation, the *farther* the score is from the mean. A deviation of 0 indicates that the score equals the mean.

When we determine the deviations of all the scores in a sample, we find the *deviations around the mean.* The **sum of the deviations around the mean** is the sum of all differences between the scores and the mean. And here's why the mean is the mathematical center of a distribution:

**The sum of the deviations around the mean always equals zero.**

For example, the scores 3, 4, 6, and 7, have a mean of 5. Table 3.1 shows how to compute the sum of the deviations around the mean for these scores. First, we subtract the mean from each score to obtain its deviation, and then we add the deviations. The sum is zero. In fact, for *any* distribution, having any shape, the sum of the deviations around the mean will equal zero. This is because the sum of the positive deviations equals the sum of the negative deviations, so the sum of all deviations is zero. In this way the mean is the center of a distribution, because in total, the mean is an equal distance from scores above and below it.

*Note:* We have a symbol for the sum of the deviations. Combining the symbol for a deviation—$(X - \overline{X})$—with the symbol for sum—$\Sigma$—gives the sum of the deviations as $\Sigma(X - \overline{X})$. This also says to first subtract the mean from each score to find each deviation, and then add all of the deviations together. Thus, in symbols, $\Sigma(X - \overline{X}) = 0$.

*REMEMBER* $\Sigma(X - \overline{X})$ is the symbol for the sum of the deviations around the mean.

The importance of the sum of the deviations equaling zero is this: Because the deviations balance out to zero, the mean is literally the score *around* which everyone in the sample scored. Therefore, we think of the mean as the typical score, because it more or less describes everyone's score. The reason the mean is such a useful summary (and why you have always used the "average" in the past) is because by using the mean, the errors that then occur will cancel out over the long run. For example, if the class average on an exam is 80, for any individual you'd estimate a score of 80. If we compare our predictions to what people actually get, sometimes we will be wrong, but our *total error* will equal zero. That is, say that one student scored 70. We would predict an 80, so we'd be off by $-10$. However, because the mean is the central score, another student would score, say, 90, and by estimating an 80, we'd be off by $+10$. In the same way, our errors will cancel out for the entire sample. A basic rule of statistics is that if we can't perfectly describe every score, then the next best thing is to have a number that more or less describes every score, with the same degrees of more and less. Thus, the mean is the best score to use when describing or predicting scores because the over- and underestimates will cancel out to equal zero.

***TABLE 3.1***
Computing Deviations Around the Mean

*The mean is subtracted from each score, resulting in the score's deviation.*

| *Score* | *minus* | *Mean Score* | *equals* | *Deviation* |
|---|---|---|---|---|
| 3 | − | 5 | = | −2 |
| 4 | − | 5 | = | −1 |
| 6 | − | 5 | = | +1 |
| 7 | − | 5 | = | +2 |
| | | | Sum = | 0 |

*REMEMBER* We use the mean when describing scores because, over the long run, the over- and underestimates cancel out, so the total error is zero.

## Summarizing an Experiment

Now you can understand how means are used in research. We compute the mean anytime we have a sample of normally distributed scores. Thus, if we've merely observed some participants, we compute the mean number of times they exhibit a particular behavior, or we compute the mean response in a survey. In a *correlational study* we compute the mean score on the $X$ variable and the mean score on the $Y$ variable. Using such means, we can describe the typical score and predict the scores of other individuals when in the same situation.

The predominant way to summarize experiments is also to compute means. As an example, say that in a study of human memory we compare the errors made when recalling lists of words. In one condition of the independent variable of list length, participants read a 5-word list and then recall it. In another condition, participants read a 10-item list and recall it, and in a third condition, they read a 15-item list and recall it. The dependent variable is the number of errors each participant made when recalling the list. Say that we obtain the idealized data shown in Table 3.2. Each column represents a condition of the independent variable, and in a column are the dependent scores for participants in that condition. A relationship appears to be present, because for each condition of list length we tend to see a different batch of recall scores: Participants having a "score" on list length of 5 items produce error scores that are around 3. But participants with 10 items have a different batch of scores around 6, and when list length is 15, scores are around 9. Thus, the longer the list, the more recall errors are produced.

Most experiments involve much larger $N$s, and so to see the relationship buried in the scores, we compute a measure of central tendency. The scores are from the *dependent variable,* so compute the mean, median, or mode depending upon (1) the scale of measurement used to measure the dependent variable and (2) for interval or ratio scores, the shape of the distribution they form. To determine the shape of the distribution, read research related to your study and see what researchers say about the population and how they computed central tendency.

*REMEMBER* The first step in summarizing an experiment is to compute a measure of central tendency using the scores from the dependent variable.

**TABLE 3.2**
Errors Made by Participants Recalling a 5-, 10-, or 15-Item List

| *Condition 1: 5-Item List* | *Condition 2: 10-Item List* | *Condition 3: 15-Item List* |
|---|---|---|
| 3 | 6 | 9 |
| 4 | 5 | 11 |
| 2 | 7 | 7 |

Usually we compute the mean of the dependent scores in each condition. In our recall experiment, we compute the mean of each column in Table 3.2, producing Table 3.3.

To interpret each mean, envision the scores that typically would produce it. In our condition 1, for example, a normal distribution producing a mean of 3 would contain scores distributed above and below 3, with most scores close to 3. (Essentially, envision raw scores as in Table 3.2.) We then use the mean to describe the scores: In condition 1, for example, we'd say participants score around 3, or the typical score is 3, and we'd predict that any participant would make about 3 errors in this situation.

To see the relationship that is present, look at the *pattern* formed by the means: Because a different mean score indicates a different batch of raw scores that produced it, a relationship is present when the means change as the conditions change. Thus, our data show a relationship, because as the conditions change from 5- to 10- to 15-item lists, the dependent scores also change from scores around 3, to scores around 6, to scores around 9, respectively. On the other hand, if the means for the three conditions had been 5, 5, and 5, this would indicate that essentially the same batch of scores occurred regardless of list length, so no relationship is present.

> ***REMEMBER*** The way to understand the relationship in an experiment is to look at the differences between the means of the conditions.

Notice that we demonstrated that, *literally,* list length makes a difference in individual recall scores and therefore in the mean scores. Although research always looks for relationships, sometimes a research report may not say so. Researchers often imply that they have found a relationship simply by saying that they have found a difference between the means. If they find no difference, they have not found a relationship. However, not all means must differ for a relationship to be present: We might find that only the mean (and scores) in the 5-item condition differs from the mean in the 15-item condition.

The above logic also applies to the median or mode. A relationship is present if a different median or mode occurs in two or more conditions, because this indicates that a different batch of raw scores occurs as the conditions change.

**Graphing the Results of an Experiment** The results of experiments are often reported using graphs. Always label the $X$ axis with the conditions of the independent variable and label the $Y$ axis as the mean (or mode or median) of the dependent scores.

> ***REMEMBER*** Plot the independent variable on the $X$ axis and the dependent variable on the $Y$ axis.

We have two types of graphs we may create. Create either a *line graph* or a *bar graph,* depending on the scale of measurement used to measure the *independent variable.*

***TABLE 3.3***
Means of Conditions in Memory Experiment

| *Condition 1: 5-Item List* | *Condition 2: 10-Item List* | *Condition 3: 15-Item List* |
|---|---|---|
| $\overline{X} = 3$ | $\overline{X} = 6$ | $\overline{X} = 9$ |

Create a line graph when the independent variable is an interval or a ratio variable. In a **line graph** adjacent data points are connected with straight lines. For example, for our previous data with the independent variable of list length (a ratio variable), we create the line graph on the left in Figure 3.7. A data point is placed above the 5-item condition opposite the mean of 3 errors, a data point is above the 10-item condition at the mean of 6 errors, and a data point is above the 15-item condition at the mean of 9 errors. Then we connect adjacent data points with straight lines.

The graph conveys the same information as the sample means did in Table 3.3. Look at the overall pattern: If the vertical positions of the data points go up or down as the conditions change, then the means are changing. Different sample means indicate different scores in each condition, so a relationship is present. However, say that instead, in every condition the mean was 5 errors, producing the line graph on the right in Figure 3.7. The result is a horizontal line, indicating that the mean error score stays the same as the conditions change, so essentially the same scores occur in each condition and no relationship is present.

> ***REMEMBER*** If data points form a line that is not horizontal, the $Y$ scores are changing as $X$ changes, and a relationship is present. If data points form a horizontal line, the $Y$ scores do not change as $X$ changes, and a relationship is not present.

On the other hand, create a **bar graph** when the independent variable is a nominal or ordinal variable. Place a bar above each condition on the $X$ axis to the height on the $Y$ axis that corresponds to the mean score for that condition. As usual, adjacent bars do not touch. For example, say that we conducted an experiment comparing the recall errors made by psychology majors, English majors, and physics majors. This independent variable involves a nominal scale, so we have the bar graph shown in Figure 3.8. Because the tops of the bars do not form a horizontal line, we know that different means and thus different scores are in each condition. We see that individual error scores are around 8 for physics majors, around 4 for psychology majors, and around 12 for English majors, so a relationship is present.

***FIGURE 3.7***

Line graphs showing (a) the relationship for mean recall errors as a function of list length and (b) showing no relationship.

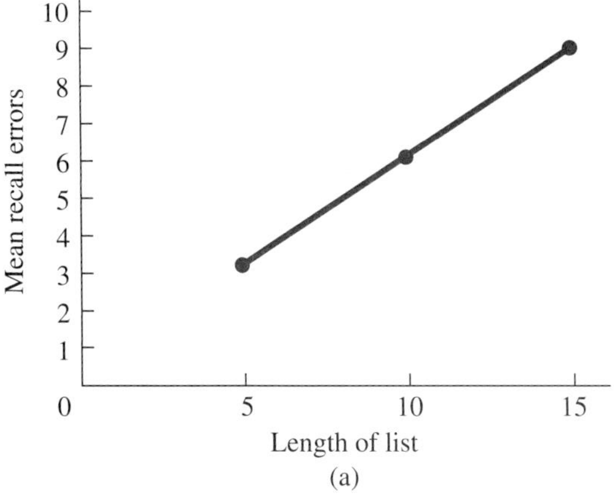


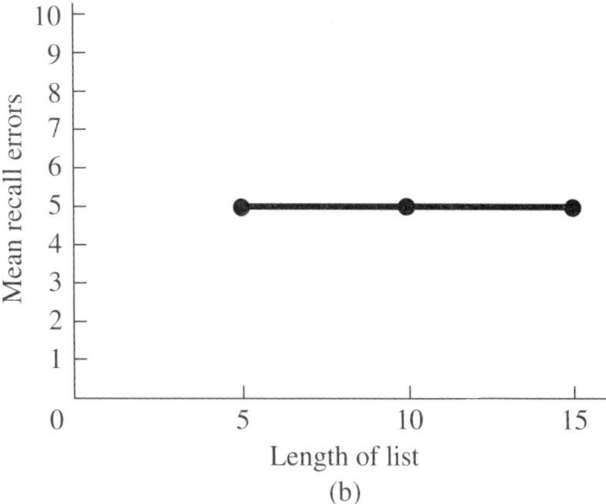

**FIGURE 3.8**
Bar graph showing mean recall errors as a function of college major
*The height of each bar corresponds to the mean score for the condition.*

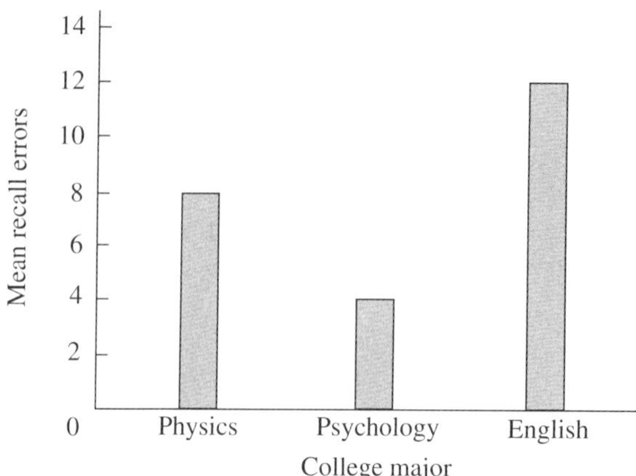


*Note:* In a different experiment we might have measured a nominal or an ordinal *dependent* variable. In that case we would plot the mode or median on the *Y* axis for each condition. Then, again depending on the characteristics of the independent variable, we would create either a line or bar graph.

**REMEMBER** The scale of measurement involved in the dependent variable determines the measure of central tendency to compute. The scale involved in the independent variable determines the type of graph to create.

## A QUICK REVIEW

- Graph the independent variable on the *X* axis and the mean, median, or mode of the dependent scores on the *Y* axis.
- Create a line graph when the independent variable is interval or ratio; produce a bar graph when it is nominal or ordinal.

### MORE EXAMPLES:

We ask males and females to rate their satisfaction with an instructor and the mean scores are 20 and 30, respectively. To graph this, gender is a nominal independent variable, so plot a bar graph, with the labels "male" and "female" on *X*, and the means for each on *Y*. Instead, say we measure the satisfaction scores of students tested with either a 10-, 40-, or 80-question final exam and, because the scores form skewed distributions, compute the median scores. Test length is a ratio independent variable, so plot a line graph, with the labels 10, 40, and 80 on *X*, and the median of each condition on *Y*.

### *For Practice:*

1. The independent variable is plotted on the ____ axis, and the dependent variable is plotted on the ____ axis.
2. A ____ shows a data point above each *X*, with adjacent data points connected with straight lines.
3. A ____ shows a discrete bar above each *X*.
4. The characteristics of the ____ variable determine whether to plot a line or bar graph.
5. Create a bar graph with ____ or ____ variables.
6. Create a line graph with ____ or ____ variables.

**Answers:**

1. *X; Y*
2. line graph
3. bar graph
4. independent
5. nominal / ordinal
6. interval / ratio

## Describing the Population Mean

Recall that ultimately we seek to describe the population of scores found in a given situation. Populations are unwieldy, so we also summarize them using measures of central tendency. Usually we have normally distributed interval or ratio scores, so usually we describe the population mean. The mean of a population is symbolized by the Greek letter $\mu$ (pronounced "mew"). Thus, to indicate that the population mean is 143, we'd say $\mu = 143$. We use $\mu$ simply to show that we're talking about a population, as opposed to a sample, but a population mean has the same characteristics as a sample mean: $\mu$ is the average of the scores in the population, it is the center of the distribution, and the sum of the deviations around $\mu$ equals zero. Thus, $\mu$ is the score around which everyone in the population scored, it is the typical score, and it is the score we predict for any individual in the population.

***REMEMBER*** The symbol for a population mean is $\mu$.

How do we determine $\mu$? If all scores in the population are known, then we compute $\mu$ using the same formula used to compute the sample mean, so $\mu = \Sigma X / N$. Usually, however, a population is infinitely large, so instead, we perform that inferential process we've discussed previously, using the mean of a sample to estimate $\mu$. Thus, if a sample's mean in a particular situation is 99, then, assuming the sample accurately represents the population, we estimate that $\mu$ in this situation is also 99.

Likewise, ultimately we wish to describe any experiment in terms of the scores that would be found if we tested the entire population in each condition. For example, assume that the data from our previous list-length study is representative. Because the mean in the 5-item condition was 3, we expect that everyone should make around 3 errors in this situation, so we estimate that if the population recalled a 5-item list, the $\mu$ would be 3. Similarly, we infer that if the population recalled a 10-item list, $\mu$ would equal the condition's mean of 6, and if the population recalled a 15-item list, $\mu$ would be 9.

We conceptualize the above populations as follows. By estimating each $\mu$, we know approximately *where* on the dependent variable each population would be located. Further, we've assumed that recall errors are normally distributed, so we also know the *shape* of each distribution. Thus, we can envision the populations of recall scores we expect for each condition as the frequency polygons shown in Figure 3.9. (These are frequency distributions, so the dependent (recall) scores are on the $X$ axis.) The figure shows a relationship because, as the conditions of the independent variable change,

**FIGURE 3.9**

Locations of populations of error scores as a function of list length

*Each distribution contains the recall scores we would expect to find if the population were tested under each condition.*

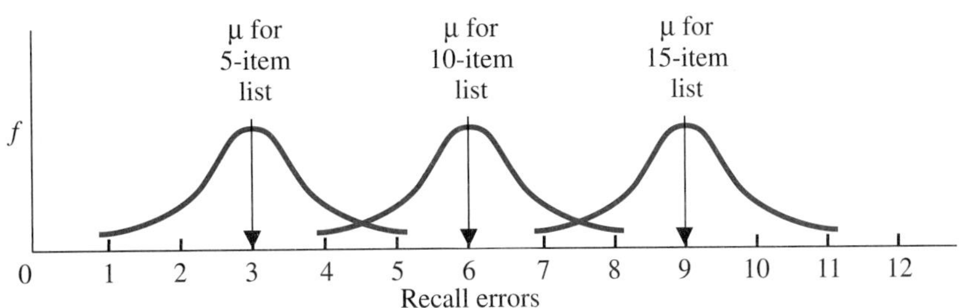

scores on the dependent variable change so that we see a different population of scores for each condition. Essentially, for every 5 items added to a list, the distributions slide to the right, going from scores around 3 to around 6 to around 9. And, at long last, because we are describing *everyone's* behavior, we have returned to the law of nature we began with: We have evidence that human memory generally works in such a way that for every 5 items, recall errors go up by about 3 errors. At this point we have basically achieved the goal of our research.

*REMEMBER* Envision the results of an experiment in the population by creating a frequency distribution located at the $\mu$ for each condition.

## CHAPTER SUMMARY

1. *Measures of central tendency* summarize the location of a distribution of scores on a variable, indicating where the center of the distribution tends to be.
2. The *mode* is a most frequently occurring score in a distribution. It is used primarily to summarize nominal data.
3. The *median,* symbolized by Mdn, is the score at the 50th percentile. It is used primarily with ordinal data and with skewed interval or ratio data.
4. The *mean* is the average score located at the mathematical center of a distribution. It is used with interval or ratio data that form a symmetrical, unimodal distribution such as a normal distribution. The symbol for a sample mean is $\overline{X}$, and the symbol for a population mean is $\mu$.
5. The amount a score *deviates* from the mean is computed as $X - \overline{X}$. The *sum of the deviations around the mean* is $\Sigma(X - \overline{X})$ and always equals zero.
6. The mean is the typical score *around* which a normal distribution is located, and is therefore the best estimate of any individual's score. Over the long run, errors when using the mean will cancel out to equal zero.
7. A relationship is present in an experiment if different means occur as the conditions change. A relationship is present in the population when different distributions, having different $\mu$s, occur as the conditions change.
8. When graphing the results of an experiment, the independent variable is placed on the $X$ axis and the dependent variable is on the $Y$ axis. A line graph is created for a ratio or interval independent variable. A bar graph is created for a nominal or ordinal independent variable.
9. If the data points on a graph form a line that is not horizontal, then a relationship is present. If the data points form a horizontal line, then a relationship is not present.

## KEY TERMS: Can You Define the Following?

$\Sigma X$ *38* Mdn *41* $\overline{X}$ *42*
$\Sigma(X - \overline{X})$ *46* $\mu$ *51*
bar graph *49*
bimodal distribution *40*
deviation *45*
line graph *49*
mean *42*
measure of central tendency *39*

median *40*
mode *39*
sum of the deviations around the mean *46*
sum of X *38*
unimodal *39*

## REVIEW QUESTIONS

(Answers for odd-numbered problems are in Appendix C.)

*1.* What does a measure of central tendency indicate?
*2.* To how many decimal places do you round off a calculation?
*3.* What is the mode, and with what type of data is it most appropriate?
*4.* What is the median, and with what type of data is it most appropriate?
*5.* What is the mean, and with what type of data is it most appropriate?
*6.* Why is it best to use the mean with a normal distribution?
*7.* Why is it inappropriate to use the mean with a skewed distribution?
*8.* Which measure of central tendency is used most often in behavioral research? Why?
*9.* What is $\mu$ and how do we usually determine it?
*10.* Why do we use the mean of a sample to estimate any score that might be found in that sample?
*11.* (a) What is the symbol for a score's deviation from the mean? (b) What is the symbol for the sum of the deviations? (c) What does it mean to say "the sum of the deviations around the mean equals zero"?
*12.* (a) When graphing an experiment, which variable is on the $X$ axis and which is on $Y$? (b) When are bar graphs or line graphs appropriate?

## APPLICATION QUESTIONS

*13.* A researcher collected the following sets of data. For each, indicate the measure of central tendency she should compute: (a) the following IQ scores: 60, 72, 63, 83, 68, 74, 90, 86, 74, 80; (b) the following error scores: 10, 15, 18, 15, 14, 13, 42, 15, 12, 14, 42; (c) the following blood types: A−, A−, O, A+, AB−, A+, O, O, O, AB+; (d) the following grades: B, D, C, A, B, F, C, B, C, D, D.
*14.* (a) When do you round off an answer to two decimal places? (b) When do you round off an answer to 3 decimal places? (c) An answer is 4.00. What do the zeros indicate?
*15.* For each sample below, compute the mean, the median, and the mode.

| Sample A | Sample B | Sample C | Sample D |
|---|---|---|---|
| 2 | 5 | 8 | 9 |
| 1 | 4 | 8 | 11 |
| 3 | 6 | 8 | 10 |
| 2 | 5 | 8 | 10 |
| | 5 | 8 | 11 |
| | 6 | | 8 |

*16.* In experiments how do we envision a relationship in the population?

*17.* For the following experimental results, interpret specifically the relationship between the independent and dependent variables:

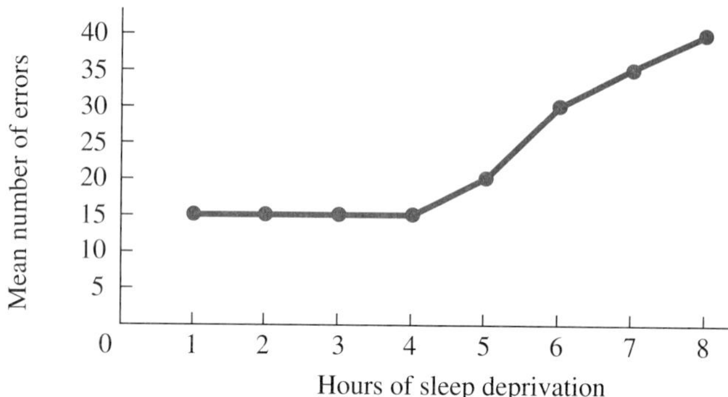


*18.* (a) If you participated in the study in problem 17 and had been deprived of 5 hours of sleep, how many errors do you think you would make? (b) If we tested all people in the world after 5 hours of sleep deprivation, how many errors do you think each would make? (c) What symbol stands for your prediction in part b?

*19.* For each of the experiments listed below, determine (1) which variable should be plotted on the $Y$ axis and which on the $X$ axis, (2) whether to use a line graph or a bar graph, and (3) how to summarize the dependent scores: (a) a study of income as a function of the independent variable of age; (b) a study of the dependent variable of politicians' positive votes on environmental issues depending on the presence or absence of a wildlife refuge in their political district; (c) a study of running speed produced by different conditions of carbohydrates consumed; (d) a study of rates of alcohol abuse found for different ethnic groups.

*20.* You hear that a line graph of scores from the Grumpy Emotionality Test slants downward with increases in the amount of sunlight present on the day subjects were tested. (a) What does this tell you about the mean scores for the conditions? (b) What does this tell you about the raw scores for each condition? (c) Assuming that the samples are representative, what does this tell you about the $\mu$s? (d) What do you conclude about if there is a relationship between emotionality and sunlight in nature?

*21.* You conduct a study to determine the impact that varying the amount of noise in an office has on worker productivity. You obtain the following productivity scores.

| *Condition 1*<br>*Low Noise* | *Condition 2*<br>*Medium Noise* | *Condition 3*<br>*Loud Noise* |
|---|---|---|
| 15 | 13 | 12 |
| 19 | 11 | 9 |
| 13 | 14 | 7 |
| 13 | 10 | 8 |

(a) Productivity scores are normally distributed ratio scores. Summarize the results of this experiment. (b) Draw the appropriate graph for these data. (c) Assuming the data are representative, draw how we would envision the populations produced by this experiment. (d) What conclusions should you draw from this experiment?

22. Assume that the data in problem 21 reflect a highly skewed interval variable. (a) Summarize these scores. (b) What conclusion would you draw from the sample data? (c) What conclusion would you draw about the populations produced by this experiment?

## SUMMARY OF FORMULAS

1. *The formula for computing the sample mean is*

$$\overline{X} = \frac{\Sigma X}{N}$$

2. *To estimate the median, rank-order the scores. If* N *is an odd number, the score in the middle position is the median. If* N *is an even number, the average of the two scores in the middle positions is the median.*

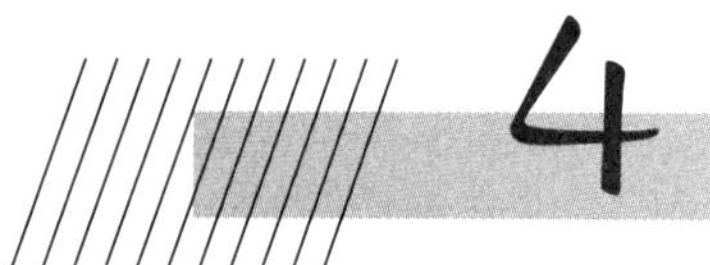

# 4 Summarizing Scores with Measures of Variability

**CHAPTER ESSENTIALS**

**Before getting started, be sure you understand**

- From Chapter 2, how to interpret the normal curve and use the proportion of the area under the curve
- From Chapter 3, what $\overline{X}$ and $\mu$ stand for, what a deviation score is, and why the sum of the deviations around the mean is zero

**Your goals in this chapter are to learn**

- What is meant by *variability*
- What the *range* is
- What the *standard deviation* and *variance* indicate about a set of scores
- How to compute the *standard deviation* and *variance* in a sample, and how to estimate each in a population

You have seen that the first steps in dealing with data are to consider the shape of the distribution and compute the mean (or other measure of central tendency). This information simplifies the distribution and describes the typical score. But not everyone will obtain the typical score, and there will be different scores. Therefore, to completely describe data you must also determine whether there are large or small differences among the scores. This chapter discusses the statistics for describing the differences among scores, which are called *measures of variability.* In the following sections we discuss (1) the concept of variability, (2) how to compute statistics that describe variability in a sample, and (3) how to estimate the variability in the corresponding population.

## UNDERSTANDING VARIABILITY

Computing a measure of variability is important because it answers the question "How large are the differences among the individual raw scores?" Without it, a measure of central tendency provides an incomplete description. The mean, for example, indicates only the central score and where the most frequent scores are. It tells us little about scores that are not at the center of the distribution and/or that occur infrequently. For example look at Table 4.1. Each sample has a mean of 6, so without looking at the raw

**TABLE 4.1**
Three Different Distributions Having the Same Mean Score

| *Sample A* | *Sample B* | *Sample C* |
|---|---|---|
| 0 | 8 | 6 |
| 2 | 7 | 6 |
| 6 | 6 | 6 |
| 10 | 5 | 6 |
| 12 | 4 | 6 |
| $\overline{X} = 6$ | $\overline{X} = 6$ | $\overline{X} = 6$ |

scores, you might think they are identical distributions. But, Sample A contains scores that differ greatly from each other and from the mean, Sample B contains scores that differ less, and in Sample C there are no differences among the scores.

Thus, to completely describe a set of data, we need to also calculate statistics called measures of variability. **Measures of variability** describe the extent to which scores in a distribution *differ* from each other. Thus, when we ask "How large are the differences among the scores?" we are asking the statistical question "How much variability is in the data?" With frequent, large differences the data are *variable* or contain a large amount of *variability.*

In Chapter 3 you saw that a score indicates a participant's location on a variable and that the difference between two scores is the distance that separates them. From this perspective, measures of variability indicate how *spread out* the scores are. For example, Sample A in Table 4.1 shows relatively large differences among the scores, so this distribution is spread out. Smaller differences occur in Sample B, so this distribution is not as spread out. With no differences in Sample C, there is no spread in this distribution.

Finally, a measure of variability describes two additional aspects of the data. First, the opposite of variability is how *consistent* the scores are. Small variability indicates there are few differences among the scores, so the scores must be rather similar and consistently close to each other. Conversely, larger variability indicates that scores are inconsistent. Second, a measure of variability indicates how accurately the mean describes the distribution. The greater the variability, the more the scores are spread out, and so the less accurately they are summarized by one central score. Conversely, the smaller the variability, the closer the scores are to each other and to the central score. Thus, by knowing the amount of variability in the above samples, we know Sample C contains consistent scores and so 6 very accurately represents it, Sample B contains less consistent scores and so 6 is not so accurate a summary, and Sample A contains very inconsistent scores and so 6 is not very close to most scores.

**REMEMBER** *Measures of variability* indicate how spread out the scores are.

Researchers have several ways to measure variability. Which specific measure you should compute depends on the type of data you have. The following sections discuss the three common measures of variability: the *range,* the *variance,* and the *standard deviation.*

## THE RANGE

One way to describe variability is to determine how far the lowest score is from the highest score. The descriptive statistic that indicates the distance between the two most extreme scores in a distribution is called the **range.**

*THE FORMULA FOR COMPUTING THE RANGE IS*

$$\text{Range} = \text{highest score} - \text{lowest score}$$

Thus, for example, the scores back in Sample A (0, 2, 6, 10, 12) have a range of $12 - 0 = 12$. The less variable scores in Sample B (4, 5, 6, 7, 8) have a range of $8 - 4 = 4$. And the perfectly consistent Sample C (6, 6, 6, 6, 6) has a range of $6 - 6 = 0$.

Thus, the range does communicate the spread in the data. However, the range is a rather crude measure. Because it involves only the two most extreme scores, the range is based on the least typical and often least frequent scores, while ignoring all other scores. Therefore, we usually use the range as our sole measure of variability only with *nominal* or *ordinal* data. With nominal data we compute the range by counting the number of categories we're examining: If the participants in our study belong to one of 4 political parties, there is more consistency than if they belong to one of 14 parties. With ordinal data the range is the distance between the lowest and highest rank: If 100 runners finish a race spanning only the 5 positions from 1st through 5th, this is a close race with many ties; if they span 75 positions, the runners are spread out.

## THE VARIANCE AND STANDARD DEVIATION

Most behavioral research involves interval or ratio scores that form a normal distribution. In such situations (when the mean is appropriate) we use two, similar measures of variability called the *variance* and the *standard deviation.*

Understand that we *use* the variance and the standard deviation to describe how different the scores are from each other. We *calculate* them, however, by measuring how much the scores differ from the mean. Because the mean is the center of a distribution, when scores are spread out from each other, they are also spread out from the mean. When scores are close to each other, they are close to the mean.

This brings us to an important point. The mean is the score *around* which a distribution is located, and the variance and standard deviation allow us to quantify "around." For example, if the grades in a statistics class form a normal distribution with a mean of 80, then you know that most of the scores are around 80. But are most scores between 79 and 81 or between 60 and 100? By measuring how spread out scores are from the mean, the variance and standard deviation will define "around."

> ***REMEMBER*** The *variance* and *standard deviation* are two measures of variability that indicate how much the scores are spread out around the mean.

Mathematically, the distance between a score and the mean is the difference between the score and the mean. This difference is symbolized by $X - \overline{X}$, which is the amount that a score *deviates* from the mean. Because some scores will deviate from the mean by more than others, it makes sense to compute the average amount the scores deviate from the mean. The larger the "average of the deviations," the greater the variability or spread between the scores and the mean.

We cannot, however, simply compute the average of the deviations. To compute an average, we first sum the scores so we would first sum the deviations. In symbols, this is $\Sigma(X - \overline{X})$. Recall, however, that the sum of the deviations, always equals zero because the positive deviations cancel out the negative deviations. This means that the average of the deviations will always be zero.

Thus, we want a statistic *like* the average of the deviations, so that we know the average amount the scores are spread out around the mean. But, because the average of the deviations is always zero, we calculate slightly more complicated statistics called the variance and standard deviation. *Think* of them, however, as each producing a number that indicates *something like* the average or typical amount that the scores differ from the mean.

## Understanding the Sample Variance

If the problem with the average of the deviations is the positive and negative deviations, then a solution is to *square* the deviations. That is, after finding the difference between each score and the mean, we square that difference. This removes all negative deviations, so the sum of the squared deviations is not necessarily zero and neither is the average squared deviation.

By finding the average squared deviation, we compute the variance. The **sample variance** is the average of the squared deviations of scores around the sample mean. The symbol for the sample variance is $S_X^2$. Always include the squared sign ($^2$). The capital $S$ indicates that we are describing a sample, and the subscript $X$ indicates that it is computed for a sample of $X$ scores.

> ***REMEMBER*** The symbol $S_X^2$ stands for the variance of a sample of scores.

*THE DEFINING FORMULA FOR THE SAMPLE VARIANCE IS*

$$S_X^2 = \frac{\Sigma(X - \overline{X})^2}{N}$$

This formula is important because it shows you what is involved when computing the variance. Later we will see a different, better formula that you'll actually use to

**TABLE 4.2**
Calculation of Variance Using the Definitional Formula

| *Age Score* | − | $\overline{X}$ | = | $(X - \overline{X})$ | $(X - \overline{X})^2$ |
|---|---|---|---|---|---|
| 2 | − | 5 | = | −3 | 9 |
| 3 | − | 5 | = | −2 | 4 |
| 4 | − | 5 | = | −1 | 1 |
| 5 | − | 5 | = | 0 | 0 |
| 6 | − | 5 | = | 1 | 1 |
| 7 | − | 5 | = | 2 | 4 |
| 8 | − | 5 | = | 3 | 9 |
| $N = 7$ | | | | | $\Sigma(X - \overline{X})^2 = 28$ |

compute variance. But first, to understand it, say that we measure the ages of some children. As shown in Table 4.2, we first, compute each deviation, $(X - \overline{X})$, by subtracting the mean (which here is 5) from each score. Next, we square each deviation. Then adding the squared deviations gives $\Sigma(X - \overline{X})^2$, which here is 28. The $N$ is 7 and so

$$S_X^2 = \frac{\Sigma(X - \overline{X})^2}{N} = \frac{28}{7} = 4$$

Thus, this sample's variance is 4. In other words, the average squared deviation of the age scores around the mean is 4.

The good news is that the variance is a legitimate measure of variability. The bad news, however, is that the variance does not make much sense as the "average deviation." There are two problems. First, squaring the deviations makes them very large, so the variance is unrealistically large. To say that our age scores differ from their mean by an *average* of 4 is silly, because not one score actually deviates from the mean by this much. The second problem is that variance is rather bizarre because it measures in squared units. We measured ages, so the variance indicates that the scores deviate from the mean by 4 *squared* years (whatever that means!).

Thus, it is difficult to interpret the variance as the "average" deviation. The variance is not a waste of time, however, because it is used extensively in statistics. Also, variance does communicate the *relative* variability of scores. If one sample has $S_X^2 = 1$ and another has $S_X^2 = 3$, you know that the second sample is more variable, because it has a larger average squared deviation. This tells you that the scores are relatively less consistent and less accurately described by their mean. Thus, think of variance as a number that generally communicates how variable the scores are: The larger the variance, the more the scores are spread out.

The measure of variability that more directly communicates the average deviation is the *standard deviation.*

## Understanding the Sample Standard Deviation

The sample variance is always an unrealistically large number because we square each deviation. To solve this problem, we take the square root of the variance. The answer is called the standard deviation. The **sample standard deviation** is the square root of the sample variance (the square root of the average squared deviation of scores around the mean). Conversely, squaring the standard deviation produces the variance.

To create the formula that defines the standard deviation, we simply add the square root to the previous defining formula for variance.

*THE DEFINING FORMULA FOR THE SAMPLE STANDARD DEVIATION IS*

$$S_X = \sqrt{\frac{\Sigma(X - \overline{X})^2}{N}}$$

Notice that the symbol for the sample standard deviation is $S_X$, which is the square root of the symbol for the sample variance.

> ***REMEMBER*** The symbol $S_X$ stands for the *sample standard deviation.*

To compute $S_X$, we first compute everything inside the square root sign to get the variance. Therefore, as we did in Table 4.2, the basis for the standard deviation is to first find the amount each score deviates from the mean, then square each deviation, then sum the squared deviations, and then divide that sum by $N$. In our previous age scores the variance ($S_X^2$) was 4. Then we take the square root of the variance to find the standard deviation. In this case

$$S_X = \sqrt{4}$$

so

$$S_X = 2$$

The standard deviation of the age scores is 2.

The standard deviation is as close as we come to the "average of the deviations." There are three related ways to interpret this statistic. First, we interpret our $S_X$ of 2 as indicating that the age scores differ from the mean by something like an "average" of 2. Further, the standard deviation measures in the same units as the raw scores, so the scores differ from the mean age by an "average" of 2 *years.*

Second, the standard deviation allows us to gauge how consistently close together the scores are and, correspondingly, how accurately they are summarized by the mean. If $S_X$ is relatively large, then we know that a large proportion of scores are relatively far from the mean. If $S_X$ is smaller, then more scores are close to the mean and relatively few are far from it.

And third, the standard deviation indicates how much the scores below the mean deviate from it and how much the scores above the mean deviate from it, so the standard deviation indicates how much the scores are spread out *around* the mean. To see this, we can further summarize a distribution by describing the scores that lie at "plus one standard deviation from the mean" ($+1S_X$) and "minus one standard deviation from the mean" ($-1S_X$). For example, our age scores of 2, 3, 4, 5, 6, 7, 8 produced a $\overline{X} = 5$ and a $S_X = 2$. The score that is $+1S_X$ from the mean is the score at $5 + 2$, or 7. The score that is $-1S_X$ from the mean is the score at $5 - 2$, or 3. Looking at the individual scores, you can see that it is accurate to say that the majority of the scores are between 3 and 7.

> ***REMEMBER*** The *standard deviation* indicates the "average deviation" from the mean, the consistency in the scores, and how far scores are spread out *around* the mean.

In fact, the standard deviation is mathematically related to the normal curve, so that describing a distribution using the scores that are between $-1S_X$ and $+1S_X$ is especially useful. Recall from Chapter 2 that the *proportion of the area under the normal curve* corresponds to the *relative frequency* of scores. On any normal distribution, approximately .34 of the area and therefore .34 of the scores are between the mean and the score that is $+1S_X$ above the mean. Likewise, approximately .34 of the area—and .34 of the scores—are between the mean and the score that is $-1S_X$ below the mean. For example, say that in the statistics class with a mean of 80, the $S_X$ is 5. The score at 80 − 5 (at $-1S_X$) is 75, and the score at 80 + 5 (at $+1S_X$) is 85. Figure 4.1 shows about where these scores are located. Thus, 34% of the scores are between 75 and 80, and 34% of the scores are between 80 and 85. Altogether, approximately 68% of the scores are always between the scores at $+1S_X$ and $-1S_X$ from the mean, so about 68% of the statistics class has scores between 75 and 85. Conversely, about 32% of the scores are outside this range, with about 16% below 75 and 16% above 85. Thus, saying that most scores are between 75 and 85 is an accurate summary because the majority of scores (68%) are here.

> ***REMEMBER*** Approximately 34% of the scores in a normal distribution are between the mean and the score that is one standard deviation from the mean.

In summary, then, here is how to describe a distribution. If you know the data form a normal distribution, you can envision its general shape. If you know that the mean is, say, 50, you know where the center of the distribution is and what the typical score is. And if you know that, for example, $S_X = 4$, you know that those participants who did not score 50 missed it by an "average" of 4 points, that scores are not so spread out, and that 68% of the scores are between 46 and 54. But, if you know that the $S_X = 12$, you know that those participants who did not score 50 missed it by an "average" of 12 points, that scores are more spread out, and that 68% of the scores are between 38 and 62.

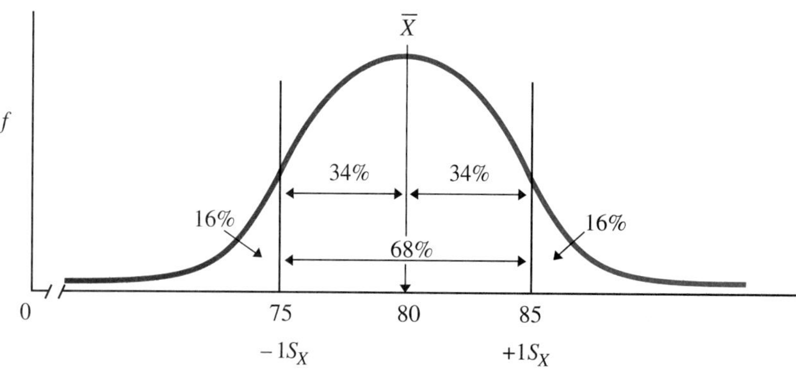


***FIGURE 4.1***
Normal distribution showing scores at plus or minus one standard deviation

*With $S_X = 5$, the score of 75 is at $-1S_X$ and the score of 85 is at $+1S_X$. The percentages are the approximate percentages of the scores falling into each portion of the distribution.*

### A QUICK REVIEW

- The sample variance ($S_X^2$) and the sample standard deviation ($S_X$) are the two statistics to use with the mean to describe variability.
- The standard deviation is interpreted as the average amount scores deviate from the mean.

#### MORE EXAMPLES

To summarize the scores 5, 6, 7, 8, 9, the $\overline{X} = 7$. The variance ($S_X^2$) is the average squared deviation of the scores around the mean (here, $S_X^2 = 2$). The standard deviation is the square root of the variance. $S_X$ is viewed as indicating the average deviation of the scores: Here, $S_X = 1.41$, so when participants missed the mean, they were above or below 7 by an average of about 1.41. Further, in a normal distribution, about 34% of the scores would be between the $\overline{X}$ and 8.41 (7 + 1.41). About 34% of the scores would be between the $\overline{X}$ and 5.59 (7 − 1.41).

***For Practice:***

1. The symbol for the sample variance is ____.
2. The symbol for the sample standard deviation is ____.
3. What is the difference between computing the standard deviation and the variance?
4. In Sample A, $S_X = 6.82$; in Sample B, $S_X = 11.41$. Sample A is ____ (more/less) variable and most scores tend to be ____ (closer to/farther from) the mean.
5. If $\overline{X} = 10$ and $S_X = 2$, then 68% of the scores fall between ____ and ____.

**Answers**

1. $S_X^2$
2. $S_X$
3. The standard deviation is the square root of the variance.
4. less; closer
5. 8; 12

## COMPUTING THE SAMPLE VARIANCE AND SAMPLE STANDARD DEVIATION

The previous defining formulas for the variance and standard deviation are important because they show that the core computation is to measure how far the raw scores are from the mean. However, by reworking the defining formulas, we have less obvious but faster *computing* formulas. They involve two new symbols that you must master for later statistics too. These symbols are introduced here:

*1.* **The Sum of the Squared *X*s:** The symbol $\Sigma X^2$ indicates to find the *sum of the squared* Xs. To do so, you first square each *X* (each raw score) and then sum—add up—the squared *X*s. Thus, to find $\Sigma X^2$ for the scores 2, 2, and 3, add $2^2 + 2^2 + 3^2$, which becomes 4 + 4 + 9, which equals 17.

*2.* **The Squared Sum of *X*:** The symbol $(\Sigma X)^2$ indicates to find the *squared sum of* X. To do so, work inside the parentheses first, so first find the sum of the *X* scores. Then square that sum. Thus, to find $(\Sigma X)^2$ for the scores 2, 2, and 3, you have $(2 + 2 + 3)^2$, which is $(7)^2$, which is 49.

***REMEMBER*** $\Sigma X^2$ indicates the sum of the squared $X$s, and $(\Sigma X)^2$ indicates the squared sum of $X$.

## Computing the Sample Variance

The computing formula for variance is derived from its defining formula by replacing the symbol for the mean with its formula and then reducing the components.

*THE COMPUTING FORMULA FOR THE SAMPLE VARIANCE IS*

$$S_X^2 = \frac{\Sigma X^2 - \frac{(\Sigma X)^2}{N}}{N}$$

The formula says to first find the sum of the $X$s, $(\Sigma X)$, square that sum, and divide the squared sum by $N$. Then subtract that result from the sum of the squared $X$s $(\Sigma X^2)$. Finally, divide that quantity by $N$.

For example, we can arrange the previous age scores as shown in Table 4.3.

**Step 1:** *Find $\Sigma X$, $\Sigma X^2$ and $N$.* Here, $\Sigma X$ is 35, $\Sigma X^2$ is 203, and $N$ is 7. Putting these quantities into the formula, we have

$$S_X^2 = \frac{\Sigma X^2 - \frac{(\Sigma X)^2}{N}}{N} = \frac{203 - \frac{(35)^2}{7}}{7}$$

**Step 2:** *Compute the squared sum of $X$.* Here the squared sum of $X$ is $35^2$, which is 1225, so

$$S_X^2 = \frac{203 - \frac{1225}{7}}{7}$$

**Step 3:** *Divide the $(\Sigma X)^2$ by $N$.* Our 1225 divided by 7 equals 175, so

$$S_X^2 = \frac{203 - 175}{7}$$

***TABLE 4.3***
Calculation of Variance Using the Computational Formula

| *X Score* | $X^2$ |
|---|---|
| 2 | 4 |
| 3 | 9 |
| 4 | 16 |
| 5 | 25 |
| 6 | 36 |
| 7 | 49 |
| 8 | 64 |
| $\Sigma X = 35$ | $\Sigma X^2 = 203$ |

**Step 4:** *Subtract in the numerator.* Because 203 minus 175 equals 28, we have

$$S_X^2 = \frac{28}{7}$$

**Step 5:** *Divide:* Here, after dividing 28/7 we have

$$S_X^2 = 4$$

Thus, again, the sample variance for these age scores is 4 and it is interpreted as we discussed previously.

Do not read any further until you understand how to work this formula!

## Computing the Sample Standard Deviation

The computing formula for the standard deviation merely adds the square root symbol to the previous formula for the variance.

*THE COMPUTING FORMULA FOR THE SAMPLE STANDARD DEVIATION IS*

$$S_X = \sqrt{\frac{\Sigma X^2 - \frac{(\Sigma X)^2}{N}}{N}}$$

This formula is used *only* when computing the *sample* standard deviation.

We'll use again those age scores from back in Table 4.3.

**Step 1:** *Find $\Sigma X$, $\Sigma X^2$, and $N$.* Here, $\Sigma X$ is 35, $\Sigma X^2$ is 203, and $N$ is 7. Thus:

$$S_X = \sqrt{\frac{203 - \frac{(35)^2}{7}}{7}}$$

Follow Steps 2–5 described previously for computing the variance. Inside the square root symbol will be the variance, which here is again 4, so

$$S_X = \sqrt{4}$$

**Step 6:** *Compute the square root.* Taking the square root

$$S_X = 2$$

Again the standard deviation of these age scores is 2. Although we get to it using a different formula, it is still the "average deviation" and is used to find the middle 68% of the scores around the mean, as discussed previously.

## A QUICK REVIEW

- $\Sigma X^2$ indicates to find the *sum of the squared* Xs.
- $(\Sigma X)^2$ indicates to find the *squared sum of* X.

### More Examples

For the scores 5, 6, 7, 8, 9,

1. To find the variance:

   1. $\Sigma X = 5 + 6 + 7 + 8 + 9 = 35$;
      $\Sigma X^2 = 5^2 + 6^2 + 7^2 + 8^2 + 9^2 = 255$;
      $N = 5$, so

   $$S_X^2 = \frac{\Sigma X^2 - \frac{(\Sigma X)^2}{N}}{N} = \frac{255 - \frac{(35)^2}{5}}{5}$$

   2. Find $(\Sigma X)^2$: $35^2 = 1225$, so $S_X^2 = \frac{255 - \frac{1225}{5}}{5}$
   3. Dividing gives $S_X^2 = \frac{255 - 245}{5}$
   4. Subtracting gives $S_X^2 = \frac{10}{5}$
   5. Dividing gives $S_X^2 = 2$

2. To find the standard deviation, perform the above 5 steps, and then find the square root, so

6.
$$S_X = \sqrt{\frac{\Sigma X^2 - \frac{(\Sigma X)^2}{N}}{N}} = \sqrt{\frac{255 - \frac{1225}{5}}{5}}$$

$$= \sqrt{2.00} = 1.41$$

***For Practice:***

For the scores 2, 4, 5, 6, 6, 7,

1. What is $(\Sigma X)^2$?
2. What is $\Sigma X^2$?
3. What is the variance?
4. What is the standard deviation?

**Answers**

1. $(30)^2 = 900$
2. $2^2 + 4^2 + 5^2 + 6^2 + 6^2 + 7^2 = 166$
3. $S_X^2 = \frac{166 - \frac{900}{6}}{6} = 2.667$
4. $S_X = \sqrt{2.667} = 1.63$

## THE POPULATION VARIANCE AND THE POPULATION STANDARD DEVIATION

Recall that our ultimate goal is to describe the population of scores. Sometimes researchers have access to a population and then they directly calculate the actual population variance and standard deviation. The symbol for the *true* or actual **population standard deviation** is $\sigma_X$. (The $\sigma$ is the lowercase Greek letter s, or sigma.) Because the squared standard deviation is the variance, the symbol for the true **population variance** is $\sigma_X^2$. (In each case the subscript $X$ indicates a population of $X$ scores.)

The defining formulas for $\sigma_X$ and $\sigma_X^2$ are similar to those we saw for a sample:

*Population Standard Deviation*

$$\sigma_X = \sqrt{\frac{\Sigma(X - \mu)^2}{N}}$$

*Population Variance*

$$\sigma_X^2 = \frac{\Sigma(X - \mu)^2}{N}$$

The only novelty here is that we have $(X - \mu)$ instead of $(X - \overline{X})$, so here we are computing how far each score deviates from the population mean, $\mu$. Otherwise, the population standard deviation and variance tell us the same things about the population that we saw previously for a sample: Both are ways of measuring how much, "on average," the scores differ from $\mu$, indicating how much the scores are spread out in the population.

***REMEMBER*** The symbols $\sigma_X^2$ and $\sigma_X$ are used when describing the *true population variability.*

These symbols (and formulas) are descriptive procedures for describing the population, signaling that you *know* what the population standard deviation or variance is. However, usually the population is infinitely large and/or unavailable, so we cannot use them. Instead, we estimate the population based on a sample.

## Estimating the Population Variance and Population Standard Deviation

We use the variability in a sample to estimate the variability we'd find if we could measure the population. However, we do *not* use the previous formulas for the sample variance and sample standard deviation as the basis for this estimate. These formulas are used only when describing the variability of a *sample.* This is because, in statistical terminology, the formulas for $S_X^2$ and $S_X$ are the **biased estimators:** When used to estimate the population, they are biased toward *underestimating* the true population parameters. Such a bias is a problem, because if we cannot be accurate, we at least want our under- and overestimates to cancel out over the long run. With the biased estimators, the underestimates and overestimates will not cancel out. Thus, although the sample variance and sample standard deviation accurately describe a sample, they are too often too small to use as estimates of the population.

The reason that $S_X$ and $S_X^2$ underestimate is because their formulas are not designed for estimating the population. When calculating them we measure variability using the mean as our reference point, and so the sum of the deviations must equal zero. Because of this, however, not all of the deviations in the sample are "free" to reflect the variability found in the population. For example, say that the mean of five scores is 6, and that four of the scores are 1, 5, 7, and 9. The sum of their deviations is $-2$. The final score must be 8, because it must have a deviation of $+2$ so that the sum of all deviations is zero. Thus, given the sample mean and the deviations of the other scores, the deviation for the score of 8 is determined by those of the other scores. Therefore, only the deviations produced by the other four scores reflect the variability found in the population. The same would be true for any four of the five scores. Thus, out of the $N$ scores in any sample, only $N - 1$ of them (the $N$ of the sample minus 1) actually reflect the variability in the population.

The problem with the biased estimators ($S_X$ and $S_X^2$) is that these formulas divide by $N$. Because we divide by too large a number, the answer tends to be too small. Instead, we should divide by $N - 1$. By doing so, we compute the ***unbiased*** **estimators** of the population variance and standard deviation.

*THE DEFINING FORMULAS FOR THE UNBIASED ESTIMATORS OF THE POPULATION VARIANCE AND STANDARD DEVIATION ARE*

***Estimated Population Variance***

$$s_X^2 = \frac{\Sigma(X - \overline{X})^2}{N - 1}$$

***Estimated Population Standard Deviation***

$$s_X = \sqrt{\frac{\Sigma(X - \overline{X})^2}{N - 1}}$$

Notice that these formulas are essentially the same as the previous defining formulas for the sample: The core computation is to determine the amount each score deviates from the sample mean, as an estimate of the deviations found in the population. The novelty here is that with the **estimated population standard deviation** and the **estimated population variance,** the final division involves $N - 1$ (the number of scores in the sample minus one).

The symbol for the unbiased estimator of the standard deviation is the lowercase $s_X$, and the symbol for the unbiased estimator of the variance is the lowercase $s_X^2$. To keep your symbols straight, remember that the symbols for the *sample* involve the capital or big *S*, and in those formulas you divide by the "big" value of *N*. The symbols for *estimates* of the population involve the lowercase or small *s*, and here you divide by the smaller quantity $N - 1$. Also, think of $s_X^2$ and $s_X$ as the inferential variance and the inferential standard deviation, because the *only* time you use them is to *infer* the variance or standard deviation of the population based on a sample. Think of $S_X^2$ and $S_X$ as the descriptive variance and standard deviation, because they are used to *describe* the sample.

*REMEMBER* $S_X^2$ and $S_X$ describe the variability in a *sample;* $s_X^2$ and $s_X$ estimate the variability in the *population.*

## Computing the Estimated Population Variance and Standard Deviation

The only difference between the computing formula for the estimated population variance and the previous computing formula for the sample variance is that here the final division is by $N - 1$.

*THE COMPUTING FORMULA FOR THE ESTIMATED POPULATION VARIANCE IS*

$$s_X^2 = \frac{\Sigma X^2 - \frac{(\Sigma X)^2}{N}}{N - 1}$$

Notice that in the numerator we still divide by *N*.

For example, previously we had the age scores of 3, 5, 2, 6, 7, 4, 8. To estimate the population variance, follow the same steps as before. As usual, the first step is to find $\Sigma X$ and $\Sigma X^2$, and here, $\Sigma X = 35$ and $\Sigma X^2 = 203$. Also, $N = 7$ so $N - 1 = 6$. Putting these quantities into the above formula gives

$$s_X^2 = \frac{\Sigma X^2 - \frac{(\Sigma X)^2}{N}}{N - 1} = \frac{203 - \frac{(35)^2}{7}}{6}$$

Work through this formula the same way you did for the sample variance: $35^2$ is 1225, and 1225 divided by 7 equals 175, so

$$s_X^2 = \frac{203 - 175}{6}$$

Next, 203 minus 175 equals 28, so

$$s_X^2 = \frac{28}{6}$$

and the final answer is

$$s_X^2 = 4.67$$

This answer is slightly larger than the sample variance for these scores, which was $S_X^2 = 4$. Thus, although 4 accurately describes the sample variance, we estimate that the variance in the corresponding population is 4.67. In other words, if we could measure all scores in the population and then compute the true population variance, we would expect $\sigma_X^2$ to be 4.67.

A standard deviation is always the square root of the corresponding variance, so the formula for the estimated population standard deviation merely adds the square root sign to the above formula for the variance.

*THE COMPUTING FORMULA FOR THE ESTIMATED POPULATION STANDARD DEVIATION IS*

$$s_X = \sqrt{\frac{\Sigma X^2 - \frac{(\Sigma X)^2}{N}}{N - 1}}$$

Above, the estimated population variance for our age scores was $s_X^2 = 4.67$. Then $s_X$ is $\sqrt{4.67}$, which is 2.16. Thus, if we could compute the standard deviation using the entire population of scores, we would expect $\sigma_X$ to equal 2.16.

## Interpreting the Estimated Population Variance and Standard Deviation

Interpret the estimated population variance and standard deviation in the same way as $S_X^2$ and $S_X$, except that here we describe how much we *expect* the scores to be spread out in the *population,* how consistent or inconsistent we *expect* the scores to be, and how accurately we *expect* the population to be summarized by $\mu$.

Notice that, assuming a sample is representative, we have reached our ultimate goal of describing the population of scores. If we can assume that the distribution is normal, we have described its overall shape. The sample mean ($\overline{X}$) provides an estimate of the population mean ($\mu$). So, for example, based on a statistics class with a mean of 80, we'd infer that the population would score at a $\mu$ of 80. The size of $s_X$ (or $s_X^2$) estimates how spread out the population is, so if $s_X$ turned out to be 6, we'd expect that the "average amount" that individual statistics scores deviate from the $\mu$ of 80 is about 6. Further, we'd expect about 34% of the scores to fall between 74 and 80 (between $\mu$ and the score at $-1s_X$) and about 34% of the scores to fall between 80 and 86 (between $\mu$ and the score at $+1s_X$) for a total of 68% of the scores between 74 and 86. Then, because scores reflect behaviors, we have a good idea of how most individuals in the population behave in this situation (which is why we conduct research in the first place).

## A QUICK REVIEW

- The symbols $s_X$ and $s_X^2$ refer to the *estimated population standard deviation* and *variance,* respectively. When computing them, the final division involves $N - 1$.

### MORE EXAMPLES

For the scores 5, 6, 7, 8, 9, to estimate the population variability:

1. $\Sigma X = 5 + 6 + 7... = 35$; $\Sigma X^2 = 5^2 + 6^2 ... = 255$. $N = 5$, so $N - 1 = 4$. So

$$s_X^2 = \frac{\Sigma X^2 - \frac{(\Sigma X)^2}{N}}{N - 1} = \frac{255 - \frac{(35)^2}{5}}{4}$$

2. $(35)^2 = 1225$, so $s_X^2 = \dfrac{255 - \frac{(1225)}{5}}{4}$

3. Dividing by 5 gives $s_X^2 = \dfrac{255 - 245}{4}$

4. Subtracting gives $s_X^2 = \dfrac{10}{4}$

5. Dividing by 4 gives $S_X^2 = 2.50$

The standard deviation is the square root of the variance, so

$$s_X = \sqrt{\frac{255 - \frac{(35)^2}{9}}{4}} = \sqrt{2.50} = 1.58$$

### *For Practice:*

1. The symbols for the biased population estimators of the variance and standard deviation are ____ and ____.
2. The symbols for the unbiased population estimators of the variance and standard deviation are ____ and ____.
3. When do you compute the unbiased estimators?
4. When do you compute the biased estimators?
5. Compute the estimated population variance and standard deviation for the scores 1, 2, 2, 3, 4, 4, 5.

**Answers**

1. $S_X^2$; $S_X$
2. $s_X^2$; $s_X$
3. To estimate the population standard deviation and variance.
4. To describe the sample standard deviation and variance.
5. $s_X^2 = \dfrac{75 - \frac{(21)^2}{7}}{6} = 2.00$; $s_X = \sqrt{2.00} = 1.41$

## SUMMARY OF THE VARIANCE AND STANDARD DEVIATION

To keep track of all of the symbols, names, and formulas for the different statistics you've seen, remember that *variability* refers to the differences between scores, and that the *variance* and *standard deviation* are two methods for describing variability. In every case we are finding the difference between each score and the mean and then calculating something like the average deviation.

Organize your thinking about the particular measures of variability using Figure 4.2. Any standard deviation is merely the square root of the corresponding variance. For either measure, compute the descriptive versions when the scores are available: When describing how far the scores are spread out from the sample $\overline{X}$, calculate the sample variance ($S_X^2$) and the sample standard deviation ($S_X$). When describing how far the scores are spread out from the population $\mu$, calculate the population variance ($\sigma_X^2$) and the population standard deviation ($\sigma_X$). When the complete population of scores is unavailable, *infer* the variability of the population based on a sample by computing the *unbiased estimators*. The difference in the formulas is that these inferential formulas require a final division by $N - 1$ instead of by $N$.

## STATISTICS IN THE RESEARCH LITERATURE: REPORTING MEANS AND VARIABILITY

The standard deviation is most often reported in published research because it more directly communicates how consistently close the individual scores are to the mean. Thus, the mean from a study might describe the number of times participants exhibited

***FIGURE 4.2***
Organizational chart of descriptive and inferential measures of variability

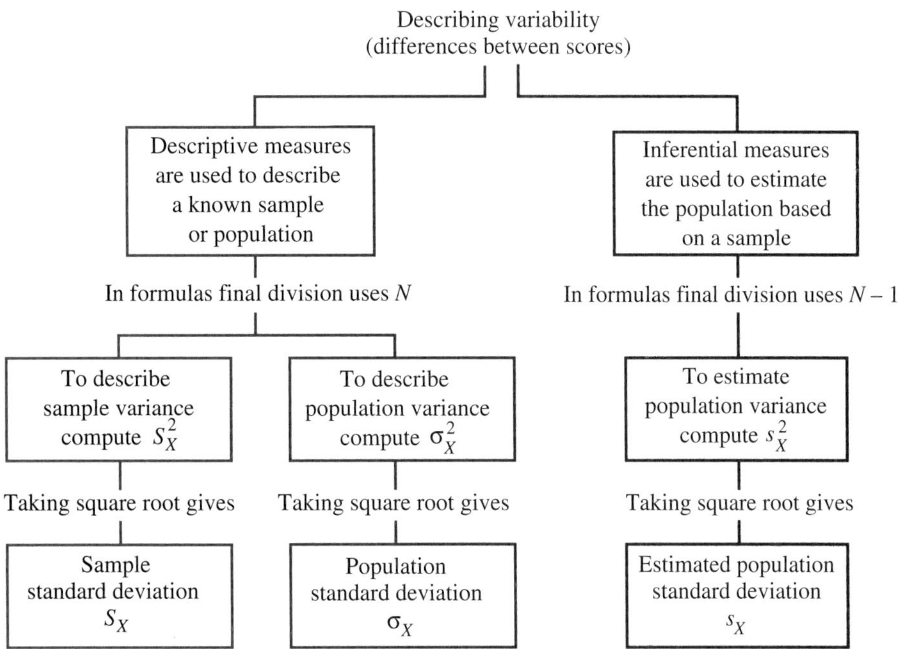

a particular behavior, and a small standard deviation indicates they consistently did so. Or, in a survey, the mean might describe the typical opinion held by participants, but a large standard deviation indicates substantial disagreement among them. The same approach is used in experiments. The mean summarizes the dependent scores, indicating around where participants in each condition scored. But for the complete picture, researchers also include the standard deviation in each condition. The sample standard deviation indicates how consistently close everyone in a condition was to the mean of that condition. Or, the estimated population standard deviation for each condition is an estimate of the variability if everyone in the population was tested under that condition.

However, as if you haven't seen enough symbols already, research journals that follow the publication guidelines of the American Psychological Association do not use our statistical symbols for the sample mean and sample standard deviation. Instead, the symbol for the mean is *M,* and the symbol for the standard deviation is *SD.* When describing the population, however, the Greek symbols $\mu$ and $\sigma$ are used.

## CHAPTER SUMMARY

1. *Measures of variability* describe how much the scores differ from each other, or how much the distribution is spread out.
2. The *range* is the difference between the highest and the lowest score.
3. The *variance* is used with the mean to describe symmetrical or normal distributions of interval or ratio scores. It is the average of the squared deviations of scores around the mean.
4. The *standard deviation* is also used with the mean to describe symmetrical or normal distributions of interval/ratio scores. It is the square root of the variance but can be thought of as the "average" amount that scores deviate from the mean.
5. There are three versions of the formula for variance. $S_X^2$ describes how the far sample of scores is spread out around the $\overline{X}$, $\sigma_X^2$ describes how far the population of scores is spread out around $\mu$, and $s_X^2$ is computed using sample data, but is the inferential, unbiased estimate of how far the scores in the population are spread out around $\mu$.
6. There are three versions of the formula for the standard deviation. $S_X$ describes how far the sample of scores is spread out around $\overline{X}$, $\sigma_X$ describes how far the population of scores is spread out around $\mu$, and $s_X$ is computed using sample data, but is the inferential, unbiased estimate of how far the scores in the population are spread out around $\mu$.
7. The formulas for descriptive measures of variability (for $S_X^2$ and $S_X$) use $N$ as the final denominator. The unbiased, inferential formulas (for $s_X^2$ and $s_X$) use $N - 1$.
8. Approximately 68% of the scores in a normal distribution lie between the scores that are at one standard deviation below the mean and one standard deviation above the mean.
9. The greater the variability, the more the distribution is spread out around the mean, the more inconsistent the scores are, and the less accurately the mean summarizes the data.
10. The usual way to summarize data is to envision a normal distribution, then compute the mean to describe its location and the standard deviation to describe its variability or spread.

## KEY TERMS: Can You Define the Following?

$\Sigma X^2$ *63*
$(\Sigma X)^2$ *63*
$S_X^2$ *59*
$S_X$ *61*
$s_X^2$ *68*
$s_X$ *68*
$\sigma_X^2$ *66*
$\sigma_X$ *66*
$\Sigma(X - \bar{X})$ *59*
biased estimators *67*
estimated population standard deviation *68*
estimated population variance *68*
measures of variability *57*
population standard deviation *66*
population variance *66*
range *58*
sample standard deviation *60*
sample variance *59*
squared sum of *X* *63*
sum of squared *X*s *63*
unbiased estimators *67*

## REVIEW QUESTIONS

(Answers for odd-numbered questions are in Appendix C.)

*1.* (a) Why is it important to describe the variability in any set of scores? (b) In any research, what three characteristics of a distribution must the researcher describe?

*2.* What do measures of variability communicate about (a) the size of differences among the scores in a distribution; (b) how consistently the participants behaved?

*3.* (a) What is the range? (b) Why is it not the most accurate measure of variability? (c) When is it used as the sole measure of variability?

*4.* (a) What do both the variance and the standard deviation tell you about a distribution? (b) Which measure will you usually want to compute? Why?

*5.* (a) What is the mathematical definition of the variance? (b) Mathematically, how is a sample's variance related to its standard deviation, and vice versa?

*6.* (a) What do $S_X$, $s_X$, and $\sigma_X$ have in common in terms of what they communicate? (b) How do they differ in terms of their use?

*7.* Why are your estimates of the population variance and standard deviation always larger than the corresponding statistics that describe a sample from that population?

*8.* In an experiment what does the size of $S_X$ in each condition indicate?

*9.* A researcher obtained the following creativity scores.

3 2 1 0 7 4 8 6 6 4

In terms of creativity, interpret the variability of these data using the following: (a) the range; (b) the variance; (c) the standard deviation.

*10.* If you could test the entire population in question 9, what would you expect each of the following to be? (a) the typical, most common creativity score; (b) the variance; (c) the standard deviation; (d) the two scores between which about 68% of all creativity scores occur in this situation.

*11.* Say the sample in question 9 had an *N* of 1000. About how many people would you expect to score below 1.59? Why?

*12.* As part of studying the relationship between mental and physical health, you obtain the following heart rates.

| | | | | | | | | | |
|---|---|---|---|---|---|---|---|---|---|
| 73 | 72 | 67 | 74 | 78 | 84 | 79 | 71 | 76 | 76 |
| 79 | 81 | 75 | 80 | 78 | 76 | 78 | | | |

In terms of differences in heart rates, interpret these data using the following: (a) the range; (b) the variance; (c) the standard deviation.

*13.* If you could test the population in question 12, what would you expect each of the following to be? (a) the shape of the distribution; (b) the typical, most common rate; (c) the variance; (d) the standard deviation; (e) the two scores between which about 68% of all heart rates fall.

## APPLICATION QUESTIONS

*14.* Foofy has a normal distribution of scores ranging from 2 to 9. (a) She computed the variance to be −.06. What should you conclude from this answer, and why? (b) She recomputes the standard deviation to be 18. What should you conclude, and why? (c) She recomputes the standard deviation to be 1.50. What should you conclude, and why?

*15.* From his statistics grades, Guchi has a $\overline{X}$ of 60 and $S_X = 20$. Pluto has a $\overline{X}$ of 60 and $S_X = 5$. (a) Who is the more inconsistent student, and why? (b) Who is more accurately described as a 60 student, and why? (c) For which student can you more accurately predict the next test score, and why? (d) Who is more likely to do either extremely well or extremely poorly on the next exam?

*16.* You correctly compute the variance of a distribution to be $S_X^2 = 0$. What should you conclude about this distribution?

*17.* Consider the results of this experiment.

| *Condition A* | *Condition B* | *Condition C* |
|---|---|---|
| 12 | 33 | 47 |
| 11 | 33 | 48 |
| 11 | 34 | 49 |
| 10 | 31 | 48 |

(a) What should you do to summarize these data? (b) These are ratio scores. Compute the appropriate descriptive statistics and summarize the relationship in the sample data. (c) Describe how consistent participants were in each condition.

*18.* Say that you conducted the previous experiment on the entire population. (a) Summarize the relationship you'd expect to observe. (b) Describe how consistently you'd expect participants to behave in each condition.

*19.* In two studies the mean is 40, but in Study A the $S_X$ is 5, and in Study B the $S_X$ is 10. (a) What is the difference in the distributions from these studies? (b) Where do you expect the majority of scores to fall in each study?

*20.* Consider these ratio scores from an experiment.

| *Condition 1* | *Condition 2* | *Condition 3* |
|---|---|---|
| 18 | 8 | 3 |
| 13 | 11 | 9 |
| 9 | 6 | 5 |

(a) What should you do to summarize the experiment? (b) Summarize the relationship in the sample data. (c) Describe how consistent the participants were in each condition.

*21.* Say that you conducted the experiment in question 20 on the entire population. (a) Summarize the relationship you'd expect to observe. (b) Describe how consistently you'd expect participants to behave in each condition.

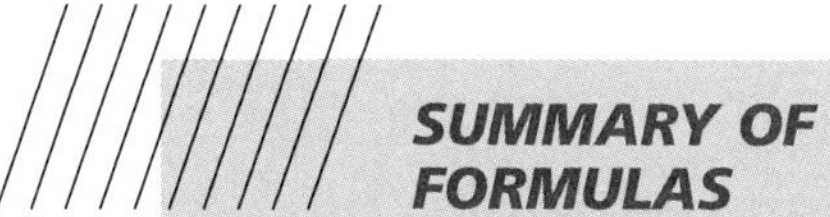

## SUMMARY OF FORMULAS

*1. The formula for the range is*

Range = Highest score − Lowest score

*2. The formula for the sample variance is*

$$S_X^2 = \frac{\Sigma X^2 - \frac{(\Sigma X)^2}{N}}{N}$$

*3. The formula for the sample standard deviation is*

$$S_X = \sqrt{\frac{\Sigma X^2 - \frac{(\Sigma X)^2}{N}}{N}}$$

*4. The formula for the estimated population variance is*

$$s_X^2 = \frac{\Sigma X^2 - \frac{(\Sigma X)^2}{N}}{N - 1}$$

*5. The formula for the estimated population standard deviation is*

$$s_X = \sqrt{\frac{\Sigma X^2 - \frac{(\Sigma X)^2}{N}}{N - 1}}$$

# 5 Describing Data with *z*-Scores and the Normal Curve

**CHAPTER ESSENTIALS**

**Before getting started, be sure you understand**

- From Chapter 2, that relative frequency is the proportion of time scores occur and it corresponds to the proportion of the area under the normal curve; that a score's percentile equals the percent of the curve to the left of the score
- From Chapter 3, that the mean is the center of a distribution and the larger a raw score's deviation, the farther the score is from the mean
- From Chapter 4, that $S_X$ and $\sigma_X$ indicate the "average" deviation of scores around $\overline{X}$ and $\mu$, respectively

**Your goals in this chapter are to learn**

- What a *z-score* is and what it tells you about a raw score's relative standing
- How the *standard normal curve* is used with *z*-scores to determine relative frequency, simple frequency, and percentile
- The characteristics of a *sampling distribution of means* and what the *standard error of the mean* is
- How a sampling distribution of means is used with *z*-scores to determine the relative frequency of sample means

In this chapter we'll combine the techniques discussed in preceding chapters to answer another question about data: How does any one score compare to the other scores in a sample or population? We answer this question by transforming raw scores into *z-scores*. In the following sections, we discuss (1) the logic of *z*-scores and their simple computation, (2) how *z*-scores are used to describe individual raw scores, and (3) how *z*-scores are used to describe sample means.

## UNDERSTANDING *z*-SCORES

Researchers *transform* raw scores into *z*-scores because we usually *don't* know how to interpret a raw score: We don't know whether, in nature, a score should be considered high or low, good or bad, or what. Instead, the best we can do is to compare a score to the other scores in the distribution, describing the score's relative standing. **Relative**

**standing** reflects the systematic evaluation of a score relative to the sample or population in which the score occurs. The way to determine the relative standing of a score is to transform it into a $z$-score. From the $z$-score we'll know whether the individual's underlying raw score was *relatively* good, bad, or in-between.

To see how this is done, say that we conduct a study at Prunepit University in which we measure the attractiveness of a sample of males. The scores form the normal curve shown in Figure 5.1. We want to interpret these scores, especially those of three men: Slug, who scored 35; Binky, who scored 65; and Biff, who scored 90. You already know that the way to do this is to use a score's location on the distribution to determine its *frequency, relative frequency,* and *percentile.* For example, Slug's score is far below the mean and has a rather low frequency. Also, the proportion of the area under the curve above his score is small, so his score has a low relative frequency. And because little of the distribution is to the left of (below) his score, he also has a low percentile. On the other hand, Binky is somewhat above the mean, so he is somewhat above the 50th percentile. Also, the height of the curve at his score is large, so his score has a rather high frequency and relative frequency. And then there's Biff: His score is far above the mean, with a low frequency and relative frequency, and a very high percentile.

The problem with the above descriptions is that they are subjective and imprecise. Instead, to precisely quantify each score's relative standing, we first calculate its $z$-score. This will indicate exactly where on the distribution a score is located, and so we can precisely determine the score's frequency, relative frequency, and percentile.

## Describing a Score's Relative Location as a z-Score

We begin by measuring how far a raw score is from the mean by computing the score's deviation, which equals $X - \overline{X}$. For example, Biff's score of 90 deviates from the mean of 60 by $90 - 60 = +30$. A deviation of $+30$ *sounds* as if it might be large, but is it? We need a frame of reference. For the entire distribution, only a few scores deviate by as much as Biff's score, and *that* makes his an impressively high score. Thus, a score is impressive if it is far from the mean, and "far" is determined by how frequently other scores deviate from the mean by such an amount.

Therefore, to interpret a score's location, we must compare its deviation to the other deviations. As you saw in Chapter 4, the standard deviation is like the "average deviation." By comparing a score's deviation to the standard deviation, we can describe the score in terms of this average deviation. For example, say that in the attractiveness data the

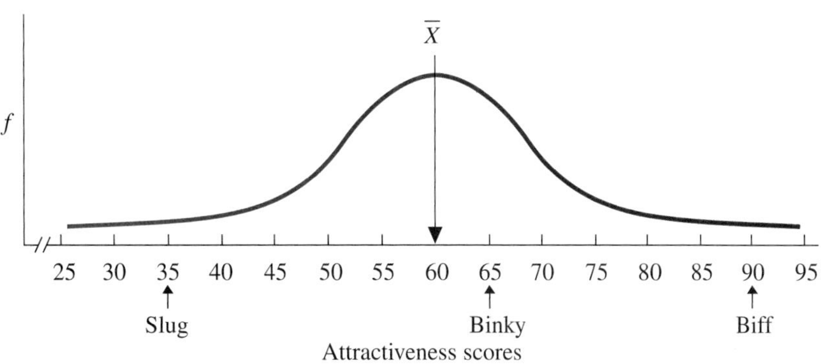


***FIGURE 5.1***
Frequency distribution of attractiveness scores at Prunepit U

*Scores for three individuals are identified on the X axis.*

sample standard deviation is 10. Biff's deviation of +30 is equivalent to 3 standard deviations, so Biff's raw score is 3 standard deviations above the mean. Thus, his raw score is impressive because it is three times as far above the mean as the "average" amount that scores were above the mean.

By transforming Biff's deviation into standard deviation units, we have computed his $z$-score. A ***z*-score** indicates the distance a raw score is from the mean when measured in standard deviations. The symbol for a $z$-score is $z$. A $z$-score always has two components: (1) either a positive or a negative sign which indicates whether the raw score is above or below the mean, and (2) the absolute value of the $z$-score (ignoring the sign) which indicates how *far* the score is from the mean when measured in standard deviations. Thus, like any score, a $z$-score is a *location* on the distribution. It is just that a $z$-score automatically communicates its *distance* from the mean.

> ***REMEMBER*** A *z-score* describes a raw score's location in terms of how far it is above or below the mean when measured in standard deviations.

## Computing *z*-Scores

We computed Biff's $z$-score by first subtracting the mean from his raw score, and then dividing by the standard deviation, so

*THE FORMULA FOR TRANSFORMING A RAW SCORE IN A SAMPLE INTO A z-SCORE IS*

$$z = \frac{X - \overline{X}}{S_X}$$

(This is both the defining and the computing formula.)

To find Biff's $z$-score,

**Step 1:** *Determine the* $\overline{X}$ *and* $S_X$: Filling in the formula gives

$$z = \frac{X - \overline{X}}{S_X} = \frac{90 - 60}{10}$$

**Step 2:** *Find the deviation in the numerator:* Always subtract $\overline{X}$ from $X$. Then

$$z = \frac{+30}{10}$$

**Step 3:** *Divide:* Then

$$z = +3$$

Likewise, Binky's raw score was 65, so

$$z = \frac{X - \overline{X}}{S_X} = \frac{65 - 60}{10} = \frac{+5}{10} = +0.50$$

Binky's raw score is literally one-half of 1 standard deviation above the mean.

And finally, Slug's raw score is 35, so

$$z = \frac{X - \overline{X}}{S_X} = \frac{35 - 60}{10} = \frac{-25}{10} = -2.50$$

Usually we compute $z$-scores for the raw scores in a sample because usually we are describing scores from data that we've collected. However, if we know a population's mean ($\mu$) and standard deviation ($\sigma_X$) we can compute $z$-scores in the population using the same logic as above. Putting the population symbols in the formula gives

*THE FORMULA FOR TRANSFORMING A RAW SCORE IN A POPULATION INTO A z-SCORE IS*

$$z = \frac{X - \mu}{\sigma_X}$$

Now the answer indicates how far a raw score lies from the population mean, measured using the population standard deviation. (*Note:* We never compute $z$-scores using the estimated population standard deviation, $s_X$.)

## Computing a Raw Score When *z* Is Known

Sometimes we know a $z$-score and want to transform it back to the raw score that produced it. Then

*THE FORMULA FOR TRANSFORMING A z-SCORE IN A SAMPLE INTO A RAW SCORE IS*

$$X = (z)(S_X) + \overline{X}$$

This says to multiply the $z$-score times the standard deviation and then add the mean.

For example, if another man had a $z$ of $+1$, then to find his attractiveness score

**Step 1:** *Determine the* $\overline{X}$ *and* $S_X$: Ours were $\overline{X} = 60$ and $S_X = 10$ so

$$X = (+1)(10) + 60$$

**Step 2:** *Multiply* z *times* $S_X$: Then

$$X = +10 + 60$$

**Step 3:** *Add:* Then

$$X = 70$$

The raw score of 70 corresponds to a $z$ of $+1$.

Instead, say that someone had a $z$-score of $-1.30$. Then with $\overline{X} = 60$ and $S_X = 10$,

$$X = (-1.30)(10) + 60$$

so

$$X = -13 + 60$$

Adding a negative number is the same as subtracting its positive value, so

$$X = 47$$

The raw score here is 47.

The above logic also applies to finding the raw score for a $z$ from a population, except we use the symbols for the population.

*THE FORMULA FOR TRANSFORMING A z-SCORE IN A POPULATION INTO A RAW SCORE IS*

$$X = (z)(\sigma_X) + \mu$$

Here, we multiply the $z$-score times the population standard deviation and then add $\mu$.

## A QUICK REVIEW

- A $+z$ indicates the raw score is above the mean, a $-z$ that it is below the mean.
- The absolute value of $z$ indicates the score's distance from the mean, measured in standard deviations.

### MORE EXAMPLES

In a sample, $\overline{X} = 25$, $S_X = 5$. To find $z$ for $X = 32$:

$$z = \frac{X - \overline{X}}{S_X} = \frac{32 - 25}{5} = \frac{+7}{5} = +1.40$$

To find the raw score for $z = -.43$:

1. $X = (z)(S_X) + \overline{X} = (-.43)(5) + 25$
   $= -2.15 + 25 = 22.85$

***For Practice:***

With $\overline{X} = 50$, $S_X = 10$,

1. What is $z$ for $X = 44$?
2. What $X$ produces $z = -1.30$?

With $\overline{X} = 100$, $S_X = 16$,

3. What is the $z$ for a score of 132?
4. What $X$ produces $z = +1.4$?

**Answers**

1. $z = (44 - 50)/10 = -.60$
2. $X = (-1.30)(10) + 50 = 37$
3. $z = (132 - 100)/16 = +2.00$
4. $X = (+1.4)(16) + 100 = 122.4$

## USING z-SCORES TO DESCRIBE RAW SCORES

$z$-scores have a number of uses in statistics and research. In the following sections you'll see how $z$-scores are used when (1) describing the relative standing of scores,

(2) comparing scores from different variables, and (3) computing the relative frequency of scores.

## Using z-Scores to Describe Relative Standing

A *z*-score automatically communicates a raw score's relative standing. The way to see this is to envision a *z*-distribution. A ***z*-distribution** is the distribution produced by transforming all raw scores in the data into *z*-scores. For example, our attractiveness scores produce the *z*-distribution shown in Figure 5.2.

Notice the two ways that the *X* axis is labeled. This shows that by creating a *z*-distribution, we only change the way that we identify each score. Saying that Biff has a *z* of +3 is merely another way to say that he has a raw score of 90. Therefore, because he is at the same location in the distribution, Biff's *z*-score has the same frequency, relative frequency, and percentile as his raw score.

The advantage of looking at *z*-scores, however, is that they directly communicate each score's relative location in the distribution. The *z*-score of 0 corresponds to the mean (here, 60): A person having the mean score is zero distance from the mean. For any other score, the sign indicates the *direction* the score lies in relation to the mean. A "+" indicates that the score is graphed to the right of the mean. A "−" indicates that the score is graphed to the left of the mean. Therefore, *z*-scores become increasingly larger numbers with a positive sign as we proceed farther to the right of the mean, **AND** such larger positive *z*-scores occur less frequently. Conversely, *z*-scores become increasingly larger numbers with a negative sign as we proceed farther to the left of the mean, **AND** such larger negative *z*-scores occur less frequently. However, as shown, most of the *z*-scores are *between* +3 and −3. Although *z*-scores greater than +3 or −3 are possible, they occur *very* infrequently. (*Note:* the symbol "±" means "plus or minus," so we can restate this by saying that most *z*-scores are between ±3.)

> ***REMEMBER*** On a normal distribution, the larger the *z*-score, whether positive or negative, the farther the raw score is from the mean, and the less frequently the *z*-score and the raw score occur.

***FIGURE 5.2***
*z*-distribution of attractiveness scores at Prunepit U

*The labels on the X axis show first the raw scores and then the z-scores.*

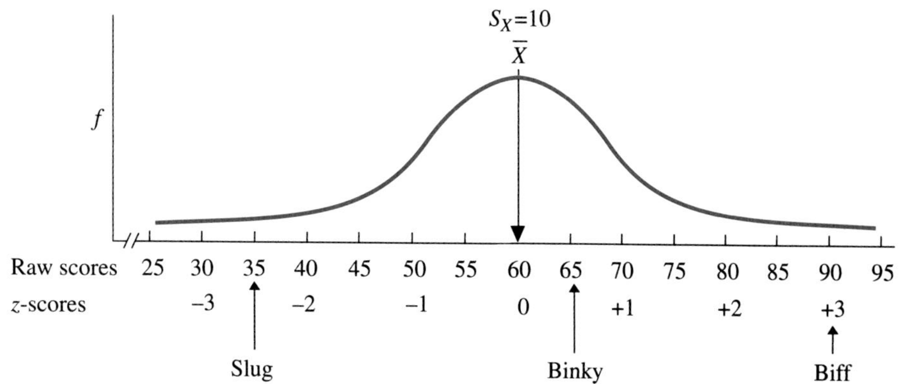

Figure 5.2 illustrates three important characteristics of any $z$-distribution.

*1. A z-distribution always has the same shape as the raw score distribution.* When the underlying raw score distribution is normal, its $z$-distribution is normal.

*2. The mean of any z-distribution is 0.* Whatever the mean of the raw scores is, it transforms into a $z$-score of 0.

*3. The standard deviation of any z-distribution is 1.* Whether the standard deviation in the raw scores is 10 or 100, it is still the standard deviation, and the standard deviation transforms into a distance in $z$-scores of 1.

Because of these characteristics, all normal $z$-distributions are similar, so that a particular $z$-score will be at the *same* relative location on *every* distribution. Therefore, the way to interpret the $z$-scores from any study is to envision the $z$-distribution in Figure 5.2. Then, for example, anytime the $z = 0$ it indicates that the raw score equals the mean (and median and mode) and is in the middle of the distribution. Or, if $z$ is +.5 then, like Binky's, the raw score is slightly above the mean, with a percentile slightly above 50%, and it has a high frequency and relative frequency. But, if any raw score produces a $z$ of $+3$ then, like Biff's, it is one of the highest scores, in the extreme upper tail of the distribution, and it has a low frequency, a low relative frequency and a high percentile. And, so on.

> ***REMEMBER*** Interpret $z$-scores by envisioning their location on the $z$-distribution.

## Using *z*-Scores to Compare Variables

A second important use of $z$-scores is when, comparing a score on one variable to a score on a different variable. Here's a new example. Say that Althea received a grade of 38 on her statistics quiz and a grade of 45 on her English paper. These scores reflect different kinds of tasks, so it's like comparing apples to oranges. The solution is to transform the raw scores from each class into $z$-scores. Then we can compare Althea's relative standing in English to her relative standing in statistics, and we are no longer comparing apples and oranges.

*Note:* The $z$-transformation equates or standardizes different distributions, so $z$-scores are often referred to as **standard scores.**

Say that for the statistics quiz, the $\overline{X}$ was 30 and the $S_X$ was 5. Althea's grade of 38 becomes $z = +1.6$. For the English paper, the $\overline{X}$ was 40 and the $S_X$ was 10, so Althea's 45 becomes $z = +.5$. You can see these results in Figure 5.3, in which the $z$-distributions from both classes are plotted on one set of axes. The corresponding raw scores are also plotted. Because the classes have different standard deviations, the raw scores for each class are spaced differently along the $X$ axis. The spacing of the $z$-scores in the two classes is the same, however, so they are comparable. Thus, Althea's $z$ of $+1.6$ in statistics is farther above the mean than her $z$ of $+.5$ in English is above the mean, so she performed relatively better in statistics.

Figure 5.3 also shows that another student, Millie, obtained raw scores that produced $z = -2$ in statistics and $z = -1$ in English. Millie did better in English because her $z$-score of $-1$ is less distance below the mean.

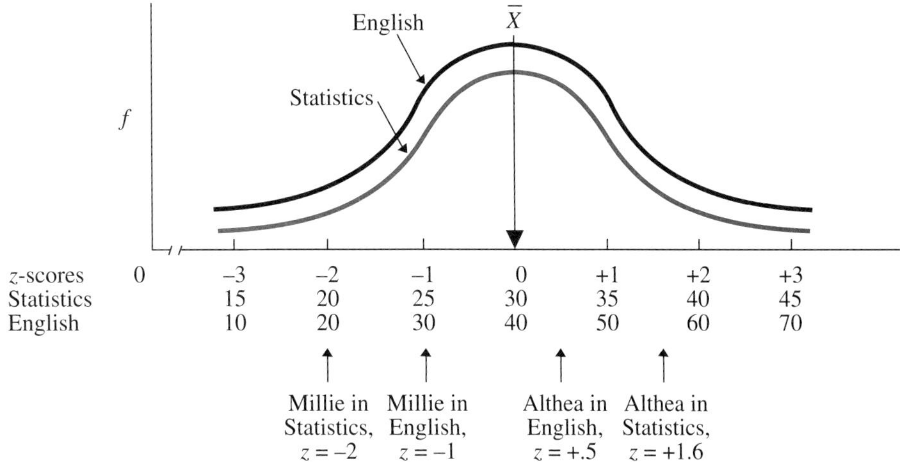


***FIGURE 5.3***
Comparison of distributions for statistics and English grades, plotted on the same set of axes

***REMEMBER*** To compare raw scores from two different variables, transform the scores into *z*-scores.

## Using *z*-Scores to Compute Relative Frequency

The third important use of *z*-scores is to determine the relative frequency of specific raw scores. Recall that relative frequency is the proportion of time that a score occurs and that the relative frequency of particular scores equals the proportion of the total area under the curve at those scores. Because a particular *z*-score is always at the same location on the normal curve, the area under the curve for that *z*-score is always the same. *Therefore, the relative frequency of a particular* z*-score will be the same on all normal* z*-distributions.*

For example, 50% of the scores on a normal curve are to the left of the mean, and scores to the left of the mean produce negative *z*-scores. In other words, the negative *z*-scores make up 50% of any distribution. Thus, the students in each class with negative *z*-scores above in Figure 5.3 constitute 50% of their respective distributions, so their scores have a relative frequency of .50. On *any* normal *z*-distribution, the relative frequency of the negative *z*-scores is .50.

Having determined the relative frequency of the *z*-scores, we work backwards to find the relative frequency of the corresponding raw scores. In the statistics distribution in Figure 5.3, students having negative *z*-scores have raw scores ranging between 15 and 30, so the relative frequency of scores between 15 and 30 is .50. In the English distribution, students having negative *z*-scores have raw scores between 10 and 40, so the relative frequency of these scores is .50.

In the same way, you can determine the relative frequencies for any other portion of a distribution, once you envision it as a *z*-distribution. To do so, we employ the *standard normal curve.*

**The Standard Normal Curve** Because all normal *z*-distributions are similar, we don't need to draw a different normal curve for every set of raw scores. Instead, we envision one standard curve that, in fact, is called the standard normal curve. The **standard normal curve** is a perfect normal $z$-distribution that serves as our model of any approximately normal $z$-distribution. The idea is that most raw scores will produce an approximately normal $z$-distribution. To simplify things, we operate as if the $z$-distribution fits our one, perfect normal curve. We use the standard normal curve to determine the relative frequency of particular $z$-scores on a perfect normal curve. Then, as above, we work backwards to determine the relative frequency of the corresponding raw scores. This provides a reasonably accurate description of our data, but how accurate the description is depends on how closely the data fit the normal curve. Therefore, this approach is best with a large sample (or population) of scores that form a reasonably normal distribution.

Statisticians have already determined the proportion of the area under the curve for any part of a normal distribution. Figure 5.4 shows the proportions for whole-number $z$-scores. The numbers above the $X$ axis indicate the proportion of the total area between the $z$-scores. The numbers below the $X$ axis indicate the proportion of the total area between the mean and the $z$-score. (You won't need to memorize them.) Each proportion is also the relative frequency of the $z$-scores—and raw scores—located in that part of the curve. Thus, between a $z$ of 0 and a $z$ of $\pm1$ is .3413 (or 34.13%) of the area; so, as we've seen, about 34% of the scores are here. Or, $z$-scores between $+1$ and $+2$ occur .1359 of the time, so this added to .3413 gives a total of .4772 of the scores between the mean and $z = +2$. Or, with .3413 of the scores between the mean and $z = -1$, and .3413 of the scores between the mean and $z = +1$, a total of .6826 or about 68% of the distribution is between $z$s of $-1$ and $+1$. And so on. (Notice that $z$-scores beyond $+3$ or beyond $-3$ occur only .0013 of the time, which is why the range of $z$ is essentially between $\pm3$.)

> ***REMEMBER*** For an approximately normal distribution, transform the raw scores to $z$-scores and use the *standard normal curve* to find the relative frequency of the scores.

In practice we usually apply the standard normal curve by beginning with a particular raw score in mind and then computing its $z$-score. For example, back in our original attractiveness scores, say that Cubby has a raw score of 80, which, with $\overline{X} = 60$ and

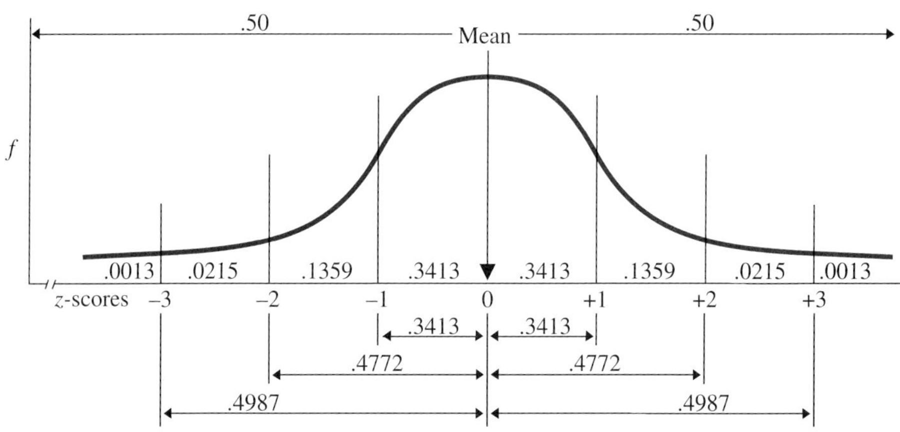


***FIGURE 5.4***
Proportions of total area under the standard normal curve

*The curve is symmetrical: 50% of the scores fall below the mean, and 50% fall above the mean.*

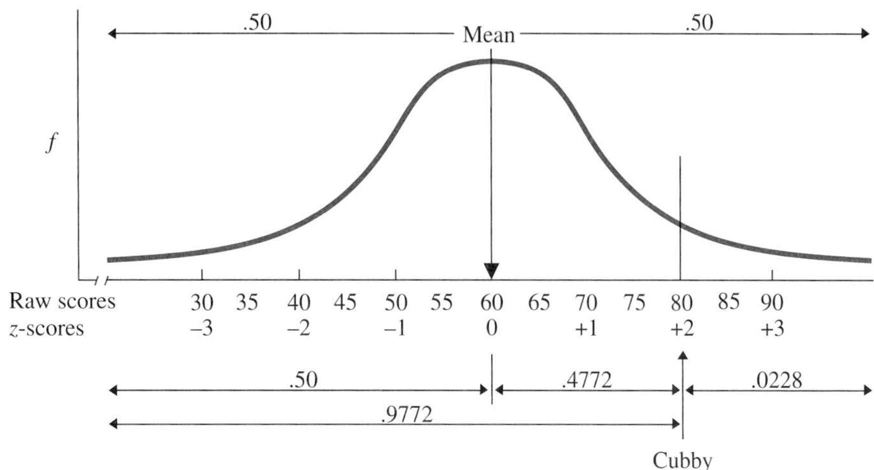


***FIGURE 5.5***

Location of Cubby's score on the *z*-distribution of attractiveness scores

*Cubby's raw score of 80 is a z-score of +2.*

$S_X = 10$, is a $z$ of $+2$. We can envision Cubby's location as in Figure 5.5. We might first ask what proportion of scores are expected to fall between the mean and Cubby's score. On the standard normal curve, .4772 of the total area falls between the mean and $z = +2$. Therefore, we also expect .4772, or 47.72%, of all attractiveness scores at Prunepit U to fall between the mean score of 60 and Cubby's score of 80. Conversely, .0228 of the area—and scores—are above his score.

We might also ask how *many* people scored between the mean and Cubby's score. Then we would convert relative frequency to *simple frequency* by multiplying the $N$ of the sample times the relative frequency. Say that our $N$ was 1000. If we expect .4772 of all scores to fall between the mean and $z = +2$, then $(.4772)(1000) = 477.2$, so we expect about 477 people to have scores between the mean and Cubby's score.

We can also use the standard normal curve to determine a score's expected *percentile* (the percent of the scores below—graphed to the left of—a score.) As in Figure 5.5, on a normal distribution the mean is the median (the 50th percentile). A positive $z$-score is above the mean, so Cubby's score of $+2$ is above the 50th percentile. In addition, Cubby's score is above the 47.72% of the scores that fall between the mean and his score. Thus, in total, 97.72% of all scores are below Cubby's score. We usually round off percentile to a whole number, so Cubby's raw score of 80 is at the 98th percentile.

Finally, we can also work in the opposite direction to find a raw score at a particular relative frequency or percentile. Say that we began by asking what attractiveness score was at the 98th percentile, or above what score was .0228 of the distribution? We have seen that a $z$-score of $+2$ is at the 98th percentile and that above $z = +2$ is .0228 of the distribution. Then to find the raw score that corresponds to this $z$, we use the formula for transforming a $z$-score into a raw score. We'd end up finding that an attractiveness score of 80 is at the 98th percentile, or that above the score of 80 is .0228 of the distribution.

**Using the *z*-Tables** So far our examples have involved whole-number $z$-scores, although with real data, a $z$-score may contain decimals. To find the proportion of the total area under the standard normal curve for any two-decimal $z$-score, look in Table 1 of Appendix B. A portion of these "$z$-tables" is reproduced in Table 5.1.

**TABLE 5.1**
Sample Portion of the z-Tables

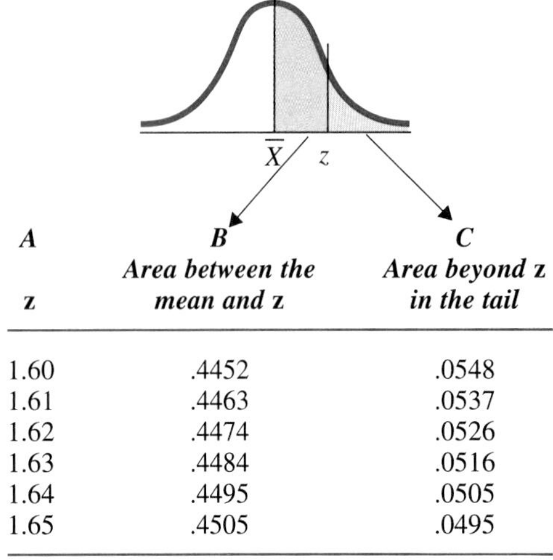


| A<br>z | B<br>Area between the mean and z | C<br>Area beyond z in the tail |
|---|---|---|
| 1.60 | .4452 | .0548 |
| 1.61 | .4463 | .0537 |
| 1.62 | .4474 | .0526 |
| 1.63 | .4484 | .0516 |
| 1.64 | .4495 | .0505 |
| 1.65 | .4505 | .0495 |

Say that you seek the area under the curve above or below a $z = +1.63$. First, locate the $z$ in column A, labeled "$z$," and then move to the right. Column B, labeled "Area between the mean and $z$," contains the proportion of the area under the curve between the mean and the $z$ identified in column A. Thus, .4484 of the curve (or 44.84% of all $z$-scores) is between the mean and the $z$ of $+1.63$. This is shown in Figure 5.6. Because our $z$ is the positive $+1.63$, we place this area between the mean and the $z$ on the *right-hand* side of the distribution. Column C, labeled "Area beyond $z$ in the tail," contains the proportion of the area under the curve that is in the tail beyond the $z$-score. Thus, .0516 of the curve (or 5.16% of all $z$-scores) is in the right-hand tail of the distribution beyond the $z$ of $+1.63$ (also shown in Figure 5.6). If you get confused when using the $z$-table, look at the normal distribution at the top of the table. The different shaded portions and arrows indicate the part of the curve described in each column.

To find the $z$-score that corresponds to a particular proportion, read the columns in the reverse order. First, find the proportion in column B or C, depending on the area you seek, and then identify the $z$-score in column A. For example, say that you seek the $z$-score corresponding to 44.84% of the curve between the mean and $z$. Find .4484 in column B of the table, and then, in column A, the $z$-score is 1.63.

**FIGURE 5.6**
Distribution showing the area under the curve for $z = -1.63$ and $z = +1.63$

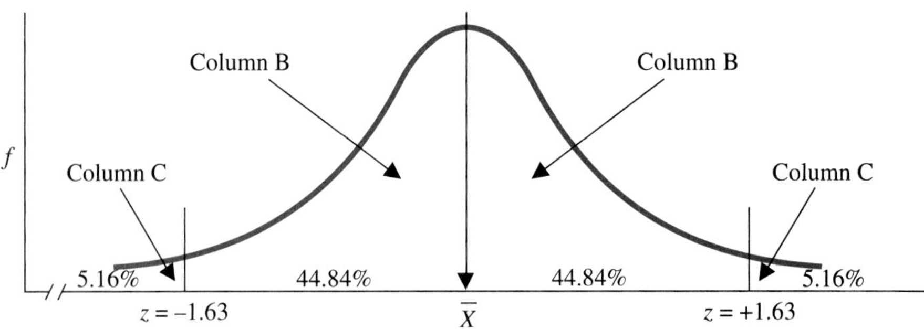

**TABLE 5.2**
Summary of Steps When Using the z-Tables

| *If You Seek* | *First, You Should* | *Then You* |
|---|---|---|
| Relative frequency of scores between $\overline{X}$ and $X$ | transform $X$ to $z$ | find area in column B* |
| Relative frequency of scores beyond $X$ in tail | transform $X$ to $z$ | find area in column C* |
| $X$ that marks a given relative frequency between $X$ and $\overline{X}$ | Find relative frequency in column B | transform $z$ to $X$ |
| $X$ that marks a given relative frequency beyond $X$ in tail | find relative frequency in column C | transform $z$ to $X$ |
| Percentile of an $X$ above $\overline{X}$ | transform $X$ to $z$ | find area in column B and add .50 |
| Percentile of an $X$ below $\overline{X}$ | transform $X$ to $z$ | find area in column C |

*To find the simple frequency of the scores, multiply relative frequency times $N$.

Sometimes you will need a proportion that is not given in the tables, or you'll need the proportion corresponding to a three-decimal $z$-score. In such cases round to the nearest value in the $z$-tables. (To compute the precise value, consult an advanced textbook to perform "linear interpolation.")

Notice that the $z$-table contains no positive or negative signs. *You* must decide whether $z$ is positive or negative, based on the problem you're working. Thus, if we had the negative $z$-score of $-1.63$, columns B and C would provide the areas shown on the *left-hand* side of Figure 5.6.

Use the information from the $z$-tables as we have done previously. For example, say that we want to examine Bucky's raw score, which transforms into the *positive* $z$-score of $+1.63$, located at the right-hand side of Figure 5.6. If we seek the proportion of scores above his score, then from column C we expect that 5.16% of the scores are above this score. If we seek the relative frequency of scores between his score and the mean, from column B we expect that 44.84% of the scores are between the mean up to his raw score. Then we can also compute simple frequency or percentile as discussed previously. Or, if we began by asking what raw score demarcates .4484 or .0516 of the curve, we would first find these proportions in column B or C, respectively, then find the $z$-score of $+1.63$ in column A, and then transform the $z$-score to find the corresponding raw score. Table 5.2 summarizes these procedures.

## A QUICK REVIEW

- To find the relative frequency of scores above or below a raw score, transform it into a *z-score.* From the $z$-tables find the proportion of the area under the curve above or below that $z$.
- To find the raw score at a specified relative frequency, find the proportion in the $z$-tables and transform the corresponding $z$ into its raw score.

### MORE EXAMPLES

With $\overline{X} = 40$ and $S_X = 4$,

To find the relative frequency of scores above 45: $z = (X - \overline{X})/S_X = (45 - 40)/4 = +1.25$. "Above" +1.25 is in the upper tail, so from column C the relative frequency is .1056.

*continued*

To find the percentile of the score of 41.5: $z = (X - \overline{X})/S_X = (41.5 - 40)/4 = +0.38$. Between this positive $z$ and $\overline{X}$ in column B is .1480. This score is at the 65th percentile because .1480 + .50 = .6480 = .65.

To find the proportion below $z = -0.38$: Below this negative $z$ is the lower tail, so from column C is .3520. (The score is at about the 35th percentile).

To find the score above the mean with 15% of the scores between the mean and the score (or the score at about the 65th percentile): From column B the proportion closest to .15 is .1517 for $z = +0.39$. Then $X = (+0.39)(4.0) + 40 = 41.56$.

***For Practice:***

For a sample: $\overline{X} = 65$, $S_X = 12$, and $N = 1000$.

1. What is the relative frequency of scores below 59?
2. What is the relative frequency of scores above 75?
3. How many scores are between the mean and 70?
4. What raw score delineates the top 3%?

**Answers**

1. $z = (59 - 65)/12 = -.50$; "below" is the lower tail, so from column C is .3085.
2. $z = (75 - 65)/12 = +.83$, "above" is the upper tail, so from column C is .2033.
3. $z = (70 - 65)/12 = +.42$; from column B is .1628; (.1628)(1000) gives about 163 scores.
4. The "top" is the upper tail, so from column C the proportion closest to .03 is .0301, with $z = +1.88$; so $X = (+1.88)(12) + 65 = 87.56$.

## USING z-SCORES TO DESCRIBE SAMPLE MEANS

We can also use the preceding logic to describe the relative standing of a sample of scores by computing a $z$-score for a sample mean. Not only does this allow us to interpret the mean, but it is also the basis for upcoming inferential statistics.

To see how the procedure works, say that we give the Scholastic Aptitude Test (SAT) to a sample of 25 students at Prunepit U. Their mean score is 520. Nationally, the mean of *individual* SAT scores is 500 (and $\sigma_X$ is 100), so it appears that at least some Prunepit students scored relatively high, pulling the mean to 520. But how do we interpret the performance of the sample as a whole? The problem is the same as when we examined individual raw scores: Without a frame of reference, we don't know whether a particular sample mean is high, low, or in-between.

The solution is to evaluate a sample mean in terms of its relative standing. Previously we compared a particular raw score to all other scores that occur in this situation. Now we'll compare our sample mean to the other sample means that occur in this situation. Therefore, the first step is to take a small detour and create a distribution showing these means. This distribution is called the *sampling distribution of means.*

### The Sampling Distribution of Means

If the national average of SAT scores is 500, then in the population, the mean ($\mu$) is 500. Because we selected a sample of 25 students and obtained their SAT scores, we essentially drew a sample of 25 scores from this population. To evaluate our sample mean, we first create a distribution showing all other possible means that occur when selecting a sample of 25 scores from the SAT population. To do so, pretend that we record all SAT scores from the population on slips of paper and put them in a large hat. Then we would select a sample with the same size $N$ as ours, compute the sample mean, replace the scores in the hat, draw another 25 scores, compute the mean, and so on.

Because the scores selected in each sample would not be identical, not all sample means would be identical. By constructing a frequency polygon of the different values of $\overline{X}$ we obtained, we would create a sampling distribution of means. The **sampling distribution of means** is the frequency distribution of all possible sample means that occur when an infinite number of samples of the same size $N$ are selected from one raw score population. Our SAT sampling distribution of means is shown in Figure 5.7. This is similar to a distribution of raw scores, except that each "score" along the $X$ axis is a sample mean.

In reality we cannot "infinitely" sample a population, but we know that it would look like Figure 5.7 because of the central limit theorem. The **central limit theorem** is a statistical principle that defines the mean, the shape, and the standard deviation of a sampling distribution. From the central limit theorem, we know the following:

*1.* **The mean of the sampling distribution equals the mean of the underlying raw score population from which we create the sampling distribution.** The sampling distribution is the *population* of sample means, so we use $\mu$. The $\mu$ of the sampling distribution is the average sample mean. When the average raw score is a particular score (here, 500), the average sample mean when using those scores will also be that score (again 500).

*2.* **A sampling distribution is an approximately normal distribution.** Most often each $\overline{X}$ will equal the raw score population's $\mu$. Sometimes, however, a sample will contain more high scores or low scores relative to the population, so the sample mean will be slightly above or below $\mu$. Less frequently, we'll obtain rather strange samples, producing a $\overline{X}$ farther above or below $\mu$.

*3.* **The standard deviation of the sampling distribution is mathematically related to the standard deviation of the raw score population.** As you'll see in a moment, the variability of the raw scores influences the variability of the sample means.

The importance of the central limit theorem is that we can describe a sampling distribution *without* having to actually infinitely sample a population of raw scores. Therefore, we can create the sampling distribution of means for any raw score population.

> *REMEMBER* The central limit theorem allows us to envision the *sampling distribution of means,* which shows all of the means that would occur through exhaustive sampling of a particular raw score population.

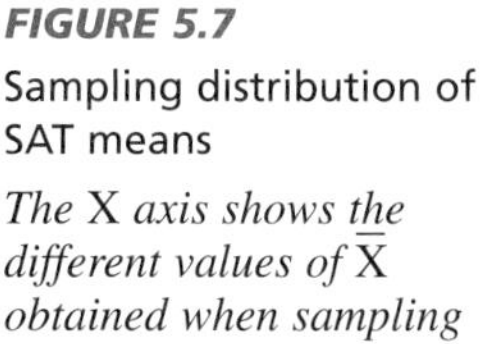

***FIGURE 5.7***
Sampling distribution of SAT means

*The* X *axis shows the different values of* $\overline{X}$ *obtained when sampling the SAT population.*

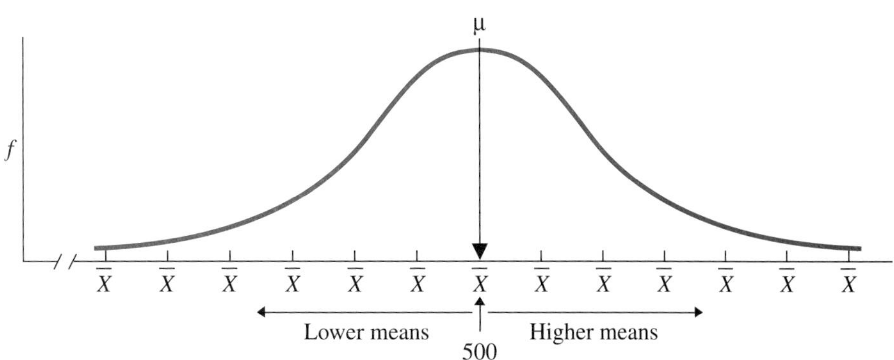

Why do we want to see the sampling distribution? Remember we took a small detour, but the original problem was to evaluate our Prunepit mean of 520. Once we envision the distribution in Figure 5.7, we have a model of the different sample means—and the frequency with which they occur—when sampling the SAT population. As we did with raw scores, once we have the frequency distribution of all possible means, we can determine the relative standing of our sample mean. To do so, we simply need to determine where a mean of 520 falls on the $X$ axis of this distribution, and then interpret the curve accordingly.

The sampling distribution is a normal distribution, and you already know how to determine the location of any "score" on a normal distribution: We use $z$-scores. That is, we determine how far the sample mean deviates from the mean of the sampling distribution, measured using the standard deviation of the distribution. Therefore, we need one more piece of information: the "standard deviation" of the sampling distribution.

## The Standard Error of the Mean

The standard deviation of the sampling distribution of means is called the **standard error of the mean.** Like a standard deviation, the standard error of the mean can be thought of as the "average" amount that the sample means deviate from the $\mu$ of the sampling distribution. That is, in some sampling distributions, the sample means may be very different from one another and deviate greatly from the average sample mean. At other times, the $\overline{X}$s may be very similar and deviate little from $\mu$.

For the moment, we'll discuss the *true* standard error of the mean, as if we had actually computed it using the entire sampling distribution. Its symbol is $\sigma_{\overline{X}}$. The $\sigma$ indicates that we are describing a population, but the subscript $\overline{X}$ indicates that we are describing a population of sample means. The central limit theorem tells us that $\sigma_{\overline{X}}$ can be found using this formula:

*THE FORMULA FOR THE TRUE STANDARD ERROR OF THE MEAN IS*

$$\sigma_{\overline{X}} = \frac{\sigma_X}{\sqrt{N}}$$

Notice that the formula involves $\sigma_X$: When we know the true standard deviation of the underlying raw score population, we will know the true "standard deviation" of the sampling distribution.

> ***REMEMBER*** The *standard error of the mean* ($\sigma_{\overline{X}}$) is computed using the true standard deviation of the population of raw scores ($\sigma_X$).

In the formula the size of $\sigma_{\overline{X}}$ depends first on the size of $\sigma_X$: The more variable the raw scores, the more likely that we'll get a very different set of scores in each sample, and so the more that the sample means will differ and the larger will be $\sigma_{\overline{X}}$. Second, the size of $\sigma_{\overline{X}}$ depends on the size of $N$: The larger the $N$, the closer the sample means will be to the population mean, and so $\sigma_{\overline{X}}$ will be smaller.

To compute $\sigma_{\overline{X}}$ for our SAT example:

**Step 1:** *Identify the* $\sigma_X$ *of the raw score population and the* N *used to create the sample:* We used an $N = 25$, and through record keeping, we know that $\sigma_X = 100$. So

$$\sigma_{\overline{X}} = \frac{\sigma_X}{\sqrt{N}} = \frac{100}{\sqrt{25}}$$

**Step 2:** *Determine the square root of* N: The square root of 25 is 5, so

$$\sigma_{\overline{X}} = \frac{100}{5}$$

**Step 3:** *Divide:* Thus

$$\sigma_{\overline{X}} = 20$$

This indicates that in the SAT sampling distribution, the individual sample means differ from the $\mu$ of 500 by an "average" of 20 points when the $N$ of each sample is 25.

Now, we can calculate a $z$-score for our sample mean.

## Computing a *z*-Score for a Sample Mean

Previously you saw that the formula for transforming a raw score in the population into a $z$-score was

$$z = \frac{X - \mu}{\sigma_X}$$

We transform a sample mean into a $z$-score using a similar formula.

*THE FORMULA FOR TRANSFORMING A SAMPLE MEAN INTO A z-SCORE IS*

$$z = \frac{\overline{X} - \mu}{\sigma_{\overline{X}}}$$

Don't be confused by this formula: All $z$-scores show how far a score is from the mean of a distribution, measured in standard deviations of that distribution. Now our "score" is a sample mean, so we find how far the sample mean is from the mean of the sampling distribution ($\mu$), measured in standard error units ($\sigma_{\overline{X}}$).

To compute the $z$-score for our Prunepit data,

**Step 1:** *Compute the standard error of the mean* ($\sigma_{\overline{X}}$) *as described above, and identify the sample mean and* $\mu$ *of the sampling distribution.* The $\mu$ of the sampling distribution equals the μ of the underlying raw score population the sample is selected from. Thus, for the sample from Prunepit U, $\overline{X} = 520$, $\mu = 500$, and $\sigma_{\overline{X}} = 20$, so we have

$$z = \frac{\overline{X} - \mu}{\sigma_{\overline{X}}} = \frac{520 - 500}{20}$$

**Step 2:** *Subtract* μ *from* $\overline{X}$: So

$$z = \frac{+20}{20}$$

**Step 3:** *Divide:*

$$z = +1$$

Thus, a sample mean of 520 has a $z$-score of +1 on the SAT sampling distribution of means that occurs when $N$ is 25.

**Here's Another Example Combining All of the Above:** Say that at Podunk U, a sample of 25 SAT scores produced a mean of 440. To find their $z$-score:

*1.* First, compute the standard error of the mean ($\sigma_{\overline{X}}$):

$$\sigma_{\overline{X}} = \frac{\sigma_X}{\sqrt{N}} = \frac{100}{\sqrt{25}} = \frac{100}{5} = 20$$

2. Then find $z$:

$$z = \frac{\overline{X} - \mu}{\sigma_{\overline{X}}} = \frac{440 - 500}{20} = \frac{-60}{20} = -3$$

The Podunk sample has a $z$-score of –3 on the sampling distribution of SAT means.

## Describing the Relative Frequency of Sample Means

Everything we said previously about a $z$-score for an individual score applies to a $z$-score for a sample mean. The $z$-score tells us our sample mean's relative location within the sampling distribution, and thus its relative standing among all means that occur in this situation. In the example, because our sample mean has a $z$-score of +1, we know that it is above the μ of the sampling distribution by an amount equal to the "average" amount that sample means deviate above μ. Our sample from Podunk U, however, has a $z$-score of –3, so its mean is one of the lowest SAT means we'd ever expect to obtain.

And here's the nifty part: Because a sampling distribution is always an approximately normal distribution, transforming *all* of the sample means in the sampling distribution into $z$-scores would produce a normal $z$-distribution. Recall that the *standard normal curve* is our model of *any* normal $z$-distribution. Therefore, as we did previously with raw scores, we can use the standard normal curve and $z$-tables to describe the relative frequency of sample means in any part of a sampling distribution.

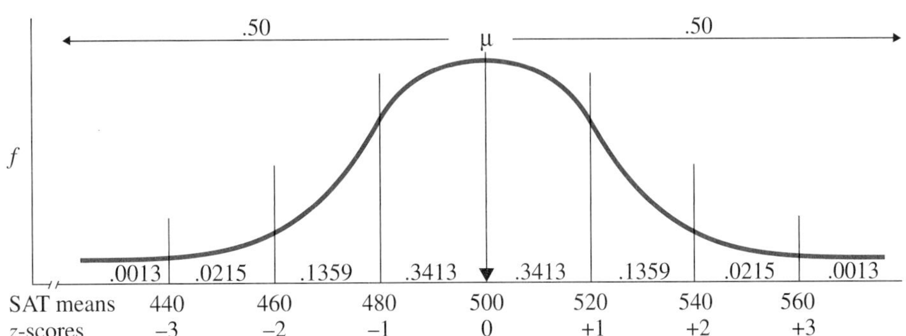


***FIGURE 5.8***
Proportions of the standard normal curve applied to the sampling distribution of SAT means

***REMEMBER*** The standard normal curve model and the *z*-tables can be used with any sampling distribution, as well as with any raw score distribution.

Figure 5.8 shows the standard normal curve applied to our SAT sampling distribution. This is the same curve, with the same proportions, that we used to describe individual raw scores. Here, however, each proportion is the expected relative frequency of the sample means that occur in this situation. For example, the sample from Prunepit U has a *z* of +1. As shown—and as in column B of the *z*-tables—.3413 of all scores fall between the mean and *z* of +1 on any normal distribution. Therefore, .3413 of all sample means are expected to fall here. Because in our data, the μ is 500 and a *z* of +1 is at the sample mean of 520, we expect .3413 of all SAT sample means to be between 500 and 520 (when *N* is 25). However, say that we asked about sample means above our sample mean. Then, as in column C of the *z*-tables, above a *z* of +1 is .1578 of the distribution. Therefore, we expect that .1578 of SAT sample means will be above 520. Similarly, a different sample mean of 460 would have a *z* of −2. As shown (and in column B of the *z*-tables), a total of .4772 of a distribution falls between the mean and this *z*-score. Therefore, we would expect 47.72% of SAT means to be between 500 and 460, with (as in column C) only .0228 of the means below 460. We can use this same procedure to describe sample means from any normally distributed variable.

## Summary of Describing a Sample Mean with a z-Score

Thus, we can describe a sample mean from any raw score population by following these steps:

*1.* Envision the sampling distribution of means (or better yet, draw it) as a normal distribution with a μ equal to the μ of the underlying raw score population.

*2.* Locate the sample mean on the sampling distribution, by computing its *z*-score.

   a. Using the $\sigma_X$ of the raw score population and your sample *N*, compute the standard error of the mean: $\sigma_{\overline{X}} = \sigma_X/\sqrt{N}$

   b. Compute *z*, finding how far your $\overline{X}$ is from the μ of the sampling distribution, measured in standard error units: $z = (\overline{X} - \mu)/\sigma_{\overline{X}}$

*3.* Use the *z*-tables to determine the relative frequency of scores above or below this *z*-score which is the relative frequency of sample means above or below your mean.

## A QUICK REVIEW

- To describe a sample mean, compute its $z$-score, and use the $z$-tables to determine the relative frequency of sample means above or below it.

### MORE EXAMPLES

On a test, $\mu = 100$, $\sigma_X = 16$, and our $N = 64$. What proportion of sample means will be above $\bar{X} = 103$?

1. Compute the standard error of the mean ($\sigma_{\bar{X}}$):

$$\sigma_{\bar{X}} = \frac{\sigma_X}{\sqrt{N}} = \frac{16}{\sqrt{64}} = \frac{16}{8} = 2$$

2. Compute $z$:

$$z = \frac{\bar{X} - \mu}{\sigma_{\bar{X}}} = \frac{103 - 100}{2} = \frac{+3}{2} = +1.33$$

3. Examine the $z$-tables: The area *above* this $z$ is the upper tail of the distribution, so from column C is .0918. This is the proportion of sample means expected to be above a mean of 103.

### *For Practice:*

A population of raw scores has $\mu = 75$ and $\sigma_X = 22$; our $N = 100$ and $\bar{X} = 80$.

1. The $\mu$ of the sampling distribution here equals ____.
2. The symbol for the standard error of the mean is ____ and here it equals ____.
3. The $z$-score for a sample mean of 80 is ____.
4. How often will sample means between 75 and 80 occur in this situation?

**Answers**

1. 75
2. $\sigma_{\bar{X}}$; $22/\sqrt{100} = 2.20$
3. $z = (80 - 75)/2.20 = +2.27$
4. From column B: .4884 of the time.

## CHAPTER SUMMARY

1. The *relative standing* of a score reflects a systematic evaluation of the score relative to a sample or population. A *z-score* indicates a score's relative standing by indicating the distance the score is from the mean when measured in standard deviations.
2. A positive $z$-score indicates the raw score is above the mean, and a negative $z$-score indicates the raw score is below the mean. The larger the absolute value of $z$, the farther the raw score is from the mean, so the less frequently the $z$-score and raw score occur.
3. $z$-scores are used to describe scores, to compare scores from different variables, and to determine the relative frequency of scores.
4. A *z-distribution* is produced by transforming all raw scores in a distribution into $z$-scores.
5. The *standard normal curve* is a perfect normal $z$-distribution that serves as a model of any approximately normal raw score distribution after it has been converted to $z$-scores. Any proportion of the area under a part of the curve (found in the $z$-tables) equals the expected relative frequency of the $z$-scores—and their corresponding raw scores—in that part of the curve.

6. A *sampling distribution of means* is the distribution of all possible sample means that occur when samples of a particular size $N$ are selected from a particular raw score population.
7. The *central limit theorem* shows that in a sampling distribution of means (a) the distribution will be approximately normal, (b) the mean of the sampling distribution will equal the mean of the underlying raw score population, and (c) the variability of the sample means is related to the variability of the raw scores.
8. The true *standard error of the mean* ($\sigma_{\bar{X}}$) is the standard deviation of the sampling distribution of means.
9. The location of a sample mean on the sampling distribution of means can be described by calculating a $z$-score. Then the standard normal curve model can be applied to the sampling distribution to determine the expected relative frequency of the sample means above or below that $z$-score.

## KEY TERMS: Can You Define the Following?

$\pm$ *81*
$z$ *78*
$\sigma_{\bar{X}}$ *90*
central limit theorem *89*
relative standing *76*
sampling distribution of means *89*
standard error of the mean *90*
standard normal curve *84*
standard scores *82*
$z$-distribution *81*
$z$-score *78*

## REVIEW QUESTIONS

(Answers for odd-numbered questions are in Appendix C.)

1. (a) What does a $z$-score indicate? (b) Why are $z$-scores important?
2. On what factors does the size of a $z$-score depend?
3. What is a $z$-distribution?
4. What are the three uses of $z$-scores?
5. Why are $z$-scores referred to as standard scores?
6. Why is using $z$-scores and the standard normal curve model so useful?
7. (a) What is the standard normal curve? (b) How is it applied to a set of data? (c) What three criteria should be met for the model to give an accurate description of a sample?
8. (a) What is a sampling distribution of means? (b) When is it used? (c) Why is it useful?
9. What three things does the central limit theorem tell us about the sampling distribution of means? (b) Why is this useful?
10. What does the standard error of the mean indicate?

## APPLICATION QUESTIONS

*11.* Poindexter received a grade of 55 on a biology test ($\overline{X} = 50$) and a grade of 45 on a philosophy test ($\overline{X} = 50$). He is considering whether to ask his two professors to curve the grades using $z$-scores. (a) What other information should he consider before making his request? (b) Does he want the $S_X$ to be large or small in biology? Why? (c) Does he want the $S_X$ to be large or small in philosophy? Why?

*12.* In freshman English, Foofy earned a 76 ($\overline{X} = 85$, $S_X = 10$). Her friend Bubbles, in a different class, earned a 60 ($\overline{X} = 50$, $S_X = 4$). Should Foofy be bragging about how much better she did? Why?

*13.* For the data 9 5 10 7 9 10 11 8 12 7 6 9, (a) Compute the $z$-score for the raw score of 10. (b) Compute the $z$-score for the raw score of 6.

*14.* For the data in question 13 find the raw scores that correspond to the following: (a) $z = +1.22$; (b) $z = -0.48$.

*15.* Which $z$-score in each of the following pairs corresponds to the smaller raw score? (a) $z = +1.0$ or $z = +2.3$; (b) $z = -2.8$ or $z = -1.7$; (c) $z = -.70$ or $z = +.20$; (d) $z = 0.0$ or $z = -2.0$.

*16.* For each pair in question 15, which $z$-score has the higher frequency?

*17.* In a normal distribution, what proportion of scores are expected to fall into each of the following areas? (a) between the mean and $z = +1.89$; (b) below $z = -2.30$; (c) between $z = -1.25$ and $z = +2.75$; (d) above $z = +1.96$ and below $-1.96$.

*18.* For a distribution in which $\overline{X} = 100$, $S_X = 16$, and $N = 500$: (a) What is the relative frequency of scores between 76 and the mean? (b) How many participants are expected to score between 76 and the mean? (c) What is the percentile of someone scoring 76?

*19.* Poindexter may be classified as having a math dysfunction—and not have to take statistics—if he scores below the 25th percentile on a diagnostic test. The $\mu$ of the test is 75 ($\sigma_X = 10$). Approximately what raw score is the cutoff score for avoiding statistics?

*20.* A researcher obtained a sample mean of 68.4 with a sample of 49 participants. In the population the mean is 65 (and $\sigma_X = 10$). How often can he expect to obtain a sample mean that is higher than 68.4?

*21.* A recent graduate has two job offers and must decide which to accept. The job in City A pays $27,000. The average cost of living there is $50,000, with a standard deviation of $15,000. The job in City B pays $12,000. The average cost of living there is $14,000, with a standard deviation of $1,000. Assuming salaries are normally distributed, which is the better job offer? Why?

*22.* You own shares of a company's stock and, over the past ten trading days, its mean selling price is $14.89. Over the years the mean price has been $10.43 ($\sigma_X = \$5.60$). Can the mean selling price over the next ten days be expected to go higher? Should you wait to sell, or should you sell now?

## SUMMARY OF FORMULAS

1. *The formula for transforming a raw score in a sample into a z-score is*

$$z = \frac{X - \overline{X}}{S_X}$$

2. *The formula for transforming a z-score in a sample into a raw score is*

$$X = (z)(S_X) + \overline{X}$$

3. *The formula for transforming a sample mean into a z-score is*

$$z = \frac{\overline{X} - \mu}{\sigma_{\overline{X}}}$$

*where the true standard error of the mean is*

$$\sigma_{\overline{X}} = \frac{\sigma_X}{\sqrt{N}}$$

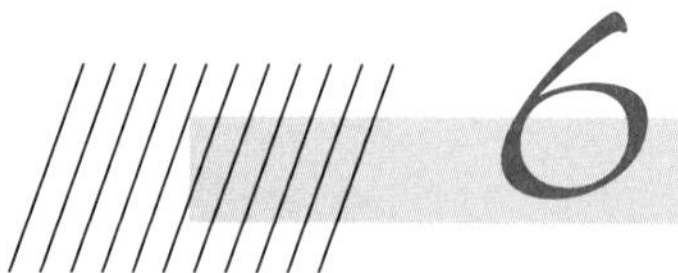

# 6 Using Probability to Make Decisions about Data

**CHAPTER ESSENTIALS**

**Before getting started, be sure you understand**

- From Chapter 1, the logic of using a sample to draw inferences about the population
- From Chapter 5, how to compute a *z*-score for a score or sample mean and how to determine relative frequency from the standard normal curve

**Your goals in this chapter are to learn**

- What *probability* communicates
- How probability is an event's relative frequency in the population
- How the probability of sample means is computed using *z*-scores and the standard normal curve
- What *sampling error* is and how random sampling can produce representative or unrepresentative samples
- How to use a *sampling distribution of means* to determine whether a sample is likely to represent a particular population

You now know most of the common descriptive statistics used in behavioral research. Therefore, you are ready to begin learning the other type of statistical procedure, called *inferential statistics*. Recall that these procedures are used to draw inferences from sample data about the scores and relationship that is found in nature—what we call the population. This chapter sets the foundation for these procedures by introducing you to probability. As you'll see, researchers combine their knowledge of probability with the standard normal curve model to make decisions about data. Therefore, although you do not need to be an expert in probability, you do need to understand the basics. In the following sections we'll discuss (1) what probability is, (2) how to determine the probability of scores and sample means, and (3) how to use probability to draw conclusions about a sample mean.

## UNDERSTANDING PROBABILITY

Probability is used to describe random or chance events. By *random* we mean that nature is being fair, with no bias toward one event over another (no rigged roulette wheels or loaded dice). Only luck operates to produce the event. In statistical terminology the event that occurs is a *random sample* from the *population* of possible events that can occur. The "event" might be drawing a playing card from a deck of cards, or tossing a coin and obtaining a particular sample of heads and tails out of the population of possible heads and tails. In research the event is obtaining a sample containing particular participants or their scores from a particular population.

A random sample is produced through random sampling. **Random sampling** is selecting a sample in such a way that all events or individuals in the population have an equal chance of being selected. Thus, in research, random sampling is anything akin to drawing participants' names from a large hat containing all names in the population. A particular sample occurs or does not occur merely because of the luck of the draw. We use probability to describe the *likelihood,* or our *confidence,* that a particular sample will occur.

But how can we describe an event that occurs only by chance? By paying attention to how *often* the event occurs *over the long run.* If event A happens frequently over the long run, we think it is likely to happen again now and say that it has a high probability. If event B happens infrequently, we think that it is unlikely to happen now and say that it has a low probability. When we describe how often an event occurs, however, we are making a relative judgment and actually describing the event's *relative frequency* (the proportion of the time that the event occurs). Thus, the **probability** of an event is equal to the event's relative frequency in the population of possible events that can occur.

> ***REMEMBER*** The *probability* of an event equals the event's relative frequency in the population.

Thus, we assume that an event's past relative frequency in the population will continue over the long run in the future. We translate this into our confidence for a *single* sample by expressing the relative frequency as a probability. For example, I am a rotten typist and I randomly make typos 80% of the time. This means that in the population of my typing, typos occur with a relative frequency of .80. We expect the relative frequency of typos to continue at a rate of .80 in anything else I type. This expected relative frequency is expressed as a probability, so the probability is .80 that I will make a typo when I type the next woid.

Notice that a probability is always expressed as a decimal. The symbol for probability is $p$. So if event A has a relative frequency of zero in a particular situation, then $p = 0$. This means that we do not expect A to occur in this situation because it never does. If A has a relative frequency of .10 in this situation, then it has a probability of .10: Because it occurs only 10% of the time in the population, we have some—but not much—confidence that A will occur in the next sample. On the other hand, if A has a probability of .95, we are confident that it will occur: It occurs 95% of the time in this situation, so we expect it in 95% of our samples. At the most extreme, event A's relative frequency can be 1: It is 100% of the population, so we are positive it will occur in this situation because it always does.

An event cannot happen less than 0% of the time nor more than 100% of the time, so a probability can *never* be less than 0 or greater than 1. Also, all events together constitute 100% of the population. This means that the relative frequencies of all events must add up to 1, and the probabilities must also add up to 1. Thus, if the probability of my making a typo is .80, then because $1 - .80 = .20$, the probability is .20 that a word will be error free.

Finally, understand that except when $p$ equals either 0 or 1, we are never certain that an event will or will not occur. The probability of an event is its relative frequency *over the long run* (in the population). It is up to chance whether a particular sample contains the event. So, even though I make typos 80% of the time, I may go for quite a while without making one. That 20% of the time when I make no typos has to occur sometime. Thus, although the probability is .80 that I will make a typo in each word, it is only over the long run that we expect to see precisely 80% typos.

People who fail to understand that probability implies *over the long run* fall victim to the "gambler's fallacy." For example, after observing my errorless typing for a while, the fallacy is thinking that errors "must" occur now, essentially concluding that errors have become more likely. Or, say we're flipping a coin and get 7 heads in a row. The fallacy is thinking that a head is now less likely to occur, because it's already occurred too often (as if the coin says, "Hold it. That's enough heads for a while!"). The mistake of the gambler's fallacy is failing to recognize that whether an event occurs or not, its probability is not altered, because probability is determined by what happens "over the long run."

## PROBABILITY DISTRIBUTIONS

To compute the probability of an event, we need only determine its relative frequency in the population. When we know the relative frequency of every event in a population, we have a probability distribution. A **probability distribution** indicates the probability of all possible events in a population.

One way to create a probability distribution is to observe the relative frequency of events, creating an *empirical probability distribution.* Typically, however, we cannot observe the entire population, so the probability distribution is based on the observed frequencies of events in a sample, that are used to represent the population. For example, say that Dr. Fraud is sometimes very cranky, and his crankiness is random. We observe him on 18 days and he is cranky on 6 of them. Relative frequency equals $f/N$, so the relative frequency of his crankiness is 6/18, or .33. We expect that he will continue to be cranky 33% of the time. Thus, the probability that he will be cranky today is $p = .33$. Conversely, he was not cranky on 12 of the 18 days, which is 12/18, or .67. Thus, $p = .67$ that he will not be cranky today. Because his cranky days plus his non-cranky days constitute all possible events, we have the complete probability distribution for his crankiness.

Another way to create a probability distribution is to devise a *theoretical probability distribution,* which is based on how we assume nature distributes events in the population. From such a model, we determine the *expected* relative frequency of each event in the population, which is then the probability of each event. For example, consider tossing a coin. We assume that nature has no bias toward heads or tails, so that over the long run we expect the relative frequency of heads to be .50 and the relative frequency of tails to be .50. Thus, we have a theoretical probability distribution for coin tosses: The probability of a head on any toss is $p = .50$ and the probability of a tail is $p = .50$.

Or, consider drawing a playing card from a deck of 52 cards. We expect each card to occur at a rate of once out of every 52 draws over the long run. Thus, each card has a relative frequency of 1/52, or .0192, so the probability of drawing any specific card on a single draw is $p = .0192$.

And that is the logic of probability: We devise a *probability distribution* based on the expected relative frequency of each event in the population. An event's expected relative frequency equals its probability of occurring in a particular sample.

## A QUICK REVIEW

- An event's probability equals its relative frequency in the population.

### MORE EXAMPLES

One hundred raffle tickets are sold. We expect that each ticket would be drawn at a rate of 1 out of 100 draws over the long run, so the probability of holding the winning ticket is $p = 1/100 = .01$.

### *For Practice:*

1. The probability of any event equals its ____ in the ____.
2. As the $p$ of an event decreases, the event's relative frequency in this situation ____, so our confidence that the event will occur now ____.
3. A ____ shows the probabilities for all events in a population.

**Answers**

1. relative frequency; population
2. decreases; decreases
3. probability distribution

## OBTAINING PROBABILITY FROM THE STANDARD NORMAL CURVE

We use probability distributions in statistics to compute the probability of obtaining particular scores in a particular situation: Selecting an individual from the population who has a particular score is a random event in the same way that selecting a particular playing card from a deck is. Recognize, however, that selecting someone from the population of individuals who then produces a particular score is the same as selecting that *score* from the population of *scores* that would be produced after we've measured everyone in the population. Therefore, to determine a particular score's probability we look at the population of scores.

For now we'll assume that the scores are normally distributed, so our probability distribution is based on the *standard normal curve.* Recall from Chapter 5 that with this curve we use $z$-scores to find the *proportion of the area under the normal curve.* This proportion corresponds to the relative frequency of scores in that part of a distribution. However, now we have seen that the relative frequency of an event *is* its probability. Therefore, the proportion of the total area under the curve for particular scores equals the probability of those scores.

For example, Figure 6.1 provides the probability distribution for a set of scores. Say that we seek the probability of randomly selecting a score below the mean of 59. To answer this, think first in terms of $z$-scores. Raw scores below the mean produce negative $z$-scores, and negative $z$-scores constitute 50% of the curve and so have a relative frequency of .50. Therefore, the probability is .50 that we will select a negative $z$-score.

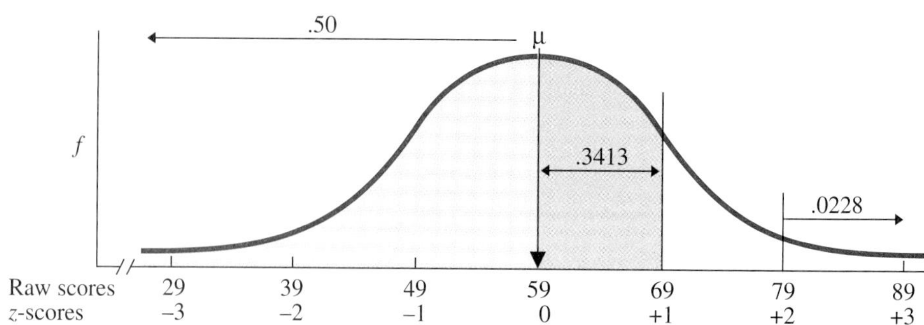


***FIGURE 6.1***
*z*-distribution showing the area for scores below the mean, between the mean and $z = +1$, and above $z = +2$

Now consider the corresponding raw scores. Because negative *z*-scores correspond to raw scores below 59, the probability is also .50 that we will select a raw score below 59.

Likewise, the area under the curve between the mean of 59 and a score of 69 in Figure 6.1 is the area between the mean and $z = +1$. From column B in the *z*-tables in Appendix B, scores in this area occur .3413 of the time, so the probability is .3413 that we will select a score between 59 and 69.

Or, say that we seek the probability of selecting a score *greater* than 79. In the right-hand tail of Figure 6.1, a raw score of 79 has a *z*-score of +2. From column C of the *z*-tables, the relative frequency of scores beyond this *z* is .0228. Therefore, the probability is .0228 that we will select a participant having a *z*-score greater than +2 or a raw score greater than 79.

In truth, researchers seldom determine the probability of an individual score. However, by understanding the preceding you can understand how *z*-scores and the normal curve are used as part of inferential statistics to determine the probability of sample means.

## Determining the Probability of Sample Means

We can compute the probability of obtaining samples that have a particular mean because a *sampling distribution of means* is another type of probability distribution. Recall that a sampling distribution is the frequency distribution of all possible sample means that occur when a particular raw score population is sampled an infinite number of times using a particular *N*. For example, Figure 6.2 shows the sampling distribution

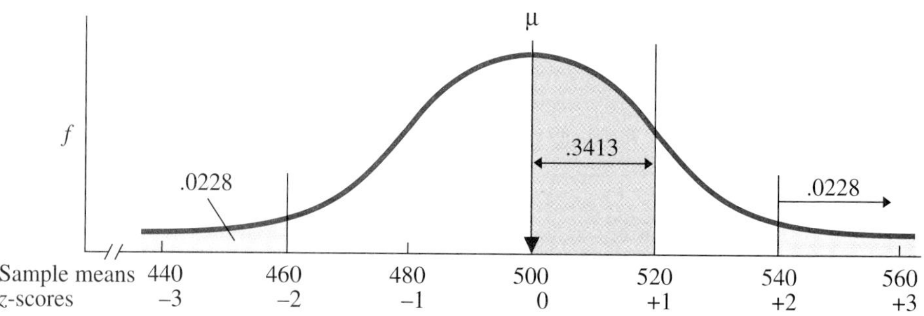


***FIGURE 6.2***
Sampling distribution of SAT means when $N = 25$

of all possible means produced from the population of SAT scores when $\mu$ is 500 and $N = 25$. Recognize that the different values of $\overline{X}$ occur here simply because of the luck of the draw of which scores are in the sample each time. Sometimes a sample mean higher than 500 occurs because, by chance, the sample contains predominantly high scores. At other times it might contain predominantly low scores, producing a mean below 500. Thus, the sampling distribution provides a picture of how often different sample means occur by chance when we draw a sample from this underlying SAT raw score population.

By using the sampling distribution, we can determine the probability of obtaining particular sample means in the same way that we previously determined the probability of obtaining particular raw scores. First, as in Chapter 5, we compute the mean's $z$-score. To do this, first compute the standard error of the mean using the formula

$$\sigma_{\overline{X}} = \frac{\sigma_X}{\sqrt{N}}$$

Then compute a $z$-score for the sample mean using the formula

$$z = \frac{\overline{X} - \mu}{\sigma_{\overline{X}}}$$

Then, by applying the standard normal curve and $z$-tables we can determine the probability of obtaining sample means that are above or below this $z$-score.

For example, for the SAT means in Figure 6.2 when $N$ is 25, say that $\sigma_X = 100$. Then the standard error of the mean is $100/\sqrt{25} = 20$. Say we're interested in means between 500 and 520, which are the means having $z$-scores between 0 and +1. The relative frequency of such $z$-scores is .3413, so the relative frequency of the sample means that produce these $z$-scores is also .3413. Therefore, the probability is .3413 that we will obtain a sample mean between 500 and 520 from this population.

Think about this: Randomly selecting a sample mean is the same as randomly selecting a sample of raw scores that produce that mean. Likewise, randomly selecting a sample of raw scores is the same as randomly selecting a sample of participants and then measuring their raw scores. Therefore, the probability of selecting the above sample means is also the probability of selecting the corresponding samples that produce those means. Thus, when we randomly select 25 participants from the SAT population, the probability of selecting a sample that produces a mean between 500 and 520 is .3413.

Likewise, say that we seek the probability of obtaining sample means above 540. As in the right-hand tail of Figure 6.2, a mean of 540 has a $z$-score of +2. As we say, the relative frequency of $z$-scores above this $z$ is .0228. Therefore, the probability is .0228 that we will select a sample of individuals whose SAT scores produce a mean higher than 540.

Or, we might seek the probability of means that are beyond a $z$ of $\pm 2$ (plus or minus 2.) Beyond $z = +2$ in the right-hand tail is .0228 of the curve, and beyond $z = -2$ in the left-hand tail is also .0228 of the curve. Therefore, adding the areas together, a total of .0456 of the curve contains the means that have $z$-scores beyond $\pm 2$. Thus, the probability that we'll obtain one of the means that lie there is $p = .0456$.

**REMEMBER** A sample mean's $z$-score on the sampling distribution indicates the relative frequency and thus the probability of obtaining samples that have means above or below this point.

Be sure that you understand that we can determine the probability of obtaining a particular sample mean from a raw score population using the mean's $z$-score. However, as with individual raw scores, we won't belabor computing the specific probabilities for different sample means. (Researchers seldom compute the precise probability of a particular mean.) Instead, understand the general logic of how $z$-scores and a sampling distribution indicate the probability of sample means.

In particular, look again at Figure 6.2 and see what happens when means have a *larger* $z$-score that places them *farther* into the tail of the sampling distribution: The height of the curve above the means decreases, indicating that the means occur less often and so their relative frequency decreases. Therefore, the probability of such means occurring in this situation also *decreases.* Thus, a sample mean having a larger $z$-score is less likely to occur when we are dealing with the underlying raw score population. For example, in Figure 6.2, an SAT mean of 560 has a $z$-score of $+3$, indicating that we are very unlikely to select a sample from the ordinary SAT population that contains such high scores and so has such a high mean.

**REMEMBER** The larger the absolute value of a sample mean's $z$-score, the less likely the mean is to occur when sampling from the underlying raw score population.

## A QUICK REVIEW

- We find the probability of obtaining a particular sample mean from a particular population by computing the mean's $z$-score, envisioning the sampling distribution, and applying the $z$-tables.
- The farther into the tail of the sampling distribution a sample mean falls, the less likely it is to occur when sampling the underlying raw score population.

### MORE EXAMPLES

The $\mu$ of a raw score population is 35. In sample A, $\overline{X}$ is 38, producing a $z$-score of $+1$. In sample B, $\overline{X}$ is 41, producing a $z$-score of $+2$. The probability of obtaining a sample with a mean above 38 is .1587 (from column C of the $z$-tables). The probability of obtaining a sample with a mean above 41 is .0228.

***For Practice:***

1. What is the probability of selecting a sample mean having a positive $z$-score?
2. Approximately, what is the probability of selecting an SAT sample mean having a $z$-score between $\pm 1$?
3. If $\mu = 100$, are we more likely to obtain a sample mean that is close to 100 or a mean that is very different from 100?
4. Which has the lower probability, a sample mean with $z = +1.75$ or a sample mean with $z = -1.82$?

**Answers**

1. With 50% of the distribution, $p = .50$.
2. With about 68% of the distribution, $p = .68$.
3. A sample close to 100 is more likely.
4. The mean at $z = -1.82$ has a lower probability.

## RANDOM SAMPLING AND SAMPLING ERROR

The procedures for using $z$-scores to compute the probability of sample means form the basis for all inferential statistics. The first step in understanding these statistics is to understand why we need them. Recall that in research we want to say that the way a sample behaves is the way that the population behaves. We need inferential statistics because there is no guarantee that the sample accurately reflects the population. In other words, we are never certain that a sample is representative of the population. In a **representative sample** the characteristics of the individuals and scores in the sample accurately reflect the characteristics of individuals and scores found in the population. Put simply, a representative sample is a miniature version of the population in terms of the types of individuals it contains and therefore in terms of the scores they produce. So, if the $\mu$ in the SAT population is 500, then the $\overline{X}$ in a representative sample will be 500.

To produce representative samples, researchers select participants using random sampling. A random sample *should* be representative because, by being unselective and random in choosing participants, we allow the characteristics of the population to occur naturally in the sample in the same ways that they occur in the population. For example, say that 20% of the population has an SAT score of 475. Then 20% of a random sample should also score 475, because that's how often that score is out there.

However, representativeness is not all or nothing. Depending on the individuals—and scores—selected, a sample can be somewhat representative, only somewhat matching the population. For example, 20% of the population may score at 475, but simply through the luck who is selected, we might obtain this score 10% or 30% of the time in our sample. In this case the sample will have characteristics that are only somewhat similar to those of the population, and although $\mu$ may be 500, the sample mean will be some other number. In the same way, depending on the scores we happen to select, any sample may not be perfectly representative of the population from which it is selected, so the sample mean will not equal the population mean it is representing.

The statistical term for communicating that chance produced an unrepresentative sample is to say that the sample reflects sampling error. **Sampling error** occurs when random chance produces a sample statistic (such as $\overline{X}$) that is not equal to the population parameter it represents (such as $\mu$). Sampling error conveys that the reason a sample mean is different from $\mu$ is because, by chance, the sample is unrepresentative of the population. That is, because of the luck of the draw, the sample contains too many high scores or too many low scores relative to the population, so the sample is in *error* to some degree in representing the population.

> **REMEMBER** *Sampling error* results when, by chance, the scores that are selected produce a sample statistic that is different from the population parameter it represents.

Here, then, is the central problem for researchers (and the reason for inferential statistics): When sampling error produces a sample that is different from the population that it comes from and represents, it has the characteristics of some other population and so it appears to come from and represent that other population. Thus, although a sample always represents some population, we are never sure *which* population it represents: Through sampling error the sample may poorly represent one population, or it may accurately represent some other population altogether.

> *REMEMBER* Any sample may poorly represent one population, or it may accurately represent a different population.

For example, say that we return to Prunepit University and in a random sample obtain a mean SAT score of 550. This is surprising because the ordinary national population of SAT scores has a $\mu$ of 500. Therefore, we should have obtained a sample mean of 500 if our sample was perfectly representative of this population. How do we explain a sample mean of 550? On the one hand, maybe we simply have sampling error. Perhaps we obtained a sample of relatively high SAT scores merely because of the luck of the draw of who was selected for the sample. Thus, it's possible that chance produced a less than perfectly representative sample, but the population being represented is still that ordinary population where $\mu$ is 500. On the other hand, perhaps the sample does not come from or represent the ordinary population of SAT scores: After all, these *are* Prunepit students, so they may belong to a very different population of students, having some other $\mu$. For example, maybe Prunepit students belong to the population where $\mu$ is 550, and their sample is perfectly representing this population.

The solution to this dilemma is to use inferential statistics to make a decision about the population being represented by our sample. The next chapter puts all of this into a research context, but in the following sections we'll examine the basics of deciding whether a sample represents a particular population.

## DECIDING WHETHER A SAMPLE REPRESENTS A POPULATION

We deal with the possibility of sampling error in this way: Because we rely on random sampling, how representative a sample is depends on random chance—the luck of the draw of which individuals and scores are selected. Therefore, using probability, we can determine whether our sample is *likely* to come from and thus represent a particular population. If the sample is *likely* to occur when that population is sampled, then we decide that it *does* represent that population. If our sample is *unlikely* to occur when that population is sampled, then we decide that the sample does *not* represent that population, and instead represents some other population.

Thus, to decide whether our Prunepit sample represents the population of SAT scores where $\mu$ is 500, we will determine the probability of obtaining a sample mean of 550 from this population. As you've seen, we determine the probability of a sample mean by computing its $z$-score on the sampling distribution of means. Thus, we first envision the sampling distribution showing the different means that occur when, using our $N$, the ordinary SAT population is sampled. This is shown in Figure 6.3.

The next step is to calculate our sample mean's $z$-score to locate it on this distribution and thus determine its likelihood. In reality we would not expect a *perfectly*

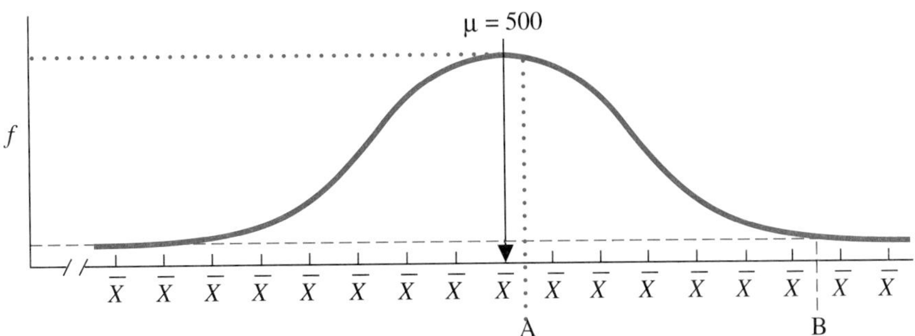


***FIGURE 6.3***
Sampling distribution of SAT means showing two possible locations of our sample mean

representative sample having a $\overline{X}$ of exactly 500.000 . . . . (Think how unlikely that is!) Instead, if our sample represents this population, the sample mean should be *close* to 500. For example, say that the *z*-score for our sample mean is at location A in Figure 6.3. Read what the frequency distribution indicates by following the dotted line: This mean has a relatively high frequency and thus is very *likely* when drawing a sample from the ordinary SAT population. Anytime you deal with this population, this mean is likely to occur, because often a sample is unrepresentative to this extent, containing slightly higher scores in the sample than occur in the population. Thus, this is exactly the kind of mean we'd expect if our Prunepit sample came from this SAT population. Therefore, we can *accept* that our sample probably comes from and represents the ordinary SAT population, accepting that the difference between our $\overline{X}$ and $\mu$ reflects chance sampling error.

However, say that instead, our sample has a *z*-score at location B in Figure 6.3: Following the dashed line shows that this is a very infrequent and *unlikely* mean: when we *are* representing the ordinary SAT population, seldom is a sample so unrepresentative as to produce this mean. Thus, our sample is unlikely to be representing this population, because this mean almost never happens with this population. Therefore, we *reject* that our sample represents this population, rejecting that the difference between the $\overline{X}$ and $\mu$ reflects sampling error. Instead, it makes more sense to conclude that the sample represents some other raw score population (having some other $\mu$), where this sample mean is more likely.

> ***REMEMBER*** The location of a $\overline{X}$ on the sampling distribution indicates how likely the sample is to come from and represent the underlying raw score population.

The above logic is used in all inferential procedures. We will always have a known, underlying raw score population that a sample may or may not represent. From the underlying raw score population we envision the sampling distribution of means that would be produced. Then we determine the location of our sample mean on the sampling distribution. The farther into the tail of the sampling distribution the sample mean is, the less likely that the sample comes from and represents the original underlying raw score population.

## A QUICK REVIEW

- If the *z-score* shows that a sample mean is *unlikely* in the sampling distribution, reject that the sample is merely poorly representing the underlying raw score population.
- If the $z$-score shows that a sample mean is *likely* in the sampling distribution, accept that the sample is representing the underlying raw score population, albeit somewhat poorly.

### More Examples

On the sampling distribution created from body weights in the United States, a sample's mean produces a $z = +5.00$! Such a mean is extremely unlikely when representing this population, so we reject that our sample represents this population. However, say another sample's mean produced a $z = -.2$. Such a mean is close to $\mu$ and very likely, so this sample is likely to be representing this population.

### *For Practice:*

1. ____ communicates that a sample mean is different from the $\mu$ it represents.
2. Sampling error occurs because of ____.
3. A sample mean has a $z = +1$ on the sampling distribution created from the population of psychology majors. Is this likely to be a sample of psychology majors?
4. A sample mean has a $z = -4.0$ on the sampling distribution. Is this likely to be a sample of psychology majors?

**Answers**

1. sampling error
2. random chance
3. Yes
4. No

## Setting Up the Sampling Distribution

To decide if our Prunepit sample represents the ordinary SAT population (with $\mu = 500$), we must perform two tasks: (1) Determine the probability of obtaining our sample from the ordinary SAT population, and (2) decide whether the sample is unlikely to be representing this population. We perform both tasks simultaneously using the sampling distribution.

We formalize the decision process in this way: At some point, a sample mean is so far above or below 500 that it is unbelievable that chance produced such an unrepresentative sample. Any samples *beyond* this point that are farther into the tail are also unbelievable. To identify this point, as shown in Figure 6.4, we literally draw a line in each tail of the distribution. In statistical terms the shaded areas beyond the lines make up the *region of rejection*. As shown, very infrequently are samples so poor at representing

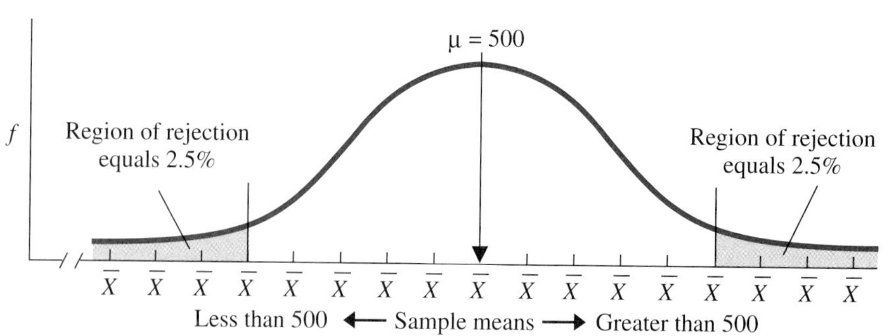


**FIGURE 6.4**
Setup of sampling distribution of means showing the region of rejection

the SAT population that they have means in the region of rejection. Therefore, the **region of rejection** is the part of a sampling distribution containing means that are so unlikely that we "reject" that they represent the underlying raw score population. Essentially, we "shouldn't" get a sample mean that lies in the region of rejection if we're representing the ordinary SAT population because such means almost never occur with this population. Therefore, if we do get such a mean, we probably aren't representing this population: We *reject* that our sample represents the underlying raw score population and decide that the sample represents some other population.

Conversely, if our Prunepit mean is not in the region of rejection, then our sample is not unlikely to be representing the ordinary SAT population. In fact, by our definition, samples not in the region of rejection are likely to represent this population, but just not perfectly. In such cases we *retain* the idea that our sample is simply poorly representing this population of SAT scores.

How do we know where to draw the line that starts the region of rejection? By defining our *criterion.* The **criterion** is the probability that defines samples as unlikely to be representing a particular population. Researchers usually use .05 as their criterion probability. Thus, by this criterion, those sample means that together occur *less* than 5% of the time when representing the ordinary SAT population are so unlikely that if we get any one of them, we'll reject that our sample represents this population.

The criterion determines the size of the region of rejection. In Figure 6.4 the sample means that occur 5% of the time are those that make up the extreme 5% of the sampling distribution. However, because we're talking about the means above *or* below 500 that together are a *total* of 5% of the curve, we divide the 5% in half. Therefore, the extreme 2.5% of the curve in each tail of the sampling distribution will form our region of rejection.

> ***REMEMBER*** The *criterion probability* that defines samples as unlikely—and also determines the size of the *region of rejection*—is usually $p = .05$.

Now the task is to determine if our sample mean falls into the region of rejection. To do this, we compare the sample's $z$-score to the *critical value.*

## Identifying the Critical Value

At the spot on the sampling distribution where the line marks the beginning of the region of rejection is a specific $z$-score. Because the absolute value of $z$-scores gets larger as we go farther into the tails, if the $z$-score for our sample is larger than the $z$-score at the line, then our sample mean lies *in* the region of rejection. The $z$-score at the line is called the critical value. A **critical value** marks the inner edge of the region of rejection and thus defines the value required for a sample to fall into the region of rejection. Essentially, it is the minimum $z$-score that defines a sample as too unlikely.

How do we determine the critical value? By considering our criterion. With a criterion of .05, the region of rejection in each tail is the extreme .025 of the total area under the curve. From column C in the $z$-tables, the extreme .025 lies beyond the $z$-score of 1.96. Therefore, in each tail, the region of rejection begins at 1.96, so $\pm 1.96$ is the critical value of $z$. Thus, as shown in Figure 6.5, labeling the inner edges of the region of rejection with $\pm 1.96$ completes how *you* should set up the sampling distribution. (*Note:* As you'll see, using both tails like this is called a *two-tailed test.*)

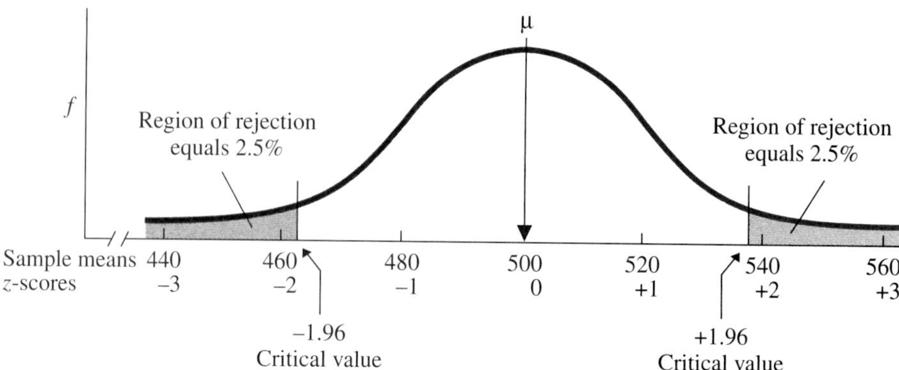


**FIGURE 6.5** Setup of sampling distribution of SAT means showing region of rejection and critical values

We'll use Figure 6.5 to determine whether our Prunepit mean lies in the region of rejection by comparing our sample's $z$-score to the critical value.

> **A sample mean lies in the region of rejection if its $z$-score is *beyond* the critical value.**

Thus, if our Prunepit sample mean has a $z$-score that is *larger* than $\pm 1.96$, then the sample lies *in* the region of rejection. If the $z$-score is *smaller than* or *equal to* the critical value, then the sample is *not* in the region of rejection.

> ***REMEMBER*** The *critical value* defines the minimum value of $z$ a sample must have in order to be in the region of rejection.

## Deciding whether the Sample Represents a Population

Now we can evaluate our sample mean of 550 from Prunepit U. First, we compute the sample's $z$-score on the sampling distribution created from the ordinary SAT population. There, $\sigma_X = 100$ and $N = 25$, so the standard error of the mean is

$$\sigma_{\overline{X}} = \frac{\sigma_X}{\sqrt{N}} = \frac{100}{\sqrt{25}} = 20$$

Then the $z$-score is

$$z = \frac{\overline{X} - \mu}{\sigma_{\overline{X}}} = \frac{550 - 500}{20} = +2.5$$

To complete the procedure, we compare the sample's $z$-score to the critical value to determine the location of the sample mean on the sampling distribution. As shown in Figure 6.6, our sample's $z$ of $+2.5$—and the underlying sample mean of 550—lies in the region of rejection. This tells us that a sample mean of 550 is among those means that are extremely unlikely to occur when the sample represents the ordinary population of SAT scores. In other words, very seldom does chance—the luck of the draw—produce such unrepresentative samples from this population, so it is not a good bet that chance produced *our* sample from this population. Therefore, we reject that our sample represents the population of SAT raw scores having a $\mu$ of 500.

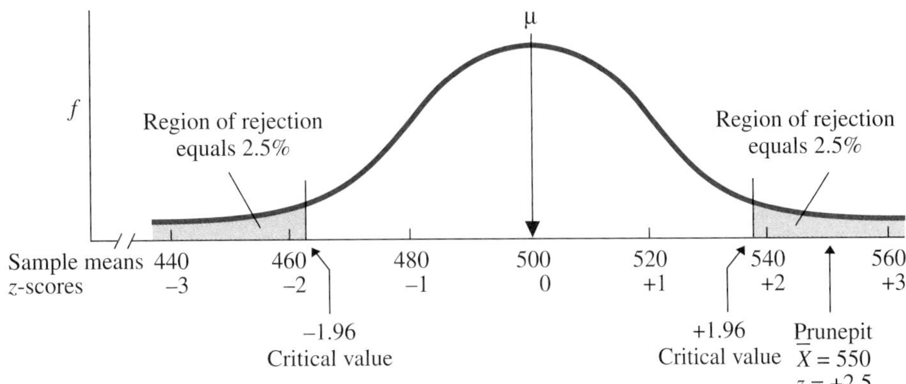


**FIGURE 6.6** Completed sampling distribution of SAT means showing location of the Prunepit U. sample relative to the critical value

Notice that we make a definitive, yes-or-no decision. Because our sample is unlikely to represent the SAT raw score population where $\mu$ is 500, we decide that no, it definitely does not represent this population. (But, in the next chapter we recognize there is *chance* that we are wrong.)

We wrap up our conclusions in this way: If the sample doesn't represent the ordinary SAT population, then it must represent some other population. For example, perhaps the Prunepit students obtained the high mean of 550 because they lied about their scores, so they may represent the population of students who lie about the SAT. Regardless, we use the sample mean to estimate the $\mu$ of the population that the sample *does* represent. A sample having a mean of 550 is most likely to come from a population having a $\mu$ of 550. Therefore, our best estimate is that the Prunepit sample represents a population of SAT scores that has a $\mu$ of 550.

On the other hand, say that our sample mean had been 474, resulting in a $z$-score of $(474 - 500)/20 = -1.30$. Because $-1.30$ does *not* lie beyond the critical value of $\pm 1.96$, this sample mean is *not* in the region of rejection. Looking at Figure 6.6 above, we see that when sampling the underlying SAT population, this sample mean is relatively frequent and thus likely. Because of this, we can accept that random chance produced a less than perfectly representative sample for us but that it probably represents the ordinary SAT population where $\mu$ is 500.

> ***REMEMBER*** When a sample's $z$-score is beyond the critical value, *reject* that the sample represents the underlying raw score population. When the $z$-score is not beyond the critical value, *retain* the idea that the sample represents the underlying raw score population.

## Summary of How to Decide About the Population Being Represented

The basic question answered by all inferential statistical procedures is "Do the sample data represent a particular raw score population?" To answer this:

*1. Envision (draw) the sampling distribution of means:* the $\mu$ equal to the $\mu$ of the underlying raw score population.

2. *Compute the sample mean, and its z-score:*
   a. Compute the standard error of the mean: $\sigma_{\bar{X}} = \sigma_X / \sqrt{N}$.
   b. Compute $z$, using $\bar{X}$ and the $\mu$ of the sampling distribution: $z = (\bar{X} - \mu)/\sigma_{\bar{X}}$
3. *Set up the sampling distribution:* Select the criterion probability (usually .05), locate the region of rejection, and determine the critical value.
4. *Compare the sample's z-score to the critical value:* If the sample's $z$ is beyond the critical value, it is in the region of rejection: Reject that the sample represents the underlying raw score population. If the sample's $z$ is not beyond the critical value, do not reject that the sample represents the underlying population.

## A QUICK REVIEW

- To decide if a sample represents a particular raw score population, compute the sample mean's $z$-score and compare it to the critical value on the sampling distribution.

### More Examples

A sample of SAT scores ($N = 25$) produces $\bar{X} = 460$. Does the sample represent the ordinary SAT population where $\mu = 500$ and $\sigma_X = 100$?

1. Compute $z$: $\sigma_{\bar{X}} = \sigma_X/\sqrt{N} = 100/\sqrt{25} = 20$; $z = (\bar{X} - \mu)/\sigma_{\bar{X}} = (460 - 500)/20 = -2.0$
2. With a criterion of .05, the region of rejection is in both tails, and the critical value is $\pm 1.96$. The sampling distribution is identical to Figure 6.6.
3. The sample's $z$ of –2 is beyond –1.96, so it is in the region of rejection. Conclusion: The sample does not represent the ordinary SAT raw score population.

### *For Practice:*

1. The ____ contains those samples considered to be likely/unlikely to represent the underlying population.
2. The ____ defines the $z$-score that is required for a sample to be in the region of rejection.
3. For a sample to be in the region of rejection, its $z$-score must be smaller/larger than the critical value.
4. On a test $\mu = 60$, $\sigma_X = 18$. A sample ($N = 100$) produces $\bar{X} = 65$. Using the .05 criterion, does this sample represent this population?

**Answers**

1. region of rejection; unlikely
2. critical value
3. larger (beyond)
4. $\sigma_{\bar{X}} = 18/\sqrt{100} = 1.80$; $z = (65 - 60)/1.80 = +2.78$. This $z$ is beyond $\pm 1.96$ in the region of rejection, so reject that the sample represents the population with $\mu = 60$; it's likely to represent the population with $\mu = 65$.

## Other Ways to Set Up the Sampling Distribution

Previously, we placed the region of rejection in both tails of the distribution because we wanted to identify unrepresentative sample means that were either too far above or too far below 500. Instead, however, we can place the region of rejection in only one tail of the distribution. (In the next chapter you'll see why you would want to use this *one-tailed test.*)

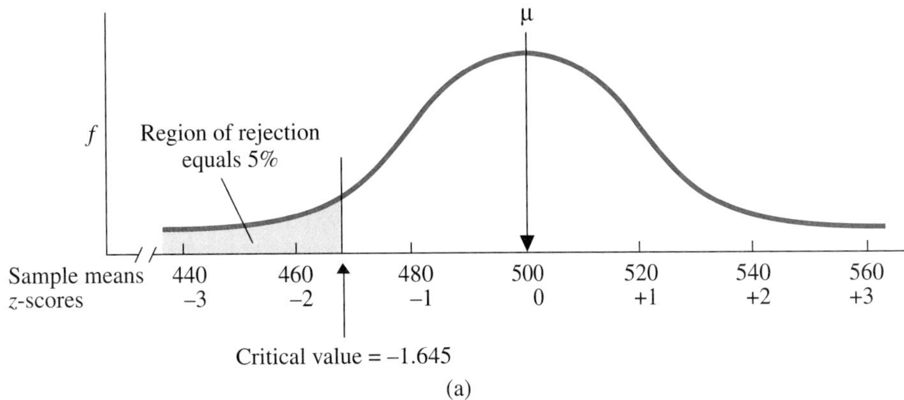


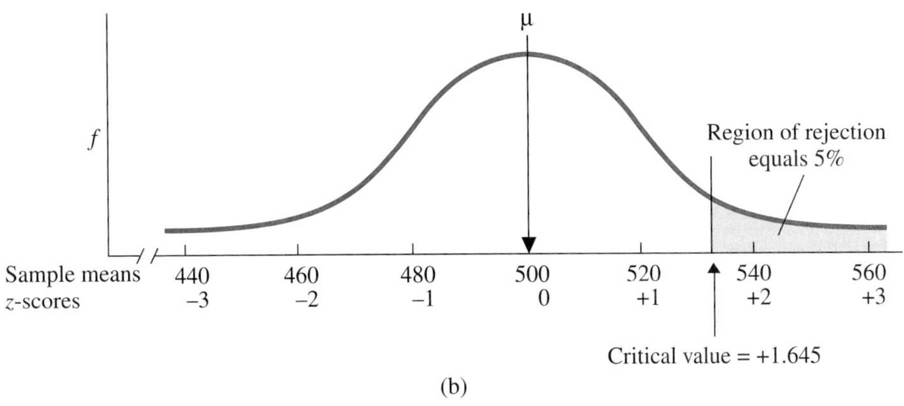


***FIGURE 6.7***
Setup of SAT sampling distribution to test (a) negative *z*-scores and (b) positive *z*-scores

Say that we are interested only in SAT means that are *less* than 500, having negative *z*-scores. Our criterion is still .05, but now we place the *entire* region of rejection in the lower, left-hand tail of the sampling distribution, as shown in part (a) of Figure 6.7. *This produces a different critical value.* The extreme lower 5% of a distribution lies beyond a *z*-score of $-1.645$. Therefore, the *z*-score for our sample must lie beyond $-1.645$ for it to be in the region of rejection. If it does, we will again conclude that the sample mean is so unlikely to occur when sampling the SAT raw score population that we'll reject that our sample represents this population. If the *z*-score is anywhere else on the sampling distribution, even far into the upper tail, we will *not* reject that the sample represents the population where $\mu = 500$.

On the other hand, say that we're interested only in sample means *greater* than 500, having positive *z*-scores. Then we place the entire region of rejection in the upper, right-hand tail of the sampling distribution, as shown in part (b) of Figure 6.7. Now the critical value is *plus* 1.645, so only if our sample's *z*-score is beyond $+1.645$ does the sample mean lie in the region of rejection. Only then do we reject the idea that our sample represents the underlying raw score population.

## CHAPTER SUMMARY

1. *Probability* $(p)$ indicates the likelihood of an event when random chance is operating. The probability of an event is equal to its relative frequency in the population.
2. *Random sampling* is selecting a sample so that all elements or individuals in the population have an equal chance of being selected.
3. A *probability distribution* is a model of the relative frequencies of all events in a population when random chance is operating.
4. A *sampling distribution of means* is a theoretical probability distribution. The proportion of the area under the curve is the probability of randomly selecting the corresponding sample means.
5. The probability of randomly selecting a particular sample mean is the same as the probability of randomly selecting a sample of participants whose scores produce that sample mean.
6. In a *representative sample* the individuals and scores in the sample accurately reflect those found in the population.
7. *Sampling error* results when chance produces a sample statistic, such as $\overline{X}$, that is different from the population parameter, $\mu$, that it represents.
8. *The region of rejection* is in the extreme tail or tails of a sampling distribution. Sample means here are unlikely to represent the underlying raw score population.
9. The *critical value* is the minimum $z$-score needed for a sample mean to lie in the region of rejection.
10. The *criterion probability* is the probability (usually .05) that defines samples as unlikely to represent the underlying raw score population and thus defines the size of the region of rejection.

## KEY TERMS: Can You Define the Following?

*p* *99*
criterion *109*
critical value *109*
probability *99*
probability distribution *100*
random sampling *99*
region of rejection *109*
representative sample *105*
sampling error *105*

## REVIEW QUESTIONS

(Answers for odd-numbered questions are in Appendix C.)

1. (a) What does a probability convey about a random event? (b) What is the probability of a random event based on?
2. Why is the proportion of the total area under the normal curve equal to probability?
3. What is a random sampling?
4. What does the term sampling error convey about a sample mean?

5. A sample produces a mean that is different from the $\mu$ of the population that we think the sample may represent. What are the two possible reasons for this difference?
6. What is (a) the criterion? (b) the region of rejection? (c) the critical value?
7. What does comparing the critical value to a sample's $z$-score indicate?
8. What is the difference between using both tails versus one tail of the sampling distribution in terms of (a) the location of the region of rejection? (b) the critical value?

## APPLICATION QUESTIONS

9. A couple with eight daughters decides to have one more baby, because they think the next one is bound to be a boy! Is this reasoning accurate?
10. Foofy read in the newspaper that there is a .05% chance of swallowing a spider while you sleep. She subsequently developed insomnia. (a) What is the probability of swallowing a spider? (b) Why isn't her insomnia justified? (c) Why is her insomnia justified?
11. Poindexter's uncle is building a house on land that has been devastated by hurricanes 160 times in the past 200 years. Because there hasn't been a major storm there in 13 years, his uncle says this is a safe investment. His nephew argues that he is wrong, because a hurricane must be due soon. What are the fallacies in the reasoning of both men?
12. Four airplanes from different airlines have crashed in the past two weeks. This terrifies Bubbles. Her travel agent claims that the probability of a plane crash is minuscule. Who is correctly interpreting the situation? Why?
13. Based on a survey of a random sample of college students, Foofy concludes that the favorite beverage in the population of college students is sauerkraut juice! What is the statistical argument for not accepting this conclusion?
14. (a) Why does random sampling produce representative samples? (b) Why does random sampling produce unrepresentative samples?
15. The mean of a population of raw scores is 18 ($\sigma_X = 12$). With $N = 30$, you obtained a sample mean of 24. Using the .05 criterion with the region of rejection in both tails of the sampling distribution, should you consider the sample to be representative of the population with $\mu = 18$? Why?
16. Foofy computes the $\overline{X}$ from data that her professor says is a random sample from population $Q$. This sample mean has a $z$-score of +41 on the sampling distribution for population $Q$ (and she computed it correctly!). Foofy claims she has *proven* that this could not be a random sample from population $Q$. Do you agree or disagree? Why?
17. In a study you obtain the following data representing the aggressive tendencies of some football players:

    40 30 39 40 41 39 31 28 33

    (a) Researchers have found that in the population of nonfootball players, $\mu$ is 30 ($\sigma_X = 5$). Using both tails of the sampling distribution, determine whether your football players represent a different population. (b) Using your sample, what do you conclude about the population of football players and its $\mu$?

*18.* You obtained a sample mean of 45 ($N = 40$). Using the .05 criterion with the region of rejection in only the lower tail of the distribution, is the sample representative of the population in which $\mu = 50$ ($\sigma_X = 18$)? Why?

*19.* (a) Why do we conclude that a low-probability sample does not represent a particular population? (b) Why do we conclude that a high-probability sample does represent a particular population?

*20.* On a test of motor coordination, a psychologist found that the population of average bowlers had a mean score of 24, with a standard deviation of 6. She tested a random sample of 30 bowlers at Fred's Bowling Alley and found a sample mean of 26. A second random sample of 30 bowlers at Ethel's Bowling Alley had a mean of 18. Using the criterion of $p = .05$ and both tails of the sampling distribution, what should she conclude about each sample's representativeness of the population of average bowlers?

*21.* (a) In question 20 if a particular sample does not represent the population of average bowlers, what is your best estimate of the $\mu$ of the population it does represent? (b) Explain the logic behind this conclusion.

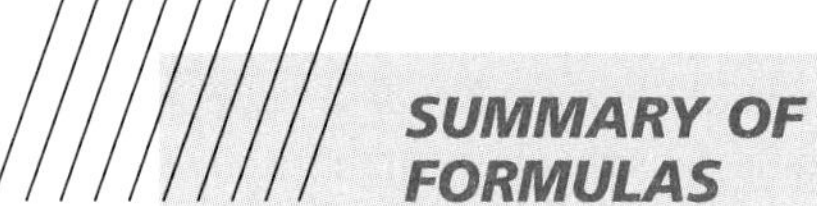

## SUMMARY OF FORMULAS

*1. The formula for transforming a sample mean into a z-score is*

$$z = \frac{\overline{X} - \mu}{\sigma_{\overline{X}}}$$

*where*

$$\sigma_{\overline{X}} = \frac{\sigma_X}{\sqrt{N}}$$

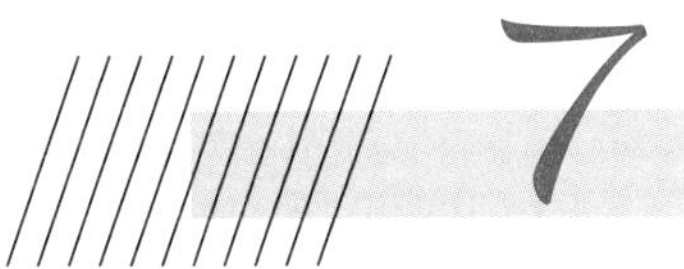

# 7 Overview of Statistical Hypothesis Testing: The *z*-Test

**CHAPTER ESSENTIALS**

**Before getting started, be sure you understand**

- From Chapter 1, what the conditions of an independent variable are and what the dependent variable is
- From Chapter 3, that a relationship in the population occurs when different means from the conditions represent different $\mu$s and thus different distributions of dependent scores
- From Chapter 6, that when a sample's *z*-score falls into the region of rejection, the sample is unlikely to represent the underlying raw score population

**Your goals in this chapter are to learn**

- Why the possibility of sampling error leads us to perform inferential statistical procedures
- When *experimental hypotheses* lead to either a *one-tailed* or a *two-tailed* test
- How to create the *null* and *alternative* hypotheses
- When and how to perform the z-*test*
- How to interpret *significant* and *nonsignificant* results
- What *Type I errors, Type II errors,* and *power* are

From the previous chapter you know the basics involved in inferential statistics. Now we'll put these procedures into a research context and present the statistical language and symbols used to describe them. Until further notice, we'll be talking about experiments. This chapter shows (1) how to set up a one-sample experiment, (2) how to perform the "*z*-test," and (3) how to interpret the results of an inferential procedure.

## THE ROLE OF INFERENTIAL STATISTICS IN RESEARCH

As you saw in the previous chapter, a random sample may be more or less representative of a population because, just by the luck of the draw, the sample may contain too many high scores or too many low scores relative to the population. Because the sample is not perfectly representative of the population, it reflects *sampling error,* so the sample mean does not equal the population mean.

*The possibility that a sample might reflect sampling error is the reason that researchers perform inferential statistics.* Recall that in an experiment, we hope to see a relationship in which, as we change the conditions of the independent variable, scores on the dependent variable change in a consistent fashion. Then, if the means for the conditions differ, we infer that, in nature, we'd see this relationship so that each condition would produce a different population of scores located at a different $\mu$. But! Maybe the sample means for the conditions differ because of sampling error, and they actually all poorly represent the *same* population having the same $\mu$. If so, then the relationship does not really exist. Or, because of sampling error, the actual relationship in the population may be different from the one in the sample data.

For example, say we compare men and women on the dependent variable of creativity. In nature, men and women don't really differ on this variable, but through the luck of the draw we might end up with some females who are more creative than our males or vice versa. Then sampling error will mislead us into thinking there's a relationship here, even though there really is not. Or, say that we measure the heights of some men and women and, by chance, obtain a sample of relatively short men and a sample of tall women. If we didn't already know that men are taller, sampling error would mislead us into concluding that women are taller.

Because of the possibility of sampling error, we must apply inferential statistics to *every* study. **Inferential statistics** are used to decide whether sample data represent a particular relationship in the population. The specific inferential procedure employed in a given situation depends upon the *study's design* and on the *scale of measurement* used to measure the *dependent variable.* There are two general categories of inferential statistics. **Parametric statistics** are procedures that require specific assumptions about the raw score populations being represented. Each procedure has its own assumptions, but two assumptions common to all parametric procedures are:

*1.* The population of dependent scores should be at least approximately normally distributed.
*2.* The scores should be interval or ratio scores.

The other category is **nonparametric statistics,** which are inferential procedures that do not require stringent assumptions about the populations being represented. These procedures are used with nominal or ordinal scores or with skewed interval or ratio distributions.

> **REMEMBER** *Parametric* and *nonparametric inferential statistics* are for deciding if the data reflect a relationship in nature, or if sampling error is misleading us into thinking there is a relationship.

In this and upcoming chapters we'll focus on parametric procedures. (Chapter 13 presents nonparametric procedures.)

## SETTING UP INFERENTIAL PROCEDURES

Researchers perform four steps in an experiment: They create the experimental hypotheses, design and conduct the experiment to test the hypotheses, translate the experimental hypotheses into statistical hypotheses, and perform the statistical test of the statistical hypotheses.

## Creating the Experimental Hypotheses

An experiment tests two **experimental hypotheses** that describe the predicted outcome we may or may not find. One hypothesis states that we will demonstrate the predicted relationship (manipulating the independent variable will work as expected). The other hypothesis states that we will not demonstrate the predicted relationship (manipulating the independent variable will not work as expected).

We can predict a relationship in one of two ways. Sometimes we predict a relationship, but we are not sure whether scores will increase or decrease as we change the independent variable. This leads to a "two-tailed" test. A **two-tailed test** is used when we do not predict the direction in which scores will change. Thus, we'd have a two-tailed hypothesis if we thought men and women differed in creativity, but were unsure who would score higher. The other approach is to predict the direction in which the scores will change. This leads to a one-tailed test. A **one-tailed test** is used when we predict the *direction* in which scores will change. We may predict that the dependent scores will only increase, or that they will only decrease. Thus, we'd have a one-tailed test if we predicted that men would be more creative than women, or if we predicted that women would score higher.

> ***REMEMBER*** A *two-tailed test* is used when you do not predict the direction that scores will change. A *one-tailed test* is used when you do predict the direction that scores will change.

Let's first examine a study involving a two-tailed test. Say we've discovered a substance related to intelligence that we will test with humans in an "IQ pill." The amount of the pill is our independent variable and the person's resulting IQ is the dependent variable. We believe this pill will affect IQ, but we are not sure whether it will make people smarter or dumber. Therefore, here are our two-tailed experimental hypotheses:

1. We will demonstrate that the pill works by either increasing or decreasing IQ scores.
2. We will not demonstrate that the pill works, because IQ scores will not change.

## Designing a One-Sample Experiment

The simplest way to design the IQ pill study is as a *one-sample experiment.* We will randomly select one sample of participants and give each person, say, one pill. Then we'll give participants an IQ test. The sample will represent the population of people when they have taken one pill, and the sample $\overline{X}$ will represent that population's $\mu$.

However, *to perform a one-sample experiment, we must already know the population mean under some other condition of the independent variable.* This is because to demonstrate a relationship, we must demonstrate that *different* conditions produce *different* populations having different $\mu$s. Therefore, we must compare the population represented by our sample to some other population receiving some other amount of the pill. One other amount of the pill is zero: Say that our IQ test has been given to many people over the years who have *not* taken the pill, and this population has a $\mu$ of 100. We will compare this population without the pill to the population with the pill represented by our sample. If the population without the pill has a different $\mu$ than the population with the pill, then we will have demonstrated a relationship in the population.

## Creating the Statistical Hypotheses

So that we can apply statistical procedures, we translate the experimental hypotheses into *statistical hypotheses.* **Statistical hypotheses** describe the population parameters that the sample data represent if the predicted relationship does or does not exist. The two statistical hypotheses are the *alternative hypothesis* and the *null hypothesis.*

**The Alternative Hypothesis** It is easier to create the alternative hypothesis first, because it corresponds to the experimental hypothesis that the experiment *does* work as predicted. The **alternative hypothesis** describes the population parameters that the sample data represent if the predicted relationship exists. It says that changing the independent variable produces the predicted difference in the populations.

For example, Figure 7.1 shows the populations if the pill *increases* IQ. By changing the conditions, everyone's IQ score is increased so that the distribution moves to the right, over to the higher scores. We don't know how much scores will increase, but we do know that the $\mu$ of the population with the pill will be *greater* than 100, because 100 is the $\mu$ of the population without the pill.

On the other hand, Figure 7.2 shows the populations if the pill *decreases* IQ. Here, the distribution is moved to the left, over to the lower scores. Again, we don't know how much scores will decrease, but we do know that the $\mu$ of the population with the pill will be *less than* 100.

The alternative hypothesis communicates all of the above. If the pill works as predicted, then the population with the pill will have a $\mu$ that is either greater than or less

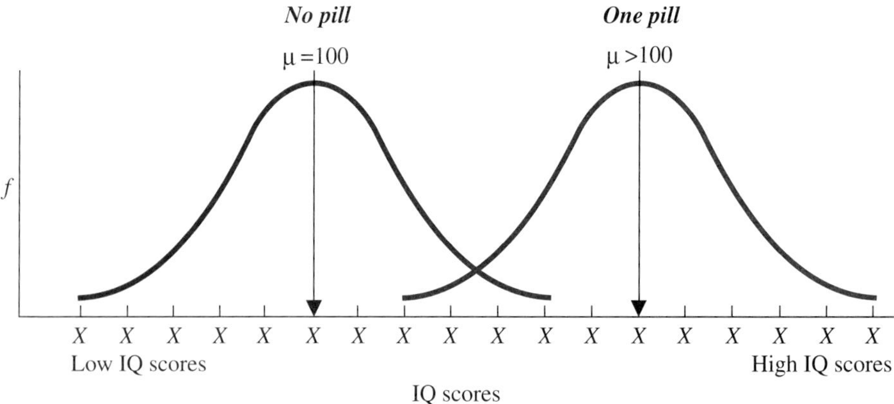


***FIGURE 7.1***
Relationship in the population if the IQ pill increases IQ scores

**FIGURE 7.2**
Relationship in the population if the IQ pill decreases IQ scores

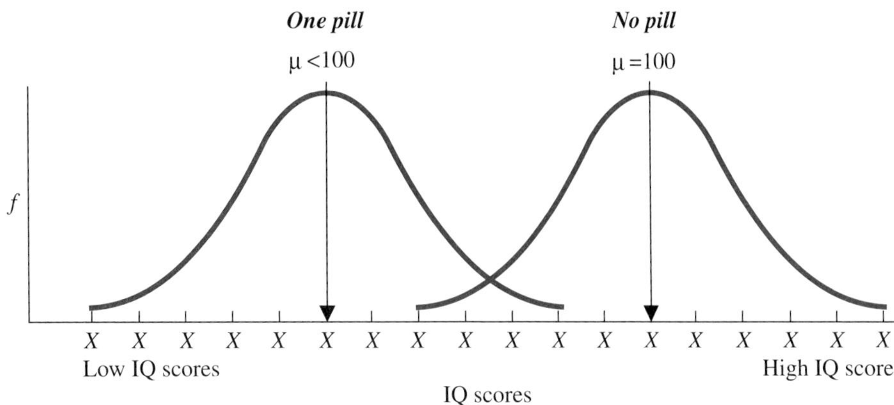


than 100. In other words, the population mean with the pill will *not equal* 100. The symbol for the alternative hypothesis is $H_a$. (The $H$ stands for hypothesis, and the subscript a stands for alternative.) The symbol for not equal is "≠," so our alternative hypothesis is

$$H_a\text{: } \mu \neq 100$$

This proposes that our sample mean represents a μ not equal to 100. Because the μ without the pill is 100, $H_a$ implies that there *is* a relationship in the population.

**The Null Hypothesis** The statistical hypothesis corresponding to the experimental hypothesis that the independent variable does *not* work as predicted is called the null hypothesis. The **null hypothesis** describes the population parameters that the sample data represent if the predicted relationship does *not* exist. It says that changing the independent variable does *not* produce the predicted difference in the population.

If the IQ pill does not work, then it would be as if the pill were not present. The population of IQ scores without the pill has a μ of 100. Therefore, if the pill does not work, then the population of scores will be unchanged and μ will still be 100. Accordingly, if we measured the population with and without the pill, we would have one population of scores, located at the μ of 100, as shown in Figure 7.3.

**FIGURE 7.3**
Population of scores if the IQ pill does not affect IQ scores

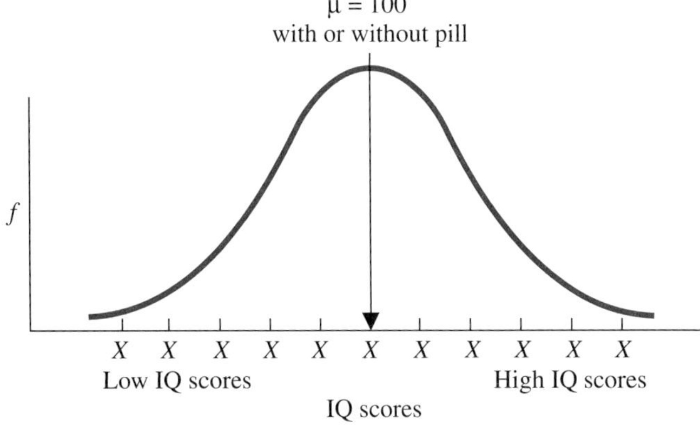

The null hypothesis communicates the above. The symbol for the null hypothesis is $H_0$. (The subscript is 0 because *null* means zero, as in zero relationship.) The null hypothesis for the IQ pill study is

$$H_0\text{: } \mu = 100$$

This proposes that our sample comes from and represents the population where $\mu$ is 100. Because this is the same population found without the pill, $H_0$ implies that the predicted relationship does *not* exist in nature.

> *REMEMBER* The *alternative hypothesis* ($H_a$) says the sample data represent a $\mu$ that reflects the predicted relationship. The *null hypothesis* ($H_0$) says the sample data represent the $\mu$ that's found when the predicted relationship is not present.

## A QUICK REVIEW

- The null hypothesis shows the value of $\mu$ that our $\overline{X}$ represents if the predicted relationship does not exist.
- The alternative hypothesis shows the value of $\mu$ that our $\overline{X}$ represents if the predicted relationship does exist.

### More Examples

In an experiment we compare a sample of men to the population of women who have a $\mu$ of 75. We predict that men are different from women, so this is a two-tailed test. The alternative hypothesis is that our men represent a different population, so their $\mu$ is not 75; thus, $H_a$: $\mu \neq 75$. The null hypothesis is that men are the same as women, so the men's $\mu$ is also 75, so $H_0$: $\mu = 75$.

### *For Practice:*

1. A ____ test is used when we do *not* predict the direction that scores will change; a ____ test is used when we *do* predict the direction that scores will change.
2. The ____ hypothesis is that the sample data represent a population where the predicted relationship exists. The ____ hypothesis is that the sample data represent a population where the predicted relationship does not exist.
3. The $\mu$ for adults on a personality test is 140. We test a sample of children to see if they are different from adults. What are $H_a$ and $H_0$?
4. The $\mu$ for days absent among workers is 15.6. We train a sample of new workers and ask whether the training changes worker absenteeism. What are $H_a$ and $H_0$?

**Answers**

1. two-tailed; one-tailed
2. alternative; null
3. $H_a$: $\mu \neq 140$; $H_0$: $\mu = 140$
4. $H_a$: $\mu \neq 15.6$; $H_0$: $\mu = 15.6$

## The Logic of Statistical Hypothesis Testing

The statistical hypotheses for the IQ pill study are

$$H_0\text{: } \mu = 100$$

$$H_a\text{: } \mu \neq 100$$

Together, $H_0$ and $H_a$ include all possibilities, so one or the other must be true. We use inferential procedures to test (choose between) these hypotheses, so these procedures are called "statistical hypothesis testing."

Say that we randomly select 36 people, gave them the pill, measured their IQ, and found that their mean was 105. We would *like* to say this: People who have not taken this pill have a mean IQ of 100, so if the pill did not work, the sample mean should have been 100. Therefore, a mean of 105 suggests that the pill does work, raising IQ scores about 5 points. If the pill does this for the sample, it should do this for the population. Therefore, we expect that a population receiving the pill would have a $\mu$ of 105. Our results appear to support our alternative hypothesis ($H_a$: $\mu \neq 100$). If we measured everyone in the population with and without the pill, we would have the two distributions shown previously in Figure 7.1, with the population that received the pill located at the $\mu$ of 105.

But hold on! We just assumed that our sample is *perfectly* representative of the population it represents. But what if we have sampling error? Maybe we obtained a mean of 105 not because the pill works, but because we inaccurately represented the situation where the pill does *not* work. Maybe the pill does nothing, but by chance we happened to select participants who *already* had an above-average IQ. Thus, maybe the null hypothesis is correct: Maybe our sample actually represents the population where $\mu$ is 100.

> ***REMEMBER*** The null hypothesis always maintains that the sample data may contain sampling error so that, regardless of the sample relationship, there is not really the predicted relationship in the population.

The only way to *prove* whether the null hypothesis is true would be to test the pill on the entire population and see whether $\mu$ was 100 or 105. We cannot do that. But, we can determine how *likely* it is to be true. That is, using the procedure discussed in the previous chapter, we always test the null hypothesis by determining how likely it is for chance to produce our sample from the population described by the null hypothesis. If the sample data are unlikely to occur, then we conclude that we are not representing this population and that the null hypothesis is the incorrect hypothesis.

All parametric and nonparametric procedures use this logic. To select the correct procedure for a particular experiment, check that the design and dependent scores fit the assumptions of the procedure. The IQ pill study meets the assumptions of the parametric procedure called the *z-test.*

## PERFORMING THE *z*-TEST

The ***z*-test** is the procedure for computing a *z*-score for a sample mean on the sampling distribution of means that we've discussed in previous chapters. The *z*-test has four assumptions:

*1.* We have randomly selected one sample.
*2.* The dependent variable is at least approximately normally distributed in the population, and involves an interval or ratio scale.
*3.* We *know* the mean of the population of raw scores under another condition of the independent variable.
*4.* We *know* the true standard deviation of the population ($\sigma_X$) described by the null hypothesis.

Say that from the research literature, we know that in the population where μ is 100, the standard deviation is 15. Therefore, the *z*-test is appropriate for our IQ pill study.

### Setting Up the Sampling Distribution for a Two-Tailed Test

To test the null hypothesis, we examine the sampling distribution of means created from the raw score population that $H_0$ says we are representing. Therefore, in the IQ pill study, it is as if, using our *N* of 36, we infinitely sampled the raw score population without the pill where μ is 100. This will produce a sampling distribution of means with a μ of 100. The μ of the sampling distribution always equals the value of μ given in the null hypothesis.

> ***REMEMBER*** The mean of the sampling distribution always equals the μ of the raw score population that $H_0$ says we are representing.

Using the sampling distribution, we set up the statistical test as we did in the previous chapter. The finished distribution is shown in Figure 7.4. To get there, we have some new symbols and terms.

*1. Choose alpha:* Recall that the *criterion* is the probability that defines sample means as unlikely to be representing the underlying raw score population. The symbol for the criterion is α, the Greek letter **alpha.** Usually the criterion is .05, so in code $\alpha = .05$.

*2. Locate the region of rejection:* Recall that we may use both tails or only one tail of the sampling distribution. Which arrangement to use depends on whether you have a two-tailed or one-tailed test. Above, we created a two-tailed hypothesis, predicting that the pill makes people either smarter or dumber. Thus, we'd be correct if our $\overline{X}$ is either larger than 100 or smaller than 100. Therefore, in the two-tailed test, part of the region of rejection is in each tail.

*3. Determine the critical value:* We abbreviate the critical value of *z* as $z_{crit}$. Recall that with $\alpha = .05$ and using both tails, the region of rejection in each tail is 2.5% of the distribution. From the *z*-tables, $z = 1.96$ demarcates this region, and so we complete Figure 7.4 by adding that $z_{crit}$ is $\pm 1.96$.

Now the test of $H_0$ boils down to comparing the *z*-score for our sample mean to the $z_{crit}$ of $\pm 1.96$. Therefore, it's time to compute our *z*-score.

**FIGURE 7.4**
Sampling distribution of IQ means for a two-tailed test

*A region of rejection is in each tail of the distribution, marked by the critical values of ±1.96*

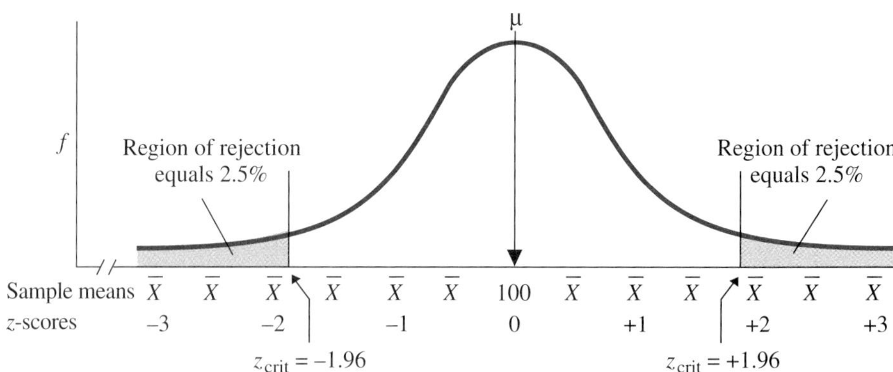

### Computing z

Here is some more code. The $z$-score we compute is "obtained" from the data, so it is called z *obtained,* which we abbreviate as $z_{obt}$. You know how to compute this from previous chapters.

*THE FORMULA FOR THE z-TEST IS*

$$z_{obt} = \frac{\overline{X} - \mu}{\sigma_{\overline{X}}}$$

The value of $\mu$ to put in the formula is the $\mu$ of the sampling distribution, which is also the $\mu$ of the underlying raw score population that $H_0$ says the sample represents. The $\overline{X}$ is computed from the scores in the sample. The $\sigma_{\overline{X}}$ is the standard error of the mean, which is computed as

$$\sigma_{\overline{X}} = \frac{\sigma_X}{\sqrt{N}}$$

where $N$ is the $N$ of the sample and $\sigma_X$ is the true population standard deviation.

For the IQ pill study, the $\sigma_X$ is 15 and $N$ is 36. Thus, $\sigma_{\overline{X}}$ is

$$\sigma_{\overline{X}} = \frac{\sigma_X}{\sqrt{N}} = \frac{15}{\sqrt{36}} = \frac{15}{6} = 2.5$$

Then the $z$-score for our sample mean of 105 is

$$z_{obt} = \frac{\overline{X} - \mu}{\sigma_{\overline{X}}} = \frac{105 - 100}{2.5} = \frac{+5}{2.5} = +2.00$$

The final step is to interpret this $z_{obt}$ by comparing it to $z_{crit}$.

### Comparing the Obtained z to the Critical Value

The sampling distribution always describes the situation *when null is true:* Here, it shows the frequency of means that occur when, as $H_0$ says, our sample comes from the population where $\mu$ is 100 (from the situation where the pill does not work). If we are to believe $H_0$, the sampling distribution should show that a $\overline{X}$ of 105 is relatively frequent and thus likely in this situation. However, Figure 7.5 shows just the opposite. A $z_{obt}$ of +2.00 tells us that a $\overline{X}$ of 105 hardly ever happens by chance when representing the population where $\mu$ is 100 (such a mean would hardly ever occur in the situation where the pill doesn't work). In fact, because a $z_{obt}$ of +2.00 is beyond the $z_{crit}$ of ±1.96, our sample is in the region of rejection. Therefore, we conclude that our sample is unlikely to have come from and thus represent the population where $\mu = 100$. Therefore, we reject that our sample is poorly representing this population (rejecting that we are poorly representing the situation where the pill does not work).

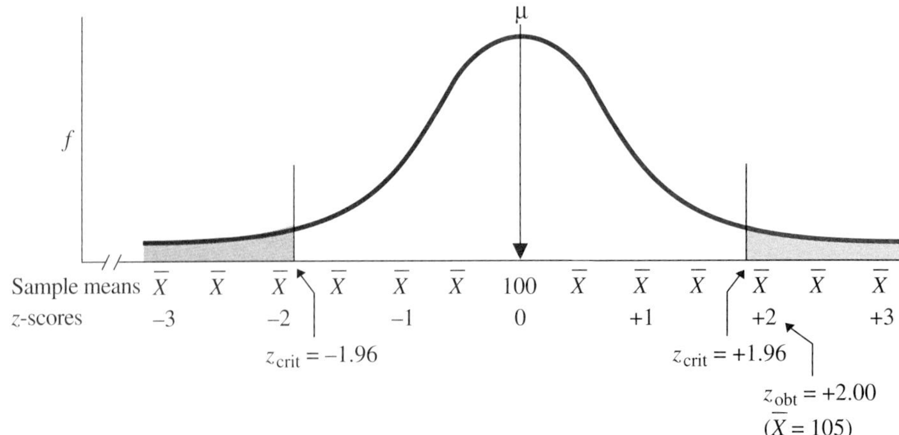


**FIGURE 7.5**
Sampling distribution of IQ means
*The sample mean of 105 is located at $z_{obt} = +2.00$.*

In statistical terms we have "rejected" the null hypothesis. If we reject $H_0$, then we are left with $H_a$, and so we "accept $H_a$." Here, $H_a$ is $\mu \neq 100$, so we accept that our sample is representing a population where μ is not 100 (accepting that we are representing the situation where the pill works).

> ***REMEMBER*** When a sample statistic falls beyond the critical value, the statistic lies in the region of rejection, so we *reject* $H_0$ *and accept* $H_a$.

By accepting the alternative hypothesis, we accept the corresponding experimental hypothesis. It appears that we have demonstrated a *relationship in nature* such that the pill would change the population of IQ scores. In fact, we can be more specific: A sample mean of 105 is most likely to represent the population where μ is 105. Thus, without the pill, the population of IQ scores is at a μ of 100, but receiving the pill would raise the population to around a μ of 105.

## INTERPRETING SIGNIFICANT RESULTS

The way to communicate that we have rejected $H_0$ and accepted $H_a$ is to use the term *significant.* Significant does *not* mean important or impressive. **Significant** indicates that our results are unlikely to occur if the predicted relationship does not exist in the population. Therefore, we imply that the relationship found in the experiment is "believable," representing a "real" relationship found in nature, and that it does not reflect sampling error from the situation in which the relationship does not exist.

> ***REMEMBER*** The term *significant* means that we have rejected the null hypothesis and believe that the data reflect a relationship found in nature.

Although we accept that a relationship exists, there are three very important restrictions on how far we can go with this claim. First, we did not *prove* that $H_0$ is false. The sampling distribution shows that means of 105 do occur once in a while when we *are* representing the population where $\mu$ is 100. Maybe the pill did not work, and our sample was simply very unrepresentative of this.

Second, although the sample may represent a population with a $\mu$ above 100, we have not proven that it was the pill that produced these scores. Some other hidden variable might have actually caused the higher scores in the sample.

Finally, assuming that the pill does increase IQ scores, the population $\mu$ would probably not be *exactly* 105. Our sample mean may contain (you guessed it) sampling error! That is, the sample may accurately reflect that the pill increases IQ, but it may not perfectly represent how *much* the pill increases scores. Therefore, we conclude that the $\mu$ produced by our pill would probably be *around* 105.

Bearing these qualifications in mind, we interpret the $\overline{X}$ of 105 the way we wanted to several pages back: *Apparently*, the pill increases IQ scores by about 5 points. But now, because the results are significant, we are confident that we are not being misled by sampling error. Therefore, after describing this significant relationship, we would return to being behavioral researchers and interpret the results in terms of the variables and behaviors reflected, describing how the ingredients in the pill affect intelligence, what brain mechanisms are involved, and so on.

## INTERPRETING NONSIGNIFICANT RESULTS

Let's say that the IQ pill had instead produced a sample mean of 99. Now the $z$-score for the sample is

$$z_{\text{obt}} = \frac{\overline{X} - \mu}{\sigma_{\overline{X}}} = \frac{99 - 100}{2.5} = \frac{-1}{2.5} = -.40$$

As in Figure 7.6, a $z_{\text{obt}}$ of $-.40$ is *not* beyond the $z_{\text{crit}}$ of $\pm 1.96$, so the sample does not lie in the region of rejection. This indicates that we will frequently obtain a sample mean of 99 when sampling the population where $\mu = 100$. Thus, our sample mean was likely to have occurred if we were representing the situation where the pill does not

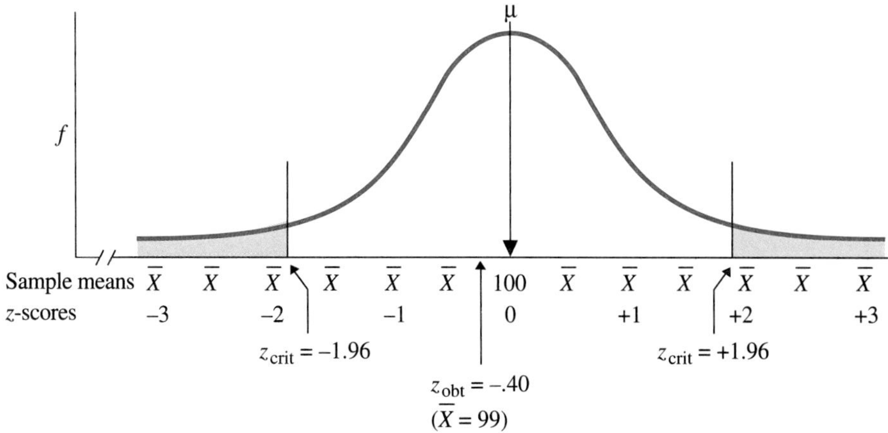


***FIGURE 7.6***
**Sampling distribution of IQ means**
*The sample mean of 99 has a $z_{obt}$ of −40.*

work. Therefore, the null hypothesis—that our sample is merely a poor representation of the population without the pill—is a reasonable hypothesis. So we will *not* conclude that the pill works. After all, it makes no sense to claim that the pill works if the results were likely to occur *without* the pill. In such situations we have "failed to reject $H_0$" or we "retain $H_0$."

The way to communicate this is to say that we have *nonsignificant* or not significant results. (Don't say *insignificant.*) **Nonsignificant** indicates that the differences reflected by our results were likely to have occurred through chance, sampling error, without there being a relationship in nature.

> ***REMEMBER*** *Nonsignificant* means that we have failed to reject $H_0$ because the results are not in the region of rejection and are thus likely to occur when there is no real relationship in nature.

Retaining $H_0$, however, does not "prove" that the independent variable does not work. We have simply failed to find convincing evidence that it *does* work. The only thing we're sure of is that sampling error *could* have produced our data. Therefore, we still have two hypotheses that are both viable: (1) $H_0$, that the results do *not* really represent a relationship, and (2) $H_a$, that the results *do* represent a relationship. Thus, maybe, in fact, the pill does work but the sample data poorly reflect this. Or, maybe the pill does not work. We simply don't know. Therefore, when you do not reject $H_0$, do not say anything about whether the independent variable influences behavior or not. All that you can say is that you have failed to demonstrate the predicted relationship in the population.

> ***REMEMBER*** Nonsignificant results provide no convincing evidence—one way or the other—as to whether a relationship exists in nature.

## SUMMARY OF THE *z*-TEST

Altogether, the preceding discussion can be summarized as follows. For a one-sample experiment that meets the assumptions of the *z*-test:

*1. Determine the experimental hypotheses and create the statistical hypothesis:* Predict the relationship the study will or will not demonstrate. Then $H_0$ describes the $\mu$ that the $\overline{X}$ represents if the predicted relationship does not exist. $H_a$ describes the $\mu$ that the $\overline{X}$ represents if the relationship does exist.

*2. Compute* $\overline{X}$ *and compute* $z_{obt}$*:* First, compute $\sigma_{\overline{X}}$. Then in the formula for $z$, the value of $\mu$ is the $\mu$ of the sampling distribution, which is also the $\mu$ of the raw score that $H_0$ says is being represented.

*3. Set up the sampling distribution:* Select $\alpha$, locate the region of rejection, and determine the critical value.

*4. Compare* $z_{obt}$ *to* $z_{crit}$*:* If $z_{\text{obt}}$ lies beyond $z_{\text{crit}}$, then reject $H_0$, accept $H_a$, and the results are "significant." Then describe the relationship. If $z_{\text{obt}}$ does not lie beyond $z_{\text{crit}}$, do not reject $H_0$ and the results are "nonsignificant." Do not draw any conclusions about the relationship.

## A QUICK REVIEW

- If $z_{obt}$ lies beyond $z_{crit}$, reject $H_0$, the results are significant, and conclude there is evidence for the predicted relationship. Otherwise, the results are not significant, and you should make no conclusion about the relationship.

### MORE EXAMPLES

We test a technique that may change a person's reading comprehension. Without it, the $\mu$ on a reading test is 220, with $\sigma_X = 15$. An $N$ of 25 participants has $\overline{X} = 211.55$.

1. This is a two-tailed test, so $H_0$: $\mu = 220$; $H_a$: $\mu \neq 220$.
2. Compute $z_{obt}$: $\sigma_{\overline{X}} = \sigma_X/\sqrt{N} = 15/\sqrt{25} = 3$. Then $z_{obt} = (\overline{X} - \mu)/\sigma_{\overline{X}} = (211.55 - 220)/3 = -2.817$.
3. With $\alpha = .05$, $z_{crit}$ is $\pm1.96$, and the sampling distribution is like Figure 7.6.
4. The $z_{obt}$ of $-2.817$ is in the lower region of rejection beyond the $z_{crit}$ of $-1.96$, so the results are significant. Thus, the data reflect a relationship, with the $\mu$ of the population using the technique at around 211.55, while those not using it are at $\mu = 220$.

Say that a different mean produced a $z = -1.83$. This $z_{obt}$ is not beyond the $z_{crit}$ of $\pm1.96$, so the results are not significant: Make no conclusion about the influence of the reading technique on comprehension.

### *For Practice:*

We test whether a sample of 36 successful dieters are more or less satisfied with their appearance than in the population of nondieters, where $\mu = 40$ ($\sigma_X = 12$).

1. What are $H_0$ and $H_a$?
2. The $\overline{X}$ for dieters is 44. Compute $z_{obt}$.
3. Set up the sampling distribution.
4. What should we conclude?

**Answers**

1. $H_0$: $\mu = 40$; $H_a$: $\mu \neq 40$
2. $\sigma_{\overline{X}} = 12/\sqrt{36} = 2$; $z_{obt} = (44 - 40)/2 = +2.00$
3. With $\alpha = .05$ the sampling distribution has a region of rejection in each tail, with $z_{crit} = \pm1.96$ (as in Figure 7.6).
4. The $z_{obt}$ of $+2.00$ is beyond $z_{crit}$ of $\pm1.96$, so the results are significant: The population of dieters are more satisfied (at a $\mu$ around 44) than the population of nondieters (at $\mu = 40$).

## STATISTICS IN THE RESEARCH LITERATURE: REPORTING *z*

When reading published reports, you'll often see statements such as "the IQ pill produced a *significant difference* in IQ scores," or "it had a *significant effect* on IQ." These are just other ways to say that the results reflect a believable relationship, because they are unlikely to occur through sampling error. However, whether a result is significant depends on the probability used to define "unlikely," so we must also indicate our $\alpha$. The convention for reporting a result is to indicate the statistic computed, the obtained value, and $\alpha$. Thus, for our previous significant $z_{obt}$ of $+2.00$, we report $z = +2.00$, $p < .05$. Notice that instead of indicating that $\alpha$ equals .05, we indicate that the probability ($p$) is *less than* .05. (We'll discuss the reason for this shortly.) For our previous nonsignificant $z_{obt}$ of $-.40$, we report $z = -0.40$, $p > .05$. Notice that with nonsignificant results, $p$ is *greater* than .05.

## THE ONE-TAILED TEST

Recall that a *one-tailed test* is used when we predict the *direction* in which scores will change. The statistical hypotheses and sampling distribution are different in a one-tailed test.

### The One-Tailed Test for Increasing Scores

Say that we had developed a "smart" pill. The experimental hypotheses are (1) the pill makes people smarter by increasing IQ, or (2) the pill does not make people smarter. For the statistical hypotheses, start with the alternative hypothesis: People without the pill produce a $\mu$ of 100, so if the pill makes them smarter, our sample will represent a population with a $\mu$ greater than 100. The symbol for greater than is "$>$" and so $H_a$: $\mu > 100$. For the null hypothesis, if the pill does not work as predicted, either it will leave IQ scores unchanged or it will decrease them (making people dumber). Then our sample mean represents a $\mu$ either equal to 100 or less than 100. The symbol for less than or equal to is "$\leq$," so $H_0$: $\mu \leq 100$.

We test $H_0$ by testing whether the sample represents the raw score population in which $\mu$ *equals* 100. This is because if the $\mu$ with the pill is above 100, then it is automatically above any value less than 100.

> *REMEMBER* A one-tailed null hypothesis always includes that $\mu$ equals some value. Test $H_0$ by testing whether the sample data represent the population with that $\mu$.

Thus, as shown in Figure 7.7, the sampling distribution again shows the means that occur if we are representing a $\mu = 100$ (the situation where the pill does nothing to IQ). We again set $\alpha = .05$, but the region of rejection is in only *one tail* of the sampling distribution. You can identify which tail to put it in by identifying the result you must have to claim that your independent variable works as predicted (to support $H_a$). To say that the smart pill works, the sample mean must be *significant* and *larger* than 100. Means that are significantly larger than 100 are in the region of rejection in the *upper* tail of the sampling distribution. Therefore, the entire region is in the upper tail of the distribution. Then, as in the previous chapter, the region of rejection is 5% of the curve, so $z_{crit}$ is $+1.645$.

Say that after testing the pill ($N = 36$) we find $\overline{X} = 106.58$. The sampling distribution is still based on the population with $\mu = 100$ and $\sigma_X = 15$, so $\sigma_{\overline{X}} = 15/\sqrt{36} = 2.5$, and then $z_{obt} = (106.58 - 100)/2.5 = +2.63$. As in Figure 7.7, this $z_{obt}$ is beyond $z_{crit}$, so it is in the region of rejection. Therefore, the sample mean is unlikely to represent the population having $\mu = 100$, and it's even less likely to represent a population that has a $\mu < 100$. Therefore, we reject the null hypothesis that $\mu \leq 100$, and accept the alternative hypothesis that $\mu > 100$. We conclude that the pill produces a *significant increase* in IQ scores, and estimate that with the pill, $\mu$ would equal about 106.58.

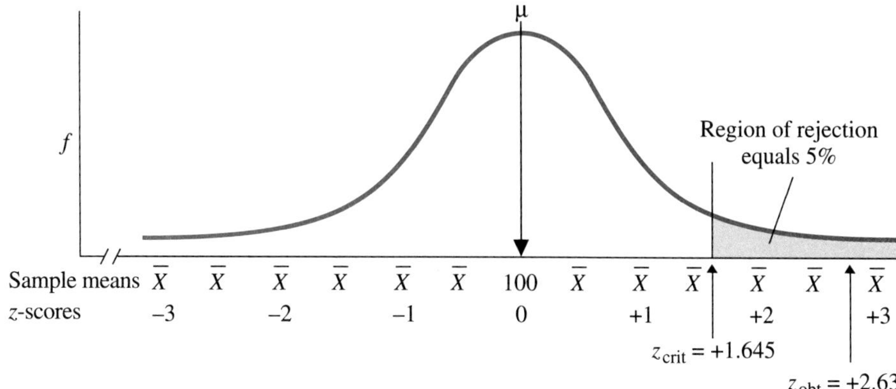


**FIGURE 7.7** Sampling distribution of IQ means for a one-tailed test of whether scores increase

*The region of rejection is entirely in the upper tail.*

If $z_{obt}$ had not been in the region of rejection, we would retain $H_0$, and would have no evidence as to whether the smart pill works or not.

## The One-Tailed Test for Decreasing Scores

Say that, instead, we had created a pill to lower IQ scores. If the pill works, then the sample mean represents a μ *less than* 100, so $H_a$: $\mu < 100$. But, if the pill does not work, either it will leave scores unchanged, or it will increase scores. Therefore, the sample mean represents a μ greater than or equal to 100. The symbol for greater than or equal to is "≥," so $H_0$: $\mu \geq 100$.

We test $H_0$ as before, except now, for us to conclude that the pill lowers IQ, our sample mean must be significantly *less* than 100. Therefore, the region of rejection is in the lower tail of the distribution, as in Figure 7.8. With $\alpha = .05$, $z_{crit}$ is now *minus* 1.645. If the sample produces a *negative* $z_{obt}$ beyond −1.645 (for example, $z_{obt} = -1.69$), then we reject the $H_0$ that the sample mean represents a μ equal to or greater than 100, and accept the $H_a$ that the sample represents a μ less than 100. However, if $z_{obt}$ does not fall in the region of rejection (for example, if $z_{obt} = -1.25$), we do not reject $H_0$, and we have no evidence as to whether the pill works or not.

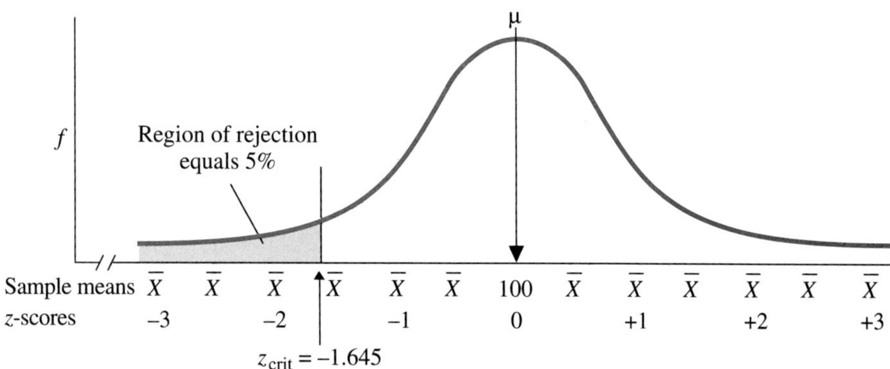


**FIGURE 7.8** Sampling distribution of IQ means for a one-tailed test of whether scores decrease

*The region of rejection is entirely in the lower tail.*

## A QUICK REVIEW

- Perform a one-tailed test when predicting the specific direction the scores will change.
- When predicting the $\overline{X}$ will be higher than $\mu$, the region of rejection is in the upper tail of the sampling distribution. When predicting the $\overline{X}$ will be lower than $\mu$, the region of rejection is in the lower tail.

### MORE EXAMPLES

I predict that learning statistics will increase a student's IQ. Those not learning statistics have $\mu = 100$ and $\sigma_X = 15$. For 25 statistics students $\overline{X} = 108.6$.

1. This is a one-tailed test, so $H_a$: $\mu > 100$; $H_0$: $\mu \leq 100$.
2. Compute $z_{obt}$: $\sigma_{\overline{X}} = \sigma_X/\sqrt{N} = 15/\sqrt{25} = 3$; $z_{obt} = (\overline{X} - \mu)/\sigma_{\overline{X}} = (108.6 - 100)/3 = +2.87$.
3. With $\alpha = .05$, and predicting scores greater than 100, $z_{crit}$ is $\pm 1.645$, and the sampling distribution is as in Figure 7.7.
4. The $z_{obt}$ of $+2.87$ is beyond $z_{crit}$, so the results are significant: A population learning statistics has a $\mu$ around 108.6, while people not learning statistics have $\mu = 100$. We report the results as $z = +2.87$, $p < .05$.

Say instead, a different mean produced $z_{obt} = +1.47$. This is not beyond $z_{crit}$, so it is not significant: We have no evidence that learning statistics raises IQ; $z = +1.47, p > .05$.

### *For Practice:*

You test the effectiveness of a new weight-loss diet.

1. Why is this a one-tailed test?
2. For the population of nondieters, $\mu = 155$. What are $H_a$ and $H_0$?
3. In which tail is the region of rejection?
4. With $\alpha = .05$, the $z_{obt}$ for the sample of dieters is $-1.86$. What do you conclude?

**Answers**

1. Because a successful diet *lowers* weight scores.
2. $H_a$: $\mu < 155$, and $H_0$: $\mu \geq 155$.
3. The left-hand tail.
4. The $z_{obt}$ is beyond $z_{crit}$ of $-1.645$, so it is significant: The $\mu$ for dieters will be less than the $\mu$ of 155 for nondieters.

## ERRORS IN STATISTICAL DECISION MAKING

There is one other issue to consider when performing hypothesis testing, and it involves potential errors in our decisions. Regardless of whether we conclude that the sample does or does not represent the predicted relationship, we may be wrong.

### Type I Errors

Sometimes the variables we investigate are *not* related in nature, and so $H_0$ is really true. When in this situation, if we obtain data that cause us to reject $H_0$, then we make an error. A **Type I error** is defined as rejecting $H_0$ when $H_0$ is true. In practical terms, we conclude that the independent variable works when it really doesn't.

In practice, we never know when we actually *make* a Type I error, because only nature knows if the variables are related or not. However, we do know that the theoretical probability of a Type I error equals $\alpha$, and this is true for a one- or two-tailed test. This is because $\alpha$ is the total size of the region of rejection. We're talking about when

$H_0$ is true, so think of the sampling distribution as showing the population of all means we will obtain in this situation if we repeatedly conduct the study over the long run. Our variable never works, but sometimes, because of extreme sampling error, we will obtain a mean that falls into the region of rejection, causing us to make a Type I error. If $\alpha = .05$, then 5% of the time over the long run we'll obtain such means, so in the population the relative frequency of Type I errors is .05. Therefore, anytime we reject $H_0$, the theoretical probability that we've just made a Type I error is .05.

You either will or will not make the correct decision when $H_0$ is true. If $\alpha$ is the probability of making a Type I error, then $1 - \alpha$ is the probability of avoiding a Type I error: retaining $H_0$ when it is true. Thus, if 5% of the time samples are in the region of rejection when $H_0$ is true, then 95% of the time they are not in the region of rejection when $H_0$ is true. Therefore, anytime you retain $H_0$, the theoretical probability is .95 that you've avoided a Type I error.

Although the *theoretical* probability of a Type I error equals $\alpha$, the *actual* probability is slightly less than $\alpha$. This is because the region of rejection includes the critical value. Yet to reject $H_0$, $z_{obt}$ must be *larger* than the critical value. We cannot determine the precise area under the curve for the point located at $z_{crit}$, so we can't remove it from our 5%. All that we can say is that when $\alpha$ is .05, a $z_{obt}$ in the region of rejection is in less than 5% of the curve. Because the actual area of the region of rejection is less than $\alpha$, the actual probability of a Type I error is also less than $\alpha$.

Thus, in our previous examples when we rejected $H_0$, the probability that we made a Type I error was slightly less than .05. That is why we reported our significant results using $p < .05$. This is code for "the probability of a Type I error is less than .05." On the other hand, we reported nonsignificant results using $p > .05$. This communicates that we did not call a result significant because to do so would require a region *greater than* .05 of the curve. But then the probability of a Type I error would be greater than our $\alpha$ of .05 and that's unacceptable.

Sometimes making a Type I error is so dangerous that we want to reduce its probability even further. Then we usually set alpha at .01, so the probability of making a Type I error is $p < .01$. For example, if the smart pill had some dangerous side effects, we could set $\alpha = .01$ so that we are even less likely to conclude that the pill works when it really does not. However, we use the term significant in an all-or-nothing fashion: A result is not "more" significant when $\alpha = .01$ than when $\alpha = .05$. If $z_{obt}$ lies *anywhere* in a region of rejection, the result is significant, period! The only difference is that when $\alpha = .01$, there is a smaller probability that we've made a Type I error.

> *REMEMBER* When $H_0$ is true: Rejecting $H_0$ is a Type I error, and its probability is $\alpha$; retaining $H_0$ is avoiding a Type I error, and its probability is $1 - \alpha$.

### Type II Errors and Power

Sometimes the variables we investigate really are related in nature and so $H_0$ really is false. When in this situation, if we obtain data that cause us to retain $H_0$, then we make a Type II error. A **Type II error** is defined as retaining $H_0$ when $H_0$ is false (and $H_a$ is true). In practical terms, we fail to identify that an independent variable that really does work. This occurs because the sample so poorly represents the relationship that is present that we—and our statistics—are fooled into concluding that the relationship is not present.

Anytime we *discuss* Type II errors, it's a given that you are in the situation where $H_0$ is false and $H_a$ *is* true. However, we never know when we actually *make* this error, because we do not know the truth about nature. (We can determine its probability, but the computations for this are beyond the introductory level.) Thus, when we retained $H_0$ and decided our pill did not work, perhaps we made a Type II error. If we reject $H_0$ in this situation, then we avoid a Type II error: We've made the correct decision by concluding that the pill works when it does work.

For help in understanding Type I and Type II errors, remember that the type of error you can potentially make is determined by your situation—what nature "says" about whether or not a relationship exists. You can be in only *one* of these situations at a time. Then whether you actually make the error depends on whether you agree or disagree with nature. Thus, four outcomes are possible in any study:

*When* $H_0$ *is true—there is no relationship:*

1. Our data cause us to *reject* $H_0$, so we make a Type I error.
2. Our data cause us to *retain* $H_0$, so we avoid a Type I error.

*When* $H_0$ *is false—the relationship exists:*

3. Our data cause us to *retain* $H_0$, so we make a Type II error.
4. Our data cause us to *reject* $H_0$, so we avoid a Type II error.

Researchers always use a small $\alpha$, because the primary concern is to minimize the probability of Type I errors. Concluding that an independent variable works when really it does not can cause untold damage. On the other hand, avoiding Type II errors is also important so that we don't miss those independent variables that do work. This ability has a special name: **Power** is the probability that we will reject $H_0$ when it is false, correctly concluding that the sample data represent a relationship. In other words, power is the probability of not making a Type II error.

Researchers always try to design a *powerful* study. Then if we retain $H_0$, we're confident that we would have found the relationship if it was there, so it must not be there. Thus, for example, it is better to design a study so that you can use parametric procedures, because *parametric procedures are more powerful than nonparametric procedures:* They are less likely to miss a relationship. Also, a *one-tailed test is more powerful than a two-tailed test:* If you can correctly predict the direction of the relationship, you are less likely to make a Type II error. And finally, *testing a larger* N *is more powerful:* With at least 30 scores per sample, you are more convinced that a relationship is present. (When you study how to design research, you'll learn of other ways to build in power.)

**REMEMBER** *Power* is the probability of not making a Type II error.

---

## CHAPTER SUMMARY

1. *Inferential statistics* are procedures for deciding whether sample data represent a particular relationship in the population.
2. *Parametric statistics* are inferential procedures that require assumptions about raw score populations the data represent. *Nonparametric statistics* are inferential procedures that do not require such assumptions.

3. *The alternative hypothesis* ($H_a$) describes the population $\mu$ being represented by our sample mean if the predicted relationship exists.
4. *The null hypothesis* ($H_0$) describes the population $\mu$ being represented by our sample mean if the predicted relationship does not exist.
5. A *two-tailed test* is used when we do not predict the direction in which the dependent scores will change. A *one-tailed test* is used when the direction of the relationship is predicted.
6. The *z-test* is the parametric procedure used in a one-sample experiment if (a) the population contains normally distributed, interval or ratio dependent scores, and (b) the standard deviation of the population ($\sigma_X$) is *known.*
7. If $z_{obt}$ lies beyond $z_{crit}$, then we *reject* $H_0$ and *accept* $H_a$. This is a *significant* result and is evidence that the predicted relationship exists in nature.
8. If $z_{obt}$ does not lie beyond $z_{crit}$, then we *retain* $H_0$. This is a *nonsignificant* result and is a failure to obtain evidence that the predicted relationship exists in nature.
9. A *Type I error* occurs when a true $H_0$ is rejected. Its theoretical probability equals $\alpha$. The probability of avoiding a Type I error by retaining a true $H_0$ is $1 - \alpha$.
10. A *Type II error* occurs when a false $H_0$ is retained. Avoiding a Type II error is rejecting a false $H_0$.
11. *Power* is the probability of rejecting a false $H_0$ (avoiding a Type II error).

## KEY TERMS: Can You Define the Following?

$\geq$ *131*
$\leq$ *130*
$\neq$ *121*
$H_0$ *122*
$H_a$ *121*
$\alpha$ *124*
$z_{crit}$ *124*
$z_{obt}$ *125*
alpha *124*
alternative hypothesis *120*
experimental hypotheses *119*
inferential statistics *118*
nonparametric statistics *118*
nonsignificant *128*
null hypothesis *121*
one-tailed test *119*
parametric statistics *118*
power *134*
significant *126*
statistical hypotheses *120*
two-tailed test *119*
Type I error *132*
Type II error *133*
*z*-test *123*

## REVIEW QUESTIONS

(Answers for odd-numbered questions are in Appendix C.)

1. Why does the possibility of sampling error present a problem to researchers when inferring a relationship in the population?
2. What are inferential statistics used for?
3. What does $\alpha$ stand for, and what two things does it determine?
4. (a) What does $H_0$ communicate? (b) What does $H_a$ communicate?
5. What are experimental hypotheses?

6. What does the term *significant* convey about the results of an experiment?
7. When do you use a one-tailed test? When do you use a two-tailed test?
8. (a) What are the advantage and disadvantage of two-tailed tests? (b) What are the advantage and disadvantage of one-tailed tests?
9. (a) What is power? (b) Why do researchers want to maximize power? (c) What situation makes us worry whether we have sufficient power?
10. (a) Why is obtaining a significant result a goal of research? (b) Why is declaring the results significant not the final step in conducting research?

## APPLICATION QUESTIONS

11. For the following experiments describe the experimental hypotheses using the independent and dependent variables: (a) Studying whether the amount of pizza consumed by college students during finals week increases relative to the rest of the semester. (b) Studying whether breathing exercises alter blood pressure. (c) Studying whether sensitivity to pain is affected by increased levels of hormones. (d) Studying whether frequency of dreaming while sleeping decreases with more light in the room.
12. For each study in question 11 indicate whether a one- or a two-tailed test should be used, and state the $H_0$ and $H_a$. Assume that $\mu = 50$ when the amount of the independent variable is zero.
13. Listening to music while taking a test may be relaxing or distracting. To determine which, 49 participants are tested while listening to music and they produce a $\overline{X} = 54.63$. In the population the $\mu$ without music is 50 ($\sigma_X = 12$). (a) Is this a one-tailed or two-tailed test? Why? (b) What are $H_0$ and $H_a$? (c) Compute $z_{obt}$. (d) With $\alpha = .05$, what is $z_{crit}$? (e) Do we have evidence of a relationship in the population? If so, describe the relationship.
14. A researcher asks whether attending a private school leads to higher or lower performance on a test of social skills. A sample of 100 students from a private school produces a mean score of 71.30. The $\mu$ for students from public schools is 75.62 ($\sigma_X = 28$). (a) Should she use a one-tailed or a two-tailed test? Why? (b) What are $H_0$ and $H_a$? (c) Compute $z_{obt}$. (d) With $\alpha = .05$, what is $z_{crit}$? (e) What should the researcher conclude about this relationship in the population?
15. (a) What is the probability that in question 13 we made a Type I error? What would the error be in terms of the independent and dependent variables? (b) What is the probability that we made a Type II error? What would the error be in terms of the independent and dependent variables?
16. (a) What is the probability that the researcher in question 14 made a Type I error? What would the error be in terms of the independent and dependent variables? (b) What would a Type II error be in terms of the independent and dependent variables?
17. Bubbles reads that Study A found: $z_{obt} = +1.97, p < .05$. She also reads about Study B, in which $z_{obt} = +14.21, p < .0001$. (a) She concludes that the results of Study B are more significant than those of Study A. Why is she correct or incorrect? (b) In terms of their conclusions, what is the difference between the two studies?

*18.* A researcher measures the self-esteem scores of a sample of statistics students, reasoning that their frustration with this course may lower their self-esteem relative to that of the typical college student where $\mu = 55$ and $\sigma_X = 11.35$. He obtains the following scores.

44 55 39 17 27 38 36 24 36

(a) Should he use a one-tailed or two-tailed test? Why? (b) What are $H_0$ and $H_a$ for this study? (c) Compute $z_{obt}$. (d) With $\alpha = .05$, what is $z_{crit}$? (e) What should the researcher conclude about the relationship between the self-esteem of statistics students and that of other students?

*19.* A researcher suggests that males and females are the same when it comes to intelligence. Why is this hypothesis impossible to test?

*20.* Researcher A finds a significant relationship between increasing stress level and ability to concentrate. Researcher B replicates this study, but finds a nonsignificant relationship. Identify the statistical error that each researcher may have made.

*21.* A report indicates that Brand X toothpaste significantly reduced tooth decay relative to other brands, with $p < .44$. (a) What does "significant" indicate about the researcher's decision about Brand X? (b) What makes you suspicious of the claim that Brand X works better than other brands?

## SUMMARY OF FORMULAS

*1. The formula for the z-test is*

$$z_{obt} = \frac{\overline{X} - \mu}{\sigma_{\overline{X}}}$$

*where*

$$\sigma_{\overline{X}} = \frac{\sigma_X}{\sqrt{N}}$$

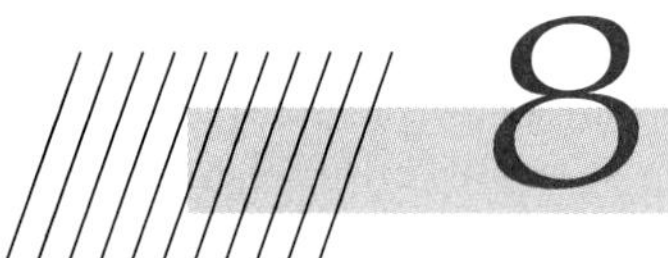

# 8 Hypothesis Testing Using the One-Sample *t*-Test

## Chapter Essentials

### Before getting started, be sure you understand

- From Chapter 4, that $s_X$ is the estimated population standard deviation, that $s_X^2$ is the estimated population variance, and that both involve dividing by $N - 1$
- From Chapter 7, the basics of significance testing

### Your goals in this chapter are to learn

- The difference between the *z-test* and the *t-test*
- How the *t-distribution* and *degrees of freedom* are used
- When and how to perform the *t-test*
- What is meant by the *confidence interval for* $\mu$, and how it is computed

The logic of hypothesis testing discussed in the previous chapter is common to all inferential statistical procedures. The goal now is for you to learn how different procedures are applied to different research designs. This chapter begins the process by introducing the inferential procedure called the *t*-test, which is very similar to the previous *z*-test. Therefore, much of this chapter contains more of a variation on a theme than new material. The chapter presents (1) the similarities and differences between the *z*-test and *t*-test, (2) when and how to perform the *t*-test, and (3) a new procedure—called the *confidence* interval—that is used to more precisely estimate $\mu$.

## UNDERSTANDING THE ONE-SAMPLE *t*-TEST

The *t*-test is important because, like the *z*-test, the *t*-test is used for significance testing in a one-sample experiment. In fact, the *t*-test is used more often in behavioral research. That is because the *z*-test required that we *know* the variability of the raw score population by knowing the standard deviation ($\sigma_X$). However, usually researchers do not know such things about the population because they're exploring uncharted areas of behavior. ("To boldly go where no one has gone . . ." and all that.) Instead, we must estimate the population variability. Recall that we have the *unbiased estimators* that involve the final division by $N - 1$. These allow us to estimate the population's standard deviation and variance. Once we've estimated the variability in the population, then the *t*-test is very similar to the *z*-test. The **one-sample *t*-test** is the parametric procedure used to test the null hypothesis for a one-sample experiment when the standard deviation of the raw score population is not known.

> ***REMEMBER*** Use the *z*-test when $\sigma_X$ is known; use the *t*-test when it is not known.

Here's an example: Say that in one of those "home-and-gardening/good-housekeeper" magazines is a test of one's housekeeping abilities. The magazine is targeted at women, and reports that nationally, the average test score for women is 10 (so their $\mu$ is 10). It does not report the standard deviation. Our question is, "How do men score on this test?" Therefore, we'll give the test to a sample of men and use their $\overline{X}$ to estimate the $\mu$ for the population of all men. Then we can compare the $\mu$ for men to the $\mu$ of 10 for women. If men score differently from women, then we've found a relationship in which, as gender changes, test scores change.

As usual, we first set up the statistical test.

1. **The statistical hypotheses:** We're open-minded and look for any kind of difference, so we have a two-tailed test. If men are different from women, then our sample represents a $\mu$ for men that will not equal the $\mu$ for women of 10, so $H_a$ is $\mu \neq 10$. If men are not different, then their $\mu$ will equal that of women, so $H_0$ is $\mu = 10$.
2. **Alpha:** We select alpha: .05 sounds good.
3. **Check the assumptions:** The one-sample *t*-test requires the following:
   a. You have a one sample experiment using interval or ratio scores.
   b. The raw score population forms a normal distribution.
   c. The variability of the raw score population is estimated from the sample.

Our study meets these assumptions, so we proceed. For simplicity, we test 9 men. (For *power,* you should never collect so few scores.) Say the sample produces a $\overline{X} = 7.78$. Based on this, we might conclude that the population of men would score around a $\mu$ of 7.78. Because females score around a $\mu$ of 10, maybe we have demonstrated a relationship between gender and housekeeping scores. On the other hand, as in $H_0$, maybe gender is not related to test scores and we are being misled by sampling error: Maybe by chance we selected some exceptionally sloppy men for our *sample,* but men in the general population are no sloppier than women, and so the sample actually poorly represents the male population, which has a $\mu = 10$.

To test this null hypothesis, we'll use the same logic we've used previously: $H_0$ says that the men's mean represents a population where $\mu$ is 10. We will compute $t_{obt}$, which will indicate the location of our sample on the sampling distribution of means when we are sampling from this raw score population. The critical value that marks the region of rejection is $t_{crit}$. If $t_{obt}$ is beyond $t_{crit}$, our sample mean lies in the region of rejection, so we'll reject the idea that the sample is poorly representing the population where $\mu = 10$.

The only novelty here is that $t_{obt}$ is calculated differently and $t_{crit}$ comes from the *t*-distribution.

## PERFORMING THE ONE-SAMPLE *t*-TEST

The computation of $t_{\text{obt}}$ consists of three steps that parallel the three steps in the $z$-test. The first step in the $z$-test was to find the true standard deviation ($\sigma_X$) of the raw score population. For the $t$-test, we could compute the estimated standard deviation ($s_X$). However, we're going to change things slightly, and instead, compute the estimated *variance,* $s_X^2$. Recall that the computing formula is

$$s_X^2 = \frac{\Sigma X^2 - \dfrac{(\Sigma X)^2}{N}}{N - 1}$$

Using the variance is better because it is more efficient and it fits later formulas.

The second step of the $z$-test was to compute the standard error of the mean ($\sigma_{\bar{X}}$), which is the "standard deviation" of the sampling distribution of means. However, because now we estimate the population variability, we compute the **estimated standard error of the mean,** which is an estimate of the "standard deviation" of the sampling distribution of means. The symbol for the estimated standard error of the mean is $s_{\bar{X}}$. (The lowercase $s$ stands for an estimate of the population, and the subscript $\bar{X}$ indicates that it is for a population of means.)

The formula for $\sigma_{\bar{X}}$ was $\sigma_X/\sqrt{N}$. The $\sigma_X$ is the square root of the population variance, which we divided by the square root of $N$. However, by using the estimated variance, we need to take the square root only once.

*THE FORMULA FOR THE ESTIMATED STANDARD ERROR OF THE MEAN IS*

$$s_{\bar{X}} = \sqrt{\frac{s_X^2}{N}}$$

This says to divide the estimated population variance by the $N$ of our sample, and then take the square root.

The third step in the $z$-test was to compute $z_{\text{obt}}$ using the formula $z = (\bar{X} - \mu)/\sigma_{\bar{X}}$. The final step in the $t$-test is to compute $t_{\text{obt}}$.

*THE FORMULA FOR THE ONE-SAMPLE t-TEST IS*

$$t_{\text{obt}} = \frac{\bar{X} - \mu}{s_{\bar{X}}}$$

$\bar{X}$ is the sample mean, $\mu$ is the mean of the sampling distribution (which equals the value of $\mu$ described in $H_0$), and $s_{\bar{X}}$ is the estimated standard error of the mean computed above.

For our housekeeping study say that we obtained the data in Table 8.1.

***TABLE 8.1***
Housekeepng Scores of Nine Males

| *Participants* | *Grades* (X) | X² |
|---|---|---|
| 1 | 9 | 81 |
| 2 | 8 | 64 |
| 3 | 10 | 100 |
| 4 | 7 | 49 |
| 5 | 8 | 64 |
| 6 | 8 | 64 |
| 7 | 6 | 36 |
| 8 | 4 | 16 |
| 9 | 10 | 100 |
| $N = 9$ | $\Sigma X = 70$ <br> $\overline{X} = 7.78$ | $\Sigma X^2 = 574$ |

**Step 1:** *Compute the* $\overline{X}$ *and the estimated variance* ($s_X^2$) *using the sample data:* Here $\overline{X} = 7.78$. The $s_X^2$ equals

$$s_X^2 = \frac{\Sigma X^2 - \frac{(\Sigma X)^2}{N}}{N - 1} = \frac{574 - \frac{(70)^2}{9}}{9 - 1} = 3.695$$

**Step 2:** *Compute the estimated standard error of the mean* ($s_{\overline{X}}$):

$$s_{\overline{X}} = \sqrt{\frac{s_X^2}{N}} = \sqrt{\frac{3.695}{9}} = \sqrt{.411} = .64$$

**Step 3:** *Compute* $t_{obt}$*:*

$$t_{\text{obt}} = \frac{\overline{X} - \mu}{s_{\overline{X}}} = \frac{7.78 - 10}{.64} = -3.47$$

So on the sampling distribution of means, where $\mu$ is 10, our sample has something like a *z*-score of $t_{\text{obt}} = -3.47$.

## *A QUICK REVIEW*

- Perform the one-sample *t*-test in a one-sample experiment when you do not know the population standard deviation.

### More Examples

In a study our $H_0$ is that $\mu = 60$. To compute $t_{\text{obt}}$:

1. Say that $\overline{X} = 62$, $s_X^2 = 25$, $N = 36$.
2. $s_{\overline{X}} = \sqrt{\frac{s_X^2}{N}} = \sqrt{\frac{25}{36}} = \sqrt{.694} = .833$
3. $t_{\text{obt}} = \frac{\overline{X} - \mu}{s_{\overline{X}}} = \frac{62 - 60}{.833} = \frac{+2}{.833} = +2.40$

***For Practice:***

In a study $H_0$ is that $\mu = 10$. The data are 6, 7, 9, 8, 8.

1. To compute the $t_{\text{obt}}$, what two statistics are computed first?
2. What do you compute next?
3. Compute the $t_{\text{obt}}$.

**Answers**

1. $\overline{X}$ and $s_X^2$
2. $s_{\overline{X}}$
3. $\overline{X} = 7.6$, $s_X^2 = 1.30$, $N = 5$; $s_{\overline{X}} = \sqrt{1.3/5} = .51$; $t_{\text{obt}} = (7.6 - 10)/.51 = -4.71$

## The *t*-Distribution and *df*

In previous chapters we described the sampling distribution of means using *z*-scores. Now the *t*-distribution is our model. Think of the *t*-distribution in the following way. Once again we infinitely draw samples of the same size *N* from the raw score population described by $H_0$. For each sample we compute the $\overline{X}$ and its $t_{obt}$. Then we plot the frequency distribution of the different means, labeling the *X* axis with $t_{obt}$ as well. Thus, the ***t*-distribution** is the distribution of all possible values of *t* computed for random sample means selected from the raw score population described by $H_0$.

You can envision the *t*-distribution as in Figure 8.1. A sample mean equal to μ has a *t* equal to zero. Means greater than μ have positive values of *t,* and means less than μ have negative values of *t.* The larger the absolute value of *t,* the farther it and the corresponding sample mean are into the tail of the distribution. To determine if our mean is far enough into a tail, we find $t_{crit}$ and create the region of rejection.

But there is one important novelty here: There are actually *many* versions of the *t*-distribution, each having a slightly different shape. The shape of a particular distribution depends on the size of the samples that are used when creating it. When using small samples, the *t*-distribution is only roughly normally distributed. With larger samples, the *t*-distribution is a progressively closer approximation to the perfect normal curve. This is because with a larger sample, our estimate of the population variance or standard deviation is closer to the true population variance and standard deviation. As we saw, when we have the true population variability as in the *z*-test, the sampling distribution *is* a normal curve.

Recall that computing the estimated variance involves dividing by the quantity $N - 1$. It is this number that determines the size of the samples and thus the shape of the *t*-distribution. We have a special name for $N - 1$: It is called the **degrees of freedom** and is symbolized as *df.*

*THE DEGREES OF FREEDOM IN THE ONE-SAMPLE* t-*TEST EQUAL*

$df = N - 1$, where *N* is the number of scores in the sample

In our housekeeping study $N = 9$, so our $df = 8$.

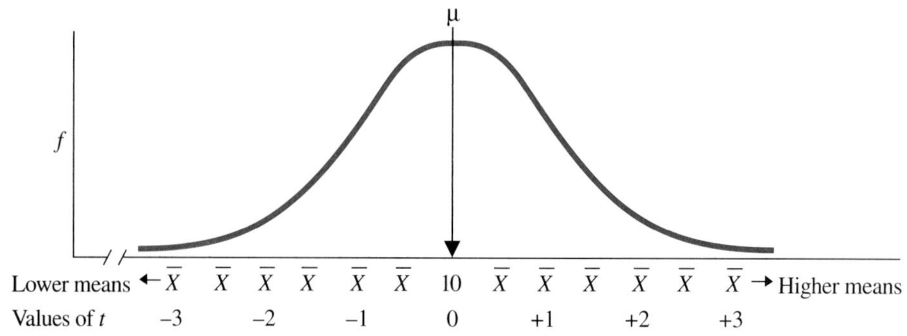


***FIGURE 8.1***
Example of a *t*-distribution of random sample means

The larger the *df,* the closer the *t*-distribution comes to forming a normal curve. However, a tremendously large sample is not required to produce a perfect normal *t*-distribution. When *df* is greater than 120, the *t*-distribution is virtually identical to the standard normal curve, and *t* is the same as *z*. But when *df* is between 1 and 120 (which is usually the case in research) we have differently shaped *t*-distributions.

> ***REMEMBER*** In a one-sample experiment the *degrees of freedom*—the *df*—equal $N - 1$ and determine the shape of the *t*-distribution.

The fact that there are differently shaped *t*-distributions is important for one reason: Our region of rejection should contain precisely that portion of the curve defined by our $\alpha$. If $\alpha = .05$, then we want to mark off precisely 5% of the curve. On distributions that are shaped differently, we mark off that 5% at different locations. Because the location of the region of rejection is marked off by the critical value, *with differently shaped* t*-distributions we will have different critical values.* For example, Figure 8.2 shows two *t*-distributions. Notice the size of the (blue) region of rejection in a tail of Distribution A. Say that this is the extreme 5% of Distribution A and has the critical value shown. If we also use this $t_{crit}$ on Distribution B, the region of rejection is larger, containing *more* than 5% of the distribution. Conversely, the $t_{crit}$ marking off 5% of Distribution B will mark off *less* than 5% of Distribution A. (The same problem exists for a one-tailed test.)

This issue is important because not only is $\alpha$ the size of the region of rejection, it is also the probability of a Type I error. Unless we use the appropriate $t_{crit}$, the actual probability of a Type I error will not equal our $\alpha$ and that is not supposed to happen! Thus, there is only one version of the *t*-distribution to use when performing a particular *t*-test: the one that would be created by using the *same df* as in our sample.

Therefore, when your *df* is between 1 and 120, you use the *df* to first identify the appropriate sampling distribution for your study. The $t_{crit}$ on that distribution

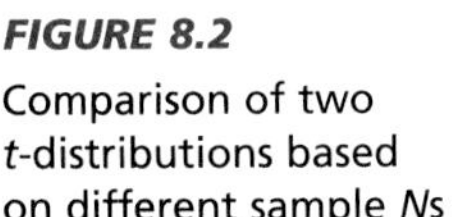

***FIGURE 8.2***
Comparison of two *t*-distributions based on different sample *N*s

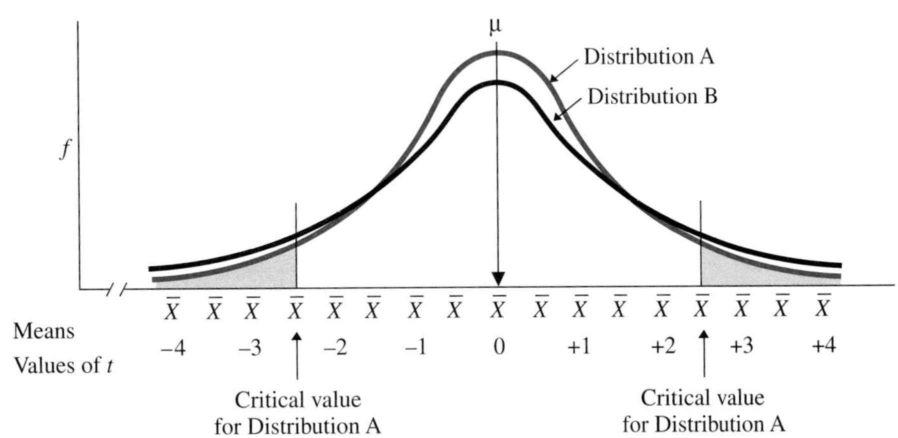

will accurately mark off the region of rejection so that the probability of a Type I error equals your $\alpha$. Thus, in the housekeeping study with an *N* of 9, we will create the sampling distribution and use the $t_{\text{crit}}$ from the *t*-distribution for $df = 8$. In a different study, however, where *N* might be 25, we create the sampling distribution and use the different $t_{\text{crit}}$ from the *t*-distribution for $df = 24$. And so on.

> *REMEMBER* The appropriate $t_{\text{crit}}$ for the one-sample *t*-test comes from the *t*-distribution that has *df* equal to $N - 1$, where *N* is the number of scores in the sample.

## Using the *t*-Tables

We obtain the different values of $t_{\text{crit}}$ from Table 2 in Appendix B, entitled "Critical Values of *t*." In these "*t*-tables" you'll find separate tables for two-tailed and one-tailed tests. Table 8.2 below contains a portion of the two-tailed table.

To find the appropriate $t_{\text{crit}}$, first locate the appropriate column under your $\alpha$ level (either .05 or .01). Then find the value of $t_{\text{crit}}$ in the row at the *df* for your sample. For example, in the housekeeping study *N* is 9, so *df* is $N - 1 = 8$. For a two-tailed test with $\alpha = .05$ and $df = 8$, $t_{\text{crit}}$ is 2.306.

Here's another example: In a different study the sample *N* is 61. Therefore, the $df = N - 1 = 60$. Look in Table 2 of Appendix B to find $t_{\text{crit}}$. With $\alpha = .05$, the two-tailed $t_{\text{crit}} = 2.000$; the one-tailed $t_{\text{crit}} = 1.671$.

The table contains no positive or negative signs. In a two-tailed test you add the "±," and in a one-tailed test you supply the appropriate "+" or "−."

Finally, you will not find a critical value for every *df* between 1 and 120. When the *df* of your sample does not appear in the table, select the *df* in the table that is nearest to your study's *df* and use the corresponding $t_{\text{crit}}$ to test your data. Usually your $t_{\text{obt}}$ will be either substantially smaller or larger than this number, and that's all you need to know to determine if $t_{\text{obt}}$ is in the region of rejection or not. If your $t_{\text{obt}}$ is very close to the substitute $t_{\text{crit}}$ (say $t_{\text{crit}} = 2.00$ and $t_{\text{obt}} = 1.99$), then you should employ the precise $t_{\text{crit}}$ for your *df*. For this consult an advanced textbook to perform "linear interpolation."

**TABLE 8.2**
A Portion of the *t*-Tables

| | *Alpha Level* | |
|---|---|---|
| *df* | $\alpha = .05$ | $\alpha = .01$ |
| 1 | 12.706 | 63.657 |
| 2 | 4.303 | 9.925 |
| 3 | 3.182 | 5.841 |
| 4 | 2.776 | 4.604 |
| 5 | 2.571 | 4.032 |
| 6 | 2.447 | 3.707 |
| 7 | 2.365 | 3.499 |
| 8 | 2.306 | 3.355 |

## INTERPRETING THE $t$-TEST

Once you've calculated $t_{obt}$ and identified $t_{crit}$, you can make a decision about your results. Remember the housekeeping study? We must decide whether or not the men's mean of 7.78 represents the same population of scores that women have. Our $t_{obt}$ was $-3.47$, and the two-tailed $t_{crit}$ is $\pm 2.306$, producing the sampling distribution in Figure 8.3. Remember, this can be interpreted as showing the frequency of all means that occur by chance when $H_0$ is true—here, when men and women belong to the same population with $\mu = 10$. But, our $t_{obt}$ lies beyond $t_{crit}$, so the results are significant: Our $\overline{X}$ of 7.78 is so unlikely to occur if our men had been representing the same population as found with women, that we reject that we were representing this population—we reject $H_0$. Then we worry that we've made a Type I error and apply the rules for interpreting significant results as discussed in the previous chapter: Because our $\overline{X}$ is 7.78, we conclude the population of men score at a $\mu$ around 7.78, but that women score at a $\mu$ of 10. The results demonstrate a relationship in the population between the independent variable (gender) and the dependent variable (housekeeping scores).

If $t_{obt}$ had not fallen beyond $t_{crit}$ (for example, if $t_{obt} = +1.32$), then it would not lie in the region of rejection and would not be significant. We would have no evidence for a relationship between gender and test scores. Then we'd worry that we've made a Type II error and apply the rules for interpreting nonsignificant results as discussed in the previous chapter.

### Performing One-Tailed Tests

As usual, we perform one-tailed tests when we predict the direction of the relationship. If, for example, we had predicted that men score *higher* than women, then $H_a$ would be that the sample represents a population $\mu$ greater than 10 ($H_a$: $\mu > 10$). $H_0$ would be that the sample represents a $\mu$ less than or equal to 10 ($H_0$: $\mu \leq 10$). We compute $t_{obt}$ as shown previously, but then we find the one-tailed $t_{crit}$ from the $t$-tables for our $df$ and $\alpha$.

**FIGURE 8.3**
Two-tailed $t$-distribution for $df = 8$ when $H_0$ is true and $\mu = 10$

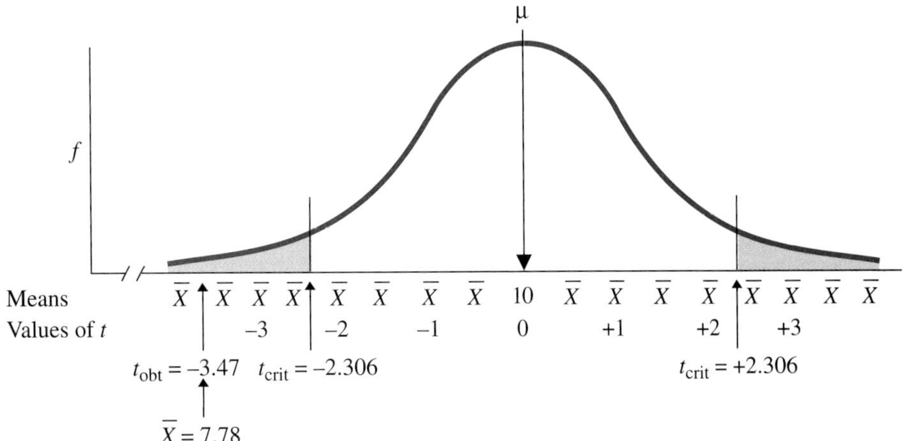

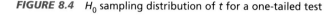

**FIGURE 8.4** $H_0$ sampling distribution of *t* for a one-tailed test

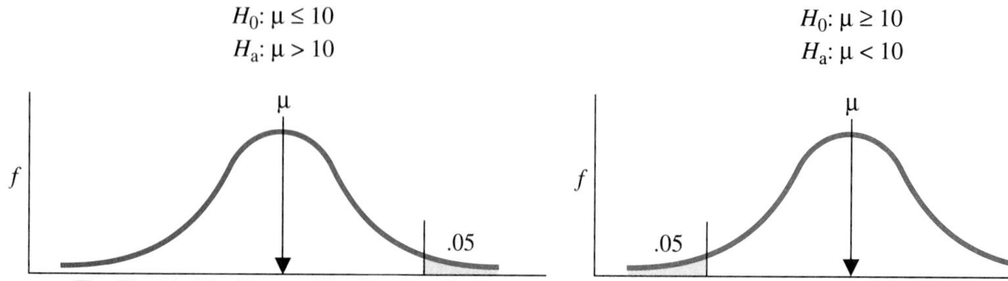


To decide which tail of the sampling distribution to put the region of rejection in, determine what's needed to support $H_a$. Here, for the sample to represent a population of higher scores, the $\overline{X}$ must be *greater* than 10 and be *significant.* As shown in the left-hand graph in Figure 8.4, such means are in the upper tail, so $t_{crit}$ is positive.

If, however, we had predicted that men score *lower* than women, we'd have the sampling distribution on the right in Figure 8.4. Now $H_a$ is that μ is less than 10, and $H_0$ is that μ is greater than or equal to 10. Because we seek a $\overline{X}$ that is *significant* and *lower* than 10, the $t_{crit}$ is negative.

In either case if the absolute value of $t_{obt}$ is larger than $t_{crit}$ and has the same sign, then the $\overline{X}$ is unlikely to be representing a μ described by $H_0$. Therefore, reject $H_0$, accept $H_a$, and the results are significant.

## SUMMARY OF THE ONE-SAMPLE *t*-TEST

The one-sample *t*-test is used with a one-sample experiment involving normally distributed interval or ratio scores and involves the following.

1. *Create either the two-tailed or one-tailed $H_0$ and $H_a$.*
2. *Compute $t_{obt}$.*
   a. Compute $\overline{X}$ and $s^2_X$.
   b. Compute $s_{\overline{X}}$.
   c. Compute $t_{obt}$.
3. *Create the sampling t-distribution and use $df = N - 1$ to find $t_{crit}$ in the t-tables.*
4. *Compare $t_{obt}$ to $t_{crit}$:* If $t_{obt}$ is beyond $t_{crit}$, the results are significant; describe the populations and interpret the relationship. If $t_{obt}$ is not beyond $t_{crit}$, the results are not significant; make no conclusion about the relationship.

## A QUICK REVIEW

- In a one-sample experiment when $\sigma_X$ is unknown, to determine if the $\overline{X}$ differs significantly from μ, perform the one-sample *t*-test.

### MORE EXAMPLES

In a one-sample study μ is 40 (but $\sigma_X$ is not known). We predict our condition will change scores relative to this μ. $N = 25$. To perform the one-sample *t*-test:

1. To "change scores" is a two-tailed test, so $H_0$: $\mu = 40$; $H_a$: $\mu \neq 40$.
2. Compute $t_{obt}$.
   Say that the scores produce $\overline{X} = 46$ and $s_X^2 = 196$.
   $$s_{\overline{X}} = \sqrt{\frac{s_X^2}{N}} = \sqrt{\frac{196}{25}} = 2.80$$
   $$t_{obt} = \frac{\overline{X} - \mu}{s_{\overline{X}}} = \frac{46 - 40}{2.80} = +2.14$$
3. Find $t_{crit}$: With $\alpha = .05$ and $df = 24$, $t_{crit} = \pm 2.064$. The sampling distribution is

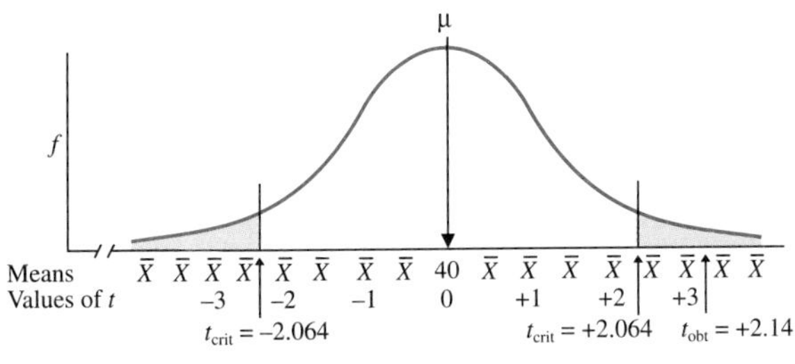


4. The $t_{obt}$ of +2.14 lies beyond the $t_{crit}$ of +2.064. Conclusion: The independent variable significantly increases scores from a μ of 40 to a μ around 46.

### *For Practice:*

We test if artificial sunlight during the winter months *lowers* one's depression. Without the light a depression test has $\mu = 8$. With the light, our sample scored 4, 5, 6, 7, 8.

1. What are the hypotheses?
2. Compute $t_{obt}$.
3. What is $t_{crit}$?
4. What is the conclusion?

**Answers**

1. To "lower" is a one-tailed test: $H_a$: $\mu < 8$; $H_0$: $\mu \geq 8$.
2. $\overline{X} = 6$; $s_X^2 = 2.5$; $s_{\overline{X}} = \sqrt{2.5/5} = .707$; $t_{obt} = (6 - 8)/.707 = -2.83$
3. With $\alpha = .05$ and $df = 4$, $t_{crit} = -2.132$.
4. $t_{obt}$ is beyond $t_{crit}$. Conclusion: Artificial sunlight significantly lowers depression scores from a μ of 8 to a μ around 6.

## ESTIMATING μ BY COMPUTING A CONFIDENCE INTERVAL

As you've seen, after rejecting $H_0$, we estimate the population μ that the sample mean represents. There are two ways to estimate μ.

The first way is **point estimation,** in which we describe a point on the variable at which the population μ is expected to fall. Earlier we estimated that the μ of the population of men is located on the variable of housekeeping scores at the *point* identified as 7.78. However, if we actually tested the population, μ would probably not be *exactly* 7.78. The problem with point estimation is that it is extremely vulnerable to sampling error. Our sample probably does not *perfectly* represent the population of men, so we can say only that the μ for men is probably *around* 7.78.

The other, better way to estimate a $\mu$ is to include the possibility of sampling error and perform interval estimation. With **interval estimation,** we specify a range of values within which we expect the population parameter to fall. You may encounter such intervals in real life, and they are usually phrased in terms of "plus or minus" some amount (called the *margin of error*). For example, when it is reported that a sample showed that 45% of the voters support the President, the margin of error may be ±3%. The pollsters have created an interval around 45%, so that if they could ask the *entire* population, the result would be within ±3% of 45%: They believe that between 42% and 48% of the population would actually support the President.

Researchers perform interval estimation in a similar way by creating a confidence interval. The **confidence interval for $\mu$** describes an interval containing values of $\mu$, any one of which our sample mean is likely to represent. Thus, instead of saying that our sample of men represents a $\mu$ somewhere *around* 7.78, a confidence interval is the way to define "around." To do so, we'll identify those values of $\mu$ above and below 7.78 that the sample mean is likely to represent, as shown here:

$$\underbrace{\mu_{\text{low}} \ldots \mu \;\; \mu \;\; \mu \;\; \mu \;\; 7.78 \;\; \mu \;\; \mu \;\; \mu \;\; \mu \ldots \mu_{\text{high}}}$$

values of $\mu$, one of which is likely to be represented by our sample mean

The $\mu_{\text{low}}$ is the lowest $\mu$ that our sample mean is likely to represent, and $\mu_{\text{high}}$ is the highest $\mu$ that the mean is likely to represent. When we compute these two values, we have the confidence interval.

When is a sample mean likely to represent a particular $\mu$? It depends on sampling error. For example, intuitively we know that sampling error is unlikely to produce a sample mean of 7.78 if $\mu$ is, say, 500. In other words, 7.78 is significantly different from 500. But sampling error *is* likely to produce a sample mean of 7.78 if, for example, $\mu$ is 8 or 9. In other words, 7.78 is not significantly different from these $\mu$s. Thus, a sample mean is likely to represent any $\mu$ that the mean is *not* significantly different from. The logic behind a confidence interval is to compute the highest and lowest values of $\mu$ that are not significantly different from the sample mean. All $\mu$s between these two values are also not significantly different from the sample mean, so the mean is likely to represent one of them.

> **REMEMBER** A *confidence interval* describes the highest and lowest values of $\mu$ that are not significantly different from our sample mean, and thus the mean is likely to represent one of them.

We usually compute a confidence interval only after finding a significant $t_{\text{obt}}$. This is because we must be sure that our sample is not representing the known $\mu$ described in $H_0$ before we estimate any other $\mu$ it might represent. Thus, we determined that our men represent a $\mu$ different from that of women and so now we can go on to describe that $\mu$. In fact, it is appropriate to compute a confidence interval in any study in which we believe a $\bar{X}$ represents a particular population $\mu$.

## Computing the Confidence Interval

The *t*-test forms the basis for the confidence interval. We seek those $\mu$s that are not significantly different from our mean. The most that a sample mean can differ from $\mu$ and still not be significant is when its $t_{obt}$ *equals* $t_{crit}$. We can state this using the formula for the *t*-test:

$$t_{crit} = \frac{\overline{X} - \mu}{s_{\overline{X}}}$$

To find the largest and smallest values of μ that do not differ significantly from our sample mean, we simply determine the values of μ that we can put into this formula. Because we are describing values above and below the sample mean, we use the two-tailed value of $t_{crit}$. Then we find the μ that produces a $-t_{obt}$ equal to $-t_{crit}$, and the μ that produces a $+t_{obt}$ equal to $+t_{crit}$. The sample mean represents a μ *between* these two values, so we have

*THE FORMULA FOR THE CONFIDENCE INTERVAL FOR μ IS*

$$(s_{\overline{X}})(-t_{crit}) + \overline{X} \leq \mu \leq (s_{\overline{X}})(+t_{crit}) + \overline{X}$$

The μ stands for the unknown value represented by the sample mean. The $\overline{X}$ and $s_{\overline{X}}$ are computed from your data. Find the two-tailed value of $t_{crit}$ in the *t*-tables at your α for $df = N - 1$, where *N* is the sample *N*.

> ***REMEMBER*** Use the *two-tailed* critical value when computing a confidence interval even if you performed a one-tailed *t*-test.

**Step 1:** *Find the two-tailed* $t_{crit}$ *and fill in the formula:* For our housekeeping study the two-tailed $t_{crit}$ for $\alpha = .05$ and $df = 8$ is $\pm 2.306$. The $\overline{X} = 7.78$ and $s_{\overline{X}} = .64$. Filling in the formula, we have

$$(.64)(-2.306) + 7.78 \leq \mu \leq (.64)(+2.306) + 7.78$$

**Step 2:** *Multiply each* $t_{crit}$ *times* $s_{\overline{X}}$: After multiplying .64 times −2.306 and +2.306 we have

$$-1.476 + 7.78 \leq \mu \leq +1.476 + 7.78$$

At this point the men's mean represents a μ of 7.78, plus or minus 1.476.

**Step 3:** *Add the above positive and negative answers to the* $\overline{X}$: After adding ±1.476 to 7.78, we have

$$6.30 \leq \mu \leq 9.26$$

Thus, our men's sample mean probably represents a μ around 7.78. But now we can define "around" as meaning that the μ represented is greater than or equal to 6.30, but less than or equal to 9.26.

Because we created this interval using the $t_{crit}$ for an α of .05, there is a 5% chance that the μ being represented by our mean is outside of this interval. On the other hand, there is a 95% chance, $(1 - \alpha)(100)$, that the μ being represented is *within* the interval. Therefore, we have created what is called the *95% confidence interval:* We are 95%

confident that the interval between 6.30 and 9.26 contains the μ represented by our sample mean. Usually this gives us sufficient confidence. However, had we used the $t_{crit}$ for $\alpha = .01$, the interval would have spanned a wider range, giving us even more confidence that it contained the μ represented by our sample. Then we would have created the 99% confidence interval.

*REMEMBER* Compute a confidence interval to estimate the μ represented by the $\overline{X}$ of a condition in an experiment.

## A QUICK REVIEW

- A confidence interval for μ provides a range of μs, one of which the $\overline{X}$ is likely to represent.

### More Examples

We find a significant $t_{obt}$ where our condition produces $\overline{X} = 50$, $N$ is 20, and from the $t$-test, $s_{\overline{X}}$ is 4.7. To compute the 95% confidence interval:

1. $df = 19$, so the two-tailed $t_{crit} = \pm 2.093$. Then:

$$(s_{\overline{X}})(-t_{crit}) + \overline{X} \leq \mu \leq (s_{\overline{X}})(+t_{crit}) + \overline{X}$$
$$= (4.7)(-2.093) + 50 \leq \mu$$
$$\leq (4.7)(+2.093) + 50$$

2. After multiplying: $(-9.837) + 50 \leq \mu \leq (+9.837) + 50$
3. After adding: $40.16 \leq \mu \leq 59.84$

***For Practice:***

1. What does this 95% confidence indicate: $15 \leq \mu \leq 20$?
2. With $N = 22$ you perform a one-tailed $t$-test ($\alpha = .05$.) What is the $t_{crit}$ for then computing the confidence interval?
3. The $t_{obt}$ is significant when $\overline{X} = 35$, $s_{\overline{X}} = 3.33$, and $N = 22$. Compute the 95% confidence interval.

**Answers**

1. We are 95% confident that our $\overline{X}$ represents a μ between 15 and 20.
2. With $df = 21$, the *two-tailed* $t_{crit} = \pm 2.080$
3. $(3.33)(-2.080) + 35 \leq \mu \leq (3.33)(+2.080) + 35 = 28.07 \leq \mu \leq 41.93$.

## STATISTICS IN THE RESEARCH LITERATURE: REPORTING *t*

Report the results of a one- or two-tailed $t$-test in the same way that you reported the $z$-test, but also include the $df$. We would report our significant results in the original housekeeping study as

$$t(8) = -3.47, p < .05$$

The $df$ is in parentheses. (Had these results not been significant, then $p > .05$.)

Note that when $\alpha$ is .01, $t_{crit}$ is $\pm 3.355$, so our $t_{obt}$ of $-3.47$ also would be significant if we had used the .01 level. Therefore, instead of saying $p < .05$ above, we provide more information by reporting that $p < .01$ because we now know that the probability of a Type I error is not in the neighborhood of .04, .03, or .02. Researchers usually report the smallest values of alpha at which a result is significant.

Further, computer programs can determine the precise, minimum size of the region of rejection that our $t_{obt}$ falls into. Then we know what the exact probability of a Type I error equals for a particular result. For example, you might see "$p = .04$." This indicates that our $t_{obt}$ falls into a region of rejection that is .04 of the curve, and therefore the probability of a Type I error here equals .04. Because this is less than our $\alpha$, this result is significant. A $p = .06$, however, would involve too large a region of rejection, so the $p$ of a Type I error would be too large, and thus the result would not be significant.

Usually, confidence intervals are reported in sentence form, but we always indicate the confidence level used. Thus, you might see: "The 95% confidence interval for $\mu$ was 45.50 to 53.72."

## CHAPTER SUMMARY

1. The *t-test* is used when (a) we have one random sample of interval or ratio data, (b) the raw score population is a normal distribution, and (c) the standard deviation of the raw score population is not known.
2. The *estimated standard error of the mean* ($s_{\overline{X}}$) is an estimate of the standard deviation of the sampling distribution.
3. A t-*distribution* is the sampling distribution of all possible values of $t$ when a raw score population is infinitely sampled using a particular $N$.
4. The appropriate $t$-distribution and thus the correct $t_{crit}$ to use for a particular study is the one identified by our *degrees of freedom* (*df*). In the one-sample $t$-test, $df = N - 1$.
5. In *point estimation* $\mu$ is assumed to equal $\overline{X}$. In *interval estimation* a $\mu$ is assumed to lie within a specified interval.
6. The *confidence interval for* $\mu$ describes a range of $\mu$s, any one of which the sample mean is likely to represent. Our confidence that the interval contains the $\mu$ equals $(1 - \alpha)(100)$.

## KEY TERMS: Can You Define the Following?

$t_{obt}$ *139*
$t_{crit}$ *139*
$s_{\overline{X}}$ *140*
*df 142*
confidence interval for $\mu$ *148*
degrees of freedom *142*
estimated standard error of the mean *140*
interval estimation *148*
one-sample $t$-test *139*
point estimation *147*
$t$-distribution *142*

## REVIEW QUESTIONS

(Answers for odd-numbered questions are in Appendix C.)

1. A scientist has conducted a one-sample experiment. (a) What two parametric procedures are available to her? (b) What is the deciding factor for selecting between them?
2. What are the assumptions of the $t$-test?

3. (a) What is the difference between $s_{\overline{X}}$ and $\sigma_{\overline{X}}$? (b) How is their use the same?
4. Why are there different values of $t_{\text{crit}}$ when samples have different *df*s?
5. (a) What does *df* symbolize? (b) Why must you compute *df* when performing the *t*-test? (c) What does *df* equal in the one-sample *t*-test?
6. Summarize the steps involved in analyzing the results of a one-sample experiment.
7. What is the final step in examining the data in any study?
8. Say you have a sample mean of 44 in a study. (a) Estimate the corresponding $\mu$ using point estimation. (b) Why is computing a confidence interval better than using a point estimate?
9. What does a confidence interval for $\mu$ indicate?
10. (a) Is the one-tailed or two-tailed $t_{\text{crit}}$ used to compute a confidence interval? (b) Why?

## APPLICATION QUESTIONS

11. You wish to determine whether a study technique is beneficial or detrimental to students learning statistics. On a national statistics exam $\mu = 68.5$. After applying the technique, 10 students produced a $\overline{X} = 78.5$ and $s_X^2 = 130.42$. (a) What are $H_0$ and $H_a$ here? (b) Compute $t_{\text{obt}}$. (c) With $\alpha = .05$, what is $t_{\text{crit}}$? (d) What do you conclude about the use of this technique? (e) Compute the confidence interval for $\mu$.
12. A researcher predicts that smoking cigarettes decreases a person's sense of smell. On a test of olfactory sensitivity, the $\mu$ for nonsmokers is 18.4. People who smoke a pack a day produced the following scores:

    16 14 19 17 16 18 17 15 18 19 12 14

    (a) What are $H_0$ and $H_a$? (b) Compute $t_{\text{obt}}$. (c) With $\alpha = .05$, what is $t_{\text{crit}}$? (d) What should the researcher conclude about this relationship? (e) Compute the confidence interval for $\mu$.
13. Foofy conducts a study to determine if hearing an argument in favor of an issue alters participants' attitudes toward the issue one way or the other. She presents a 30-second speech in favor of an issue to 8 people. In a national survey the mean attitude score toward this issue was $\mu = 50$. She obtains the following scores:

    10 33 86 55 67 60 44 71

    (a) What are $H_0$ and $H_a$? (b) Compute $t_{\text{obt}}$. (c) With $\alpha = .05$, what is $t_{\text{crit}}$? (d) What are the statistical results? (e) If appropriate, compute the confidence interval for $\mu$. (f) What conclusions should Foofy draw about the relationship?
14. For the study in question 13, (a) What statistical principle should Foofy be concerned with? (b) Why?
15. We ask whether a computer word-processing program leads to more or fewer grammatical errors. On a typing test without a computer $\mu = 12$. A sample using a computer scores 8, 12, 10, 9, 6, 7. (a) Perform the *t*-test and draw the appropriate conclusion. (b) Compute the confidence interval.

*16.* While reading a published research report, you encounter the following. Identify the $N$, the procedure performed and the outcome, the relationship, and the type of error possibly being made. "When we examined the perceptual skills data, the mean of 55 for the sample of adolescents differed significantly from the population mean of 70 for adults, $t(45) = 3.76$, $p < .01$."

*17.* In a one-tailed test ($\alpha = .05$) our $N = 33$. Is $t_{obt}$ significant if it equals: (a) $+1.61$? Why? (b) $+1.785$? Why?

*18.* Poindexter performed a two-tailed experiment in which $N = 20$. He couldn't find his $t$-tables, but somehow he remembered the $t_{crit}$ at $df = 10$. He decided to compare his $t_{obt}$ to this $t_{crit}$. Why is this a correct or incorrect approach? (*Hint:* Consider whether $t_{obt}$ turns out to be significant or nonsignificant at this $t_{crit}$.)

*19.* (a) How would you report your results if $\alpha = .01$, $N = 43$, and the $t_{obt} = +6.72$ is significant? (b) How would you report your results if $\alpha = .05$, $N = 6$, and the $t_{obt} = -1.72$ is not significant?

*20.* A research report indicates that for a $t$-test, $p = .03$. What does this indicate?

## SUMMARY OF FORMULAS

*1. The formula for the one-sample* t*-test is*

$$t_{obt} = \frac{\overline{X} - \mu}{s_{\overline{X}}}$$

*where*

$$s_{\overline{X}} = \sqrt{\frac{s_X^2}{N}}$$

$$s_X = \sqrt{\frac{\Sigma X^2 - \frac{(\Sigma X)^2}{N}}{N - 1}}$$

$$df = N - 1$$

*2. The formula for the confidence interval for* $\mu$ *is*

$$(s_{\overline{X}})(-t_{crit}) + \overline{X} < \mu < (s_{\overline{X}})(+t_{crit}) + \overline{X}$$

# 9 Hypothesis Testing Using the Two-Sample *t*-Test

**CHAPTER ESSENTIALS**

**Before getting started, be sure you understand**

- From Chapter 1, what a condition, independent variable, and dependent variable are
- From Chapter 8, how to perform the one-sample *t*-test using the *t*-distribution and *df*

**Your goals in this chapter are to learn**

- The logic of a two-sample experiment
- The difference between *independent samples* and *related samples*
- When and how to perform the *independent-samples t-tests*
- When and how to perform the *related-samples t-test*
- How to summarize a two-sample experiment

This chapter presents the two-sample *t*-test, which is the major parametric procedure used when an experiment involves *two* samples. As the name implies, this test is similar to the one-sample *t*-test you saw in Chapter 8, except that the characteristics of a two-sample design require that we use slightly different formulas. This chapter discusses (1) one version of the two-sample *t*-test called the *independent-samples* t*-test,* (2) the other version of two-sample *t*-test called the *related-samples* t*-test,* and (3) how to summarize the results of any two-sample experiment.

## UNDERSTANDING THE TWO-SAMPLE EXPERIMENT

The one-sample experiment discussed in previous chapters requires that we know the value of $\mu$ for a population under one condition of the independent variable. However, because researchers explore new behaviors and variables, they usually do not know $\mu$ ahead of time. Instead, the simplest alternative is to conduct a two-sample experiment, measuring participants' scores under two conditions of the independent variable. Condition 1 produces one sample mean—call it $\overline{X}_1$—that represents $\mu_1$, the $\mu$ we would find if we tested everyone in the population under Condition 1. Condition 2 produces another sample mean—call it $\overline{X}_2$—that represents $\mu_2$, the $\mu$ we would find if we tested everyone in the population under Condition 2. A possible outcome from such an

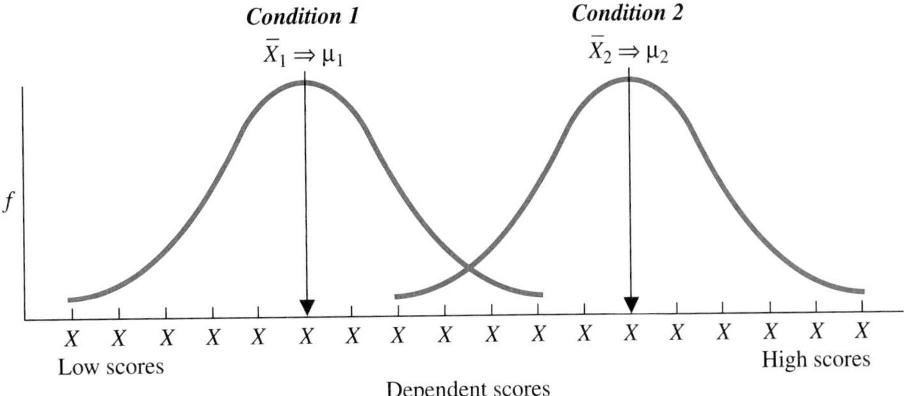


**FIGURE 9.1**
Relationship in the population in a two-sample experiment
*As the conditions change, the population tends to change in a consistent fashion.*

experiment is shown in Figure 9.1. If each sample represents a different population for each condition, then the experiment has demonstrated a relationship in nature.

However, there's the usual problem of sampling error. Even though we may have different sample means, the independent variable may not change scores, and the relationship may not exist in the population. Instead, if we tested the population, we might find the *same* population of scores under both conditions. In Figure 9.1 we might find only the lower or upper distribution, or we might find one in between. Then there would be only one value of $\mu$: Call it $\mu_1$ or $\mu_2$, it wouldn't matter because it's the *same* $\mu$. Therefore, before we make any conclusions about the experiment, we must determine whether the difference between the sample means reflects sampling error.

The parametric statistical procedure for determining whether the results of a two-sample experiment are significant is the two-sample *t*-test. However, we have two different ways to create the samples, so we have two different versions of the *t*-test: One is called the "independent-samples *t*-test" and the other is the "related-samples *t*-test."

> **REMEMBER** The two ways to calculate the two-sample *t*-test are the *independent-samples* t-*test* or the *related-samples* t-*test.*

## THE INDEPENDENT-SAMPLES *t*-TEST

The **independent-samples *t*-test** is the parametric procedure for testing two sample means from **independent samples.** Two samples are independent when we randomly select participants for a sample, without regard to who else has been selected for either sample. Then the scores occurring in one sample are not influenced by—are "independent" of—the scores in the other sample. You can recognize independent samples by the absence of anything fancy when selecting participants, such as matching the participants in one condition with those in the other or repeatedly testing the same participants in both conditions.

Here is a study that calls for the independent-samples *t*-test. People who witness a crime or other event may recall the event differently when they are hypnotized. We'll create two samples of participants who watch a videotape of a supposed robbery. Later, one group will be hypnotized and then answer 30 questions about the event. The other

**TABLE 9.1**

Diagram of Hypnosis Study using an Independent-Samples Design

*The independent variable is amount of hypnosis, and the dependent variable is recall.*

| | No Hypnosis | Hypnosis |
|---|---|---|
| Recall Scores → | $X$ | $X$ |
| | $X$ | $X$ |
| | $X$ | $X$ |
| | $X$ | $X$ |
| | $X$ | $X$ |
| | $\overline{X}$ | $\overline{X}$ |

group will answer the questions without being hypnotized. Thus, the conditions of the independent variable are the presence or absence of hypnosis, and the dependent variable is the number of times information is correctly recalled. This design is shown in Table 9.1. We will compute the mean of each condition (in each column). If the means differ, we'll have evidence of a relationship where, as amount of hypnosis changes, recall scores also change.

First, as always we check that the study meets the assumptions of the statistical test. In addition to requiring independent samples, this $t$-test also requires

1. The dependent scores measure an interval or ratio variable.
2. The populations of raw scores form at least roughly normal distributions.
3. And here's a new one: The populations have homogeneous variance. **Homogeneity of variance** means that the variances ($\sigma^2_X$) of the populations being represented are equal.

Determine if your data meet these assumptions by seeing how your variables are treated in the research literature related to your study.

## Statistical Hypotheses for the Independent-Samples *t*-Test

As usual, we may perform either a one- or a two-tailed test. Let's begin with a two-tailed test: We predict that the samples will be different, representing different populations that have different $\mu$s.

First, the alternative hypothesis: The predicted relationship exists if one population mean ($\mu_1$) is larger or smaller than the other ($\mu_2$); that is, $\mu_1$ should not equal $\mu_2$. We could state this as $H_a$: $\mu_1 \neq \mu_2$, but there is a better way. If the two $\mu$s are not equal, then their *difference* does not equal zero. Thus, the two-tailed alternative hypothesis is

$$H_a\colon \mu_1 - \mu_2 \neq 0$$

$H_a$ implies that the means from our two conditions each represent a different population of recall scores, so a relationship is present.

Now, the null hypothesis: If no relationship exists, then if we tested everyone under the two conditions, we would find the same population and $\mu$. In other words, $\mu_1$ *equals* $\mu_2$. We could state this as $H_0$: $\mu_1 = \mu_2$, but, again, there is a better way. If the two $\mu$s are equal, then their *difference* is zero. Thus, the two-tailed null hypothesis is

$$H_0\colon \mu_1 - \mu_2 = 0$$

$H_0$ implies that both sample means represent the same population, so no relationship is present.

Notice that these hypotheses do not contain a specific value of μ. Therefore, these are the two-tailed hypotheses for *any* independent variable. However, this is true only when you test whether the data might actually represent *zero difference* between your conditions in the population. This is the most common approach and the one we'll use. (You can also test for nonzero differences: You might know of an existing difference between two populations and test if the independent variable alters that difference. Consult an advanced statistics book for the details of this test.)

As usual, we test the null hypothesis, and to do that we examine the sampling distribution.

## The Sampling Distribution for the Independent-Samples *t*-Test

To understand the sampling distribution, let's say that we find a mean recall score of 20 in the no-hypnosis condition, and a mean of 23 in the hypnosis condition. Thus, changing from no hypnosis to hypnosis results in a *difference* in mean recall of 3 points. We always test $H_0$ by finding the probability of obtaining our results when no relationship is present, so here we will determine the probability of obtaining a *difference* of 3 between two $\overline{X}$s when they both actually represent the same μ.

> *REMEMBER* The independent-samples *t*-test determines the probability of obtaining our *difference* between $\overline{X}$s when $H_0$ is true.

Think of the sampling distribution as being created in the following way. We select *two* random samples from *one* raw score population, compute the means, and arbitrarily subtract one from the other. The result is the *difference between the means,* symbolized by $\overline{X}_1 - \overline{X}_2$. We do this an infinite number of times and plot a frequency distribution of these differences. We then have the **sampling distribution of differences between means,** which is the distribution of all possible differences between two means when samples are drawn from the raw score population described by $H_0$. You can envision this sampling distribution as in Figure 9.2.

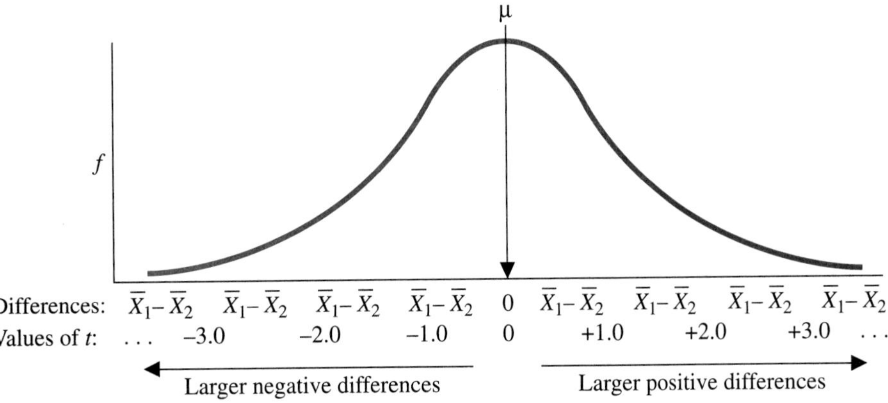


***FIGURE 9.2***

Sampling distribution of differences between means when $H_0$: $\mu_1 - \mu_2 = 0$

*The X axis has two labels: Each $\overline{X}_1 - \overline{X}_2$ symbolizes the difference between two sample means; when labeled as t, a larger ±t indicates a larger difference between means that is less likely when $H_0$ is true.*

The mean of the sampling distribution is stated in $H_0$, and here it is zero. This is because, most often, both sample means will equal the $\mu$ of the population of raw scores, so their difference will be zero. Sometimes, however, both sample means will not equal $\mu$ or each other. Depending on whether $\overline{X}_1$ or $\overline{X}_2$ is larger, the difference will be positive or negative. Small negative or positive differences occur frequently when $H_0$ is true, but larger ones do not.

To test $H_0$, we compute a new version of $t_{obt}$ to determine where on this sampling distribution the difference between our sample means lies. As in Figure 9.2, the larger the absolute value of $\pm t_{obt}$, the farther into the tail of the distribution our difference lies, and so the less likely it is that $H_0$ is true for our study.

## Computing the Independent-Samples *t*-Test

In the previous chapter you computed $t_{obt}$ by performing three steps: (1) estimating the variance of the raw score population, (2) computing the estimated standard error of the sampling distribution, and (3) computing $t_{obt}$. You perform similar steps in the two-sample $t$-test. Estimating the population variance, however, requires two steps.

**Step 1:** *Compute the mean and estimated population variance in each condition:* Calculate $\overline{X}_1$ and $\overline{X}_2$. Then calculate the estimated population variance for *each* condition.

However, we have some new symbols here. Previously, the estimated population variance was $s_X^2$. Now we'll use $s_1^2$ and $s_2^2$ for the respective conditions. Also, $N$ has stood for the number of scores in a sample, but actually $N$ is the number of scores in the *study* (with only one sample, $N$ was also the number of scores in the sample.) However, now we have two samples, so $n$ with a subscript stands for the number of scores in each sample. Thus, $n_1$ is the number of scores in Sample 1, and $n_2$ is the number of scores in Sample 2. $N$ is the total number of scores in the experiment, so adding the $n$s together equals $N$.

> ***REMEMBER*** $N$ stands for the total number of scores in an experiment; $n$ stands for the number of scores in a condition.

Using $n$, the formula for calculating $s_X^2$ in a condition is

$$s_X^2 = \frac{\Sigma X^2 - \frac{(\Sigma X)^2}{n}}{n - 1}$$

Each time, use the $X$s from only one condition, and $n$ is the number of scores in that condition.

**Step 2:** *Compute the pooled variance:* Each $s_X^2$ estimates the population variance, but it may contain sampling error. Therefore, to obtain the best estimate, we compute an average of the two. Each variance is "weighted" based on the size of $df$ in the sample. The weighted average of the sample variances is the **pooled variance,** and its symbol is $s^2_{pool}$.

*THE FORMULA FOR THE POOLED VARIANCE IS*

$$s^2_{\text{pool}} = \frac{(n_1 - 1)s^2_1 + (n_2 - 1)s^2_2}{(n_1 - 1) + (n_2 - 1)}$$

This says for Sample 1, determine $n_1 - 1$ and multiply this times the $s^2_1$ that you computed above. Likewise, for Sample 2, find $n_2 - 1$ and multiply it times $s^2_2$. Add the results together and divide by the sum of $(n_1 - 1) + (n_2 - 1)$.

For example, say that the hypnosis study produced the results shown in Table 9.2. The hypnosis condition produces $\overline{X}_1$, $s^2_1$, and $n_1$. The no-hypnosis condition produces $\overline{X}_2$, $s^2_2$, and $n_2$. Filling in the above formula, we have

$$s^2_{\text{pool}} = \frac{(17 - 1)9.0 + (15 - 1)7.5}{(17 - 1) + (15 - 1)}$$

After subtracting we have

$$s^2_{\text{pool}} = \frac{(16)9.0 + (14)7.5}{16 + 14}$$

In the numerator 16 times 9 is 144, and 14 times 7.5 is 105. In the denominator 16 plus 14 is 30, so

$$s^2_{\text{pool}} = \frac{144 + 105}{30} = \frac{249}{30} = 8.3$$

The $s^2_{\text{pool}}$ is our estimate of the variability in the raw score population that $H_0$ says we are representing. As in previous procedures, once we know how spread out the underlying raw score population is, we can determine how spread out the sampling distribution is by computing the standard error.

**Step 3:** *Compute the standard error of the difference:* The **standard error of the difference** is the "standard deviation" of the sampling distribution of differences between means (of the distribution back in Figure 9.2). The symbol for the standard error of the difference is $s_{\overline{X}-\overline{X}}$.

In previous chapters the formula for the standard error involved dividing by *N*. Now the formula is more complicated. First, dividing by *N* is the same as multiplying by the fraction 1/*N*. Second, we have two samples and two *n*s, so the result is

***TABLE 9.2***
Data from the Hypnosis Study

| | *Sample 1: Hypnosis* | *Sample 2: No Hypnosis* |
|---|---|---|
| Mean recall score | $\overline{X}_1 = 23$ | $\overline{X}_2 = 20$ |
| Number of participants | $n_1 = 17$ | $n_2 = 15$ |
| Estimated variance | $s^2_1 = 9.0$ | $s^2_2 = 7.5$ |

*THE FORMULA FOR THE STANDARD ERROR OF THE DIFFERENCE IS*

$$s_{\bar{X}_1-\bar{X}_2} = \sqrt{(s^2_{\text{pool}})\left(\frac{1}{n_1} + \frac{1}{n_2}\right)}$$

To compute $s_{\bar{X}_1-\bar{X}_2}$, first reduce the fractions $1/n_1$ and $1/n_2$ to decimals. Then add them together. Then multiply the sum times $s^2_{\text{pool}}$. Then find the square root.

For the hypnosis study, $s^2_{\text{pool}}$ is 8.3, $n_1$ is 17, and $n_2$ is 15. Filling in the formula gives

$$s_{\bar{X}_1-\bar{X}_2} = \sqrt{8.3\left(\frac{1}{17} + \frac{1}{15}\right)}$$

First, 1/17 is .059 and 1/15 is .067, so

$$s_{\bar{X}_1-\bar{X}_2} = \sqrt{8.3(.059 + .067)}$$

After adding

$$s_{\bar{X}_1-\bar{X}_2} = \sqrt{8.3(.126)} = \sqrt{1.046} = 1.023$$

**Step 4:** *Compute* $t_{obt}$: In previous chapters we've calculated how far the result of the study ($\bar{X}$) was from the mean of the $H_0$ sampling distribution ($\mu$), measured in standard error units. In general this formula is

$$t_{\text{obt}} = \frac{(\text{Result of the study}) - (\text{Mean of } H_0 \text{ sampling distribution})}{\text{Standard error}}$$

Now the "result of the study" is the *difference* between the two sample means. So in place of "result of the study" we put "$(\bar{X}_1 - \bar{X}_2)$." The mean of the $H_0$ sampling distribution is the *difference* between the two $\mu$s described by $H_0$. Thus, we replace "mean of $H_0$ sampling distribution" with "$(\mu_1 - \mu_2)$." Finally, we replace "standard error" with "$s_{\bar{X}_1-\bar{X}_2}$." All together, we have

*THE FORMULA FOR THE INDEPENDENT-SAMPLES t-TEST IS*

$$t_{\text{obt}} = \frac{(\bar{X}_1 - \bar{X}_2) - (\mu_1 - \mu_2)}{s_{\bar{X}_1-\bar{X}_2}}$$

Here, $\bar{X}_1$ and $\bar{X}_2$ are the sample means, $s_{\bar{X}_1-\bar{X}_2}$ is computed as shown previously, and the value of $\mu_1 - \mu_2$ is the difference specified by the null hypothesis. We write $H_0$ as $\mu_1 - \mu_2 = 0$ so that it indicates the value of $\mu_1 - \mu_2$ to put into this formula. (This value is always 0 unless your $H_0$ says that $\mu_1 - \mu_2$ equals some other number.) Then the formula measures how far our difference between $\bar{X}$s is from the zero difference between the $\mu$s that $H_0$ says we are representing, measured in standard error units.

For the hypnosis study, our sample means were 23 and 20, the difference between $\mu_1$ and $\mu_2$ is 0, and $s_{\bar{X}_1-\bar{X}_2}$ is 1.023. Putting these values into the above formula gives

$$t_{obt} = \frac{(23 - 20) - 0}{1.023}$$

After subtracting the means

$$t_{obt} = \frac{(+3) - 0}{1.023} = \frac{+3}{1.023} = +2.93$$

Our $t_{obt}$ is +2.93. Thus, our difference of +3 is located at something like a $z$-score of +2.93 on the sampling distribution of differences when $H_0$ is true and both samples represent the same population.

## A QUICK REVIEW

To compute the independent-samples $t_{obt}$:

- Compute $\bar{X}_1$, $s_1^2$, and $n_1$; $\bar{X}_2$, $s_2^2$, and $n_2$.
- Then compute the pooled variance ($s^2_{pool}$).
- Then compute the standard error of the difference ($s_{\bar{X}_1-\bar{X}_2}$).
- Then compute $t_{obt}$.

### More Examples

An independent-samples study produced the following data.

1. $\bar{X}_1 = 27$ $s_1^2 = 36$, $n_1 = 11$, $\bar{X}_2 = 21$, $s_2^2 = 33$, $n_2 = 11$

2. $$s^2_{pool} = \frac{(n_1 - 1)s_1^2 + (n_2 - 1)s_2^2}{(n_1 - 1) + (n_2 - 1)} = \frac{(10)36 + (10)33}{10 + 10} = 34.5$$

3. $$s_{\bar{X}_1-\bar{X}_2} = \sqrt{s^2_{pool}\left(\frac{1}{n_1} + \frac{1}{n_2}\right)} = \sqrt{34.5\left(\frac{1}{11} + \frac{1}{11}\right)} = 2.506$$

4. $$t_{obt} = \frac{(\bar{X}_1 - \bar{X}_2) - (\mu_1 - \mu_2)}{s_{\bar{X}-\bar{X}}} = \frac{(27 - 21) - 0}{2.506} = +2.394$$

### For Practice:

After testing two conditions, $\bar{X}_1 = 33$, $s_1^2 = 16$, $n_1 = 21$, $\bar{X}_2 = 27$, $s_2^2 = 13$, $n_2 = 21$.

1. Compute the pooled variance ($s^2_{pool}$).
2. Compute the standard error of the difference ($s_{\bar{X}_1-\bar{X}_2}$).
3. Compute $t_{obt}$.

**Answers**

1. $$s^2_{pool} = \frac{(20)16 + (20)13}{20 + 20} = 14.5$$

2. $$s_{\bar{X}_1-\bar{X}_2} = \sqrt{14.5\left(\frac{1}{21} + \frac{1}{21}\right)} = 1.18$$

3. $$t_{obt} = \frac{(33 - 27) - 0}{1.18} = +5.08$$

## Interpreting the Independent-Samples t-Test

To determine if $t_{obt}$ is significant, compare it to $t_{crit}$ from the $t$-tables (Table 2 in Appendix B). As usual, obtain $t_{crit}$ using degrees of freedom, but with two samples, the $df$ are computed differently.

> *THE DEGREES OF FREEDOM IN THE INDEPENDENT-SAMPLES* t*-TEST EQUAL*
>
> $df = (n_1 - 1) + (n_2 - 1)$, where each $n$ is the number of scores in a condition.

For the hypnosis study, $n_1 = 17$ and $n_2 = 15$, so $df$ equals $(17 - 1) + (15 - 1)$, which is 30. With alpha at .05, the two-tailed $t_{crit}$ is $\pm 2.042$.

Figure 9.3 shows the completed sampling distribution. $H_0$ says that the difference between our sample means is merely a poor representation of no difference in the population. But, the sampling distribution shows that you'll hardly ever get a difference of +3 when your samples represent no difference in the population. Therefore, because $t_{obt}$ is in the region of rejection, we reject $H_0$ and conclude that our difference of +3 is unlikely to be representing zero difference in the population. In other words, the difference between our means is significantly different from zero.

We now accept the alternative hypothesis that our data represent a difference between μs that is *not* zero. This is the same as saying that the two means differ significantly *from each other*. Therefore, we conclude that increasing the amount of hypnosis leads to significantly higher recall scores.

If $t_{obt}$ was not beyond $t_{crit}$, we would not reject $H_0$, and we would have no evidence of a relationship between hypnosis and recall.

Because we did find a significant result, we describe the relationship. From the sample means, we expect that if we tested the entire population in this experiment, we would find the μ for no hypnosis at around 20 and the μ for hypnosis at around 23. To more precisely describe these μs, we could compute a *confidence interval* for each μ, using the formula in the previous chapter and the data from one condition at a time. Also, another less common confidence interval that can be used here is the *confidence interval for the difference between two μs*. It describes the differences between the population μs that the difference between our sample means represents. (The computations of this confidence interval are presented in Appendix A.1.)

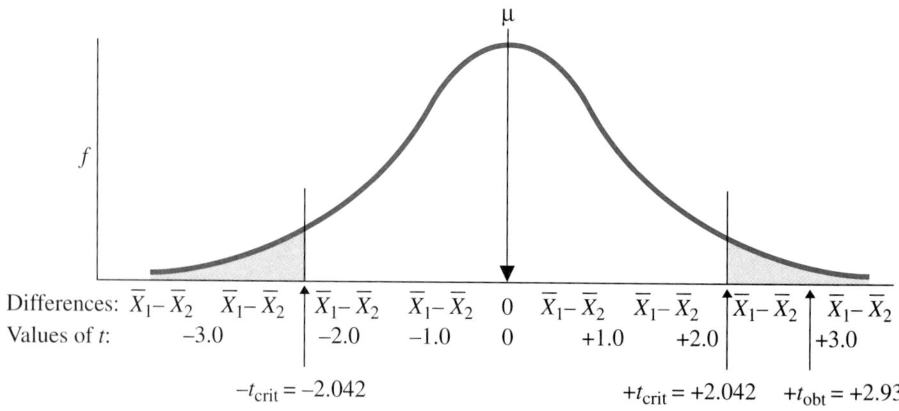


**FIGURE 9.3**
$H_0$ sampling distribution of differences between means when $\mu_1 - \mu_2 = 0$
*The $t_{obt}$ shows the location of a difference of +3.0*

### Performing One-Tailed Tests on Independent Samples

We could have conducted the hypnosis study using a one-tailed test if, for example, we predicted a positive relationship such that the greater the degree of hypnosis, the higher the recall scores. Everything discussed above applies here, but to prevent confusion, use more meaningful subscripts than 1 and 2. For example, use the subscript h for hypnosis and n for no-hypnosis. Then follow these steps:

1. Decide which $\overline{X}$ and corresponding $\mu$ is expected to be larger. (We think the $\mu$ for hypnosis ($\mu_h$) is larger.)
2. Arbitrarily decide which condition to subtract from the other. (We'll subtract no-hypnosis *from* hypnosis.)
3. Decide whether the difference will be positive or negative. (Subtracting the smaller $\mu_n$ from the larger $\mu_h$ should produce a positive difference, *greater* than zero.)
4. Create $H_a$ and $H_0$ to match this prediction. (Our $H_a$ is that $\mu_h - \mu_n > 0$; $H_0$ is that $\mu_h - \mu_n \leq 0$.)
5. Locate the region of rejection based on your predictions and subtraction. (We expect a positive difference which is in the right-hand tail of the sampling distribution, so $t_{crit}$ is positive.)
6. Complete the *t*-test as above. Subtract the $\overline{X}$s in the same way the $\mu$s are subtracted! (We used $\mu_h - \mu_n$, so we'd compute $\overline{X}_h - \overline{X}_n$.)

Confusion arises because, while *still predicting a larger* $\mu_h$, we could have reversed $H_a$, saying $\mu_n - \mu_h < 0$. Subtracting the larger $\mu_h$ from the smaller $\mu_n$ should produce a difference less than zero, so now the region of rejection is in the left-hand tail, and $t_{crit}$ is negative.

## SUMMARY OF THE INDEPENDENT-SAMPLES *t*-TEST

After checking that as a study meets the assumptions, the independent-samples *t*-test involves the following.

1. *Create either the two-tailed or one-tailed $H_0$ and $H_a$.*
2. *Compute $t_{obt}$ by following these four steps:*
   a. Compute $\overline{X}_1$, $s_1^2$, and $n_1$; $\overline{X}_2$, $s_2^2$, and $n_2$.
   b. Compute the pooled variance ($s^2_{pool}$).
   c. Compute the standard error of the difference ($s_{\overline{X}-\overline{X}}$).
   d. Compute $t_{obt}$.
3. *Examine the sampling distribution and, using $df = (n_1 - 1) + (n_2 - 1)$, find $t_{crit}$ in the t-tables.*
4. *Compare $t_{obt}$ to $t_{crit}$:* If $t_{obt}$ is beyond $t_{crit}$, the results are significant; describe the relationship. If $t_{obt}$ is not beyond $t_{crit}$, the results are not significant; make no conclusion about the relationship.

## A QUICK REVIEW

- Perform the independent-samples *t*-test in experiments that test two independent conditions.

### MORE EXAMPLES

We perform a two-tailed experiment with two samples.

1. It is two-tailed, so $H_0$: $\mu_1 - \mu_2 = 0$, $H_a$: $\mu_1 - \mu_2 \neq 0$.
2. Say that the sample data produce $\overline{X}_1 = 24$, $s_1^2 = 9$, $n_1 = 14$, $\overline{X}_2 = 21$, $s_2^2 = 9.4$, $n_2 = 16$. Then

$$s^2_{\text{pool}} = \frac{(n_1 - 1)s_1^2 + (n_2 - 1)s_2^2}{(n_1 - 1) + (n_2 - 1)}$$

$$= \frac{(13)9 + (15)9.4}{13 + 15} = 9.214$$

$$s_{\overline{X}-\overline{X}} = \sqrt{s^2_{\text{pool}}\left(\frac{1}{n_1} + \frac{1}{n_2}\right)}$$

$$= \sqrt{9.214\left(\frac{1}{14} + \frac{1}{16}\right)} = 1.111$$

$$t_{\text{obt}} = \frac{(\overline{X}_1 - \overline{X}_2) - (\mu_1 - \mu_2)}{s_{\overline{X}-\overline{X}}} = \frac{(24 - 21) - 0}{1.111}$$

$$= +2.70$$

3. With $\alpha = .05$ and $df = (n_1 - 1) + (n_2 - 1) = 28$, $t_{\text{crit}} = \pm 2.048$. The sampling distribution is below.

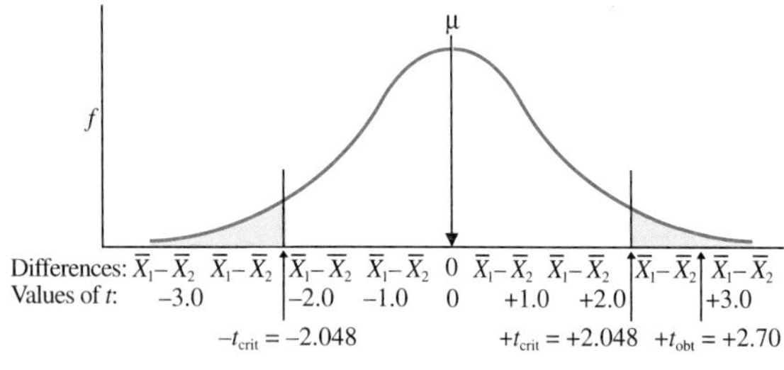


4. The $t_{\text{obt}}$ is beyond $t_{\text{crit}}$ and is significant: We expect $\mu_1$ to be around 24 and $\mu_2$ to be around 21.

### *For Practice:*

To test whether "cramming" for an exam is beneficial or harmful to grades, Condition 1 crams for a pretend exam but Condition 2 does not. Each $n = 31$, the cramming $\overline{X}$ is 43 ($s^2_X = 64$), and the no-cramming $\overline{X}$ is 48 ($s^2_X = 83.6$).

1. What are $H_0$ and $H_a$?
2. Compute $t_{\text{obt}}$.
3. What do you conclude about this relationship?
4. If we predicted cramming would *lower* grades, what are $H_0$ and $H_a$ if we subtract cramming from no cramming?
5. Would the $t_{\text{crit}}$ be positive or negative?

**Answers**

1. $H_0$: $\mu_1 - \mu_2 = 0$, $H_a$: $\mu_1 - \mu_2 \neq 0$.
2. $s^2_{\text{pool}} = (1920 = 2508)/60 = 73.8$.
   $s_{\overline{X}-\overline{X}} = \sqrt{73.8(.064)} = 2.173$.
   $t_{\text{obt}} = (43 - 48)/2.173 = -2.30$.
3. With $\alpha = .05$ and $df = 60$, $t_{\text{crit}} = \pm 2.00$. $t_{\text{obt}}$ is significant: $\mu$ when cramming is around 43; $\mu$ when not cramming is around 48.
4. $H_a$: $\mu_{nc} - \mu_c > 0$; $H_0$: $\mu_{nc} - \mu_c \leq 0$.
5. Positive.

## THE RELATED-SAMPLES *t*-TEST

Now we will discuss the other version of the two-sample *t*-test. The **related-samples *t*-test** is the parametric procedure used with two related samples. **Related samples** occur when we pair each score in one sample with a particular score in the other sample. Researchers create related samples to have more equivalent and thus comparable samples. The two types of research designs that produce related samples are *matched-samples designs* and *repeated-measures designs.*

In a **matched-samples design** the researcher matches each participant in one condition with a particular participant in the other condition. For example, say we wish to match participants on the variable of their height. We would select pairs of people who are the same height, and assign a member of the pair to each condition. Thus, if two people are six feet tall, one is assigned to one condition and one to the other condition. Likewise, a four-foot person in one condition is matched with a four-footer in the other condition, and so on. Then, overall the conditions are comparable in height so we'd proceed with the experiment. In the same way, we might match participants using their age or physical ability, or we might use naturally occurring pairs, such as roommates or identical twins.

The other way to create related samples is with a **repeated-measures design,** in which each participant is tested under all conditions of the independent variable. That is, first participants are tested under Condition 1 and then the *same* participants are tested under Condition 2. Although we have one sample of participants, we have two samples of scores.

Matched-groups and repeated-measures designs are analyzed in the same way. (Such related samples are also called *dependent samples.*) Except for requiring related samples, the assumptions of the related-samples $t$-test are the same as those for the independent-samples $t$-test: (1) The dependent variable involves an interval or ratio scale, (2) scores are normally distributed, and (3) the populations being represented have homogeneous variance. Because related samples form pairs of scores, the $n$ in the two samples must be equal.

## The Logic of the Related-Samples $t$-Test

Let's say that we have a new therapy to test on spider-phobics—people who are overly frightened by spiders. From the local phobia club we randomly select the unpowerful $N$ of five spider-phobics, and test our therapy using repeated measures of two conditions: before therapy and after therapy. Before therapy we measure each person's fear response to a picture of a spider, measuring heart rate, perspiration, etc., and compute a "fear" score between 0 (no fear) and 20 (holy terror!). After the therapy we again measure the person's fear response to the picture. (A before-and-after, or *pretest/posttest,* design such as this always uses the related-samples $t$-test.)

In Table 9.3 the two columns to the left of the equals signs show the fear scores from the two conditions. First, compute the mean of each condition. Before therapy the mean fear score is 14.80, and after therapy the mean is 11.20. It looks as if therapy reduces fear scores by an average of $14.80 - 11.20 = 3.6$ points. But, conversely, maybe therapy does nothing; maybe this difference reflects sampling error from the one population of fear scores we'd have with or without therapy. To test these hypotheses, we first transform the data. Then we perform the test using the transformed scores.

As in the right side of Table 9.3 we transform the data by first finding the difference between the two fear scores for each participant. This *difference score* is symbolized by

***TABLE 9.3***

Finding the Difference Scores in the Phobia Study

*Each $D$ = Before − After*

| *Participant* | *Before Therapy* | − | *After Therapy* | = | D | $D^2$ |
|---|---|---|---|---|---|---|
| 1 (Foofy) | 11 | − | 8 | = | +3 | 9 |
| 2 (Biff) | 16 | − | 11 | = | +5 | 25 |
| 3 (Millie) | 20 | − | 15 | = | +5 | 25 |
| 4 (Althea) | 17 | − | 11 | = | +6 | 36 |
| 5 (Slug) | 10 | − | 11 | = | −1 | 1 |
| | $\overline{X} = 14.80$ | | $\overline{X} = 11.20$ | | $\Sigma D = +18$ | $\Sigma D^2 = 96$ |
| $N = 5$ | | | | | $\overline{D} = +3.6$ | |

$D$. Here, we arbitrarily subtracted after-therapy from before-therapy. You could subtract in the reverse order, but subtract all scores in the same way. If this were a matched-samples design, we'd subtract the scores in each pair of matched participants.

Next, compute the *mean difference,* symbolized as $\overline{D}$. Add the positive and negative differences to find the sum of the differences, symbolized by $\Sigma D$. Then divide by $N$, the number of difference scores. In Table 9.3 $\overline{D}$ equals 18/5, which is +3.6: The before scores were, on average, 3.6 points higher than the after scores. (As in the far right-hand column of Table 9.3, later we'll need to square each difference and then find the sum, finding $\Sigma D^2$.)

Finally, here's a surprise: We have one sample mean ($\overline{D}$) from one random sample of (difference) scores. As in the previous chapter, with one sample we perform the one-sample *t*-test! The fact that we have difference scores is irrelevant, so we create the statistical hypotheses and test them in virtually the same way that we did with the one-sample *t*-test.

> ***REMEMBER*** The *related-samples* t-*test* is performed by applying the one-sample *t*-test to the difference scores.

## Statistical Hypotheses for the Related-Samples *t*-Test

Our sample of difference scores represents the population of difference scores that would result if we could measure the population's fear scores under each condition and then subtract the scores in one population from the corresponding scores in the other population. The population of difference scores has a $\mu$ that we identify as $\mu_D$. To create the statistical hypotheses, we determine the predicted values of $\mu_D$ in $H_0$ and $H_a$.

In reality we expect the therapy to reduce fear scores, but for illustration let's first perform a two-tailed test. $H_0$ always says no relationship is present, so it says the population of before-scores is the same as the population of after-scores. However, when we subtract them as we did in the sample, not every $D$ will equal zero because, due to random physiological or psychological fluctuations, some participants would not score identically when tested before and after. Therefore, we would have a *population* of different $D$s, as shown on the left of Figure 9.4.

**FIGURE 9.4**
Population of difference scores described by $H_0$ and the resulting sampling distribution of mean differences

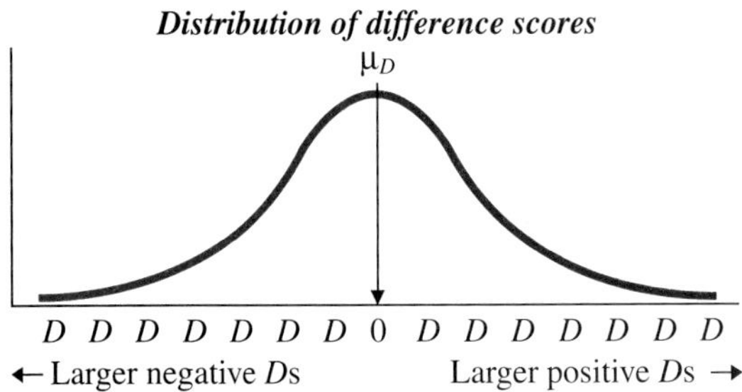


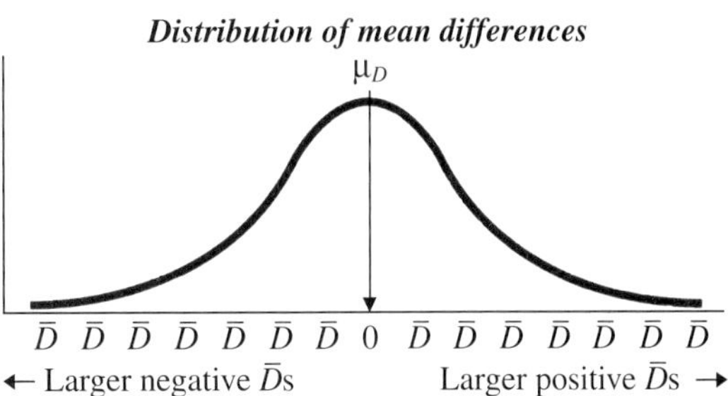


On average, the positive and negative differences should cancel out to produce a $\mu_D = 0$. This is the population that $H_0$ says our sample of *D*s represents, and that our $\bar{D}$ represents this $\mu_D$. Therefore, $H_0$: $\mu_D = 0$. For the alternative hypothesis, if the therapy alters fear scores in the population, then either the before-scores or the after-scores will be higher. Then, after subtracting them, the population of *D*s will tend to contain only positive or only negative scores. Therefore, $\mu_D$ will be a positive or negative number and not zero. Therefore, $H_a$: $\mu_D \neq 0$.

We test $H_0$ by examining the sampling distribution, which here is the *sampling distribution of mean differences*. Shown on the right side of Figure 9.4, it is as if we infinitely sampled the population of *D*s on the left of the figure that $H_0$ says our sample represents. It shows the different values of $\bar{D}$ that occur through sampling error when $H_0$ is true. For the phobia study it essentially shows all values of $\bar{D}$ we might get simply by chance when the therapy does not work. The $\bar{D}$s that are farther into the tails of the distribution are less likely to occur if $H_0$ was true and the therapy did not work. We test $H_0$ by locating our $\bar{D}$ on this sampling distribution by computing $t_{obt}$.

Notice that the hypotheses $H_0$: $\mu_D = 0$ and $H_a$: $\mu_D \neq 0$ and the above sampling distribution are appropriate for the two-tailed test for *any* independent variable when you are testing whether the data represent *zero difference* between your conditions in the population. This is the most common approach and the one we'll discuss. (You can also test whether your independent variable alters an existing, nonzero difference. Consult an advanced statistics book for the details.)

## Computing the Related-Samples *t*-Test

Computing $t_{obt}$ here is identical to computing the one-sample *t*-test discussed in Chapter 8—only the symbols have been changed from *X* to *D*. There, we first computed the estimated population variance ($s_X^2$), then the standard error of the mean ($s_{\bar{X}}$), and then $t_{obt}$. We perform the same three steps here.

**Step 1:** Find $s_D^2$, which is the estimated variance of the population of difference scores. Replacing the *X*s with *D*s in the formula for variance gives

*THE FORMULA FOR $s_D^2$ IS*

$$s_D^2 = \frac{\Sigma D^2 - \frac{(\Sigma D)^2}{N}}{N - 1}$$

Using the phobia data back in Table 9.3, we have

$$s_D^2 = \frac{\Sigma D^2 - \frac{(\Sigma D)^2}{N}}{N - 1} = \frac{96 - \frac{(18)^2}{5}}{4} = 7.8$$

Thus, it is as if for our example the distribution of *D*s on the left-hand side back in Figure 9.4 has a $s_D^2$ of 7.8. As usual, once we know the variability of the raw scores, we determine how spread out the sampling distribution is.

**Step 2:** Compute the **standard error of the mean difference,** which is the "standard deviation" of the sampling distribution of $\overline{D}$. This is symbolized by $s_{\overline{D}}$. Thus, $s_{\overline{D}}$ indicates how spread out the means are back in the sampling distribution on the right-hand side of Figure 9.4.

*THE FORMULA FOR THE STANDARD ERROR OF THE MEAN DIFFERENCE IS*

$$s_{\overline{D}} = \sqrt{\frac{s_D^2}{N}}$$

For the phobia study $s_D^2 = 7.8$, and $N = 5$, so

$$s_{\overline{D}} = \sqrt{\frac{s_D^2}{N}} = \sqrt{\frac{7.8}{5}} = \sqrt{1.56} = 1.249$$

**Step 3:** Find $t_{obt}$.

*THE FORMULA FOR THE RELATED-SAMPLES t-TEST IS*

$$t_{obt} = \frac{\overline{D} - \mu_D}{s_{\overline{D}}}$$

For the phobia study $\overline{D}$ is +3.6, $s_{\overline{D}}$ is 1.249, and $\mu_D$ equals 0. In fact, $\mu_D$ is always 0 unless your $H_0$ says that $\mu_D$ equals some other number. Then we are measuring how far our $\overline{D}$ is from the $\mu_D$ of zero that $H_0$ says we are representing (which is the $\mu$ of the sampling distribution), measured in standard error units. So

$$t_{obt} = \frac{\bar{D} - \mu_D}{s_{\bar{D}}} = \frac{+3.6 - 0}{1.249} = +2.88$$

Our sample is located at a $t_{obt}$ of $+2.88$ on the sampling distribution of $\bar{D}$.

## Interpreting the Related-Samples *t*-Test

Interpret $t_{obt}$ by comparing it to $t_{crit}$ from the *t*-tables in Appendix B.

> *THE DEGREES OF FREEDOM IN THE RELATED-SAMPLES t-TEST EQUAL*
>
> $df = N - 1$, where $N$ is the number of difference scores.

For the phobia study, with $\alpha = .05$ and $df = 4$, the $t_{crit}$ is $\pm 2.776$. The completed sampling distribution is shown in Figure 9.5. The $t_{obt}$ is in the region of rejection, so our $\bar{D}$ of $+3.6$ is unlikely to be representing the population of *D*s where $\mu_D = 0$. Therefore, the results are significant: We reject $H_0$ and accept $H_a$, concluding that the sample represents a $\mu_D$ around $+3.6$.

Now we work backwards to our original before- and after-therapy fear scores. One way that a $\mu_D$ around $+3.6$ would occur is if the population of before-scores had a $\mu$ of 14.80 and the population of after-scores had a $\mu$ of 11.20. These $\mu$s are based on our original sample means of 14.80 and 11.20, respectively. Because the mean difference of $+3.6$ is significant, the difference between these means is also significant. Therefore, we conclude that the sample data represent a relationship in the population such that fear scores go from a $\mu$ around 14.80 before therapy to a $\mu$ around 11.20 after therapy.

Instead of merely saying that $\mu$ is *around* 14.80 or 11.20, previously we've been more precise by computing a confidence interval for $\mu$. However, that procedure is appropriate only for *independent* samples. The confidence interval that is appropriate for related samples is called the *confidence interval for* $\mu_D$: It describes the values of $\mu_D$ that our $\bar{D}$ is likely to represent. (The computations for this confidence interval are presented in Appendix A.1.)

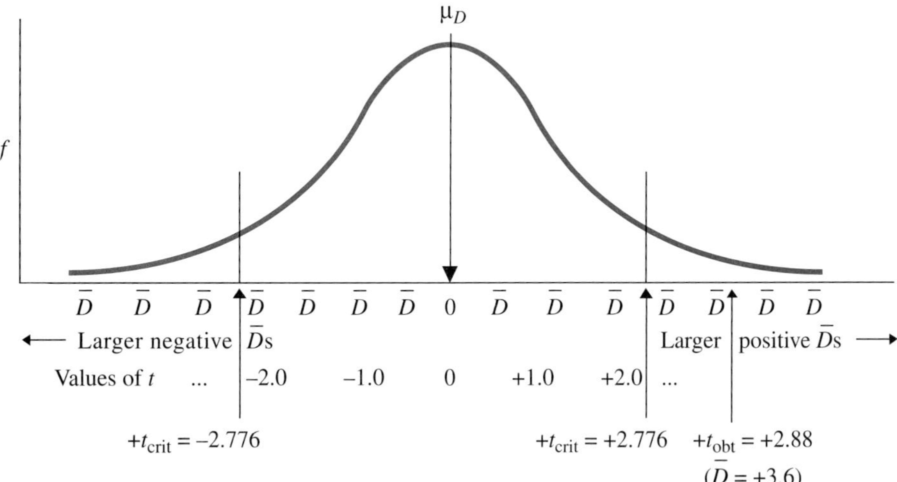


***FIGURE 9.5***
Two-tailed sampling distribution of $\bar{D}$s when $\mu_D = 0$

### One-Tailed Hypotheses with the Related-Samples *t*-Test

The phobia study would have involved a one-tailed test if, for example, we had predicted that fear scores would be lower after therapy. For $H_0$ and $H_a$, first decide which condition to subtract from which. We subtracted *after* from *before,* so lower after-scores would produce positive differences, so $\overline{D}$ should be positive, representing a positive $\mu_D$. Therefore, $H_a$: $\mu_D > 0$. Then $H_0$: $\mu_D \leq 0$.

As usual, we examine the sampling distribution that occurs when $\mu_D = 0$ (as we did in the two-tailed test). Obtain the one-tailed $t_{crit}$ from Table 2 in Appendix B. We predict a positive $\overline{D}$, so the region of rejection is in the upper tail and $t_{crit}$ is positive.

Had we predicted *higher* after-scores, then (subtracting as above) $\overline{D}$ should be negative, representing a negative $\mu_D$, so $H_a$: $\mu_D < 0$, and $H_0$: $\mu_D \geq 0$. Now the region of rejection is in the lower tail and $t_{crit}$ is negative.

## SUMMARY OF THE RELATED-SAMPLES *t*-TEST

After checking that the design is matched-samples or repeated-measures and meets the assumptions, the related-samples *t*-test involves the following.

1. *Create either the two-tailed or one-tailed $H_0$ and $H_a$.*
2. *Compute $t_{obt}$:*
   a. Compute the *difference score* for each pair of scores.
   b. Compute $\overline{D}$ and $s_D^2$.
   c. Compute $s_{\overline{D}}$.
   d. Compute $t_{obt}$.
3. *Create the sampling distribution and using $df = N - 1$, find $t_{crit}$ in the t-tables.*
4. *Compare $t_{obt}$ to $t_{crit}$:* If $t_{obt}$ is beyond $t_{crit}$, the results are significant; describe the populations of raw scores and interpret the relationship. If $t_{obt}$ is not beyond $t_{crit}$, the results are not significant; make no conclusion about the relationship.

### *A QUICK REVIEW*

- With a matched-groups or repeated-measures design, perform the related-samples *t*-test.
- Find the difference between each pair of raw scores and then perform the one-sample *t*-test on the difference scores.

#### More Examples

In a two-tailed study we compare husband-and-wife pairs.

1. $H_0$: $\mu_D = 0$ and $H_a$: $\mu_D \neq 0$.
2. Subtracting wife − husband produces the following difference scores.

| *Wife* | *Husband* | **D** |
|---|---|---|
| 4 | 6 | −2 |
| 5 | 8 | −3 |
| 3 | 9 | −6 |
| 5 | 8 | −3 |
| $\overline{X} = 4.25$ | $\overline{X} = 7.75$ | $\overline{D} = -3.5$ |

$\overline{D} = -14/4 = -3.5.$

$$s_D^2 = \frac{\Sigma D^2 - \frac{(\Sigma D)^2}{N}}{N - 1} = \frac{58 - \frac{(-14)^2}{4}}{3} = 3.0$$

3. $s_{\bar{D}} = \sqrt{\frac{s_D^2}{N}} = \sqrt{3/4} = .866$

4. $t_{obt} = \frac{\bar{D} - \mu_D}{s_{\bar{D}}} = (-3.5 - 0)/.866 = -4.04.$

With $\alpha = .05$ the sampling distribution is like that back in Figure 9.5, except with $df = 3$, the two-tailed $t_{crit}$ is $\pm 3.182$. The $t_{obt}$ of $-4.04$ is beyond $-3.182$. Therefore, in the population, for wives we expect $\mu$ is around 4.25, and for husbands we expect $\mu$ is around 7.75.

### *For Practice:*

In a two-tailed study we test the same participants in both Conditions A and B, with these data:

| A | B |
|---|---|
| 8 | 7 |
| 10 | 5 |
| 9 | 6 |
| 8 | 5 |
| 11 | 6 |

1. This way of producing related samples is called ____.
2. What are $H_0$ and $H_a$?
3. Subtracting A − B, perform the $t$-test.
4. What $\mu$s do you expect in the raw score populations?
5. Subtracting A − B, what are $H_0$ and $H_a$ if we predicted that B would lower scores?

**Answers**

1. repeated-measures
2. $H_0$: $\mu_D = 0$, $H_a$: $\mu_D \neq 0$.
3. $\bar{D} = 17/5 = +3.4$; $s_D^2 = 2.8$: $s_{\bar{D}} = \sqrt{2.80/5}$ $= .748$; $t_{obt} = (3.4 - 0)/.748 = +4.55$. With $\alpha = .05$, $t_{crit} = \pm 2.776$ and $t_{obt}$ is significant.
4. With A, $\mu = 9.2$ and with B, $\mu = 5.8$.
5. $H_0$: $\mu_D \leq 0$, $H_a$: $\mu_D > 0$.

## STATISTICS IN THE RESEARCH LITERATURE: REPORTING A TWO-SAMPLE STUDY

Report the results of an independent- or related-samples $t$-test using the same format used previously. For example, in our hypnosis study, the $t_{obt}$ of $+2.93$ was significant with 30 $df$, so we report $t(30) = +2.93$, $p < .05$. As usual, $df$ is in parentheses, and because $\alpha = .05$, the probability is less than .05 that we've made a Type I error.

In addition, as in Chapter 3, we report the mean and standard deviation from each condition. Also, with two or more conditions, researchers often include graphs of their results. Recall that we graph the results of an experiment by plotting the mean of each condition on the $Y$ axis and the conditions of the independent variable on the $X$ axis. *Note:* In a related-samples study, report the means and standard deviations of the original raw scores—not the $D$s—and graph these means.

## A WORD ABOUT EFFECT SIZE: THE PROPORTION OF VARIANCE ACCOUNTED FOR

An important statistic for describing a significant relationship is called a *measure of effect size.* The "effect" is the influence of the independent variable on dependent scores. **Effect size** indicates the amount of influence that changing the conditions of the independent variable had on dependent scores. Thus, for example, the extent to which changing the amount of hypnosis produced differences in recall scores is the effect size of hypnosis.

The larger the effect size, the larger is the independent variable's impact, so effect size indicates how important the independent variable is in determining participants' dependent scores. Remember that *significant* does not mean important, only that the sample relationship is unlikely to reflect sampling error. Although a relationship must be significant to be potentially important, *it can be significant and still be unimportant.* Measures of effect size indicate which independent variables have the greatest effect on behavior and are thus most important for understanding it.

> ***REMEMBER*** The larger the *effect size,* the larger is the influence and importance of the independent variable in determining dependent scores.

A common way to measure effect size is to measure the "proportion of variance accounted for." Recall that variance reflects the differences in scores. In an experiment, the **proportion of variance accounted for** is the proportion of all differences in dependent scores that occur with, and seem to be caused by, changing the conditions of the independent variable. The proportion can be near 0, indicating that few of the differences in scores seem to be produced by changing the conditions (with many different scores occurring within the same condition). Or it may be as high as 1.0, indicating that 100% of the differences in scores occur *only* with, and presumably are produced by, changing the independent variable.

We compute the proportion of variance accounted for by squaring a *correlation coefficient,* which is a statistic for summarizing a relationship that we discuss in the next chapter. In the two-sample experiment we compute the squared **point-biserial correlation coefficient,** and its symbol is $r^2_{pb}$.

*THE FORMULA FOR COMPUTING EFFECT SIZE IN A TWO-SAMPLE EXPERIMENT IS*

$$r^2_{pb} = \frac{(t_{obt})^2}{(t_{obt})^2 + df}$$

This can be used with either the independent-samples or related-samples $t$-test. In the numerator square $t_{obt}$. In the denominator add $(t_{obt})^2$ to the $df$ from the study. For independent samples $df = (n_1 - 1) + (n_2 - 1)$, but for related samples $df = N - 1$.

In our hypnosis study $t_{obt} = +2.94$ with $df = 30$. So

$$r^2_{pb} = \frac{(t_{obt})^2}{(t_{obt})^2 + df} = \frac{(2.93)^2}{(2.93)^2 + 30} = \frac{8.585}{38.585} = .22$$

Thus, .22 or 22% of the differences in our recall scores are accounted for by changing our hypnosis conditions. This means that of all differences among recall scores, 22% of them consistently occured when we changed the amount of hypnosis, and 78% of the differences were not associated with changing the conditions. We assume that everything has a cause, so other variables must be producing these unaccounted for differences (perhaps their IQ, memory ability, or motivation played a role). Therefore, we would conclude that amount of hypnosis is only one of a number of variables that influence memory here, and thus, it is only somewhat important in determining recall scores.

On the other hand, in the phobia study $t_{\text{obt}} = +2.88$ and $df = 4$, so

$$r^2_{\text{pb}} = \frac{(t_{\text{obt}})^2}{(t_{\text{obt}})^2 + df} = \frac{(2.88)^2}{(2.88)^2 + 4} = .68$$

This indicates that of all the differences in our fear scores, 68% of them are associated with before- or after-therapy. Therefore, whether or not phobics have received our therapy has a rather large effect on their fear score.

Further, we use effect size to compare the importance of different independent variables: The phobia therapy accounts for 68% of the variance in fear scores, but the hypnosis variable accounts for only 22% of the variance in recall scores. Therefore, in their respective relationships, the therapy variable more consistently changed dependent scores, so it has a larger effect size and is a more important variable.

> **REMEMBER** *Effect size* as measured by the *proportion of variance accounted for* indicates how important a role an independent variable plays in determining dependent scores.

## CHAPTER SUMMARY

1. Two samples are *independent* when participants are randomly selected for a sample without regard to who is selected for the other sample.
2. The independent-samples $t$-test requires (a) independent samples, (b) normally distributed interval or ratio scores, and (c) homogeneous variance.
3. *Homogeneity of variance* means that the $\sigma^2_X$ in the populations being represented are equal.
4. A significant $t_{\text{obt}}$ from the independent-samples $t$-test indicates that the difference between $\overline{X}_1$ and $\overline{X}_2$ is unlikely to represent the difference between $\mu_1$ and $\mu_2$ described by $H_0$.
5. Two samples are *related* when each participant in one condition is *matched* with someone in the other condition, or when we have *repeated measures* of the same participants under both conditions.
6. The *related-samples* t*-test* is a one-sample $t$-test performed on the difference scores. A significant $t_{\text{obt}}$ indicates that the mean of the difference scores ($\overline{D}$) is significantly different from the $\mu_D$ described by $H_0$. Therefore, the means of the raw scores in the conditions also differ significantly.
7. *Effect size* indicates the amount of influence (and importance) of the independent variable in determining dependent scores. A way to measure effect size is to compute the proportion of variance accounted for.
8. In an experiment, the *proportion of variance accounted for* is the proportion of all differences in dependent scores that occur with, and seem to be caused by, changing the conditions of the independent variable.
9. In a two-sample experiment, the proportion of variance accounted for equals the *squared point biserial correlation coefficient* or $r^2_{\text{pb}}$.

## KEY TERMS: Can You Define the Following?

$n$ *158*
$N$ *158*
$s^2_{\text{pool}}$ *158*
$s_{\bar{X}_1-\bar{X}_2}$ *159*
$\bar{D}$ *166*
$s^2_D$ *167*
$s_{\bar{D}}$ *168*
$r^2_{\text{pb}}$ *172*
effect size *171*
homogeneity of variance *156*
independent samples *155*
independent-samples *t*-test *155*
matched-samples design *165*
point-biserial correlation coefficient *172*
pooled variance *158*
proportion of variance accounted for *172*
related samples *164*
related-samples *t*-test *164*
repeated-measures design *165*
sampling distribution of differences between means *157*
standard error of the difference *159*
standard error of the mean difference *168*

## REVIEW QUESTIONS

(Answers for odd-numbered questions are in Appendix C.)

*1.* A scientist has conducted a two-sample experiment. (a) What two parametric procedures are available to him? (b) What is the deciding factor for selecting between them?

*2.* How do you create independent samples?

*3.* What are the two ways to create related samples?

*4.* How are matched samples created?

*5.* How is a repeated-measures study conducted?

*6.* In addition to independent or related samples, the two-sample *t*-test has what other assumptions?

*7.* What is homogeneity of variance?

*8.* What is the difference between $n$ and $N$?

*9.* (a) What is $s_{\bar{X}_1-\bar{X}_2}$? (b) What is $s_{\bar{D}}$?

*10.* (a) What does effect size indicate? (b) What does *the proportion of variance accounted for* indicate? (c) How do we compute the proportion of variance accounted for in a two-sample experiment?

*11.* With $\alpha = .05$ and $df = 40$, a significant independent-samples $t_{\text{obt}}$ was $+4.55$. How would this be reported in the literature?

## APPLICATION QUESTIONS

*12.* For each of the following, which type of *t*-test is required? (a) An investigation of the effects of a new memory-enhancing drug on the memory of Alzheimer's patients, testing a group of patients before and after administration of the drug. (b) An investigation of the effects of alcohol on motor coordination, comparing one group of participants given a moderate dose of alcohol to the population $\mu$ for people given no alcohol. (c) An investigation of whether males and females rate differently the persuasiveness of an argument delivered by a female speaker. (d) The study described in part c, but with the added requirement that for each male of a particular age, there is a female of the same age.

*13.* In an experiment a researcher seeks to demonstrate a relationship between hot or cold baths and the amount of relaxation they produce. He obtains the following relaxation scores from two independent samples.

Sample 1 (hot): $\overline{X} = 43$, $s_X^2 = 22.79$, $n = 15$
Sample 2 (cold): $\overline{X} = 39$, $s_X^2 = 24.6$, $n = 15$

(a) What are $H_0$ and $H_a$? (b) Compute $t_{obt}$. (c) With $\alpha = .05$, what is $t_{crit}$? (d) What should the researcher conclude about this relationship? (e) What is the proportion of variance accounted for by changing the bath temperature? (f) Is this variable important in determining someone's relaxation score?

*14.* A researcher investigates whether a period of time feels longer or shorter when people are bored compared to when they are not bored. Using independent samples, the researcher obtains the following estimates of the time period (in minutes):

Sample 1 (bored): $\overline{X} = 14.5$, $s_X^2 = 10.22$, $n = 28$
Sample 2 (not bored): $\overline{X} = 9.0$, $s_X^2 = 14.6$, $n = 34$

(a) What are $H_0$ and $H_a$? (b) Compute $t_{obt}$. (c) With $\alpha = .05$, what is $t_{crit}$? (d) What should the researcher conclude about this relationship? (e) What is the proportion of variance accounted for by boredom levels? (f) Is this variable important in determining someone's time estimate?

*15.* Foofy predicts that students who use a computer program that corrects spelling errors will receive higher grades on a term paper. She uses an independent-samples design in which Group A uses a spelling checker and Group B does not. She tests $H_0$: $\mu_A - \mu_B \leq 0$ and $H_a$: $\mu_A - \mu_B > 0$. She obtains a negative value of $t_{obt}$. (a) What should she conclude about this study? (b) Say that her sample means actually support her predictions. What miscalculation is she likely to have made?

*16.* A rather dim student proposes testing the conditions of "male" and "female" using a repeated-measures design. What's wrong with this idea?

*17.* We ask whether people will score higher or lower on a questionnaire of their well-being when they are exposed to sunshine compared to when they're not exposed to sunshine. A sample of 8 people is first measured after low levels of sunshine exposure and then again after high levels of exposure. We get the following pairs of scores:

| Low: | 14 | 13 | 17 | 15 | 18 | 17 | 14 | 16 |
|---|---|---|---|---|---|---|---|---|
| High: | 18 | 12 | 20 | 19 | 22 | 19 | 19 | 16 |

(a) Subtracting low from high, what are $H_0$ and $H_a$? (b) Compute the appropriate $t$-test. (c) What should we conclude about these results? (d) Report your results using the correct format. (e) What is the predicted well-being score for anyone tested under low sunshine and under high sunshine? (f) Compute the statistic that reflects the amount of influence that changing sunshine has on well-being.

*18.* A researcher investigates whether classical music is more or less soothing than modern music. He plays a classical selection to one group and a modern selection to another (each $n = 6$.) He gives each person an irritability questionnaire and, after computing the independent-samples $t$-test, he finds $t_{obt} = +1.38$. (a) Are the results significant? (b) Report the results using the correct format. (c) What should he conclude about the relationship in nature between listening to music and irritability? (d) What error and statistical principle (from previous chapters) should concern him?

*19.* A researcher investigates whether children exhibit a higher number of aggressive acts after watching a violent television show. The aggressive acts for the same 10 participants before and after watching the show are as follows:

| *Sample 1 (After)* | *Sample 2 (Before)* |
|---|---|
| 5 | 4 |
| 6 | 6 |
| 4 | 3 |
| 4 | 2 |
| 7 | 4 |
| 3 | 1 |
| 2 | 0 |
| 1 | 0 |
| 4 | 5 |
| 3 | 2 |

(a) Subtracting before-scores from after-scores, what are $H_0$ and $H_a$? (b) Compute $t_{obt}$. (c) With $\alpha = .05$, what is $t_{crit}$? (d) What should the researcher conclude about this relationship? (e) If you want to understand children's aggression, how important is it to consider whether they watch violent television shows?

*20.* You investigate whether the older or younger male in pairs of brothers tends to be more extroverted. You obtain the following extroversion scores:

| *Sample 1 (Younger)* | *Sample 2 (Older)* |
|---|---|
| 10 | 18 |
| 11 | 17 |
| 18 | 19 |
| 12 | 16 |
| 15 | 15 |
| 13 | 19 |
| 19 | 13 |
| 15 | 20 |

(a) What are $H_0$ and $H_a$? (b) Compute $t_{obt}$. (c) With $\alpha = .05$, what is $t_{crit}$? (d) What should you conclude about this relationship? (e) What statistic would indicate how important the variable of age is in producing differences in extroversion scores?

*21.* We investigate the effects of sensitivity training on a policeman's effectiveness at resolving domestic disputes (comparing independent samples of policemen who had or had not completed the training). The dependent variable was their ability to successfully resolve domestic disputes. The following scores were obtained:

| *No Course* | *Course* |
|---|---|
| 11 | 13 |
| 14 | 16 |
| 10 | 14 |
| 12 | 17 |
| 8 | 11 |
| 15 | 14 |
| 12 | 15 |
| 13 | 18 |
| 9 | 12 |
| 11 | 11 |

(a) Should a one-tailed or a two-tailed test be used? (b) What are $H_0$ and $H_a$? (c) Subtracting the $\overline{X}$ for course from the $\overline{X}$ for no course, compute $t_{obt}$ and determine whether it is significant. (d) What conclusions can the experimenter draw from these results? (e) Compute the effect size and interpret it.

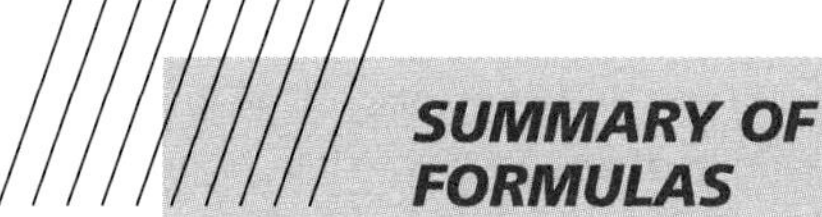

## SUMMARY OF FORMULAS

*1. The formula for the independent-samples* t*-test is*

$$t_{obt} = \frac{(\overline{X}_1 - \overline{X}_2) - (\mu_1 - \mu_2)}{s_{\overline{X}-\overline{X}}}$$

*where*

$$s_{\overline{X}-\overline{X}} = \sqrt{s^2_{pool}\left(\frac{1}{n_1} + \frac{1}{n_2}\right)}$$

$$s^2_{pool} = \frac{(n_1 - 1)s_1^2 + (n_2 - 1)s_2^2}{(n_1 - 1) + (n_2 - 1)}$$

$$s^2_X = \frac{\Sigma X^2 - \frac{(\Sigma X)^2}{n}}{n - 1}$$

$$df = (n_1 - 1) + (n_2 - 1)$$

*2. The formula for the related-samples* t*-test is*

$$t_{obt} = \frac{\overline{D} - \mu}{s_{\overline{D}}}$$

*where*

$$s_{\overline{D}} = \sqrt{\frac{s^2_D}{N}}$$

$$s^2_D = \frac{\Sigma D^2 - \frac{(\Sigma D)^2}{N}}{N - 1}$$

$$df = N - 1$$

*3. The formula for the proportion of variance accounted for is*

$$r^2_{pb} = \frac{(t_{obt})^2}{(t_{obt})^2 + df}$$

# 10 Describing Relationships Using Correlation and Regression

### CHAPTER ESSENTIALS

**Before getting started, be sure you understand**

- From Chapter 1, the difference between an experiment and a correlational study, and how to recognize a relationship between the scores of two variables
- From Chapter 4, understand that greater variability indicates that scores are not close to each other
- From the previous chapters, the basics of significance testing

**Your goals in this chapter are to learn**

- How to create and interpret a *scatterplot*
- What a *regression line* is
- When and how to compute the *Pearson* r
- How to perform significance testing of the Pearson $r$
- The logic of *linear regression* and $r^2$

Recall that in a relationship, as the scores on one variable change, we see a consistent pattern of change in the scores on the other variable. In research, in addition to demonstrating a relationship, we also want to describe and summarize the relationship. This chapter presents a new descriptive statistic for summarizing a relationship, called the *correlation coefficient.* In conjunction with this, we have a new way to graph a relationship, called the *regression line.* In the following sections we will discuss (1) what a correlation coefficient is and how to interpret it, (2) how to compute the most common coefficient, (3) how to perform inferential hypothesis testing of it, and (4) the logic behind using the regression line to predict unknown scores.

## UNDERSTANDING CORRELATIONS

Whenever we find a relationship, we then want to know its characteristics: What pattern is formed, how consistently do the scores change together, what direction do the scores change, and so on? The best—and easiest—way to answer these questions is by computing a correlation coefficient. The term *correlation* means relationship, and a correlation coefficient is a number that describes a relationship. The **correlation coefficient** is the statistic that describes the important characteristics of a relationship. That is, the correlation coefficient *quantifies* the pattern in a relationship, summarizing the entire relationship at once. Thus, the correlation coefficient is important because it simplifies a complex relationship involving many scores into one, easily interpreted statistic.

Correlation coefficients are most commonly used to summarize the relationship found in a *correlational design,* but computing a correlation coefficient does not create this type of study. Recall from Chapter 1 that, unlike in an experiment, in a correlational design, we simply measure participants' scores on two variables. For example, typically as people drink more coffee they become more nervous. To study this in a correlational study, we might simply ask participants the amount of coffee they had consumed that day and also measure how nervous they were. In an experiment, however, we would *manipulate* coffee consumption by assigning some people to a one-cup condition, others to a two-cup condition, and so on, and then measuring their nervousness. In either case a correlation coefficient would, in one number, summarize the important aspects of the relationship.

## Distinguishing Characteristics of Correlational Analysis

There are four major differences between how we handle data in a correlational analysis versus in an experiment. First, in our coffee experiment we would examine the mean of the nervousness score (of the $Y$ scores) for each condition of the amount of coffee consumed (each $X$). With correlational data, however, we do not compute a mean $Y$ score at each $X$. Instead, the correlation coefficient summarizes the *entire* relationship formed by all pairs of $X$-$Y$ scores in the data.

A second difference is that, because we examine all pairs of $X$-$Y$ scores, correlational procedures involve *one* sample:

**In correlational analysis $N$ stands for the number of *pairs* of scores in the data.**

Third, in a correlational study, neither variable is called the independent or dependent variable, and either variable may be the $X$ or $Y$ variable. How do we decide? In a relationship the $X$ scores are the "given" scores. Thus, if we ask, "For a given amount of coffee, what are the nervousness scores?" then amount of coffee is the $X$ variable and nervousness is the $Y$ variable. Conversely, if we ask, "For a given nervousness score, what is the amount of coffee consumed?" then nervousness is the $X$ variable and amount of coffee is the $Y$ variable.

Finally, the data are graphed differently in correlational research. We use the individual pairs of scores to create a *scatterplot.* A **scatterplot** is a graph that shows the location of each data point formed by a pair of $X$-$Y$ scores. The scatterplot in Figure 10.1 shows data from studying nervousness and coffee consumption. (Real research typically involves a larger $N$, and the data points will not form such a pretty pattern.) To create this scatterplot, the first person in the table had 1 cup of coffee and a nervousness score of 1, so we place a data point above an $X$ of 1 cup at the height of a score of 1 on the $Y$ variable of nervousness. And so on. Then we examine the overall pattern. Reading Figure 10.1 from left-to-right, as the $X$ scores increase, the data points move *higher* on the graph, indicating that the corresponding $Y$ scores are higher. Thus, the scatterplot reflects a relationship. As you saw in Chapter 1, in a relationship one or close to one value of $Y$ tends to be paired with one value of $X$; as the $X$ scores increase, the $Y$ scores change such that a different value of $Y$ tends to be paired with a different value of $X$.

***FIGURE 10.1***
Scatterplot showing nervousness as a function of coffee consumption

*Each data point is created using a participant's coffee consumption as the X score and nervousness as the Y score.*

| *Cups of Coffee:* X | *Nervousness Scores:* Y |
|---|---|
| 1 | 1 |
| 1 | 1 |
| 1 | 2 |
| 2 | 2 |
| 2 | 3 |
| 3 | 4 |
| 3 | 5 |
| 4 | 5 |
| 4 | 6 |
| 5 | 8 |
| 5 | 9 |
| 6 | 9 |
| 6 | 10 |

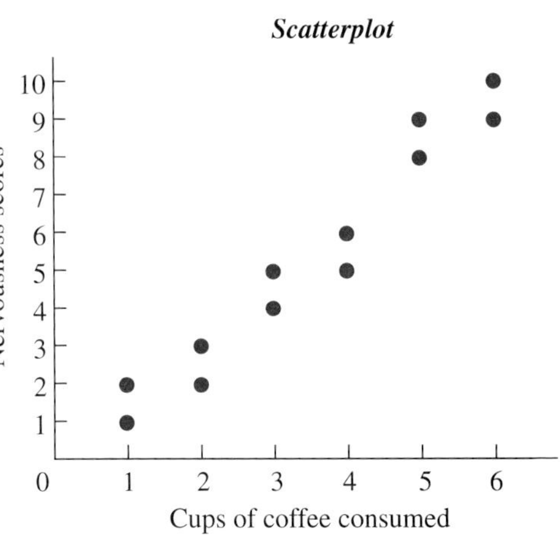


Drawing the scatterplot allows you to see a particular relationship and to map out the best way to summarize it. This is because the shape and orientation of a scatterplot reflect the characteristics of the relationship formed by the data, and it is these characteristics that are summarized by the correlation coefficient. The correlation coefficient communicates two important characteristics of a relationship: the *type* and the *strength* of the relationship. The following sections discuss these characteristics.

> ***REMEMBER*** A correlation coefficient indicates the *type* and *strength* of the relationship.

## Types of Relationships

The **type of relationship** that is present in a set of data is the overall direction in which the *Y* scores change as the *X* scores change. There are two general types of relationships: *linear* and *nonlinear* relationships.

**Linear Relationships** The term *linear* means "straight line," and a linear relationship forms a pattern that follows a straight line. This is because in a **linear relationship,** as the *X* scores increase, the *Y* scores tend to change in only *one* direction. Figure 10.2 shows two linear relationships: between the amount of time that students study and their test performance, and between the number of hours that students watch television and the amount of time they sleep. These are linear because as students study longer, their grades tend only to increase, and as they watch more television, their sleep time tends only to decrease.

To better see the overall pattern in a scatterplot, visually summarize it by drawing a line around its outer edges. As in Figure 10.2, a scatterplot that forms a slanted ellipse that follows a straight line indicates a linear relationship: By slanting, it indicates that the *Y* scores are changing as the *X* scores increase; the straight line indicates it is a linear relationship.

*FIGURE 10.2* Scatterplots showing positive and negative linear relationships

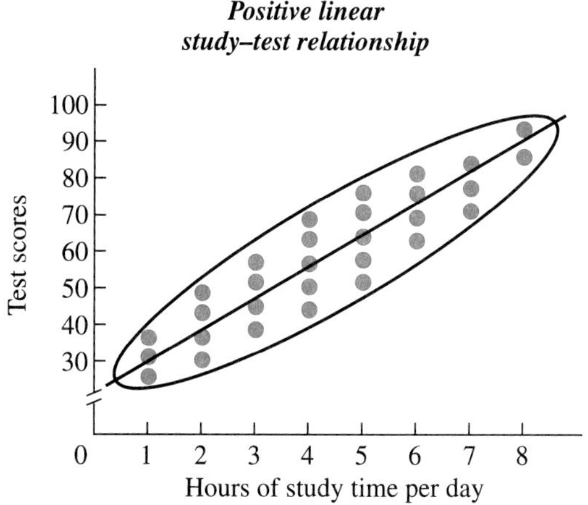


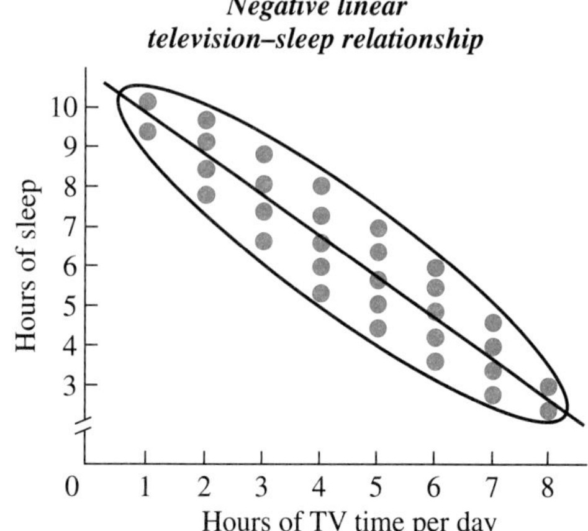


Further, as shown, we also summarize a relationship by drawing a line through the scatterplot. This line is called the *regression line.* While the correlation coefficient is the *statistic* that summarizes a relationship, the regression line is the *line* that summarizes the relationship. The **linear regression line** is the straight line that summarizes a relationship by passing through the center of the scatterplot. That is, although not all data points are *on* the line, the distance that some are above the line equals the distance that others are below it, so that the regression line passes through the center of the scatterplot. Therefore, think of the regression line as reflecting the pattern that all data points more or less follow, so it shows the linear—straight-line—relationship hidden in the data: It is how we visually summarize the general pattern in the relationship.

> *REMEMBER* The **linear regression line** summarizes the relationship by passing through the center of the scatterplot.

Finally, the two scatterplots in Figure 10.2 illustrate the two subtypes of linear relationships that occur. The type that we have depends on the *direction* in which the *Y* scores change. The study–test relationship is a positive relationship. In a **positive linear relationship,** as the *X* scores increase, the *Y* scores also tend to increase. Any relationship that fits the pattern "the more *X,* the more *Y*" is a positive linear relationship. On the other hand, the television–sleep relationship is a negative relationship. In a **negative linear relationship,** as the *X* scores increase, the *Y* scores tend to decrease. Any relationship that fits the pattern "the more *X,* the less *Y*" is a negative linear relationship. (*Note:* the term *negative* does not mean that there is something wrong with the relationship: It merely indicates the direction in which the *Y* scores change as the *X* scores increase.)

**Nonlinear Relationships** If a relationship is not linear, then it is *nonlinear,* meaning that the data cannot be summarized by a *straight* line. Thus, another name for a nonlinear relationship is a curvilinear relationship. In a **nonlinear,** or **curvilinear, relationship,** as the *X* scores change, the *Y* scores do not *only* increase or *only* decrease: At some point, the *Y* scores alter their direction of change.

***FIGURE 10.3*** Scatterplots showing nonlinear relationships

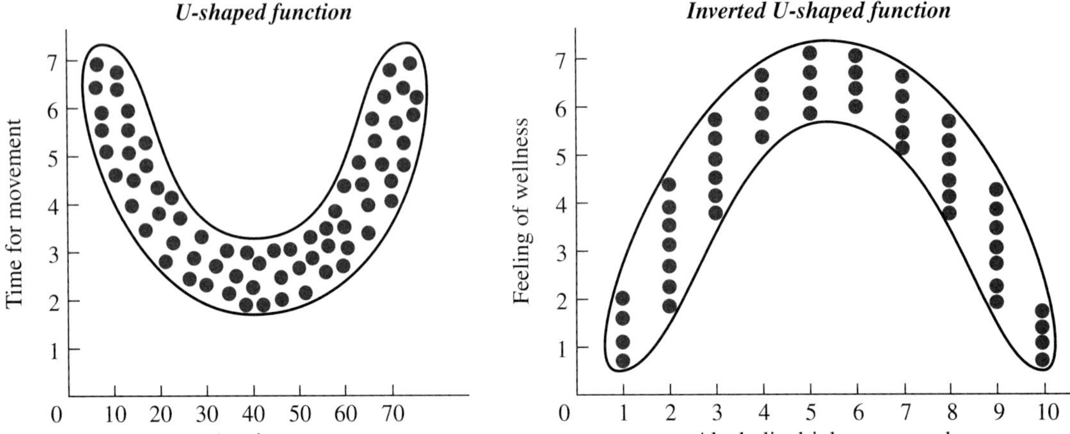


Nonlinear relationships come in many different shapes, but Figure 10.3 shows two common ones. On the left is the relationship between a person's age and the amount of time required to move from one place to another. At first, as age increases, movement time decreases; but, beyond a certain age, the time scores change direction and begin to increase. (Such a pattern is called *U-shaped.*) The scatterplot on the right shows the relationship between the number of alcoholic drinks consumed and feeling well. At first, people tend to feel better as they drink, but beyond a certain point, drinking more makes them feel progressively worse. (This pattern reflects an *inverted U-shaped relationship.*) Curvilinear relationships may be more complex than those above, producing a wavy pattern that repeatedly changes direction.

Note that the preceding terminology is also used to describe the type of relationship found in experiments. If, as the amount of the independent variable ($X$) increases, the dependent scores ($Y$) also increase, then you have a positive relationship. If the dependent scores decrease as the independent variable ($X$) increases, then you have a negative relationship. And if, as the independent variable ($X$) increases, the dependent scores alter their direction of change, then you have a nonlinear relationship.

**How the Coefficient Describes the Type of Relationship** Behavioral research focuses primarily on linear relationships, so we'll discuss only linear correlation coefficients. How do you know whether data form a linear relationship? If the scatterplot is best summarized by a straight line, then linear correlation is appropriate. Do not summarize a nonlinear relationship by computing a linear correlation coefficient. The relationship won't fit the straight line very well, so the coefficient won't accurately describe the relationship.

The correlation coefficient communicates two things about the type of relationship. First, by computing a linear correlation coefficient, we communicate that we are describing a linear relationship. Second, the coefficient itself indicates whether the relationship is positive or negative. The coefficient—the number we compute—either will have a minus sign ($-$) in front of it, or it will have no sign because it's positive, so we add a plus sign ($+$). A positive correlation coefficient indicates a positive linear relationship, and a negative correlation coefficient indicates a negative linear relationship.

The other characteristic of a relationship communicated by the correlation coefficient is the *strength* of the relationship.

## Strength of the Relationship

Recall that a relationship can exhibit varying degrees of consistency. The **strength of a relationship** is the extent to which one value of $Y$ is consistently paired with one and only one value of $X$. (This is also referred to as the *degree of association.*) The strength of a relationship is indicated by the absolute value of its correlation coefficient (ignoring the sign). The larger the coefficient, the stronger, more consistent, the relationship is. The largest possible value of a correlation coefficient is 1, and the smallest value is 0. When you include the sign, the correlation coefficient can be any value between $-1$ and $+1$. Thus, the closer the coefficient is to $\pm 1$, the more consistently one value of $Y$ is paired with one and only one value of $X$.

> ***REMEMBER*** A *correlation coefficient* has two components: the sign, indicating a positive or a negative relationship, and the absolute value, indicating the strength of the relationship.

Recognize that correlation coefficients do not directly measure units of "consistency." Thus, if one correlation coefficient is $+.40$ and another is $+.80$, you *cannot* conclude that one is only half as consistent as the other. Instead, evaluate any correlation coefficient by comparing it to the extreme values of 0 and $\pm 1$. The starting point is a perfect relationship.

**The Perfect Correlation** A correlation coefficient of $+1$ or $-1$ describes a perfectly consistent linear relationship. Figure 10.4 shows an example of each. In this and the following figures first look at the scores to see how they pair up; then look at the scatterplot. Other data having the same correlation coefficient will produce similar patterns having similar scatterplots.

The correlation coefficient communicates three things: First, a coefficient of $\pm 1$ indicates that everyone who obtains a particular $X$ score obtains one and only one value of $Y$. In other words, different $Y$ scores do not occur with one $X$, so there is no *variability* in the $Y$ scores paired with an $X$. Second, the coefficient of $\pm 1$ tells us that, with this absence of variability, the scatterplot has one data point above each $X$, and because it is a perfect straight-line relationship, all of the data points lie *on* the regression line. Third, a coefficient of $\pm 1$ indicates that we have perfect predictability of $Y$ scores. That is, a goal of behavioral science is to predict the specific behaviors—and the scores that reflect them—that occur in a particular situation. We do this using relationships because a particular $Y$ score is naturally paired with a particular $X$ score. Therefore, once we've identified a relationship, if we know someone's $X$ score, then using the relationship we can predict that individual's $Y$ score. In a perfect relationship only one value of $Y$ occurs with an $X$, so by knowing anyone's $X$, we can predict exactly what his or her $Y$ will be. Here, for example, in both graphs an $X$ of 3 is always paired with a $Y$ of 5, so we predict that *anyone* scoring an $X$ of 3 will have a $Y$ score of 5. All coefficients communicate the extent to which a relationship has these three characteristics.

*FIGURE 10.4*
Data and scatterplots reflecting perfect positive and negative correlations

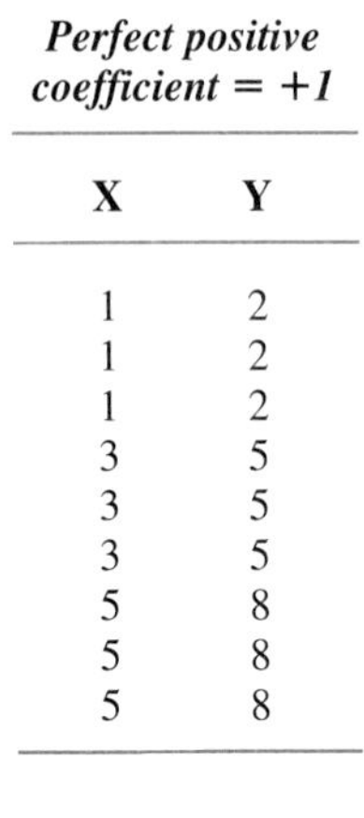

| *Perfect positive coefficient = +1* | |
|---|---|
| X | Y |
| 1 | 2 |
| 1 | 2 |
| 1 | 2 |
| 3 | 5 |
| 3 | 5 |
| 3 | 5 |
| 5 | 8 |
| 5 | 8 |
| 5 | 8 |

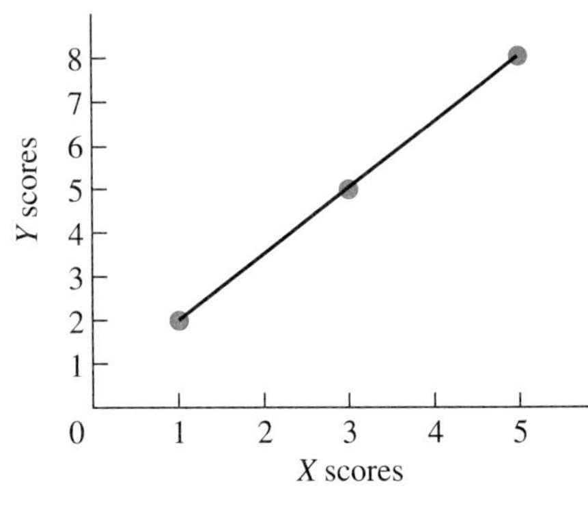


| *Perfect negative coefficient = −1* | |
|---|---|
| X | Y |
| 1 | 8 |
| 1 | 8 |
| 1 | 8 |
| 3 | 5 |
| 3 | 5 |
| 3 | 5 |
| 5 | 2 |
| 5 | 2 |
| 5 | 2 |

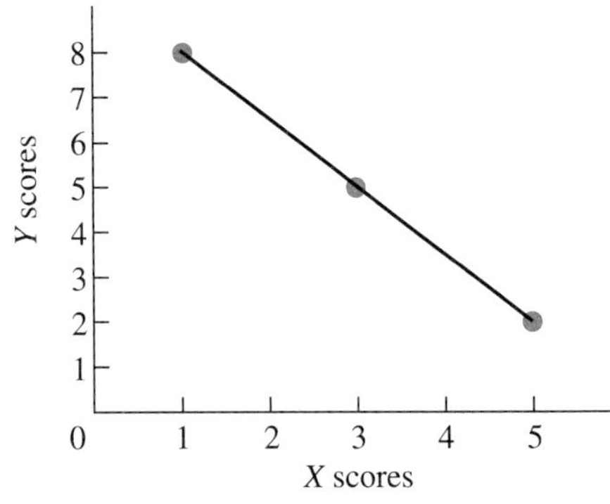


*REMEMBER* By knowing the strength of a relationship we know the degree of variability in *Y* scores, the shape of the scatterplot, and the amount of error in our predictions.

**Intermediate Strength** A correlation coefficient that is not ±1 indicates that the data form a linear relationship to only some degree. The key to understanding the strength of any relationship is this:

**As the variability—differences—in the *Y* scores paired with each *X* becomes larger, the relationship becomes weaker.**

The correlation coefficient communicates this because, as the variability in the *Y*s at each *X* becomes larger, the correlation coefficient becomes smaller.

For example, Figure 10.5 shows data that produce a correlation coefficient of +.98. Here, different *Y* scores are paired with an *X* score, so there is variability among the *Y* scores at each *X*. In the scatterplot this variability results in *groups* of data points at each *X* that are vertically spread out above and below the regression line. Because different *Y* scores occur with an *X*, knowing an individual's *X* score allows us to predict only *around* what his or her *Y* score will be, so predictions will contain some error. (For an *X* of 1, we cannot predict whether someone scores a *Y* of 1 or 2.) However, a coefficient of +.98 is close to +1, indicating that the variability is relatively small, so the *Y* scores at each *X* are relatively close to each other. Therefore, we know the data points at

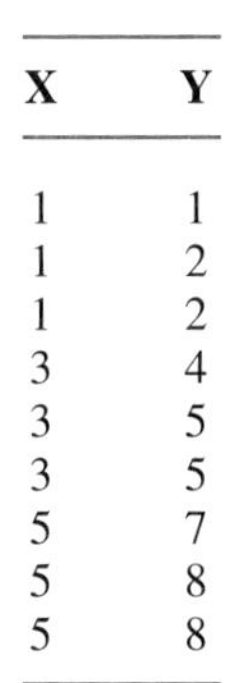

| X | Y |
|---|---|
| 1 | 1 |
| 1 | 2 |
| 1 | 2 |
| 3 | 4 |
| 3 | 5 |
| 3 | 5 |
| 5 | 7 |
| 5 | 8 |
| 5 | 8 |

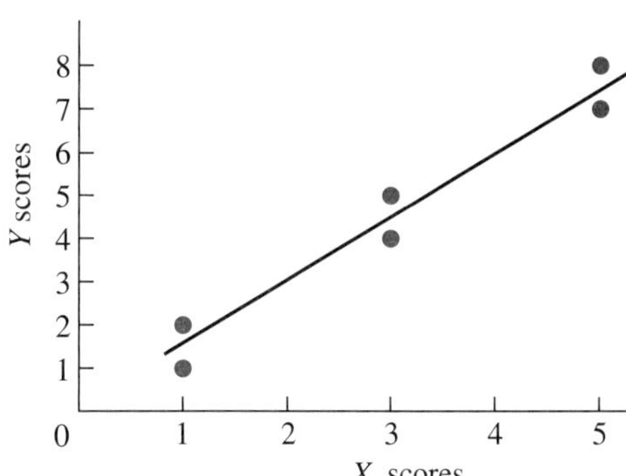


***FIGURE 10.5***
Data and scatterplot reflecting a correlation coefficient of +.98

each *X* are relatively close together, resulting in a narrow scatterplot that hugs the regression line. And, the predicted *Y* scores will be close to the actual *Y* scores that participants obtained, and so our error when predicting the scores will be relatively small.

On the other hand, Figure 10.6 shows data that produce a coefficient of −.28. Because −.28 is not very close to −1, we know that this relationship is not very close to forming a perfectly consistent linear relationship. Therefore, we know that (1) the variability in the *Y* scores paired with each *X* is relatively large, so only barely does one or close to one value of *Y* tend to be associated with one value of *X*. (2) These large differences produce data points on the scatterplot at each *X* that are vertically very spread out above and below the regression, forming a relatively wide scatterplot. (3) Because each *X* score is paired with many different *Y* scores, knowing a participant's *X* will not get us close to his or her exact *Y*, and so our predictions will contain large amounts of error.

> ***REMEMBER*** Greater *variability* in the *Y* scores at each *X* reduces the strength of a relationship and the size of the correlation coefficient.

**Zero Correlation** The lowest possible value of the correlation coefficient is 0, indicating that no relationship is present. Figure 10.7 shows data that produce such a coefficient. A correlation coefficient of 0 is as far as possible from ±1, telling us the scatterplot is as far as possible from forming a slanted straight line. Therefore, we know that no *Y* score tends to be consistently associated with only one *X*, and instead, virtually the same batch of *Y* scores is paired with every *X*. Therefore, the spread in *Y* at any *X* equals the overall spread of *Y* in the data, producing a scatterplot that is a circle

| X | Y |
|---|---|
| 1 | 9 |
| 1 | 6 |
| 1 | 3 |
| 3 | 8 |
| 3 | 6 |
| 3 | 3 |
| 5 | 7 |
| 5 | 5 |
| 5 | 1 |

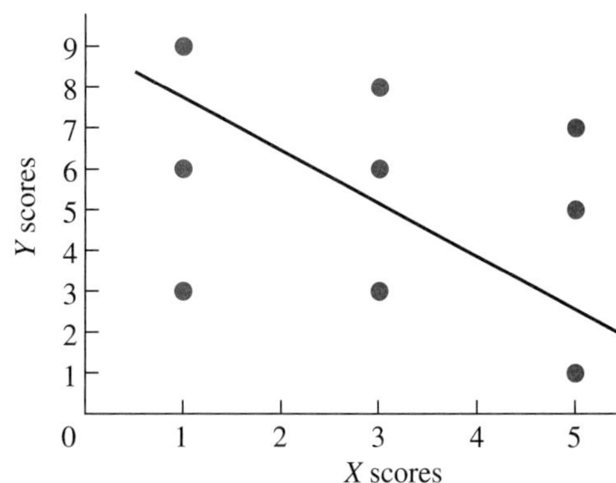


***FIGURE 10.6***
Data and scatterplot reflecting a correlation coefficient of −.28.

***FIGURE 10.7***
Data and scatterplot reflecting a correlation coefficient of 0.

| X | Y |
|---|---|
| 1 | 3 |
| 1 | 5 |
| 1 | 7 |
| 3 | 3 |
| 3 | 5 |
| 3 | 7 |
| 5 | 3 |
| 5 | 5 |
| 5 | 7 |

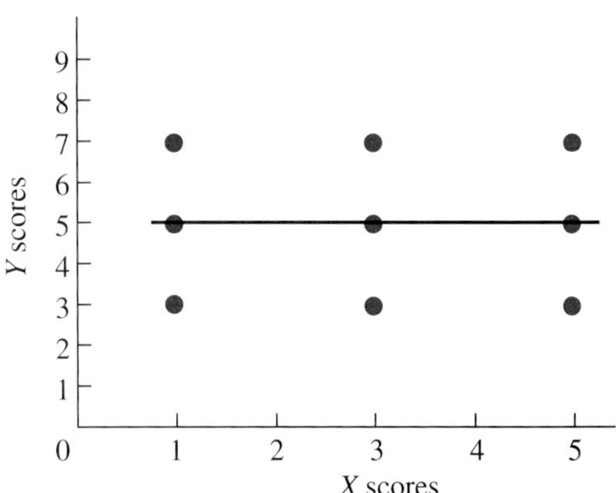


or horizontal ellipse that in no way hugs the horizontal regression line. And, because each $X$ is paired with virtually all $Y$ scores, knowing someone's $X$ score is no help in predicting his or her $Y$ score.

> ***REMEMBER*** The larger a correlation coefficient (whether positive or negative), the stronger the linear relationship, because the less the *Y*s are spread out at each *X,* and so the closer the data come to forming a straight line.

## *A QUICK REVIEW*

- As $X$ scores increase, in a positive linear relationship the $Y$ scores tend to increase, and in a negative linear relationship the $Y$ scores tend to decrease.
- The larger the correlation coefficient, the smaller the variability in $Y$ scores at each $X$, the narrower the scatterplot, and the more accurate our predictions.

### More Examples

A correlation coefficient of +.84 indicates (1) as $X$ increases, $Y$ consistently increases, with everyone at a particular $X$ having close to the same $Y$ score; (2) by knowing an individual's $X$ we can closely predict his/her $Y$ score; and (3) the scatterplot is a narrow ellipse, with the data points lying near the upward slanting regression line. However, a coefficient of +.38 indicates (1) as $X$ increases, $Y$ somewhat consistently increases, with a wide variety of $Y$ scores paired with a particular $X$; (2) knowing an $X$ score does not produce accurate predictions of the paired $Y$ score; and (3) the scatterplot is a wide ellipse around the upward slanting regression line.

***For Practice:***

1. In a ____ relationship, the $Y$ scores increase or decrease only. This is not true in a ____ relationship.
2. The more that you smoke cigarettes, the lower is your healthiness. This is a ____ linear relationship, producing a scatterplot that slants ____ as $X$ increases.
3. The more that you exercise, the better is your muscle tone. This is a ____ linear relationship, producing a scatterplot that slants ____ as $X$ increases.
4. In a stronger relationship the variability among the $Y$ scores at each $X$ is ____, producing a scatterplot that forms a ____ ellipse.
5. The ____ line summarizes the scatterplot.

**Answers**

1. linear; nonlinear
2. negative; down
3. positive; up
4. smaller; narrower
5. regression

## THE PEARSON CORRELATION COEFFICIENT

Statisticians have developed a number of different correlation coefficients that are used with different scales of measurement and in different kinds of studies. However, the most common correlation in behavioral research is the **Pearson correlation coefficient,** which describes the linear relationship between two interval variables, two ratio variables, or one interval and one ratio variable. (Technically, this statistic is the *Pearson Product Moment Correlation Coefficient,* but it's usually called the Pearson correlation coefficient.) The symbol for the Pearson correlation coefficient is the lowercase $r$. When you see $r$, think *relationship.* (All of the example coefficients in the previous section were $r$s.)

***REMEMBER*** Compute the *Pearson correlation coefficient* ($r$) to describe the linear relationship between interval and/or ratio variables.

In the following sections we discuss how to compute the Pearson $r$, and then how to perform significance testing of it.

### Computing the Pearson Correlation Coefficient

The basis for $r$ is that it compares how consistently each value of $Y$ is paired with each value of $X$. In Chapter 5 you saw that we compare scores from different variables by transforming them into $z$-scores. Essentially, calculating $r$ involves transforming each $Y$ score and each $X$ score into a $z$-score, and then determining the "average" amount of correspondence between each pair of $z$-scores. The following formula simultaneously accomplishes all of that.

*THE FORMULA FOR THE PEARSON CORRELATION COEFFICIENT IS*

$$r = \frac{N(\Sigma XY) - (\Sigma X)(\Sigma Y)}{\sqrt{[N(\Sigma X^2) - (\Sigma X)^2][N(\Sigma Y^2) - (\Sigma Y)^2]}}$$

In the numerator the $N$ (the number of pairs of scores) is multiplied times a new term, $\Sigma XY$: This is the *sum of the cross products,* which indicates to first multiply each $X$ score in a pair times its corresponding $Y$ in the pair, and then to sum all of the resulting products. Then subtract the quantity $(\Sigma X)(\Sigma Y)$: First, find the sum of the $X$s and the sum of the $Y$s, multiply the sums together, and then subtract. In the denominator, in the left brackets multiply $N$ times the sum of the squared $X$s or $\Sigma X^2$, and from that, subtract the squared sum of $X$ or $(\Sigma X)^2$. In the right bracket, multiply $N$ times the *sum of the squared* $Y$s or $\Sigma Y^2$, and from that subtract the *squared sum of* $Y$ or $(\Sigma Y)^2$. Multiply the answers from the two brackets together, and take the square root. Then divide the denominator into the numerator and, voila, the answer is the Pearson correlation coefficient.

For example, say that we ask 10 people the number of times they visited a doctor in the last year and the number of glasses of orange juice they drink daily. We want to

***TABLE 10.1***
Sample Data for Computing the *r* Between Orange Juice Consumed (the *X* variable) and Doctor Visits (the *Y* variable)

| | Glasses of Juice per Day | | Doctor Visits per Year | | |
|---|---|---|---|---|---|
| *Participant* | **X** | **$X^2$** | **Y** | **$Y^2$** | **XY** |
| 1 | 0 | 0 | 8 | 64 | 0 |
| 2 | 0 | 0 | 7 | 49 | 0 |
| 3 | 1 | 1 | 7 | 49 | 7 |
| 4 | 1 | 1 | 6 | 36 | 6 |
| 5 | 1 | 1 | 5 | 25 | 5 |
| 6 | 2 | 4 | 4 | 16 | 8 |
| 7 | 2 | 4 | 4 | 16 | 8 |
| 8 | 3 | 9 | 4 | 16 | 12 |
| 9 | 3 | 9 | 2 | 4 | 6 |
| 10 | 4 | 16 | 0 | 0 | 0 |
| $N = 10$ | $\Sigma X = 17$ | $\Sigma X^2 = 45$ | $\Sigma Y = 47$ | $\Sigma Y^2 = 275$ | $\Sigma XY = 52$ |
| | $(\Sigma X)^2 = 289$ | | $(\Sigma Y)^2 = 2209$ | | |

describe the linear relationship between juice drinking and doctor visits, so we compute *r*. Table 10. 1 shows a good way to set up the data for computing the correlation coefficient.

**Step 1:** *Compute* $\Sigma X$, $(\Sigma X)^?$, $\Sigma X^2$, $\Sigma Y$, $(\Sigma Y)^2$, $\Sigma Y^2$, $\Sigma XY$, *and* N: As in Table 10.1, in addition to the columns for *X* and *Y*, make a column for each $X^2$ and $Y^2$. Also, make a column for *XY* and here, multiply each *X* times its paired *Y*. Then sum all of the columns. Then square $\Sigma X$ and $\Sigma Y$.

Filling in the formula for *r* we get

$$r = \frac{N(\Sigma XY) - (\Sigma X)(\Sigma Y)}{\sqrt{[N(\Sigma X^2) - (\Sigma X)^2][N(\Sigma Y^2) - (\Sigma Y)^2]}} = \frac{10(52) - (17)(47)}{\sqrt{[10(45) - 289][10(275) - 2209]}}$$

**Step 2:** *Compute the numerator:* Multiplying 10 times 52 is 520, and 17 times 47 is 799. Rewriting the formula, we have

$$r = \frac{520 - 799}{\sqrt{[10(45) - 289][10(275) - 2209]}}$$

Complete the numerator by subtracting 799 *from* 520, which is $-279$. (Note the negative sign.)

**Step 3:** *Compute the denominator and then divide:* First, perform the operations within each bracket. In the left bracket, 10 times 45 is 450. In the right bracket 10 times 275 is 2750.

This gives

$$r = \frac{-279}{\sqrt{[450 - 289][2750 - 2209]}}$$

On the left, subtracting $450 - 289$ gives 161. On the right, subtracting $2750 - 2209$ gives 541. So

$$r = \frac{-279}{\sqrt{[161][541]}}$$

Now multiply the quantities in the brackets together: 161 times 541 equals 87,101. After taking the square root we have

$$r = \frac{-279}{295.129} = -.95$$

Thus, our correlation coefficient between orange juice drinks and doctor visits is $-.95$. (*Note:* We usually round off a correlation coefficient to two decimals.) Thus, on a scale of 0 to $\pm 1$, a $-.95$ indicates that this is an extremely strong negative linear relationship: Each amount of orange juice is associated with a very small range of doctor visits, and as juice scores increase, doctor visits consistently decrease.

## A QUICK REVIEW

- The Pearson correlation coefficient ($r$) describes the linear relationship between two interval and/or ratio variables.

### More Examples

| X | Y |
|---|---|
| 1 | 3 |
| 1 | 2 |
| 2 | 4 |
| 2 | 5 |
| 3 | 5 |
| 3 | 6 |

To compute $r$ for the above scores:

1. $\Sigma X = 12$, $(\Sigma X)^2 = 144$, $\Sigma X^2 = 28$, $\Sigma Y = 25$, $(\Sigma Y)^2 = 625$, $\Sigma Y^2 = 115$, $\Sigma XY = 56$, and $N = 6$, so

$$r = \frac{N(\Sigma XY) - (\Sigma X)(\Sigma Y)}{\sqrt{[N(\Sigma X^2) - (\Sigma X)^2][N(\Sigma Y^2) - (\Sigma Y)^2]}}$$
$$= \frac{6(56) - (12)(25)}{\sqrt{[6(28) - 144][6(115) - 625]}}$$

2. In the numerator 6 times 56 is 336, and 12 times 25 is 300, so

$$r = \frac{336 - 300}{\sqrt{[(6(28) - 144][6(115) - 625]}}$$
$$= \frac{+36}{\sqrt{[6(28) - 144][6(115) - 625]}}$$

3. In the denominator 6 times 28 is 168; 6 times 115 is 690, so

$$r = \frac{+36}{\sqrt{[168 - 144][690 - 625]}} = \frac{+36}{\sqrt{[24][65]}}$$
$$= \frac{+36}{\sqrt{1560}} = \frac{+36}{39.497} = +.91$$

***For Practice:***

1. Compute $r$ for the following:

| X | Y |
|---|---|
| 1 | 1 |
| 1 | 3 |
| 2 | 2 |
| 2 | 4 |
| 3 | 4 |

**Answers**

1. $r = \frac{5(28) - (9)(14)}{\sqrt{[5(19) - 81][5(46) - 196]}} = \frac{+14}{\sqrt{[14][34]}}$

$$= \frac{+14}{21.817} = +.64$$

## Significance Testing of the Pearson *r*

The correlation coefficient we calculate describes a *sample*. Ultimately, however, we wish to describe the relationship as it occurs in nature—in the population. But, before we can believe that any sample correlation coefficient accurately represents the relationship found in the population, we must first perform statistical hypothesis testing and conclude that $r$ is significant.

> ***REMEMBER*** Never accept that a sample correlation coefficient reflects a real relationship in nature unless it is significant.

Here's a new example. We're interested in the relationship between a man's age and his physical agility. We select 25 men, measure their age and their agility, and using the previous formula, compute that $r = -.45$. Based on this, we might conclude that for all men, the older a man is, the lower his agility score.

In fact, we use the sample's correlation coefficient to estimate the population correlation coefficient we'd expect to find if we computed the correlation for the entire population. The symbol for the Pearson population correlation coefficient is the Greek letter ρ, called "rho." A ρ is interpreted in the same way as $r$: It is a number between 0 and $\pm 1$, indicating either a positive or a negative linear relationship in the population. The larger the absolute value of ρ, the stronger the relationship, and the more closely the population's scatterplot hugs the regression line.

Thus, we might estimate that ρ would equal $-.45$ if we measured the agility and age of all men. On the other hand, maybe these variables are not really related in nature, but sampling error is misleading us to believe they are. This leads to our statistical hypotheses. As usual, we can perform either a one- or two-tailed test. The two-tailed test is used when we do not predict the direction of the relationship, predicting that the correlation will be either positive or negative. First, the alternative hypothesis always says the predicted relationship exists. Thus, if the correlation in the population is either positive or negative, then ρ does not equal zero.

$$H_a\colon \rho \neq 0.$$

As usual, the null hypothesis is that the predicted relationship does not exist, so the correlation in the population should be zero. Thus,

$$H_0\colon \rho = 0.$$

Regardless of our sample $r$, $H_0$ maintains that we are simply poorly respresenting this population correlation.

These are the two-tailed hypotheses whenever you test that the sample either does or does not represent a relationship. This is the most common approach and the one we'll use. (You can also test the $H_0$ that your sample represents a nonzero ρ. Consult an advanced statistics book for the details.) The assumptions for testing $r$ are

*1.* In a random sample of $X$-$Y$ pairs, each variable is a normally distributed, interval or ratio variable.

*2.* The null hypothesis is that the population correlation is zero.

Our agility and age scores meet these assumptions, so we set alpha at .05 and test $r$.

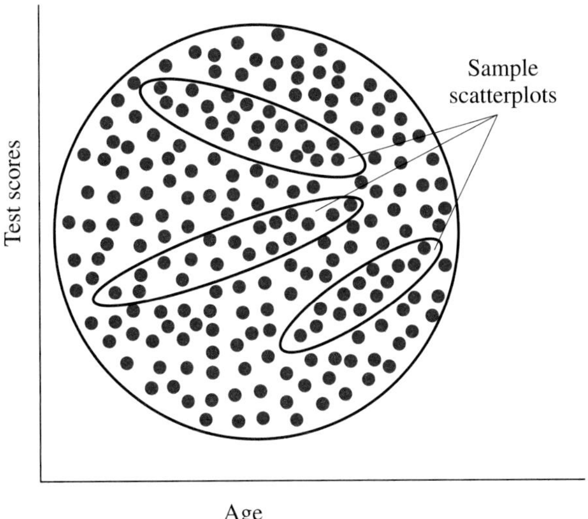


**FIGURE 10.8**
Scatterplot of a population for which $\rho = 0$, as described by $H_0$

*Any* r *is a result of sampling error when selecting a sample from this scatterplot.*

**The Sampling Distribution of *r*** Our $H_0$ implies that if *r* does not equal zero, it's because of sampling error. You can understand this by looking at the population scatterplot in Figure 10.8. There is no relationship here, and so ρ is 0. However, the null hypothesis implies that, by chance, we obtained an elliptical *sample* scatterplot from this population that produced our *r*. Thus, our $H_0$ says that age and agility are not really related, but the scores in our sample happen to pair up so that it looks as though they're related. (On the other hand, $H_a$ essentially says that the population's scatterplot would be similar to the sample's scatterplot.)

As usual, we test $H_0$, so here we determine the likelihood of obtaining our sample *r* from the population where ρ is zero. To do so, we envision the sampling distribution. To create this, it is as if we infinitely sampled the population in Figure 10.8, each time computing *r*. Then the **sampling distribution of *r*** is the frequency distribution showing all possible values of the *r* that occur when samples are drawn from a population in which ρ is zero. Such a distribution is shown in Figure 10.9. The only novelty here is that along the *X* axis are now different values of *r*. When $\rho = 0$, the most frequent sample *r* is also 0, so the mean of the sampling distribution—the average *r*—is 0. Because

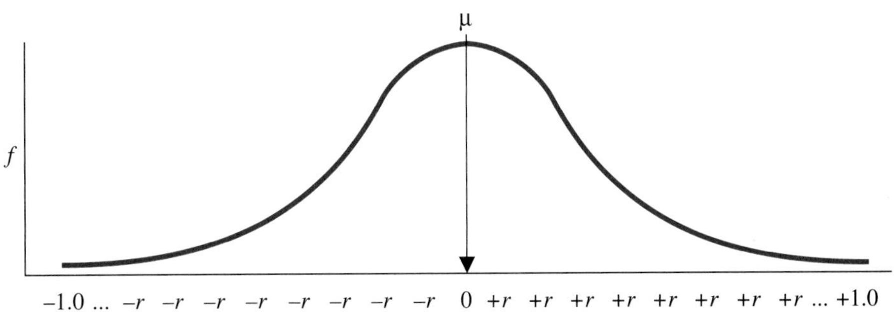


**FIGURE 10.9**
Sampling distribution of $r$ when $\rho = 0$

*It is an approximately normal distribution, with values of* r *plotted along the* X *axis.*

of sampling error, however, sometimes we might obtain a positive $r$, and sometimes a negative $r$. Most often the $r$ will be relatively small (close to 0), but less frequently we may obtain a larger $r$ that falls more into the tails of the distribution. Thus, the larger the $r$ (whether positive or negative), the less likely it is to occur when the sample represents a population where $\rho = 0$.

To test $H_0$, we determine where our $r$ is located in this sampling distribution. To do so, we could compute a variation of the $t$-test, but that is not necessary. Instead, the $r$ directly communicates its location on the sampling distribution. The mean of the sampling distribution is always 0, so, for example, our $r$ of $-.45$ is a distance of .45 below the mean. Therefore, we test $H_0$ simply by examining our obtained $r$, which is $r_{obt}$. To determine whether $r_{obt}$ is in the region of rejection, we compare it to $r_{crit}$.

**Drawing Conclusions About *r*** As with the $t$-distribution, the shape of the $r$-distribution is slightly different for each *df*, so there is a different value of $r_{crit}$ for each *df*. Table 3 in Appendix B gives the critical values of the Pearson correlation coefficient. Use these "$r$-tables" in the same way you've used the $t$-tables: Find $r_{crit}$ for either a one- or a two-tailed test at the appropriate $\alpha$ and *df*.

*THE DEGREES OF FREEDOM IN THE PEARSON CORRELATION COEFFICIENT EQUAL*

$df = N - 2$, where $N$ is the number of $X$-$Y$ pairs in the data

For our example, $N$ was 25, so $df = 23$. For $\alpha = .05$, the two-tailed $r_{crit}$ is $\pm.396$. We set up the sampling distribution as in Figure 10.10. An $r_{obt}$ of $-.45$ is beyond the $r_{crit}$ of $\pm.396$, so it is in the region of rejection. Thus, our $r$ is so unlikely to occur if we had been representing the population where $\rho$ is 0, that we reject the $H_0$ that we were representing this population. We conclude that the $r_{obt}$ is "significantly different from zero."

The rules for interpreting a significant result here are the same as with previous statistics. In particular, $\alpha$ is again the theoretical probability of a Type I error. Here, a Type I error is *rejecting* the $H_0$ that the population correlation is zero, when in fact the correlation is zero. Also, as usual, rejecting $H_0$ does not *prove* anything. In particular, we have not proven that changes in age *cause* test scores to change. In fact, we have not even proven that there is a relationship in the population. Instead, we are simply more confident

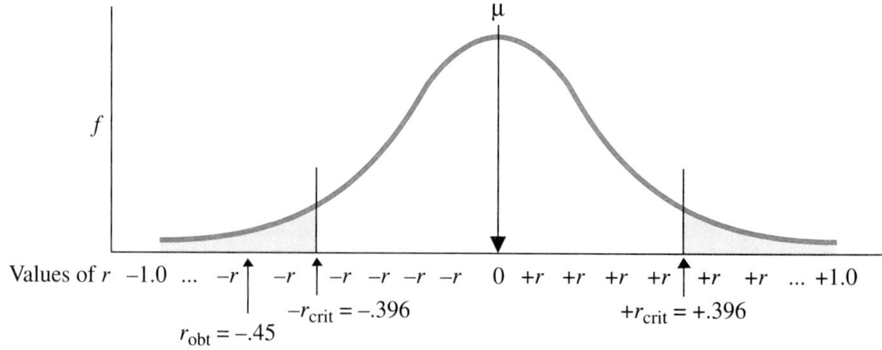


**FIGURE 10.10**
$H_0$ sampling distribution of $r$ when $H_0$: $\rho = 0$
*For the two-tailed test, there is a region of rejection for positive values of* $r_{obt}$ *and for negative values of* $r_{obt}$.

that the $r_{obt}$ does not merely reflect some quirk of sampling error, and that instead, it represents a "real" relationship in nature.

Because the sample $r_{obt}$ is $-.45$, our best estimate is that in the population, $\rho$ equals $-.45$. However, recognizing that the sample may contain sampling error, we expect that $\rho$ is probably *around* $-.45$. (We could more precisely describe this $\rho$ by computing a confidence interval for $\rho$. This confidence interval is computed using a different procedure from that discussed previously.)

If our $r_{obt}$ did not lie beyond $r_{crit}$, then we would retain $H_0$ and conclude that the sample may represent a population where $\rho = 0$. As usual, we have not proven there is no relationship in the population, we have simply failed to convincingly demonstrate that there *is* one. Therefore, we make no claims about the relationship that may or may not exist.

**One-Tailed Tests of *r*** If we had predicted only a positive correlation or only a negative correlation, then we would have performed a one-tailed test.

*THE ONE-TAILED HYPOTHESES FOR TESTING A CORRELATION COEFFICIENT ARE*

| ***Predicting positive correlation*** | ***Predicting negative correlation*** |
|---|---|
| $H_0$: $\rho \leq 0$ | $H_0$: $\rho \geq 0$ |
| $H_a$: $\rho > 0$ | $H_a$: $\rho < 0$ |

Test each $H_0$ by again testing whether the sample represents a population in which there is zero relationship—so again examine the sampling distribution for $\rho = 0$. From the *r*-tables in Appendix B, find the one-tailed critical value for *df* and $\alpha$, and set up one of the sampling distributions shown in Figure 10.11. When predicting a positive correlation, use the left-hand distribution: $r_{obt}$ is significant if it falls beyond the positive $r_{crit}$. When predicting a negative correlation, use the right-hand distribution: $r_{obt}$ is significant if it falls beyond the negative $r_{crit}$.

***FIGURE 10.11*** $H_0$ sampling distribution of *r* where $\rho = 0$ for one-tailed test

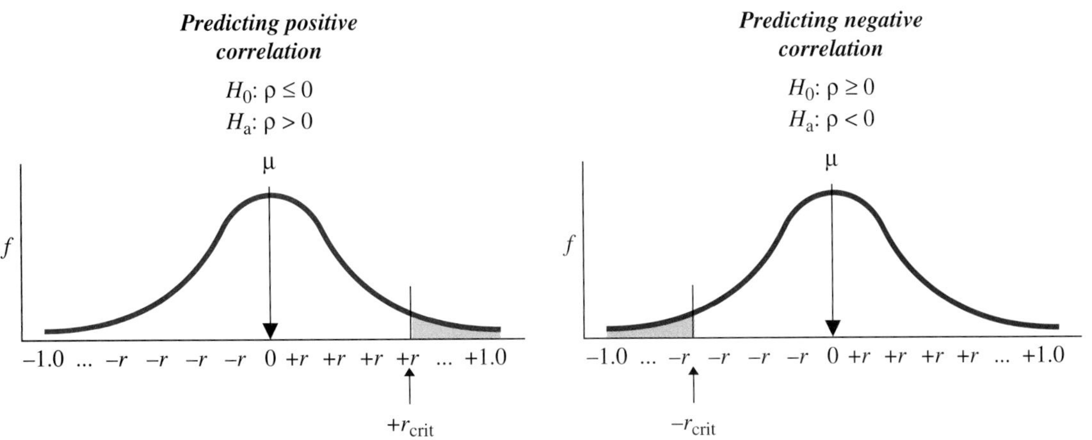

### Summary of the Pearson Correlation Coefficient

The Pearson correlation coefficient describes the strength and type of linear relationship between normally distributed interval/ratio variables.

1. Compute $r_{obt}$.
2. Create either the two-tailed or one-tailed $H_0$ and $H_a$.
3. Set up the sampling distribution and, using $df = N - 1$ (where $N$ is the number of *pairs*), find $r_{crit}$ in the $r$-tables.
4. If $r_{obt}$ is beyond $r_{crit}$, the results are significant, so describe the relationship and population correlation coefficient ($\rho$). If $r_{obt}$ is not beyond $r_{crit}$, the results are not significant, and you should make no conclusion about the relationship.

## A QUICK REVIEW

- Always perform hypothesis testing on the Pearson $r$ so that we are confident that we are not being misled by sampling error.

### More Examples

We compute an $r = +.32$, using $N = 42$. We predicted some kind of relationship, so $H_0$: $\rho = 0$; $H_a$: $\rho \neq 0$. With $\alpha = .05$ and $df = 42 - 2 = 40$, the two-tailed $r_{crit} = \pm.304$. The sampling distribution is:

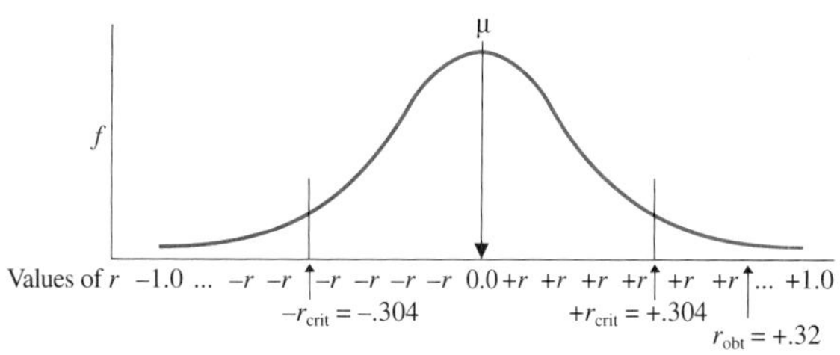


Because $r_{obt}$ is beyond $r_{crit}$, the results are significant: In the population, we expect the correlation coefficient ($\rho$) would be around $+.32$.

### For Practice:

We predict a negative relationship and obtain $r_{obt} = -.44$.

1. What are $H_0$ and $H_a$?
2. With $\alpha = .05$ and $N = 10$, what is $r_{crit}$?
3. What is the conclusion about $r_{obt}$?
4. What is the conclusion about the relationship in the population?

**Answers**

1. $H_0$: $\rho \geq 0$; $H_a$: $\rho < 0$.
2. $df = 8$, $r_{crit} = .549$.
3. Not significant.
4. Make no conclusion about the relationship in the population.

## STATISTICS IN THE RESEARCH LITERATURE: REPORTING *r*

Report the Pearson correlation coefficient using the same format as with previous statistics. Thus, in our agility study, the $r_{obt}$ of $-.45$ was significant with 23 *df.* We report this as $r(23) = -.47, p < .05$. As usual, *df* is in parentheses and because $\alpha = .05$, the probability is less than .05 that we've made a Type I error.

Understand that, although theoretically a correlation coefficient may be as large as ±1, in real research such values do not occur. Our scores reflect the behaviors of living organisms who always show variability. Therefore, adjust your expectations about real correlation coefficients: Typically, researchers obtain coefficients in the neighborhood of ±.30 to ±.50, so below ±.30 is considered rather weak and above ±.50 is considered extremely strong.

Finally, often published research involves a rather large *N*, producing a complex scatterplot that is difficult to read. Therefore, instead, a graph showing only the regression line may be included. Also, often the mathematical formula for producing the regression line, called the *linear regression equation*, will be included, especially when the report focuses on predicting *Y* scores, as discussed in the next section.

## A WORD ABOUT LINEAR REGRESSION

Recall that we use a relationship and an individual's *X* score to predict his or her *Y* score. Not only is the regression line the summary of the scatterplot, it is also the basis for making such predictions. **Linear regression** is the procedure used to predict unknown *Y* scores based on correlated *X* scores. For example, the reason that students take the Scholastic Aptitude Test (SAT) when applying to some colleges is because researchers have previously established that SAT scores are moderately positively correlated with college grades: We know the typical college grade average that is paired with a particular SAT score. Therefore, through regression techniques, the SAT scores of applying students are used to predict their future college performance. If the predicted grades are too low, the student is not admitted to the college.

To draw a regression line, we use the *linear regression equation.* This equation is also used to predict *Y* scores from the *X* scores. Consult an advanced text for the calculations and applications of the equation, but you can understand its basic logic from Figure 10.12.

**FIGURE 10.12**

Graphs showing the actual *Y* scores and the predicted *Y* scores from the regression line.

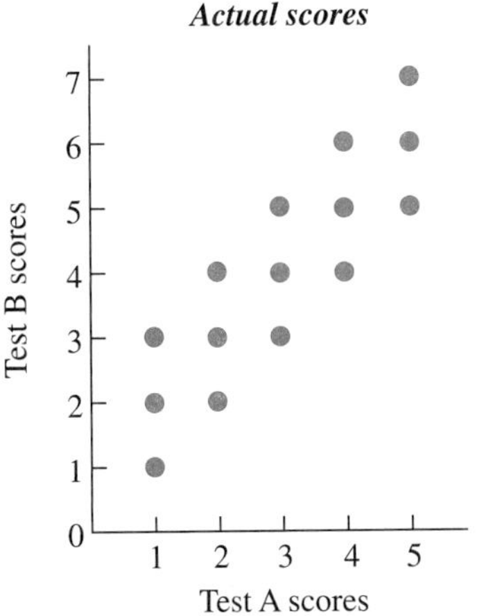


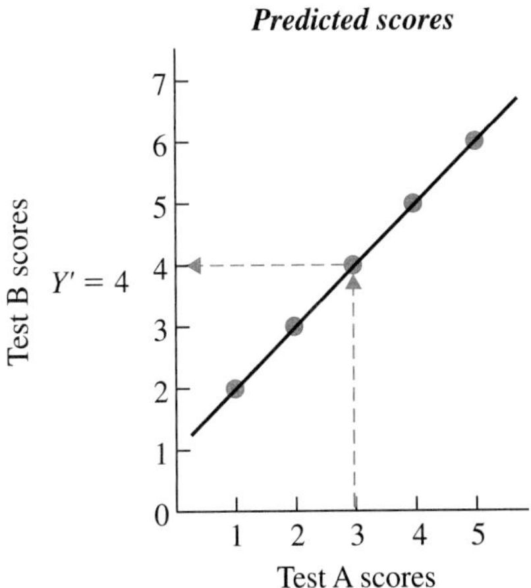

On the left is the scatterplot showing the relationship between scores on Test A and scores on Test B. A regression line passes through the center of the scatterplot so that the individuals at a particular $X$ score have $Y$ scores that are literally *around* (above and below) the line. For example, people scoring an $X$ of 3 have $Y$s of 3, 4, and 5, so the regression line will go through the middle of these scores at 4. Thus, think of the regression line in the graph on the right as the summary of this relationship, composed of a series of data points itself, with each $Y$ on the line located in the middle of the $Y$ scores paired with that $X$. Thus, following the dotted lines, it shows that people at an $X$ of 3 scored a $Y$ around 4. Therefore, for anyone else scoring an $X$ of 3, we'd predict a $Y$ of 4 for them also. Notice that the symbol for this **predicted Y score** is $Y'$ (pronounced Y *prime*).

Real data won't form such a perfectly balanced scatterplot as shown here, but each $Y'$ is still the central, summary $Y$ score at an $X$ based on the linear relationship in the data. Thus, even if no one at the $X$ of 3 had actually scored a $Y$ of 4, the line shows that participants scored *around* 4, so 4 is still our best prediction. Likewise, in the left-hand graph, people at $X = 1$ scored $Y$s around 2, so in the right-hand graph, for anyone scoring this $X$, we'd predict for them a $Y' = 2$. In the same way, using the linear regression equation is the equivalent of us traveling vertically from an $X$ to the regression line and then horizontally to determine the predicted $Y'$ score for that $X$.

Finally, recall that the larger the correlation coefficient and the stronger a relationship, the more accurate will be our predictions. This is because in a stronger relationship, the data points at each $X$ are *closer* to the regression line. Then the $Y$ scores that participants actually obtain are closer to the $Y'$ scores that we predict for them, so we have greater accuracy.

> ***REMEMBER*** *Linear regression* is used to produce a $Y'$ score, which is our predicted $Y$ score based on an individual's $X$ score from a correlated variable. The stronger the correlation, the more accurate the predictions.

---

## A WORD ABOUT THE PROPORTION OF VARIANCE ACCOUNTED FOR: $r^2$

From the correlation coefficient we can compute one more piece of information about a relationship, called the *proportion of variance accounted for.* In the previous chapter we saw that, with experiments, this measured the "effect size." With correlational studies, we don't call it effect size, because we don't have an independent variable that has an "effect." The logic, however, is the same. In any relationship, **the proportion of variance accounted for** describes the proportion of all differences in $Y$ scores that are associated with changing the $X$ variable. We've seen that in a relationship, to some extent the $Y$ scores change along with changing $X$ scores, but to some extent the $Y$ scores change when $X$ doesn't—different $Y$ scores occur at the *same* $X$. Together, these are all of the differences in $Y$ scores. The proportion of variance accounted for is the proportion of all differences in $Y$ scores that are those differences associated with—that occur with—changes in $X$ scores.

With the Pearson correlation coefficient, the proportion of variance accounted for is easy to compute.

*THE FORMULA FOR THE PROPORTION OF VARIANCE ACCOUNTED FOR IS*

$$\text{Proportion of variance accounted for} = r^2$$

Not too tough! Compute $r$ and then square it. For example, previously our age and agility scores produced $r = -.45$, so $r^2 = (.45)^2 = .20$. Thus, out of all of the differences in the agility scores, .20 or 20% of them are associated with differences in our men's ages. (80% of the differences in agility scores do *not* occur along with changes in age.)

The $r^2$ can be as low as 0 (when $r = 0$), indicating that no differences in $Y$ scores are associated with $X$, to as high as 1 (when $r = \pm 1$), indicating that 100% of the changes in $Y$ occur when $X$ changes, with no differences in $Y$ occuring at the same $X$. Thus, while $r$ describes the consistency of the pairing of a particular $X$ with a particular $Y$ in a relationship, $r^2$ is slightly different: It indicates the extent to which the differences in $Y$ occur along with changes in $X$.

**REMEMBER** $r^2$ indicates the *proportion of variance accounted for* by the relationship. This is the proportion of all differences in $Y$ that occur with changes in $X$.

The proportion of variance accounted for is used to judge the usefulness and scientific importance of a relationship. Although a relationship must be significant in order to be potentially important (and for us to even compute $r^2$), it can be significant and still be unimportant. The $r^2$ indicates the importance of a relationship because the larger it is, the closer the relationship gets us to our goal of understanding behavior. By understanding the differences in $Y$ scores that are associated with changes in $X$, we are actually describing the differences in *behaviors* that are associated with changes in $X$.

Further, we compare different relationships by comparing each $r^2$. Say that we had also correlated a man's weight with his physical agility, finding a significant $r_{\text{obt}} = -.60$, so $r^2 = .36$. Thus, a greater proportion of the differences in agility scores are associated with a man's weight than with his age. Therefore, a man's weight is the more useful and important variable to consider when trying to predict and understand differences in physical agility.

**REMEMBER** Evaluate the importance of a relationship by computing $r^2$.

## CHAPTER SUMMARY

1. A *scatterplot* is a graph that shows the location of each pair of $X$-$Y$ scores in the data.
2. The *regression line* is the line that summarizes a relationship by passing through the center of the scatterplot.
3. In a *positive linear relationship,* as the $X$ scores increase, the $Y$ scores tend to increase. In a *negative linear relationship,* as the $X$ scores increase, the $Y$ scores tend to decrease. In a *nonlinear relationship,* as the $X$ scores increase, the $Y$ scores do not only increase or only decrease.

4. The *strength* of a relationship is the extent to which one value of $Y$ is consistently paired with only one value of $X$.
5. A *Pearson correlation coefficient* describes the strength and type of linear relationship that is present between two interval and/or ratio variables: $r$ stands for the sample correlation coefficient, and $\rho$ stands for the population correlation coefficient.
6. A smaller absolute value of the correlation coefficient indicates a weaker relationship, with greater variability in $Y$ scores at each $X$, greater vertical spread in the scatterplot, and less accuracy in predicting $Y$ scores based on correlated $X$ scores.
7. *Linear regression* is the procedure used to predict $Y$ scores based on correlated $X$ scores. For each $X$, we obtain $Y'$ which is the *predicted Y score.*
8. The *proportion of variance accounted for* equals $r^2$. It indicates the proportion of all differences in $Y$ scores that occur with changes in the $X$ scores.

## KEY TERMS: Can You Define the Following?

$\Sigma XY$ *187*
$r$ *187*
$\rho$ *190*
$Y'$ *196*
correlation coefficient *178*
curvilinear relationship *181*
linear regression *195*
linear regression line *181*
linear relationship *180*
negative linear relationship *181*
nonlinear relationship *181*
Pearson correlation coefficient *187*
positive linear relationship *181*
predicted $Y$ score *196*
proportion of variance accounted for *196*
sampling distribution of $r$ *191*
scatterplot *179*
strength of a relationship *183*
type of relationship *180*

## REVIEW QUESTIONS

(Answers for odd-numbered questions are in Appendix C.)

1. What is the difference between an experiment and a correlational study in terms of how the researcher (a) collects the data? (b) examines the relationship?
2. (a) You have collected data that you think show a relationship. What do you do next? (b) What is the advantage of computing a correlation coefficient? (c) What two characteristics of a linear relationship are described by a correlation coefficient?
3. (a) What is a scatterplot? (b) What is a regression line?
4. When do you compute a Pearson correlation coefficient?
5. (a) Define a positive linear relationship. (b) Define a negative linear relationship. (c) Define a curvilinear relationship.
6. As the value of $r$ approaches $\pm 1$, what does it indicate about the following? (a) the shape of the scatterplot; (b) the variability of the $Y$ scores at each $X$; (c) the accuracy with which we can predict $Y$ if $X$ is known.
7. (a) What does $\rho$ stand for? (b) How is the value of $\rho$ determined?
8. Why can't you obtain a correlation coefficient greater than $\pm 1$?

9. Summarize the steps involved in hypothesis testing of the Pearson correlation coefficient.
10. (a) How do researchers use linear regression to predict unknown $Y$ scores? (b) What is the symbol for a predicted $Y$ score?
11. (a) What is the proportion of variance accounted for ? (b) How is it measured in a correlational study? (c) How do we use the size of $r^2$ to judge a relationship?

## APPLICATION QUESTIONS

12. For each of the following, indicate whether it is a positive linear, negative linear, or nonlinear relationship: (a) Quality of performance ($Y$) increases with increased arousal ($X$) up to an optimal level; then quality of performance decreases with increased arousal. (b) Heavier jockeys ($X$) tend to win fewer horse races ($Y$). (c) As number of minutes of exercise increases each week ($X$), dieting individuals lose more pounds ($Y$). (d) The number of bears in an area ($Y$) decreases as the area becomes increasingly populated by humans ($X$).
13. Poindexter wondered if there is a relationship between the quality of sneakers worn by 20 volleyball players and their average number of points scored per game. He computed $r = +.21$ and immediately claimed this was evidence that better-quality sneakers are related to better performance. (a) What did he forget to do? (b) What are his $H_0$ and $H_a$? (c) With $\alpha = .05$, what is $r_{crit}$? (d) Report the results and what should he conclude? (e) What other computations should he perform to describe this relationship?
14. A researcher has just completed a correlational study, measuring the number of boxes of tissue purchased per week and the number of vitamin tablets consumed per week for each participant. (a) Which is the independent and which is the dependent variable? (b) Which variable is $X$? Which is $Y$?
15. You want to know if a nurse's absences from work in one month ($Y$) are positively correlated with her score on a test of psychological "burnout" ($X$). (a) Compute the correlation coefficient using the following sample data. (b) What are $H_0$ and $H_a$? (c) With $\alpha = .05$, what is $r_{crit}$? (d) Report the results, and what do you conclude about the relationship? (e) What do you conclude about the relationship that occurs in the population? (f) How scientifically useful is this relationship?

| *Participant* | *Burnout* X | *Absences* Y |
|---|---|---|
| 1 | 2 | 4 |
| 2 | 1 | 7 |
| 3 | 2 | 6 |
| 4 | 3 | 9 |
| 5 | 4 | 6 |
| 6 | 4 | 8 |
| 7 | 7 | 7 |
| 8 | 7 | 10 |
| 9 | 8 | 11 |

*16.* A researcher asks if there is a relationship between the $X$ variable of number of errors on a math test and the $Y$ variable of the person's level of satisfaction with the performance. (a) Summarize the relationship in the data below. (b) What are $H_0$ and $H_a$? (c) With $\alpha = .05$, what is $r_{crit}$? (d) Report the results, and what do you conclude about the relationship? (e) What do you conclude about the relationship in the population? (f) What proportion of the differences in satisfaction scores occurs with different test scores?

| *Participant* | *Errors* X | *Satisfaction* Y |
|---|---|---|
| 1 | 9 | 3 |
| 2 | 8 | 2 |
| 3 | 4 | 8 |
| 4 | 6 | 5 |
| 5 | 7 | 4 |
| 6 | 10 | 2 |
| 7 | 5 | 7 |

*17.* A scientist suspects that as a person's stress level changes, so does the amount of his or her impulse buying. He collects data from 72 people and obtains an $r = +.38$. (a) What are $H_0$ and $H_a$? (b) With $\alpha = .05$, what is $r_{crit}$? (c) Report these results using the correct format. (d) What conclusions should he draw? (e) What other calculations should be performed to describe the relationship in these data?

*18.* Foofy computes the correlation between participants' physical strength and their college grade average, obtaining a significant $r = +.08$. She claims she has uncovered a useful tool for predicting which college applicants are likely to succeed academically. Do you agree or disagree? Why?

*19.* Poindexter finds $r = +.80$ for the variables of number of hours studied and number of errors on a statistics test, and $r = +.40$ for the variables of speed of taking the test and the number of errors on the test. He concludes that study time forms twice as strong a relationship and is therefore twice as important as the speed of taking the test. (a) Why is he incorrect? (b) Compare these relationships and draw the correct conclusion.

*20.* (a) Why must a relationship be significant in order to be important? (b) Why can a relationship be significant and still be unimportant?

## SUMMARY OF FORMULAS

*1. The formula for the Pearson correlation coefficient is*

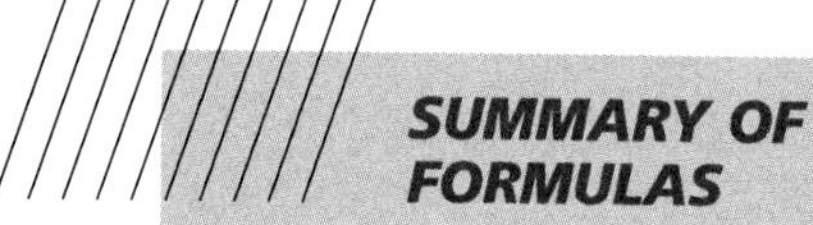

$$r = \frac{N(\Sigma XY) - (\Sigma X)(\Sigma Y)}{\sqrt{[N(\Sigma X^2) - (\Sigma X)^2][N(\Sigma Y^2) - (\Sigma Y)^2]}}$$

$df = N - 2$

*2. The proportion of variance accounted for equals* $r^2$.

# 11 Hypothesis Testing Using the One-Way Analysis of Variance

**CHAPTER ESSENTIALS**

**Before getting started, be sure you understand**

- From Chapter 1, what an independent and dependent variable is, and what a condition is
- From Chapter 4, that variance measures the differences between scores
- From Chapter 7, why we limit the probability of a Type I error to .05
- From Chapter 9, what independent samples and related samples are

**Your goals in this chapter are to learn**

- The terminology and logic of *analysis of variance*
- When and how to compute $F_{\text{obt}}$
- When and how to compute *Tukey's HSD*

In this chapter we will return to analyzing experiments. We have only one more common type of inferential procedure to learn, and it is called the *analysis of variance.* It is used in experiments involving more than two conditions. This chapter will show you (1) the general logic behind the analysis of variance, (2) how to perform this procedure, and (3) an additional part to this analysis called *post hoc tests.*

## AN OVERVIEW OF THE ANALYSIS OF VARIANCE

It is important to know about analysis of variance because it is *the* most common inferential statistical procedure used to analyze experiments. Why? Because there are actually many versions of this procedure, so it can be used with many different designs: It can be applied to independent or related samples, to an independent variable involving any number of conditions, and to a study involving any number of independent variables. Such complex designs are common, so you'll often encounter this statistic when conducting your own research or when reading that of others.

The analysis of variance has its own language that is also commonly used in research publications:

1. Analysis of variance is abbreviated as **ANOVA.**
2. An independent variable is called a **factor.**
3. Each condition of the independent variable is also called a **level** or a **treatment,** and differences produced by the independent variable are a **treatment effect.**
4. The symbol for the number of levels in a factor is **k.**
5. A **one-way ANOVA** is performed when one independent variable is tested. (A "two-way" ANOVA is used with two independent variables, and so on.)
6. When an independent variable is studied using independent samples, it is called a **between-subjects factor** and involves using the formulas from a **between-subjects ANOVA.**
7. When a factor is studied using related samples, it is called a **within-subjects factor** and requires the formulas for a **within-subjects ANOVA.**

In this chapter we discuss the one-way, between-subjects ANOVA. As an example, let's examine how people perform a task, depending on how difficult they believe the task will be (the "perceived difficulty" of the task). We'll create three conditions containing the unpowerful $n$ of 5 participants each and provide them with the same easy 10 math problems. However, we will tell participants in Level 1 that the problems are easy, in Level 2 that the problems are of medium difficulty, and in Level 3 that the problems are difficult. Our dependent variable is the number of problems that participants solve within an allotted time.

The way to diagram a one-way ANOVA is shown in Table 11.1. Each column is a level of the factor, containing the scores of participants tested under that condition (here, symbolized by $X$). The mean of each level is the mean of the scores from that column. Because we have three levels, $k = 3$. (Notice that the general format is to label the factor as factor A, with levels $A_1$, $A_2$, $A_3$, and so on.)

As usual, the purpose here is to demonstrate a relationship between the independent variable and the dependent variable. Ideally, we'll find a different mean for each condition, suggesting that if we tested the entire population under each level of difficulty, we would find three different populations of scores located at three different $\mu$s. But

***TABLE 11.1***

Diagram of a Study Having Three Levels of One Factor

*Each column represents a condition of the independent variable.*

*Factor A: Independent Variable of Perceived Difficulty*

| *Level $A_1$: Easy* | *Level $A_2$: Medium* | *Level $A_3$: Difficult* | ← *Conditions* $k = 3$ |
|---|---|---|---|
| $X$ | $X$ | $X$ | |
| $X$ | $X$ | $X$ | |
| $X$ | $X$ | $X$ | |
| $X$ | $X$ | $X$ | |
| $X$ | $X$ | $X$ | |
| $\overline{X}_1$ | $\overline{X}_2$ | $\overline{X}_3$ | |

there's the usual problem: Differences between the means may reflect sampling error, so that actually we would find one population of scores, having the same $\mu$, for all levels of difficulty. Therefore, the first step is to eliminate the idea that the differences between our sample means reflect sampling error. The **analysis of variance** is the parametric procedure for determining whether significant differences occur in an experiment containing two or more sample means. Don't be confused by this: When you have only two conditions, you can use either a two-sample $t$-test or the ANOVA. However, you *must* use ANOVA when you have more than two conditions.

The one-way between-subjects ANOVA requires that

*1.* all conditions contain independent samples,

*2.* the dependent scores are normally distributed, interval or ratio scores, and

*3.* the variances of the populations are homogeneous.

Although the $n$ in all conditions need not be equal, the $n$s should not be massively different. However, these procedures are *much* easier to perform with equal $n$s.

## Controlling the Experiment-Wise Error Rate

You might be wondering why we even need ANOVA. Couldn't we use the independent-samples $t$-test to find significant differences among the three means above? That is, we might test whether $\overline{X}_1$ differs from $\overline{X}_2$, then whether $\overline{X}_2$ differs from $\overline{X}_3$, and finally whether $\overline{X}_1$ differs from $\overline{X}_3$. We cannot use this approach because of the resulting probability of making a Type I error (rejecting a true $H_0$).

To understand this, we must first distinguish between making a Type I error *when comparing a pair of means,* and making a Type I error *somewhere* in the experiment. With $\alpha = .05$, the probability of a Type I error in a *single* $t$-test is .05. But here, we can make a Type I error when comparing $\overline{X}_1$ to $\overline{X}_2$, $\overline{X}_2$ to $\overline{X}_3$, or $\overline{X}_1$ to $\overline{X}_3$. The *overall* probability of making a Type I error somewhere in the experiment is called the **experiment-wise error rate.**

We use the $t$-test when comparing only two means in an experiment because with only one comparison, the experiment-wise error rate equals $\alpha$. But with more than two means in the experiment, performing multiple $t$-tests results in an experiment-wise error rate that is much larger than our $\alpha$. Because of the importance of avoiding Type I errors, we do not want the error rate to be larger than we think it is, and it should never be larger than .05. Therefore, we perform ANOVA. With it the experiment-wise error rate will equal the alpha we've chosen.

> ***REMEMBER*** The reason for performing ANOVA is that it keeps the *experiment-wise error rate* equal to $\alpha$.

## Statistical Hypotheses in ANOVA

ANOVA tests only two-tailed hypotheses. The null hypothesis is that there are no differences between the populations represented by the conditions. Thus, for our perceived difficulty study with the three levels of easy, medium, and difficult, we have

$$H_0: \mu_1 = \mu_2 = \mu_3$$

In general, when we perform ANOVA on a factor with $k$ levels, the null hypothesis is $H_0$: $\mu_1 = \mu_2 = \cdots = \mu_k$. The "$\ldots = \mu_k$" indicates that there are as many $\mu$s as there are levels.

However, the alternative hypothesis is not $\mu_1 \neq \mu_2 \neq \mu_3$. A study may demonstrate differences between *some* but not *all* conditions. (Perhaps our data represent a difference between $\mu_1$ and $\mu_2$, but not between $\mu_1$ and $\mu_3$, or perhaps only $\mu_2$ and $\mu_3$ differ.) To communicate this idea, the alternative hypothesis is

$H_a$: not all $\mu$s are equal

$H_a$ implies that a relationship is present because the population mean represented by one of the level means is different from the population mean represented by at least one other mean.

As usual, we test $H_0$, so ANOVA tests whether all sample means represent the same population mean.

## The *F* Statistic and Post Hoc Comparisons

Completing an ANOVA requires two major steps. First, we compute the statistic called F, which simultaneously compares all levels to determine whether any of the means represent different $\mu$s. We calculate $F_{obt}$ which we compare to $F_{crit}$.

When $F_{obt}$ is not significant, it indicates there are no significant differences between any means. Then, the experiment has failed to demonstrate a relationship and it's back to the drawing board.

When $F_{obt}$ is significant, it indicates only that *somewhere* among the means *at least two* of them differ significantly. But, $F_{obt}$ does not indicate *which* specific means differ significantly. Thus, if $F_{obt}$ for the perceived difficulty study is significant, then we have one or more significant differences somewhere among the means of the easy, medium, and difficult levels, but we won't know where they are.

Therefore, when $F_{obt}$ is significant, we perform a second statistical procedure, called *post hoc comparisons*. **Post hoc comparisons** are like *t*-tests, in which we compare all possible *pairs* of level means from a factor, one pair at a time, to determine which means differ significantly. Thus, for the difficulty study we'll compare the means from easy and medium, from easy and difficult, and from medium and difficult to determine which means differ significantly from each other. However, perform post hoc comparisons *only* when $F_{obt}$ is significant. A significant $F_{obt}$ followed by post hoc comparisons ensures that the experiment-wise probability of a Type I error will equal our alpha.

***REMEMBER*** If $F_{obt}$ is significant, perform *post hoc comparisons* to determine which means differ significantly.

The one exception to this rule is when you have only two levels in the factor. Then the significant difference indicated by $F_{obt}$ must be between the only two means in the study, so it is unnecessary to perform post hoc comparisons.

## A QUICK REVIEW

- The one-way ANOVA is performed when testing two or more conditions from one independent variable.
- A significant $F_{obt}$ followed by post hoc comparisons indicates which level means differ significantly, with the experiment-wise error rate equal to $\alpha$.

### More Examples

We measure the mood of participants after they have won 0, 10, or 20 dollars in a rigged card game. With one independent variable, a *one-way* design is involved, and the *factor* is the amount of money won. The *levels* are \$0, \$10, or \$20. If independent samples receive each *treatment,* we perform the *between-subjects ANOVA*. (Otherwise, perform the *within-subjects ANOVA*.) A significant $F_{obt}$ will indicate that at least two of the conditions produced significant differences in mean mood scores. Perform *post hoc comparisons* to determine which levels differ significantly, comparing the mean mood scores for each pair of conditions: \$0 vs. \$10, \$0 vs. \$20, and \$10 vs. \$20. The probability of a Type I error in the study—the *experiment-wise error rate*—equals $\alpha$.

### For Practice:

1. A study involving one independent variable is a ____ design.
2. Perform the ____ when a study involves independent samples; perform the ____ when it involves related samples.
3. An independent variable is also called a ____ and a condition is also called a ____ or ____.
4. The ____ will indicate whether any of the conditions differ, and then the ____ will indicate which specific conditions differ.
5. The probability of a Type I error in the study is called the ____.

**Answers**

1. one-way
2. between-subjects ANOVA; within-subjects ANOVA
3. factor; level; treatment
4. $F_{obt}$; post hoc comparisons
5. experiment-wise error rate

## COMPONENTS OF THE ANOVA

The analysis of variance does just that—it analyzes variance. It involves computing variance from two perspectives in the sample data, so that we can estimate two components in the population. But, we do not *call* them an estimated variance. Instead, each is called a *mean square*. (This is shortened from "mean of the squared deviations," which is what variance actually is.) The symbol for a mean square is *MS*. The two mean squares that we compute are the *mean square within groups* and the *mean square between groups*.

### The Mean Square Within Groups

The **mean square within groups** describes the variability in scores *within* the conditions of an experiment. It is symbolized by $MS_{wn}$. Recall that variance is a way to measure the differences among the scores. Here, we find the differences among the scores within each condition and "pool" them (like we did in the independent-samples *t*-test). Thus, the $MS_{wn}$ is the "average" variability of the scores within each condition.

The $MS_{wn}$ is an estimate of the variability within each population that is represented by our conditions. Because we look at scores within one condition at a time, $MS_{wn}$ stays the same regardless of whether $H_0$ is true or false. Thus, the $MS_{wn}$ describes the variability of individual scores in any of the populations being represented.

> ***REMEMBER*** The $MS_{wn}$ describes the differences among individual scores in the population.

## The Mean Square Between Groups

The other variance we compute is the mean square between groups. **The mean square between groups** describes the differences *between* the levels in a factor. It is symbolized by $MS_{bn}$. Essentially, the computations of $MS_{bn}$ measure how much the means of the conditions differ from each other. Then $MS_{bn}$ is used to estimate the differences between the populations that are represented by our conditions. Therefore, the size of $MS_{bn}$ will change, depending on whether $H_0$ is true or false. The larger the $MS_{bn}$, the more it *appears* that $H_0$ is false and that the conditions of the independent variable produce different populations of scores.

> ***REMEMBER*** The $MS_{bn}$ describes the differences produced by changing the levels of a factor.

## Comparing the Mean Squares: The Logic of the *F*-Ratio

The key to understanding the ANOVA is understanding what $MS_{bn}$ will equal when $H_0$ is true or false. First, when $H_0$ is true, the differences between the means of our levels reflected by $MS_{bn}$ will not be zero. In fact, statisticians have shown that when $H_0$ is true and the scores in all conditions come from one population, the amount the means differ should *equal* the amount that the individual scores differ. The reason for this is that when we select individual scores, because there is variability in the population, the scores will differ from the population's $\mu$ and from each other. Then, when we examine samples of such scores, their means will differ from the population's $\mu$ and each other to the same degree. The $MS_{bn}$ reflects the amount the sample (level) means differ, and $MS_{wn}$ reflects the amount that individual scores differ. Therefore, when $H_0$ is true, the $MS_{bn}$ should *equal* the $MS_{wn}$.

Thus, the smallest that $MS_{bn}$ should be is equal to $MS_{wn}$ when $H_0$ is true. However, when $H_0$ is false and changing the independent variable produces differences between the conditions, this will increase the differences among the means over and above this starting point. That is, now the level means differ because they represent different $\mu$s, plus they differ because of the variability in the scores in each population. Therefore, when $H_0$ is false (and $H_a$ is true) the $MS_{bn}$ should be *larger* than $MS_{wn}$.

However, we're not all that interested in the actual values of $MS_{bn}$ and $MS_{wn}$. Instead, we are interested in their ratio, called the $F$-ratio. The ***F*-ratio** equals the mean square between groups divided by the mean square within groups.

*THE FORMULA FOR THE* F-*RATIO IS*

$$F_{obt} = \frac{MS_{bn}}{MS_{wn}}$$

$MS_{bn}$ is always on top!

The $F$-ratio allows us to compare these components in order to make a decision about $H_0$. When $H_0$ is true, the $MS_{bn}$ should equal the $MS_{wn}$, and with the same number in both the numerator and denominator, the $F_{obt}$ equals 1. On the other hand, when $H_0$ is false, the $MS_{bn}$ should be larger than the $MS_{wn}$, and then the $F_{obt}$ is greater than 1. (An $F_{obt}$ between 0 and 1 is possible, but this can occur only when $H_0$ is true and $MS_{bn}$ and/or $MS_{wn}$ poorly represent this. $F_{obt}$ cannot be less than zero because mean squares are variances, which cannot be negative numbers.)

> ***REMEMBER*** When $H_0$ is true, the $MS_{bn}$ should equal the $MS_{wn}$ and so $F_{obt}$ should equal 1; when $H_0$ is false, the $MS_{bn}$ should be larger than the $MS_{wn}$ and so $F_{obt}$ should be greater than 1.

Unfortunately, in addition to the above there is another reason why $F_{obt}$ can be larger than 1, and that is (here we go again) sampling error! When $H_0$ is true, $F_{obt}$ "should" equal 1 if the data are perfectly representative. But what if they're not? Perhaps $H_0$ is true, so there is only one population of scores present, but by chance, the scores we obtain produce an $MS_{bn}$ that is larger than $MS_{wn}$. Then $F_{obt}$ will be larger than 1 simply because of sampling error.

This all boils down to the same old problem of significance testing. An $F_{obt}$ greater than 1 may accurately reflect the situation in which two or more conditions represent different populations (and there really is a treatment effect). Or, because of sampling error, an $F_{obt}$ greater than 1 may inaccurately reflect the situation in which all conditions represent the same population (and there only appears to be a treatment effect). The larger the $F_{obt}$, however, the less likely it is that we are poorly representing only one population and the more likely that we are representing two or more populations. Therefore, as with previous statistics, after computing $F_{obt}$, we will compare it to $F_{crit}$. If $F_{obt}$ is beyond $F_{crit}$, then our $MS_{bn}$ (and the differences between our level means that produced it) is unlikely to merely reflect sampling error, and instead is likely to reflect a real relationship in nature.

> ***REMEMBER*** An $F_{obt}$ equal to (or less than) 1 indicates that $H_0$ is true. An $F_{obt}$ greater than 1 may result from sampling error, or it may indicate a relationship in the population. A significant $F_{obt}$ indicates that the level means represent two or more different $\mu$s.

## PERFORMING THE ANOVA

When we computed the estimated variance in Chapter 4, the quantity $\Sigma(X - \overline{X})^2$ was called the "sum of the squared deviations." In calculating the mean squares, we perform a similar operation, so this name is shortened to the **sum of squares.** The symbol for the sum of squares is *SS*. Then the general formula for a mean square is the fraction formed by the sum of squares divided by the degrees of freedom or

$$MS = \frac{SS}{df}$$

Adding subscripts, we compute the mean square between groups ($MS_{\text{bn}}$) by computing the sum of squares between groups ($SS_{\text{bn}}$) and dividing by the degrees of freedom between groups ($df_{\text{bn}}$). Likewise, we compute the mean square within groups ($MS_{\text{wn}}$) by computing the sum of squares within groups ($SS_{\text{wn}}$) and dividing by the degrees of freedom within groups ($df_{\text{wn}}$). With $MS_{\text{bn}}$ and $MS_{\text{wn}}$, we compute $F_{\text{obt}}$.

If all this strikes you as the most confusing thing ever devised, you'll find an ANOVA summary table very helpful. Here is the general format.

Summary Table of One-Way ANOVA

| *Source* | *Sum of Squares* | **df** | *Mean Square* | **F** |
|---|---|---|---|---|
| Between | $SS_{\text{bn}}$ | $df_{\text{bn}}$ | $MS_{\text{bn}}$ | $F_{\text{obt}}$ |
| Within | $SS_{\text{wn}}$ | $df_{\text{wn}}$ | $MS_{\text{wn}}$ | |
| Total | $SS_{\text{tot}}$ | $df_{\text{tot}}$ | | |

The "source" column identifies each source of variation, either *between* or *within,* and we also consider the *total.* Using the following formulas, we'll compute the components for the other columns.

## Computing $F_{\text{obt}}$

Say that we performed the perceived difficulty study discussed earlier, telling participants that some math problems were easy, of medium difficulty, or difficult, and measuring the number of problems they solved. The data are presented in Table 11.2. As shown in the following sections, there are four parts to computing the $F_{\text{obt}}$, finding: (1) the sum of squares, (2) the degrees of freedom, (3) the mean squares, and (4) $F_{\text{obt}}$.

**Computing the Sums of Squares** The computations here require 4 steps.

**Step 1:** *Compute the sums and means:* As in Table 11.2, compute $\Sigma X$, $\Sigma X^2$, and $\overline{X}$ for each level (each column). Each *n* is the number of scores in the level. Then add together the $\Sigma X$ from all levels to get the total, which is "$\Sigma X_{\text{tot}}$." Also, add together the $\Sigma X^2$ from all levels to get the total, which is "$\Sigma X^2_{\text{tot}}$." And, add the *n*s together to obtain *N*.

**Step 2:** *Compute the total sum of squares* ($SS_{tot}$):

*THE FORMULA FOR THE TOTAL SUM OF SQUARES IS*

$$SS_{\text{tot}} = \Sigma X^2_{\text{tot}} - \frac{(\Sigma X_{\text{tot}})^2}{N}$$

**TABLE 11.2**
Data from Perceived Difficulty Experiment

| *Factor A: Perceived Difficulty* | | | |
|---|---|---|---|
| *Level $A_1$: Easy* | *Level $A_2$: Medium* | *Level $A_3$: Difficult* | |
| 9 | 4 | 1 | |
| 12 | 6 | 3 | |
| 4 | 8 | 4 | |
| 8 | 2 | 5 | |
| 7 | 10 | 2 | *Totals* |
| $\Sigma X = 40$ | $\Sigma X = 30$ | $\Sigma X = 15$ | $\Sigma X = 85$ |
| $\Sigma X^2 = 354$ | $\Sigma X^2 = 220$ | $\Sigma X^2 = 55$ | $\Sigma X^2 = 629$ |
| $n_1 = 5$ | $n_2 = 5$ | $n_3 = 5$ | $N = 15$ |
| $\bar{X}_1 = 8$ | $\bar{X}_2 = 6$ | $\bar{X}_3 = 3$ | $k = 3$ |

Using the data from Table 11.2, $\Sigma X^2_{\text{tot}} = 629$, $\Sigma X_{\text{tot}} = 85$, and $N = 15$, so

$$SS_{\text{tot}} = 629 - \frac{(85)^2}{15}$$

$$SS_{\text{tot}} = 629 - \frac{7225}{15}$$

$$SS_{\text{tot}} = 629 - 481.67$$

Thus, $SS_{\text{tot}} = 147.33$.

**Step 3:** *Compute the sum of squares between groups* ($SS_{bn}$):

*THE FORMULA FOR THE SUM OF SQUARES BETWEEN GROUPS IS*

$$SS_{\text{bn}} = \Sigma\left(\frac{(\Sigma X \text{ in column})^2}{n \text{ in column}}\right) - \frac{(\Sigma X_{\text{tot}})^2}{N}$$

Above in Table 11.2, each column represents a level of the factor. Thus, find the $\Sigma X$ for a level, square that $\Sigma X$, and then divide by the $n$ in that level. After doing this for all levels, add the results together and subtract the quantity $(\Sigma X_{\text{tot}})^2/N$. Thus, we have

$$SS_{\text{bn}} = \left(\frac{(40)^2}{5} + \frac{(30)^2}{5} + \frac{(15)^2}{5}\right) - \frac{(85)^2}{15}$$

so

$$SS_{\text{bn}} = (320 + 180 + 45) - 481.67$$

and

$$SS_{\text{bn}} = 545 - 481.67$$

So $SS_{\text{bn}} = 63.33$.

**Step 4:** *Compute the sum of squares within groups* ($SS_{wn}$): Mathematically, $SS_{\text{tot}}$ equals $SS_{\text{bn}}$ plus $SS_{\text{wn}}$. Therefore, the total minus the between leaves the within.

*THE FORMULA FOR THE SUM OF SQUARES WITHIN GROUPS IS*

$$SS_{wn} = SS_{tot} - SS_{bn}$$

In the example, $SS_{tot}$ is 147.33 and $SS_{bn}$ is 63.33, so

$$SS_{wn} = 147.33 - 63.33 = 84.00$$

Thus, $SS_{wn} = 84.00$.

**Computing the Degrees of Freedom** Compute $df_{bn}$, $df_{wn}$, and $df_{tot}$, so here there are three steps.

**Step 1:** *The degrees of freedom between groups equals* k $-$ *1,* where $k$ is the number of levels in the factor. In the example there are three levels of perceived difficulty (easy, medium, and difficult), so $k = 3$. Thus, $df_{bn} = 2$.

**Step 2:** *The degrees of freedom within groups equals N* $-$ *k,* where $N$ is the total $N$ in the experiment and $k$ is the number of levels in the factor. In the example $N$ is 15 and $k$ is 3, so $df_{wn} = 15 - 3 = 12$.

**Step 3:** *The degrees of freedom total equals N* $-$ *1,* where $N$ is the total $N$ in the experiment. In the example $N$ is 15, so $df_{tot} = 15 - 1 = 14$.

The $df_{tot}$ must equal the $df_{bn}$ plus the $df_{wn}$. At this point the ANOVA summary table looks like this:

| *Source* | *Sum of Squares* | df | *Mean Square* | F |
|---|---|---|---|---|
| Between | 63.33 | 2 | $MS_{bn}$ | $F_{obt}$ |
| Within | 84.00 | 12 | $MS_{wn}$ | |
| Total | 147.33 | 14 | | |

**Computing the Mean Squares** You can work directly from the summary table to compute the mean squares.

**Step 1:** *Compute the mean square between groups:*

*THE FORMULA FOR THE MEAN SQUARE BETWEEN GROUPS IS*

$$MS_{bn} = \frac{SS_{bn}}{df_{bn}}$$

From the summary table

$$MS_{bn} = \frac{63.33}{2} = 31.67$$

so $MS_{bn}$ is 31.67.

**Step 2:** *Compute the mean square within groups:*

*THE FORMULA FOR THE MEAN SQUARE WITHIN GROUPS IS*

$$MS_{\text{wn}} = \frac{SS_{\text{wn}}}{df_{\text{wn}}}$$

For the example

$$MS_{\text{wn}} = \frac{84}{12} = 7.00$$

so $MS_{\text{wn}}$ is 7.00.

Do *not* compute the mean square for $SS_{\text{tot}}$ because it has no use.

**Computing the *F*** Finally, compute $F_{\text{obt}}$.

*THE FORMULA FOR* $F_{obt}$ *IS*

$$F_{\text{obt}} = \frac{MS_{\text{bn}}}{MS_{\text{wn}}}$$

In the example $MS_{\text{bn}}$ is 31.67 and $MS_{\text{wn}}$ is 7.00, so

$$F_{\text{obt}} = \frac{MS_{\text{bn}}}{MS_{\text{wn}}} = \frac{31.67}{7.00} = 4.52$$

Thus, $F_{\text{obt}}$ is 4.52.

Now the completed ANOVA summary table is

| *Source* | *Sum of Squares* | df | *Mean Square* | F |
|---|---|---|---|---|
| Between | 63.33 | 2 | 31.67 | 4.52 |
| Within | 84.00 | 12 | 7.00 | |
| Total | 147.33 | 14 | | |

The $F_{\text{obt}}$ is always placed in the row labeled "Between."

As discussed in the following section, the final, Step 5 is to compare $F_{\text{obt}}$ to $F_{\text{crit}}$.

## Interpreting $F_{\text{obt}}$

We interpret $F_{\text{obt}}$ by comparing it to $F_{\text{crit}}$, and for that we examine the *F*-distribution. The ***F*-distribution** is the sampling distribution showing the various values of *F* that occur when $H_0$ is true and all conditions represent one population. To create it, it is as if, using our *n*s and *k*, we select the scores for all of our conditions from one raw score population (like $H_0$ says we did in our experiment), and compute $MS_{wn}$, $MS_{bn}$ and then $F_{obt}$. We do this an infinite number of times, and plotting the $F$s produces the sampling distribution, as shown in Figure 11.1.

The $F$-distribution is skewed because there is no limit to how large $F_{obt}$ can be, but it cannot be less than zero. The mean of the distribution is 1 because, most often when $H_0$ is true, $MS_{bn}$ will equal $MS_{wn}$, and so $F$ will equal 1. The right-hand tail, however, shows that sometimes, by chance, $F$ is greater than 1. Because our $F_{obt}$ can reflect a relationship in the population only when it is greater than 1, the entire region of rejection is in this upper tail of the $F$-distribution. (That's right, ANOVA involves two-tailed hypotheses, but they are tested using only the upper tail of the sampling distribution.) If $F_{obt}$ is larger than $F_{crit}$, then $F_{obt}$—and the differences between our level means—is so unlikely when $H_0$ is true that we reject $H_0$.

The $F$-distribution is actually a family of curves, each having a slightly different shape, depending on our degrees of freedom. However, two values of $df$ determine the shape of an $F$-distribution: the $df$ used when computing the mean square between groups ($df_{bn}$) and the $df$ used when computing the mean square within groups ($df_{wn}$). Therefore, to obtain $F_{crit}$, turn to Table 4 in Appendix B, entitled "Critical Values of $F$." A portion of these "$F$-tables" is presented in Table 11.3. Across the top of the tables, the columns are labeled "$df$ between groups." Along the left-hand side, the rows are labeled "$df$ within groups." Locate the appropriate column and row using the $df$s from your study. The critical values in dark type are for $\alpha = .05$, and those in light type are for $\alpha = .01$. For our example, $df_{bn} = 2$ and $df_{wn} = 12$. For $\alpha = .05$, the $F_{crit}$ is 3.88. (If your $df_{wn}$ are not in the table, then for $df$ between 30 and 50 your $F_{crit}$ is the average of the two critical values shown for the bracketing even $df$ that are given. For $df$ above 50, use the $F_{crit}$ for the $df$ that is closest to your $df$.)

Thus, our $F_{obt}$ is 4.52 and $F_{crit}$ is 3.88, producing the complete sampling distribution in Figure 11.1. The $H_0$ says that our $F_{obt}$ is greater than 1 because of sampling error: The differences between the means of our levels are due to sampling error, and all means poorly represent one population mean. However, our $F_{obt}$ is in the region of rejection, telling us that such differences between $\bar{X}$s hardly ever occur when $H_0$ is true. Because $F_{obt}$ is larger than $F_{crit}$, we reject $H_0$. Thus, we conclude that the $F_{obt}$ is significant and that the factor of perceived difficulty produces a significant difference in mean performance scores. (Had $F_{obt}$ been less than $F_{crit}$, then the corresponding differences between our means would *not* be unlikely to occur when $H_0$ is true, so we would not reject $H_0$.)

***FIGURE 11.1***

Sampling distribution of $F$ when $H_0$ is true for $df_{bn} = 2$ and $df_{wn} = 12$

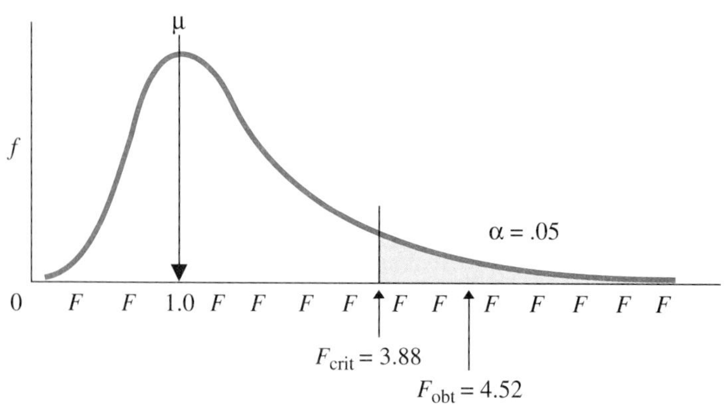

**TABLE 11.3**
Portion of Table 4 in Appendix B, "Critical Values of *F*."

| *Degrees of Freedom Within Groups (degrees of freedom in denominator of* **F**-*ratio)* | *Degrees of Freedom Between Groups (degrees of freedom in numerator of* **F**-*ratio)* | | | | | |
|---|---|---|---|---|---|---|
| | α | *1* | *2* | *3* | *4* | *5* |
| 1 | **.05** | **161** | **200** | **216** | **225** | **230** |
| | .01 | 4,052 | 4,999 | 5,403 | 5,625 | 5,764 |
| — | — | — | — | — | — | — |
| — | — | — | — | — | — | — |
| 11 | **.05** | **4.84** | **3.98** | **3.59** | **3.36** | **3.20** |
| | .01 | 9.65 | 7.20 | 6.22 | 5.67 | 5.32 |
| 12 | **.05** | **4.75** | **3.88** | **3.49** | **3.26** | **3.11** |
| | .01 | 9.33 | 6.93 | 5.95 | 5.41 | 5.06 |

Because we rejected $H_0$ and accepted $H_a$, we return to the means from the levels:

***Perceived Difficulty***

| *Easy* | *Medium* | *Difficult* |
|---|---|---|
| $\overline{X}_1 = 8$ | $\overline{X}_2 = 6$ | $\overline{X}_3 = 3$ |

To see the *treatment effect,* look at the overall pattern: Because the means change, the scores that produce them are changing, so a relationship is present in which as perceived difficulty increases, performance scores decrease. However, we do not know if *every* increase in difficulty results in a *significant* decrease in scores. To determine that, we must perform the post hoc comparisons. But first . . .

## A QUICK REVIEW

- To compute $F_{obt}$, compute the $SS_{tot}$, $SS_{bn}$, and $SS_{wn}$, and $df_{tot}$, $df_{bn}$, and $df_{wn}$. Dividing $SS_{bn}$ by $df_{bn}$ gives the $MS_{bn}$; dividing $SS_{wn}$ by $df_{wn}$ gives $MS_{wn}$. Dividing $MS_{bn}$ by $MS_{wn}$ gives $F_{obt}$. Compare $F_{obt}$ to $F_{crit}$.

### More Examples

We test participants under conditions $A_1$ and $A_2$.

| $A_1$ | $A_2$ | |
|---|---|---|
| 4 | 6 | |
| 5 | 8 | |
| 3 | 9 | |
| 5 | 8 | |
| $\overline{X}_1 = 4.25$ | $\overline{X} = 7.75$ | |
| $\Sigma X = 17$ | $\Sigma X = 31$ | $\Sigma X_{tot} = 48$ |
| $\Sigma X^2 = 75$ | $\Sigma X^2 = 245$ | $\Sigma X^2_{tot} = 320$ |
| $n_1 = 4$ | $n_2 = 4$ | $N = 8$ |

1. *Compute the sums of squares:*

   1. $SS_{\text{tot}} = \Sigma X^2_{\text{tot}} - \frac{(\Sigma X_{\text{tot}})^2}{N} = 320 - \left(\frac{48^2}{8}\right) = 32$

   2. $SS_{\text{bn}} = \Sigma\left(\frac{(\Sigma X \text{ in column})^2}{n \text{ in column}}\right) - \frac{(\Sigma X_{\text{tot}})^2}{N}$

      $= \left(\frac{17^2}{4} + \frac{31^2}{4}\right) - \left(\frac{48^2}{8}\right) = 24.5$

   3. $SS_{\text{wn}} = 32 - 24.5 = 7.5$

2. *Compute the degrees of freedom:*

   1. $df_{\text{bn}} = k - 1 = 2 - 1 = 1$
   2. $df_{\text{wn}} = N - k = 8 - 2 = 6$
   3. $df_{\text{tot}} = N - 1 = 8 - 1 = 7$

3. *Compute the mean squares:*

   1. $MS_{\text{bn}} = SS_{\text{bn}}/df_{\text{bn}} = 24.5/1 = 24.5$
   2. $MS_{\text{wn}} = SS_{\text{wn}}/df_{\text{wn}} = 7.5/6 = 1.25$

4. *Compute* $F_{obt}$*:*

   $F_{\text{obt}} = MS_{\text{bn}}/MS_{\text{wn}} = 24.5/1.25 = 19.60$

5. *Compare* $F_{obt}$ *to* $F_{crit}$*:* With $\alpha = .05$, and $df_{\text{bn}} = 1$ and $df_{\text{wn}} = 6$, $F_{\text{crit}} = 5.99$. The sampling distribution is similar to that back in Figure 11.1, except that the $F_{\text{obt}}$ of 19.60 is beyond the $F_{\text{crit}}$ of 5.99. Therefore, the means of the conditions differ significantly.

### *For Practice:*

1. What are the two components that are needed to compute a mean square?
2. Then next, to compute the ____, divide the ____ by the ____. To compute the ____, divide the ____ by the ____.
3. Finally, $F_{\text{obt}}$ is computed by dividing the ____ by the ____.

**Answers**

1. The sums of squares and the *df*
2. $MS_{\text{bn}}$, $SS_{\text{bn}}$, $df_{\text{bn}}$; $MS_{\text{wn}}$, $SS_{\text{wn}}$, $df_{\text{wn}}$
3. $MS_{\text{bn}}$, $MS_{\text{wn}}$

## Tukey Post Hoc Comparisons

Remember that a significant $F_{\text{obt}}$ indicates at least one significant difference somewhere among the level means. To determine which means differ, we perform post hoc comparisons. Statisticians have developed a variety of post hoc procedures which differ in how likely they are to produce Type I or Type II errors. One common procedure that has reasonably low error rates is the **Tukey *HSD* multiple comparisons test.** It is used only when the *n*s in all levels of the factor are equal. The *HSD* is a rearrangement of the *t*-test that computes the minimum difference between two means that is required for them to differ significantly. (*HSD* stands for the Honestly Significant Difference.) There are four steps to performing the *HSD* test.

**Step 1:** *Find* $q_k$: Use Table 5 in Appendix B, entitled "Values of Studentized Range Statistic." Locate the column labeled with the *k* corresponding to the number of means in your factor. Find the row labeled with the $df_{\text{wn}}$ used to compute your $F_{\text{obt}}$. (If your *df* is not in the Table, use the *df* in the table that is closest to it.) Then find the $q_k$ for the appropriate $\alpha$. For our study above, $k = 3$, $df_{\text{wn}} = 12$, and $\alpha = .05$, so $q_k = 3.77$.

**Step 2:** *Compute the* HSD:

*THE FORMULA FOR TUKEY'S* HSD *IS*

$$HSD = (q_k)\left(\sqrt{\frac{MS_{\text{wn}}}{n}}\right)$$

$MS_{wn}$ is the denominator from your significant $F$-ratio, and $n$ is the number of scores in each level of the factor.

In the example $MS_{wn}$ was 7.0 and $n$ was 5, so

$$HSD = (q_k)\left(\sqrt{\frac{MS_{wn}}{n}}\right) = (3.77)\left(\sqrt{\frac{7.0}{5}}\right) = (3.77)(\sqrt{1.4}) = (3.77)(1.183) = 4.46$$

Thus, $HSD$ is 4.46.

**Step 3:** *Determine the differences between each pair of means:* Subtract each mean from every other mean. Ignore whether differences are positive or negative (this is a two-tailed test of the $H_0$ that $\mu_1 - \mu_2 = 0$).

The differences for the perceived difficulty study can be diagramed as shown below.

***Perceived Difficulty***

| *Easy* | *Medium* | *Difficult* |
|---|---|---|
| $\bar{X}_1 = 8$ | $\bar{X}_2 = 6$ | $\bar{X}_3 = 3$ |

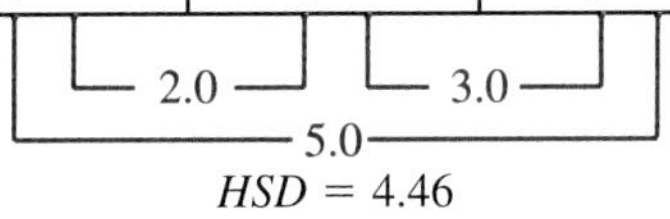

2.0 3.0

5.0

$HSD = 4.46$

On the line connecting any two levels is the absolute difference between their means.

**Step 4:** *Compare each difference to the* HSD: If the absolute difference between two means is *greater than* the *HSD,* then these means differ significantly. (It's as if you performed a $t$-test on them and $t_{obt}$ was significant.) If the absolute difference between two means is less than or equal to the *HSD,* then it is *not* a significant difference (and would not produce a significant $t_{obt}$).

Above, the *HSD* was 4.46. The means from the easy level (8) and the difficult level (3) differ by more than 4.46, so they differ significantly. The mean from the medium level (6), however, differs from the other means by less than 4.46, so it does not differ significantly from them.

Thus, our final conclusion about the study is that we did demonstrate a relationship between performance and perceived difficulty, but only when we changed from the easy to the difficult condition. If everyone in the population were tested under each of these conditions, we would expect to find two populations of scores, one for the easy condition at a $\mu$ around 8, and one for the difficult condition at a $\mu$ around 3. (In fact, recall from Chapter 8 that we can compute a *confidence interval* to describe the range of $\mu$s that is likely to be represented by the $\bar{X}$ of a condition.) However, we cannot say anything about the population produced by the medium condition, because it did not produce any significant differences.

## A QUICK REVIEW

- Post hoc comparisons indicate which specific levels differ significantly.
- Perform the Tukey *HSD* test when $F_{obt}$ is significant, there are more than two levels, and all *n*s are equal.

### MORE EXAMPLES

In an experiment the $F_{obt}$ is significant, and the level means are $\overline{X}_1 = 4.0$, $\overline{X}_2 = 1.5$, and $\overline{X}_3 = 6.8$. In the ANOVA, $n = 11$, $MS_{wn} = 20.61$, and $df_{wn} = 30$. To compute Tukey's *HSD:*

1. Find $q_k$ in Table 5: For $k = 3$ and $df_{wn} = 30$, $q_k = 3.49$.
2. Compute *HSD.*

$$HSD = (q_k)\left(\sqrt{\frac{MS_{wn}}{n}}\right) = (3.49)\left(\sqrt{\frac{20.61}{11}}\right) = 4.78$$

3. Find the differences

$\overline{X}_1 - \overline{X}_2 = 4.0 - 1.5 = 2.5.$
$\overline{X}_2 - \overline{X}_3 = 1.5 - 6.8 = -5.3.$
$\overline{X}_1 - \overline{X}_3 = 4.0 - 6.8 = -2.8$

4. Compare the differences to *HSD.* Only the difference between $\overline{X}_2$ and $\overline{X}_3$ of $-5.3$ is greater than the *HSD* of 4.78, so changing only from level 2 to level 3 produced significant differences in scores.

### *For Practice:*

We have level means of $\overline{X}_1 = 16.50$, $\overline{X}_2 = 11.50$, and $\overline{X}_3 = 8.92$ (with $n = 21$, $MS_{wn} = 63.44$, and $df_{wn} = 60$).

1. What is $q_k$ here?
2. What is the *HSD?*
3. Which means differ significantly?

**Answers**

1. For $k = 3$ and $df_{wn} = 60$, $q_k = 3.40$.
2. $HSD = 3.40(\sqrt{63.44/21}) = 5.91$.
3. Only the difference for $\overline{X}_1 - \overline{X}_3$ of 7.58 is larger than 5.91, so only these means differ significantly.

## SUMMARY OF THE ONE-WAY ANOVA

It's been a long haul, but after checking the assumptions here is how to perform a one-way ANOVA:

*1.* The null hypothesis is $H_0$: $\mu_1 = \mu_2 = \ldots = \mu_k$, and the alternative hypothesis is $H_a$: not all $\mu$s are equal.

*2.* Compute $F_{obt}$.

a. Compute the sums of squares and the degrees of freedom.

b. Compute the mean squares.

c. Compute $F_{obt}$.

*3.* Compare $F_{obt}$ to $F_{crit}$, found in Appendix B, Table 4, using $df_{bn}$ and $df_{wn}$. If $F_{obt}$ is larger than $F_{crit}$, then $F_{obt}$ is significant, indicating that the means in at least two conditions differ significantly.

*4.* With a significant $F_{obt}$, more than two levels, and equal *n*s, perform the Tukey *HSD* test.

a. Find $q_k$ in Appendix B, Table 5, using *k* and $df_{wn}$.

b. Compute the *HSD.*

c. Find the difference between each pair of level means.

d. Any differences larger than the *HSD* are significant.

*5.* Draw conclusions about the influence of your independent variable by considering the significant means of your levels.

## STATISTICS IN THE RESEARCH LITERATURE: REPORTING ANOVA

In research reports, an $F_{obt}$ is reported using the same format as previous statistics, except that we include both the $df_{bn}$ and the $df_{wn}$. In the perceived-difficulty study the significant $F_{obt}$ was 4.52, with $df_{bn} = 2$, and $df_{wn} = 12$. We report this as

$$F(2, 12) = 4.52, p < 05$$

*Note:* In the parentheses always report $df_{bn}$ *and then* $df_{wn}$.

Usually the *HSD* value is not reported. Instead, indicate that the Tukey *HSD* was performed, the alpha level used, and identify which levels differ significantly. However, for completeness, the means and standard deviations from all levels are reported, even those that do not differ significantly. Likewise, when graphing the results, the means from all levels are plotted.

## A WORD ABOUT EFFECT SIZE AND ETA²

Recall from Chapter 9 that in experiments we report the *effect size,* which indicates the amount of influence that changing the conditions of the independent variable had on dependent scores. A common way to measure effect size is the "proportion of variance accounted for," which, in an experiment, is the proportion of all differences in dependent scores that occur with—and presumably are produced by—changing the conditions of the independent variable.

In ANOVA, effect size is computed by squaring the correlation coefficient symbolized by the Greek letter "eta" (pronounced "ay-tah"). The symbol for eta squared is $\eta^2$. **Eta squared** indicates the proportion of variance in dependent scores that is accounted for by changing the levels of a factor. This is analogous to other measures we've discussed in previous chapters, except that $\eta^2$ can be used to describe any linear or nonlinear relationship containing two or more levels of a factor. In a particular experiment, $\eta^2$ will be a proportion between 0 and 1, indicating the extent to which dependent scores change as the independent variable changes.

*THE FORMULA FOR ETA SQUARED IS*

$$\eta^2 = \frac{SS_{bn}}{SS_{tot}}$$

In the ANOVA, the $SS_{bn}$ reflects the differences between the conditions. The $SS_{tot}$ reflects the differences between all scores in the experiment. Then $\eta^2$ reflects the proportion of all differences in scores that are associated with changing the conditions.

For example, for the perceived-difficulty study, $SS_{bn}$ was 63.33 and $SS_{tot}$ was 147.33. So

$$\eta^2 = \frac{SS_{bn}}{SS_{tot}} = \frac{63.33}{147.33} = .43$$

The larger the $\eta^2$, the larger a role the factor plays in determining differences among participants' scores, so the more important the variable is for understanding differences in participants' corresponding behaviors. Thus, 43% of all differences in our scores were accounted for (produced) by changing the levels of perceived difficulty. Because 43% is a substantial amount, this factor is important in determining participants' performance, so it is important for scientific study.

*REMEMBER* $\eta^2$ (*eta squared*) measures the *effect size* of a factor by indicating the proportion of all differences in dependent scores that is accounted for by changing the levels of a factor.

## CHAPTER SUMMARY

1. The general terms used previously and their corresponding ANOVA terms are shown in this table:

| *General Term* | = | *ANOVA Term* |
|---|---|---|
| independent variable | = | factor |
| one independent variable | = | one-way design |
| independent samples | = | between-subjects |
| related samples | = | within-subjects |
| condition | = | level (treatment) |
| sum of squared deviations | = | sum of squares (*SS*) |
| variance ($s_X^2$) | = | mean square (*MS*) |
| effect of independent variable | = | treatment effect |

2. The *experiment-wise error rate* is the probability that a Type I error will occur in an experiment. ANOVA keeps the experiment-wise error rate equal to $\alpha$.
3. The ANOVA tests the $H_0$ that all $\mu$s being represented are equal; $H_a$ is that not all $\mu$s are equal.
4. The one-way, between-subjects ANOVA assumes (1) normally distributed, interval or ratio dependent scores, (2) one independent variable is tested using independent samples, and (3) the populations being represented have homogeneous variance.
5. The $MS_{wn}$ describes the differences among individual scores in the population. The $MS_{bn}$ describes the differences produced by changing the levels of a factor.
6. $F_{obt}$ is computed using the F-*ratio,* which equals the mean square between groups divided by the mean square within groups.
7. The F-*distribution* is the sampling distribution of all possible values of $F_{obt}$ when $H_0$ is true.
8. The $F_{obt}$ may be greater than 1 because either (a) there is no treatment effect, but the level means are not perfectly representative of this, or (b) the means from

two or more levels represent different $\mu$s. If $F_{obt}$ is significant, the level means are so unlikely to represent the same population mean that we conclude that a relationship is present.

9. If $F_{obt}$ is significant with more than two levels, perform *post hoc comparisons* to determine which means differ significantly. If all *n*s are equal, perform *Tukey's* HSD *test.*
10. *Eta squared* ($\eta^2$) describes the *effect size*—the *proportion of variance* in dependent scores accounted for by changing the levels of the independent variable.

## KEY TERMS: Can You Define the Following?

*k* *202*
$F_{obt}$ *204*
$F_{crit}$ *204*
$MS_{wn}$ *205*
$MS_{bn}$ *206*
$df_{bn}$ *210*
$df_{wn}$ *210*
$\eta^2$ *218*
$SS_{bn}$ *209*
$SS_{wn}$ *210*
*HSD* *214*
$q_k$ *215*
analysis of variance *203*
ANOVA *202*
between-subjects ANOVA *202*
between-subjects factor *202*
eta squared *218*
experiment-wise error rate *203*
factor *202*
*F*-distribution *212*
*F*-ratio *206*
level *202*
mean square between groups *206*
mean square within groups *205*
one-way ANOVA *202*
post hoc comparisons *204*
sum of squares *207*
treatment *202*
treatment effect *202*
Tukey's *HSD* multiple comparisons test *214*
within-subjects ANOVA *202*
within-subjects factor *202*

## REVIEW QUESTIONS

(Answers for odd-numbered questions are in Appendix C.)

1. What does each of the following terms mean? (a) ANOVA (b) one-way design (c) factor (d) level (e) treatment (f) between-subjects factor (g) within-subjects factor
2. (a) What is the difference between *n* and *N?* (b) What does *k* stand for?
3. (a) What is the experiment-wise error rate? (b) Why does ANOVA solve the problem with the experiment-wise error rate created by multiple *t*-tests?
4. Summarize the steps involved in analyzing an experiment when $k > 2$.
5. (a) When is it necessary to perform post hoc comparisons? Why? (b) When is it unnecessary to perform post hoc comparisons?
6. What are the two types of mean squares, and what does each one estimate?
7. What does the *F*-ratio compare?

8. (a) Why should $F_{obt}$ equal 1 if the data represent the $H_0$ situation? (b) Why is $F_{obt}$ greater than 1 when the data represent the $H_a$ situation? (c) What does a significant $F_{obt}$ indicate about differences between the levels of a factor?
9. What does $\eta^2$ indicate?
10. With $\alpha = .05$, $F_{obt} = 6.31$ is significant, with $df_{bn} = 4$ and $df_{wn} = 30$. How is this result reported in the literature?

## APPLICATION QUESTIONS

11. (a) In a study comparing four conditions, what is $H_0$? (b) What is $H_a$? (c) In words what do $H_0$ and $H_a$ say for this study?
12. In an experiment, scores are measured under two conditions. (a) How will the researcher know whether to perform a parametric or nonparametric procedure? (b) Which two types of parametric procedures are available? (c) If the experiment involves three levels, which two versions of a parametric procedure are available? (d) How does the researcher choose between them?
13. (a) Poindexter computes an $F_{obt}$ of .63. How should this be interpreted? (b) He computes another $F_{obt}$ of $-1.7$. How should this be interpreted?
14. Foofy obtained a significant $F_{obt}$ from an experiment with five levels. She says she's demonstrated a relationship in which changing each condition of the independent variable results in a significant change in the dependent variable. (a) Is she correct? (b) What must she do?
15. (a) Why must the relationship in a one-way ANOVA be significant in order to be potentially important? (b) What does "significant" tell you about the relationship? (c) Why can the relationship be significant yet unimportant?
16. In a research report the between-subjects factor of participants' salary produced significant differences in judgments of self-esteem. (a) What does this tell you about the design? (b) What does it tell you about the results?
17. An article reports that, using a within-subjects design, a diet led to a significant decrease in weight for a group of participants. (a) What does this tell you about the design? (b) Which ANOVA was computed here?
18. A researcher investigated the number of viral infections people contract as a function of the amount of stress they experienced during a six-month period. She obtained the following data:

*Amount of Stress*

| *Negligible Stress* | *Minimal Stress* | *Moderate Stress* | *Severe Stress* |
|---|---|---|---|
| 2 | 4 | 6 | 5 |
| 1 | 3 | 5 | 7 |
| 4 | 2 | 7 | 8 |
| 1 | 3 | 5 | 4 |

(a) What are $H_0$ and $H_a$? (b) Compute $F_{obt}$ and complete the ANOVA summary table. (c) With $\alpha = .05$, what is $F_{crit}$? (d) Perform the post hoc comparisons. (e) What do you conclude about this study? (f) Describe the effect size and interpret it.

***19.*** Here are data from an experiment studying the effect of age on creativity scores:

| *Age 4* | *Age 6* | *Age 8* | *Age 10* |
|---|---|---|---|
| 3 | 9 | 9 | 7 |
| 5 | 11 | 12 | 7 |
| 7 | 14 | 9 | 6 |
| 4 | 10 | 8 | 4 |
| 3 | 10 | 9 | 5 |

(a) Compute $F_{obt}$ and create an ANOVA summary table. (b) With $\alpha = .05$ what do you conclude about $F_{obt}$? (c) Perform the post hoc comparisons. What should you conclude about the treatments? (d) How important is the relationship in this study?

***20.*** In a study in which $k = 3$, $n = 21$, $\overline{X}_1 = 45.3$, $\overline{X}_2 = 16.9$, and $\overline{X}_3 = 8.2$, you compute the following sums of squares:

| *Source* | *Sum of Squares* | df | *Mean Square* | F |
|---|---|---|---|---|
| Between | 147.32 | ____ | ____ | ____ |
| Within | 862.99 | ____ | ____ | |
| Total | 1010.31 | ____ | | |

(a) Complete the ANOVA. (b) With $\alpha = .05$ what do you conclude about $F_{obt}$? (c) Perform the post hoc comparisons. (d) What do you conclude about this relationship? (e) What is the effect size, and what does it tell you about the influence of this independent variable?

***21.*** We investigated the effect of volume of background noise on participants' accuracy rates while performing a boring task. Three groups produced the following means and sums of squares:

| | *Low Volume* | *Moderate Volume* | *High Volume* |
|---|---|---|---|
| $\overline{X}$ | 61.5 | 65.5 | 48.25 |
| $n$ | 5 | 5 | 5 |

| *Source* | *Sum of Squares* | df | *Mean Square* | F |
|---|---|---|---|---|
| Between groups | 652.16 | ____ | ____ | ____ |
| Within groups | 612.75 | ____ | ____ | |
| Total | 1264.92 | ____ | | |

(a) Complete the ANOVA. (b) At $\alpha = .05$, what is $F_{crit}$? (c) Report the statistical results in the proper format. (d) Perform the post hoc test. (e) What do you conclude about the influence of changing the levels of volume? (f) Compute $\eta^2$ and interpret it.

## SUMMARY OF FORMULAS

1. *The formulas for the one-way ANOVA are*

   a. *For computing the sums of squares,*

$$SS_{\text{tot}} = \Sigma X^2_{\text{tot}} - \frac{(\Sigma X_{\text{tot}})^2}{N}$$

$$SS_{\text{bn}} = \Sigma\left(\frac{(\Sigma X \text{ in column})^2}{n \text{ in column}}\right) - \frac{(\Sigma X_{\text{tot}})^2}{N}$$

$$SS_{\text{wn}} = SS_{\text{tot}} - SS_{\text{bn}}$$

   b. *For computing the mean squares,*

$$MS_{\text{bn}} = \frac{SS_{\text{bn}}}{df_{\text{bn}}} \qquad df_{bn} = k - 1$$

$$MS_{\text{wn}} = \frac{SS_{\text{wn}}}{df_{\text{wn}}} \qquad df_{wn} = N - k$$

   c. *For computing the* F-*ratio*

$$F_{\text{obt}} = \frac{MS_{\text{bn}}}{MS_{\text{wn}}}$$

   Critical values of $F$ are found in Table 4 in Appendix B for $df_{\text{bn}}$ and $df_{\text{wn}}$.

2. *The formula for the* HSD *is*

$$HSD = (q_k)\left(\sqrt{\frac{MS_{\text{wn}}}{n}}\right)$$

   Values of $q_k$ are found in Table 5 for $df_{\text{wn}}$ and $k$.

3. *The formula for eta squared is*

$$\eta^2 = \frac{SS_{\text{bn}}}{SS_{\text{tot}}}$$

# 12 A Brief Introduction to the Logic of the Two-Way Analysis of Variance

## Chapter Essentials

### Before getting started, be sure you understand

- From Chapter 11, the terms factor and level, what a significant $F$ indicates, and when to perform post hoc tests

### Your goals in this chapter are to learn

- What a *two-way factorial* ANOVA is
- How to *collapse* across a factor
- What *cell means* and *main effect means* are
- What a significant *main effect* indicates
- What a significant *interaction* indicates
- How to interpret the results of a two-way experiment

Researchers often conduct studies that simultaneously involve more than one independent variable. Therefore, this chapter briefly introduces the ANOVA used when experiments involve two factors. *The good news is that we will NOT focus on computations.* Nowadays, we usually analyze such experiments using a statistical computer program (although the formulas for a version of this are presented in Appendix A.2). You will frequently encounter such designs in research publications, however, so you need to understand their basic logic and terminology. The following sections present (1) the general layout of a two-factor experiment, (2) the logic of what the ANOVA indicates, and (3) how to interpret such a study.

## UNDERSTANDING THE TWO-WAY ANOVA

The **two-way ANOVA** is the parametric inferential procedure that is applied to designs that involve two independent variables. When both factors involve independent samples, we perform the **two-way, between-subjects ANOVA.** When both factors involve related samples, we perform the **two-way, within-subjects ANOVA.** If one factor is tested using independent samples, and the other factor involves related samples, we perform the **two-way, mixed-design ANOVA.** The logic of these ANOVAs is identical except for slight variations in the formulas.

A specific design is described using the number of levels in each factor. If, for example, factor A has two levels and factor B has two levels, we have a two-by-two ANOVA, which is written as $2 \times 2$. Or, with four levels of one factor and three levels of the other, we have a $4 \times 3$ ANOVA, and so on. Each factor can involve any number of levels.

Here's an example of a two-way, between-subjects design: Television commercials are often much louder than the programs themselves because increased volume may make the commercial more persuasive. To test this, we play a recording of an advertising message to participants at each of three volumes—either soft, medium, or loud. We're also interested in the differences between how males and females are persuaded, so our other factor is the gender of the listener. The dependent variable measures how persuasive each person believes the message to be, with higher scores indicating more persuasive.

The way to organize such a $3 \times 2$ design is shown in Table 12.1.
In the diagram:

*1.* Each *column* represents a level of the volume factor. (In general we'll call the column factor "factor A.") Thus, any score in column $A_1$ is from someone tested under soft volume.

*2.* Each *row* represents a level of the gender factor. (In general we'll call the row factor "factor B.") Thus, any score in row $B_1$ is from a male participant.

*3.* Each small square produced by combining a level of factor A with a level of factor B is called a **cell.** Here, we have six cells, each containing a sample of three participants who are one gender and given one volume. For example, the highlighted cell contains scores from 3 females presented with medium volume. (With 3 participants per cell, we have a total of 9 males and 9 females, so $N = 18$.)

*4.* Combining all levels of one factor with all levels of the other factor produces a **complete factorial design.** Here, all levels of gender are combined with all levels of our volume factor. However, in an **incomplete factorial design,** not all levels of the two factors are combined (e.g., if we had not tested females at the loud volume). Incomplete designs require procedures not discussed here.

We perform the two-way, between-subjects ANOVA if (1) each *cell* is an independent sample, and (2) we have normally distributed interval or ratio scores that have homogeneous variance. Then, as in the following sections, any two-way ANOVA involves examining three things: the two *main effects* and the *interaction effect.*

***TABLE 12.1***

A $3 \times 2$ Design for the Factors of Volume and Gender

*Each column represents a level of the volume factor; each row represents a level of the gender factor; each cell contains the dependent scores of participants tested under a particular combination of a level of volume and gender.*

| | | *Factor A: Volume* | | |
|---|---|---|---|---|
| | | *Level $A_1$: Soft* | *Level $A_2$: Medium* | *Level $A_3$: Loud* |
| *Factor B: Gender* | *Level $B_1$: Male* | 9<br>4<br>11 | 8<br>12<br>13 | 18<br>17<br>15 |
| | *Level $B_2$: Female* | 2<br>6<br>4 | 9<br>10<br>17 | 6<br>8<br>4 |

One of the six cells ↑ (the shaded Level $A_2$/Level $B_2$ cell)

$N = 18$

## The Main Effect of Factor A

The **main effect** of a factor is the effect that changing the levels of that factor has on dependent scores while ignoring all other factors in the study. In the persuasiveness study, to find the main effect of factor A (volume), we will ignore the levels of factor B (gender). Literally, we erase the horizontal line that separates the rows of males and females back in Table 12.1, and treat the experiment as if it were this one-way design:

***Factor A: Volume***

| *Level $A_1$: Soft* | *Level $A_2$: Medium* | *Level $A_3$: Loud* |
|---|---|---|
| 9 | 8 | 18 |
| 4 | 12 | 17 |
| 11 | 13 | 15 |
| 2 | 9 | 6 |
| 6 | 10 | 8 |
| 4 | 17 | 4 |
| $\overline{X}_{A_1} = 6$ | $\overline{X}_{A_2} = 11.5$ | $\overline{X}_{A_3} = 11.33$ |

For now, we ignore the distinction between males and females, so we simply have six *people* in each column (so $n = 6$.) We have one factor with three levels of volume (so $k_A = 3$.) Averaging the scores in each column yields the **main effect means** for the column factor. Here, we have the main effect mean of the persuasiveness scores for each volume level.

In statistical terminology we created the main effect means for volume by *collapsing* across the factor of gender. **Collapsing** across a factor refers to averaging together all scores from all levels of that factor. When we collapse across one factor, we have the main effect means for the remaining factor.

> *REMEMBER* When we examine the *main effect of factor A,* we look at the overall mean of each level of A.

Once we have the main effect means, we can see the *main effect* of a factor by looking at the overall pattern in the means. For the main effect of volume, we see how persuasiveness scores change as volume increases: Scores go up from around 6 (at soft) to around 11.5 (at medium), but then scores drop slightly to around 11.3 (at high). To determine if these are significant differences—if there is a *significant main effect of the volume factor*—we essentially perform a one-way ANOVA that compares these main effect means. In general $H_0$ says there is no difference between the levels of factor A in the population, so $H_0$: $\mu_{A_1} = \mu_{A_2} = \mu_{A_3}$. The $H_a$ is that at least two of the main effect means reflect different populations, so $H_a$: not all $\mu_A$ are equal.

We test this $H_0$ by computing an $F_{obt}$, which, in general, is $F_A$. We compare this to $F_{crit}$, and if $F_A$ is significant, it indicates that at least two main effect means from factor A differ significantly. Then, if needed, we determine which specific conditions differ by performing *post hoc tests* (such as the Tukey *HSD*). Then we describe and interpret the relationship (here describing how volume influences persuasiveness scores).

### The Main Effect of Factor B

After analyzing the main effect of factor A, we examine the main effect of factor B. Here, we *collapse* across the levels of factor A (volume), so we erase the vertical lines separating the levels of volume back in Table 12.1, producing this:

| Factor B: Gender | | | | | |
|---|---|---|---|---|---|
| *Level $B_1$: Male* | 9 | 8 | 18 | |
| | 4 | 12 | 17 | $\overline{X}_{B_1} = 11.89$ |
| | 11 | 13 | 15 | |
| *Level $B_2$: Female* | 2 | 9 | 6 | |
| | 6 | 10 | 8 | $\overline{X}_{B_2} = 7.33$ |
| | 4 | 17 | 4 | |

For now, we simply have the persuasiveness scores of 9 males and 9 females, ignoring the fact that some of each heard the message at different volumes. Thus, we have one factor with two levels, so $k_B = 2$. With 9 scores in each row, $n = 9$. Averaging the scores in each row yields the mean persuasiveness score for each gender of 11.89 and 7.33. These are the *main effect means for factor B.*

**REMEMBER** When we examine the *main effect of factor B,* we look at the overall mean for each level of B.

To see the main effect of this factor, we again look at the pattern of the means: Apparently, changing from males to females leads to a drop in scores from around 11.89 to around 7.33. To determine if this is a significant difference—if there is a significant *main effect of the gender factor*—we perform essentially another one-way ANOVA that compares these main effect means. Our $H_0$ says there is no difference between the levels of factor B in the population, so $H_0$: $\mu_{B_1} = \mu_{B_2}$. Our $H_a$ is that at least two of the main effect means reflect different populations, so $H_a$: not all $\mu_B$ are equal.

We test this $H_0$ by computing another $F_{obt}$, which, in general, is $F_B$. We compare this to $F_{crit}$, and if $F_B$ is significant, it indicates that at least two main effect means from factor B differ significantly. Then, if needed, we perform *post hoc tests* (such as the Tukey *HSD*) to determine the specific means that differ, and we describe and interpret this relationship (here describing how gender influences persuasiveness scores).

## A QUICK REVIEW

- Collapsing (averaging together) the scores from the levels of factor B produces the main effect means for factor A. Differences among these means reflect the main effect of A. Collapsing the scores from the levels of A produces the main effect means for factor B. Differences among these means reflect the main effect of B.

### More Examples

We study the influence of taking 1 or 2 "smart pills." We also study participant's age, either 10- or 20-year-olds. The IQ scores in this 2 × 2 design are:

| | | Factor A: Dose | | |
|---|---|---|---|---|
| | | *One Pill* | *Two Pills* | |
| *Factor B: Age* | *10 years* | 100<br>105<br>110 | 140<br>145<br>150 | $\overline{X} = 125$ |
| | *20 years* | 110<br>115<br>120 | 110<br>115<br>120 | $\overline{X} = 115$ |
| | | $\overline{X} = 110$ | $\overline{X} = 130$ | |

The means of the columns are the main effect means for dose level: The main effect here is that mean IQ increases from 110 to 130 as dosage increases. The means in the rows are the main effect means for age: The main effect here is that mean IQ decreases from 125 to 115 as age increases.

### *For Practice:*

In this study:

| | $A_1$ | $A_2$ |
|---|---|---|
| $B_1$ | 2<br>2<br>2 | 5<br>4<br>3 |
| $B_2$ | 11<br>10<br>9 | 7<br>6<br>5 |

1. The means produced by collapsing across factor B are ____ and ____. They are called the ____ means for factor ____.
2. What is the main effect of A?
3. The means produced by collapsing across factor A are ____ and ____. They are called the ____ means for factor ____.
4. What is the main effect of B?

**Answers**

1. $\overline{X}_{A_1} = 6$; $\overline{X}_{A_2} = 5$; main effect; A.
2. Changing from $A_1$ to $A_2$ produces a decrease in scores.
3. $\overline{X}_{B_1} = 3$; $\overline{X}_{B_2} = 8$; main effect; B.
4. Changing from $B_1$ to $B_2$ produces an increase in scores.

## The Interaction Effect

After you've examined the main effects of factors A and B, you examine the effect of their interaction. The interaction of two factors is called a *two-way interaction.* It is created by combining each level of factor A with each level of factor B. In the example it is combining each volume with each gender. An interaction is identified as A × B. Here, factor A has 3 levels and factor B has 2 levels, so it is a 3 × 2 (say "3 *by* 2") interaction.

Because an interaction examines the influence of combining the levels of the factors, we do not collapse across, or ignore, either factor. Instead, we treat each *cell* in the study as a level of the interaction and compare the cell means. A **cell mean** is the mean of the scores from one cell. The cell means for the interaction between volume and gender are shown in Table 12.2. Therefore, we ask whether the scores in male–soft are different from those in male–medium or from the scores in female–soft, etc. (Notice that with six cells, $k_{A\times B} = 6$, and with 3 scores per cell, $n = 3$.)

> ***REMEMBER*** For the *interaction effect,* you compare the cell means. For a *main effect,* you compare the level means.

Interpreting an interaction is difficult because both independent variables are changing, as well as the dependent scores. To simplify the process, look at the influence of

***TABLE 12.2***
The Volume by Gender Interaction

| | | *Factor A: Volume* | | |
|---|---|---|---|---|
| | | ***Soft*** | ***Medium*** | ***Loud*** |
| ***Factor B: Gender*** | ***Male*** | $\overline{X} = 8$ | $\overline{X} = 11$ | $\overline{X} = 16.67$ |
| | ***Female*** | $\overline{X} = 4$ | $\overline{X} = 12$ | $\overline{X} = 6$ |

changing the levels of factor A under *one* level of factor B. Then see if this effect—pattern—for factor A is *different* when you look at the other levels of factor B. For example, here is the first row of Table 12.2, showing the relationship between volume and scores for the males. As volume increases, mean persuasiveness scores also increase, in a positive, linear relationship.

| | ***Factor A: Volume*** | | |
|---|---|---|---|
| | ***Soft*** | ***Medium*** | ***Loud*** |
| ***$B_1$: Male*** | $\overline{X} = 8$ | $\overline{X} = 11$ | $\overline{X} = 16.67$ |

Now look at the relationship between volume and scores for females, using the cell means from the bottom row of Table 12.2.

| | ***Factor A: Volume*** | | |
|---|---|---|---|
| | ***Soft*** | ***Medium*** | ***Loud*** |
| ***$B_2$: Female*** | $\overline{X} = 4$ | $\overline{X} = 12$ | $\overline{X} = 6$ |

Here, as volume increases, mean persuasiveness scores first increase but then decrease, producing a nonlinear relationship.

Thus, there is a different relationship between volume and persuasiveness scores for each gender level. A **two-way interaction effect** is present when the relationship between one factor and the dependent scores changes with, or depends on, the level of the other factor that is present. (Thus, whether increasing the volume increases scores *depends* on whether we're talking about males or females.) In other words, there's an interaction effect when the influence of changing one factor is not the same for each level of the other factor. (Increasing volume does not have the same effect for males as it does for females.)

You can also see the interaction by looking at the difference between males and females at each level of volume. Sometimes the males score higher, sometimes the females do; it *depends* on which level of volume we're talking about.

Conversely, an interaction effect would not be present if the cell means formed the *same* pattern for males and females. For example, say the cell means had been as follows.

| | | ***Factor A: Volume*** | | |
|---|---|---|---|---|
| | | ***Soft*** | ***Medium*** | ***Loud*** |
| ***Factor B: Gender*** | ***Male*** | $\overline{X} = 5$ | $\overline{X} = 10$ | $\overline{X} = 15$ |
| | ***Female*** | $\overline{X} = 20$ | $\overline{X} = 25$ | $\overline{X} = 30$ |

Here, increasing the volume increases scores by about 5 points, *regardless* of whether it's for males or females. (Or, females always score higher, regardless of volume.) Thus, an interaction effect is not present when the influence of changing the levels of one factor does not depend on which level of the other variable we are talking about. Or, in other words, there's no interaction when we see the same relationship between the dependent scores and one factor for each level of the other factor.

REMEMBER *A two-way interaction effect* indicates that the influence that one factor has on scores depends on which level of the other factor is present.

To determine if we have a *significant interaction effect,* we perform essentially another one-way ANOVA that compares the cell means. To write the $H_0$ and $H_a$ in symbols is complicated, but in words, $H_0$ is that the cell means do not represent an interaction effect in the population, and $H_a$ is that at least some of the cell means do represent an interaction effect in the population.

To test $H_0$, we compute another $F_{obt}$, called $F_{A \times B}$. If $F_{A \times B}$ is significant, it indicates that at least two of the cell means differ significantly in a way that produces an interaction effect. Then we perform *post hoc tests* (such as the Tukey *HSD*) to determine which specific cell means differ, and we describe and interpret the relationship (here describing how the different combinations of volume and gender influence persuasiveness scores).

## A QUICK REVIEW

- We examine the interaction by looking at the pattern in the cell means. An interaction effect is present if the relationship between one factor and the dependent scores changes as the levels of the other factor change.

### More Examples

Here are the data again when factor A is the amount of the smart pill, and factor B is age of participants.

| | | *Factor A: Dose* | |
|---|---|---|---|
| | | *One Pill* | *Two Pills* |
| *Factor B: Age* | *10 years* | 100<br>105<br>110<br>$\bar{X} = 105$ | 140<br>145<br>150<br>$\bar{X} = 145$ |
| | *20 years* | 110<br>115<br>120<br>$\bar{X} = 115$ | 110<br>115<br>120<br>$\bar{X} = 115$ |

Looking at the cell means in one row at a time, we see an interaction effect because the influence of increasing dose depends on participants' age: Increasing dose increases mean IQ for 10-year-olds from 105 to 145, but increasing dose does not change mean IQ for 20-year-olds (it stays at 115). Or, looking at each column, the influence that increasing age has depends on participants' dosage level: with one pill, 20-year-olds score higher (115) than 10-year-olds (105), but with two pills 10-year-olds score higher (145) than 20-year-olds (115).

### For Practice:

A study produces these cell means:

| | $A_1$ | $A_2$ |
|---|---|---|
| $B_1$ | 2<br>2<br>2<br>$\bar{X} = 2$ | 5<br>4<br>3<br>$\bar{X} = 4$ |
| $B_2$ | 11<br>10<br>9<br>$\bar{X} = 10$ | 7<br>6<br>5<br>$\bar{X} = 6$ |

1. The means to examine in the interaction are the _____ means.
2. What is the influence of changing the levels of A at $B_1$ and then at $B_2$?
3. Why is this an interaction effect?

**Answers**

1. cell
2. For $B_1$, changing from $A_1$ to $A_2$ increases the means from 2 to 4. For $B_2$, changing from $A_1$ to $A_2$ decreases the means from 10 to 6.
3. Because the influence of changing from $A_1$ to $A_2$ depends on which level of B is present.

## INTERPRETING THE TWO-WAY EXPERIMENT

As you've seen, in the two-way ANOVA we compute three *F*s: one for the main effect of factor A, one for the main effect of factor B, and one for the interaction of A × B. The logic and calculations for these are the same as in the one-way ANOVA, because any *F* equals the mean square between groups divided by the mean square within groups, and any mean square equals the sum of squares divided by *df*. (The formulas for the two-way, between-subjects ANOVA applied to our persuasiveness data are presented in Appendix A.2.)

Each $F_{obt}$ is tested by comparing it to $F_{crit}$ from the *F*-tables in Appendix B. The *dfs* are those used in computing each particular $F_{obt}$. Because factor A and B may have different *dfs*, usually you will have a different $F_{crit}$ for each main effect and for the interaction. *Note:* Whether one $F_{obt}$ is significant does not influence whether any other one is significant, so any combination of significant main effects and/or the interaction is possible.

As shown in Appendix A.2, the persuasiveness data produced significant *F*s for A (volume), for B (gender), and for their interaction. We interpret the two-way ANOVA by examining the means from the significant main effects and/or interaction. Table 12.3 shows the means for the persuasiveness study.

### Completing the Main Effects

Approach each main effect as the one-way ANOVA that we originally diagrammed. As usual, a significant $F_{obt}$ merely indicates differences *somewhere* among the means. Therefore, if the *n*s are equal, determine which specific means differ by performing Tukey's *HSD* test. Use the formula and procedure described in the previous chapter. *Note:* You saw that the *n* and *k* may be different for each factor. If so, this requires computing a separate *HSD* for each factor.

For the persuasiveness study, comparing the three main effect (column) means for the volume factor indicates that the soft condition (6) differs significantly from both the medium (11.5) and loud (11.33) levels, but that medium and loud do not differ significantly.

For the gender factor the *HSD* test is not necessary: It must be that the mean for males (11.89) differs significantly from the mean for females (7.33). If factor B had more than two levels, however, we would compute a new *HSD* and proceed as usual.

***TABLE 12.3***
Main Effect and Interaction Means from the Persuasiveness Study

| | | *Factor A: Volume* | | | |
|---|---|---|---|---|---|
| | | *Level $A_1$: Soft* | *Level $A_2$: Medium* | *Level $A_3$: Loud* | |
| *Factor B: Gender* | *Level $B_1$: Male* | 8 | 11 | 16.67 | $\overline{X}_{male} = 11.89$ |
| | *Level $B_2$: Female* | 4 | 12 | 6 | $\overline{X}_{female} = 7.33$ |
| | | $\overline{X}_{soft} = 6$ | $\overline{X}_{med} = 11.5$ | $\overline{X}_{loud} = 11.33$ | |

In the research literature each $F_{obt}$ is reported in the usual format. Also, it is appropriate to compute the effect size (eta$^2$) for each main effect. Further, researchers may produce a separate graph for each main effect. As you saw in Chapter 3, we show the relationship between the levels of the factor (independent variable) on the $X$ axis, and the main effect means (dependent variable) on the $Y$ axis. Include all means, even those that do not differ significantly.

We examine interaction effects in the same ways, but they involve slightly different procedures.

## Graphing the Interaction Effect

An interaction can be a beast to interpret, so always graph it! As usual, label the $Y$ axis with the mean of the dependent variable. Then place the factor with the most levels on the $X$ axis. For the persuasiveness study the $X$ axis is labeled with the three volume levels. Then plot the *cell* means. The resulting graph is shown in Figure 12.1. Remember that any graph shows the relationship between the $X$ variable and the $Y$ variable. Here, you show the relationship between the $X$ factor and the dependent scores, but you do this separately for each level of the other factor. Thus, approach this in the same way that you examined the means for the interaction effect. There you first looked at the relationship between volume and persuasiveness scores for only *males:* From Table 12.3 their cell means are $\overline{X}_{soft} = 8$, $\overline{X}_{medium} = 11$, and $\overline{X}_{loud} = 16.67$. Plot these three means and connect the adjacent data points with straight lines. Then look at the relationship between volume and scores for *females:* Their cell means are $\overline{X}_{soft} = 4$, $\overline{X}_{medium} = 12$, and $\overline{X}_{loud} = 6$. Plot these means and connect their adjacent data points with straight lines. (*Notice:* Always provide a key to identify each line.)

The way to read the graph is to look at one line at a time. For males (the dashed line), as volume increases, mean persuasiveness scores increase. However, for females (the solid line), as volume increases, persuasiveness scores first increase but then decrease.

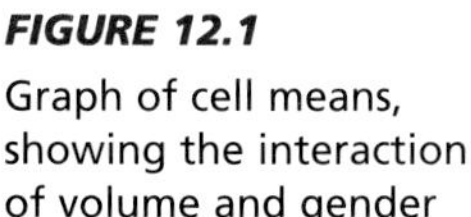

***FIGURE 12.1***

Graph of cell means, showing the interaction of volume and gender

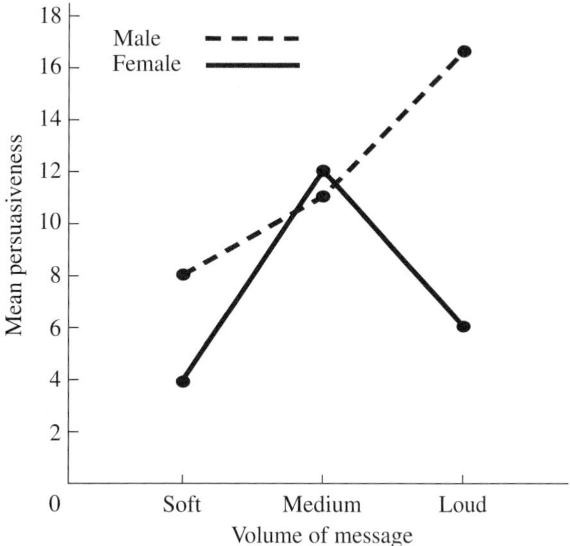

Thus, we see one relationship for males and a different relationship for females. Therefore, the graph also shows an interaction effect by showing that the effect that increasing volume has on persuasiveness scores depends on whether the participants are male or female.

> *REMEMBER* Graph the interaction by drawing a separate line that shows the relationship between the factor on the *X* axis and the dependent (*Y*) scores for each level of the other factor.

**Here is another example** Say that a 2 × 2 experiment produces the cell means on the left. To produce the graph of the interaction on the right, we plot data points at 2 and 6

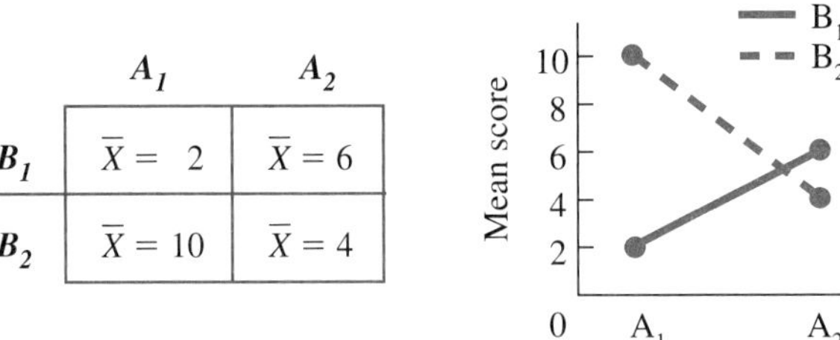

|  | $A_1$ | $A_2$ |
|---|---|---|
| $B_1$ | $\overline{X} = 2$ | $\overline{X} = 6$ |
| $B_2$ | $\overline{X} = 10$ | $\overline{X} = 4$ |



(the cell means at $A_1$ and $A_2$ for $B_1$) and connect them with the solid line. We plot data points at 10 and 4 (the cell means at $A_1$ and $A_2$ for $B_2$) and connect them with the dashed line.

*Note:* An interaction effect can produce an infinite variety of different graphs, but when it is present, it produces lines that are not parallel. Each line summarizes the relationship, and a line that is shaped or oriented differently from another line indicates a different relationship. Therefore, lines that are not parallel indicate that the relationship between *X* and *Y* changes, depending on the level of the second factor, so that an interaction effect is present. Conversely, when an interaction effect is not present, the lines will be essentially parallel, with each line depicting essentially the same relationship. (Think of significance testing of the interaction as testing whether the lines are significantly different from parallel.)

> *REMEMBER* An *interaction effect* is present when its graph produces lines that are *not parallel.*

## Performing Unconfounded Post Hoc Comparisons on the Interaction

The Tukey *HSD* is also used with a significant interaction effect so that we can determine which of the *cell* means differ significantly. However, we do not compare every cell mean to every other cell mean. Look at Table 12.4. We would not, for example, compare the mean for males at loud volume to the mean for females at soft volume. Because the two cells differ both in terms of gender and volume, we cannot determine what caused the difference. Therefore, we are confused or "confounded." A **confounded**

**TABLE 12.4**
Interaction Means for Persuasiveness Study

*Any horizontal or vertical comparison is unconfounded; any diagonal comparison is confounded.*

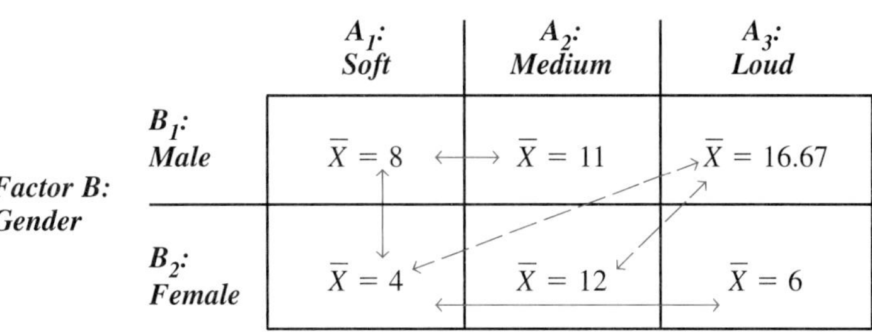

| | | Factor A: Volume | | |
|---|---|---|---|---|
| | | $A_1$: Soft | $A_2$: Medium | $A_3$: Loud |
| Factor B: Gender | $B_1$: Male | $\overline{X} = 8$ | $\overline{X} = 11$ | $\overline{X} = 16.67$ |
| | $B_2$: Female | $\overline{X} = 4$ | $\overline{X} = 12$ | $\overline{X} = 6$ |

**comparison** occurs when two cells differ along more than one factor. Instead, we perform only **unconfounded comparisons,** in which two cells differ along only one factor. Therefore, compare only cell means within the same column because these differences result from factor B. Compare means within the same row because these differences result from factor A. Do not, however, make any diagonal comparisons, because these are confounded comparisons.

Thus, we find the difference between all pairs of cell means in the same column or in the same row to compare to the *HSD*. (*Note:* As shown in Appendix A.2, the *HSD* is computed slightly differently for an interaction than for a main effect.) For the persuasiveness study, only three significant differences occur between the cell means: (1) between females at soft volume and females at medium volume, (2) between males at soft volume and males at loud volume, and (3) between males at loud volume and females at loud volume.

## Interpreting the Experiment

The way to interpret an experiment is to look at the significant differences between means from the post hoc comparisons for all significant main effects and interaction effects. All of the differences found in the persuasiveness study are summarized in Table 12.5. Each line connecting two means indicates that they differ significantly.

*Usually the interpretation of a two-way study rests with the significant interaction, even when main effects are significant.* This is because the conclusions about main

**TABLE 12.5**
Summary of Significant Differences in the Persuasiveness Study

*Each line connects two means that differ significantly.*

| | | Factor A: Volume | | | |
|---|---|---|---|---|---|
| | | Level $A_1$: Soft | Level $A_2$: Medium | Level $A_3$: Loud | |
| Factor B: Gender | Level $B_1$: Male | 8.0 | 11 | 16.67 | $\overline{X} = 11.89$ |
| | Level $B_2$: Female | 4.0 | 12 | 6 | $\overline{X} = 7.33$ |
| | | $\overline{X}_{soft} = 6$ | $\overline{X}_{med} = 11.5$ | $\overline{X}_{loud} = 11.33$ | |

effects are contradicted by the interaction. For example, our main effect means for gender suggest that males scored higher than females. However, the cell means of the interaction show that gender differences *depend* on volume: Only in the loud condition is there a significant difference between males and females. Therefore, we cannot make an overall, general conclusion about differences between males and females. Likewise, the main effect means for volume showed that increasing volume from soft to medium and from soft to loud produced significant differences in scores. However, the interaction indicates that increasing volume from soft to medium actually produced a significant difference only for females; increasing the volume from soft to loud produced a significant difference only for males.

Thus, as above, usually you cannot draw any conclusions about significant main effects when the interaction is significant. After all, the interaction indicates that the influence of one factor *depends* on the levels of the other factor and vice versa, so you should not act like either factor has a consistent effect by itself. When the interaction is not significant, then you focus on any significant main effects. For completeness however, always perform the entire ANOVA and report all results.

> ***REMEMBER*** The primary interpretation of a two-way ANOVA rests on the interaction when it is significant.

Thus, we conclude that increasing the volume of a message beyond soft tends to increase persuasiveness scores in the population, but this increase occurs for females with medium volume and for males with loud volume. Further, we conclude that differences in persuasiveness scores occur between males and females in the population, but only if the volume of the message is loud. (And, after all of the above shenanigans, for all of these conclusions together, the probability of a Type I error in the study—the *experimentwise error rate*—is still $p < .05$.)

## CHAPTER SUMMARY

1. A *two-way, between-subjects ANOVA* involves two independent variables, and all conditions of both factors contain independent samples. A two-way, *within-subjects* ANOVA is used when both factors involve related samples. A two-way, *mixed-design* ANOVA is used when one factor is tested using independent samples and one factor is tested using related samples.
2. In a *complete factorial design,* each level of one factor is combined with all levels of the other factor. Each *cell* is formed by a particular combination of a level from each factor.
3. A *main effect* is the influence of manipulating an independent variable alone. The *main effect means* for a factor are obtained by *collapsing* across (combining the scores from) the levels of the other factor.
4. Collapsing across factor B produces the main effect means for factor A: the overall mean for participants tested under $A_1$, the mean for those under $A_2$, etc.

A significant $F_{obt}$ for this factor indicates that differences among the means result from changing the levels of A.

*5.* Collapsing across factor A produces the main effect means for factor B: the overall mean for participants tested under $B_1$, the mean for those under $B_2$, etc. A significant $F_{obt}$ for this factor indicates that differences among these means result from changing the levels of B.

*6.* An *interaction effect* indicates that the *cell means* differ such that the relationship between one factor and the dependent scores depends on the level of the other factor that is present. When graphed, an interaction effect produces nonparallel lines.

*7.* Post hoc comparisons are performed on each significant effect having more than two levels. In the interaction perform only *unconfounded comparisons,* in which the cells differ along only one factor. Two means are *confounded* if the cells differ along more than one factor.

*8.* Main effects are graphed by plotting the main effect means on $Y$ and the levels of the factor on $X$. The interaction is graphed by plotting cell means on $Y$ and the levels of one factor on $X$. Then a separate line connects the data points for the cell means from each level of the other factor.

*9.* Conclusions in a two-way ANOVA are usually based on the interaction effect when it is significant, because overall conclusions about main effects are contradicted by the interaction.

## KEY TERMS: Can You Define the Following?

$F_A$ *225*
$F_B$ *226*
$F_{A \times B}$ *229*
cell *224*
cell mean *227*
collapsing *225*
complete factorial design *224*
confounded comparison *232*
incomplete factorial design *224*
main effect *225*
main effect means *225*
two-way ANOVA *223*
two-way, between-subjects ANOVA *223*
two-way interaction effect *228*
two-way, mixed-design ANOVA *223*
two-way, within-subjects ANOVA *223*
unconfounded comparison *233*

## REVIEW QUESTIONS

(Answers for odd-numbered questions are in Appendix C.)

*1.* (a) A researcher conducts a study involving one independent variable. What are the two types of parametric procedures available to her? (b) She next conducts a study involving two independent variables. What are the three versions of the parametric procedure available to her? (c) In part b what aspect of her design determines which version she should perform?

2. Identify the following terms (a) Two-way design (b) Complete factorial (c) Cell (d) Two-way between-subjects design
3. What is the difference between a main effect mean and a cell mean?
4. Which type of ANOVA is used in a two-way design when: (a) both factors are tested using independent samples? (b) one factor involves independent samples and one factor involves related samples? (c) both factors involve related samples?
5. (a) What is a confounded comparison, and when does it occur in a study's diagram? (b) What is an unconfounded comparison, and when does it occur? (c) Why don't we perform post hoc tests on confounded comparisons?
6. Why do we usually base the interpretation of a two-way design on the interaction effect when it is significant?
7. For a $2 \times 2$ ANOVA describe the following in words: (a) the statistical hypotheses for factor A; (b) the statistical hypotheses for factor B; (c) the statistical hypotheses for $A \times B$.
8. What does it mean to collapse across a factor?
9. (a) A significant main effect indicates what about a study? (b) A significant interaction effect indicates what about a study?

## APPLICATION QUESTIONS

10. A student hears that a $2 \times 3$ design was conducted and concludes that six factors were examined. Is this conclusion correct? Why or why not?
11. Below are the cell means of three experiments. For each experiment compute the main effect means and indicate whether there appears to be an effect of A, B, and/or $A \times B$.

*Study 1*

| | $A_1$ | $A_2$ |
|---|---|---|
| $B_1$ | 2 | 4 |
| $B_2$ | 12 | 14 |

*Study 2*

| | $A_1$ | $A_2$ |
|---|---|---|
| $B_1$ | 10 | 5 |
| $B_2$ | 5 | 10 |

*Study 3*

| | $A_1$ | $A_2$ |
|---|---|---|
| $B_1$ | 8 | 14 |
| $B_2$ | 8 | 2 |

12. In question 11, if we label the $X$ axis with factor A and graph the cell means, what pattern will we see for each interaction?
13. After performing a $3 \times 4$ ANOVA with equal $n$s, you find that all $F$s are significant. What other procedures should you perform?
14. A $2 \times 2$ design studies participants' frustration levels when solving problems depending on the difficulty of the problem and whether they are math or logic problems. The results are that logic problems produce significantly more frustration than math problems, that greater difficulty leads to significantly greater frustration, and that when difficult, the math problems produce significantly greater

frustration than the logic problems, but the reverse is true for easy problems. In the ANOVA for this study, what effects are significant?

*15.* In question 14 say instead that the researcher found no difference between math and logic problems, that frustration significantly increases with greater difficulty, and that this is true for both math and logic problems. In the ANOVA performed for this study, what effects are significant?

*16.* In an experiment you measure the popularity of two brands of soft drinks (factor A), and for each brand you test males and females (factor B). The following table shows the cell means from the study:

| | | *Factor A* | |
|---|---|---|---|
| | | *Level $A_1$: Brand X* | *Level $A_2$: Brand Y* |
| *Factor B* | *Level $B_1$: Males* | 14 | 23 |
| | *Level $B_2$: Females* | 25 | 12 |

(a) Describe the graph of the interaction means when factor A is on the *X* axis. (b) Does there appear to be an interaction effect? Why? (c) What is the main effect (and means) of changing brands? (d) What is the main effect (and means) of changing gender? (e) Why will a significant interaction prohibit you from making conclusions based on the main effects?

*17.* We examine performance on an eye–hand coordination task as a function of three levels of reward and three levels of practice, obtaining the following cell means.

| | | *Reward* | | |
|---|---|---|---|---|
| | | *Low* | *Medium* | *High* |
| *Practice* | *Low* | 4 | 10 | 7 |
| | *Medium* | 5 | 5 | 14 |
| | *High* | 15 | 15 | 15 |

(a) What are the main effect means for reward, and what do they indicate? (b) What are the main effect means for practice, and what do they indicate? (c) Is there apparently an interaction effect? (d) How would you perform unconfounded post hoc comparisons of the cell means?

*18.* (a) In question 17 why does the interaction contradict your conclusions about the effect of reward? (b) Why does the interaction contradict your conclusions about practice?

*19.* A study compared the performance of males and females tested by either a male or a female experimenter. Here are the data:

| | | *Factor A: Participants* | |
|---|---|---|---|
| | | *Level $A_1$: Males* | *Level $A_2$: Females* |
| *Factor B: Experimenter* | *Level $B_1$: Male Experimenter* | 6<br>11<br>9<br>10<br>9 | 8<br>14<br>17<br>16<br>19 |
| | *Level $B_2$: Female Experimenter* | 8<br>10<br>9<br>7<br>10 | 4<br>6<br>5<br>5<br>7 |

(a) What are the main effect means for participants' gender? Interpret the main effect. (b) What are the main effect means for experimenter's gender? Interpret the main effect. (c) What are the means in the interaction? Interpret the effect.

# 13 Chi Square and Nonparametric Procedures

**Chapter Essentials**

**Before getting started, be sure you understand**

- From Chapter 1, the four types of measurement scales (nominal, ordinal, interval, and ratio)
- From Chapter 8, the concepts of Type I errors and power

**Your goals in this chapter are to learn**

- When to use *nonparametric* statistics.
- The logic and use of the *one-way chi square.*
- The logic and use of the *two-way chi square.*
- The names of the common nonparametric procedures for ranked data.

Previous chapters have discussed the category of inferential statistics called *parametric procedures.* Now we'll turn to the other category called *nonparametric statistics.* Nonparametric procedures are still inferential statistics for deciding whether the relationships in the sample accurately represents the relationship in the population. Therefore, $H_0$ and $H_a$, sampling distributions, Type I and Type II errors, alpha, critical values, and significance all apply. Although a number of different nonparametric procedures are available, we'll focus on the most common ones. This chapter presents (1) the one-way chi square, (2) the two-way chi square, and (3) a brief review of the procedures for ordinal scores.

## PARAMETRIC VERSUS NONPARAMETRIC STATISTICS

Previous parametric procedures have required that dependent scores involve an interval or ratio scale, that the scores are normally distributed, and that the population variances are homogeneous. But, sometimes researchers obtain data that do not fit parametric procedures. Some dependent variables are nominal variables (e.g., whether someone is male or female). Sometimes we can measure a dependent variable only by assigning ordinal scores (e.g., judging this participant as showing the most of an attribute, this one the second-most, and so on). And sometimes a variable involves an interval or ratio scale, but the populations are severely skewed and/or do not have homogeneous variance (e.g., we saw that yearly income forms a severely positively skewed distribution).

It is better to design a study that allows you to use parametric procedures, because they are more *powerful* than nonparametric procedures (we are less likely to miss a relationship and make a Type II error). In fact, parametric procedures will tolerate some violation of their assumptions, so usually we can use them. But if the data severely violate the rules, then we increase the probability of making a Type I error (rejecting $H_0$ when it's true), so that the actual probability of a Type I error will be larger than the alpha level you've set. Therefore, when data do not fit a parametric procedure, we turn to nonparametric procedures. **Nonparametric statistics** do not assume a normal distribution or homogeneous variance, and the data may be nominal or ordinal. Using nonparametric procedures with such data will keep the probability of a Type I error equal to your alpha.

> ***REMEMBER*** Use *nonparametric statistics* when dependent scores form very nonnormal distributions, when the population variances are not homogeneous, or when scores are measured using ordinal or nominal scales.

Nonparametric procedures fall into one of two groups: those that are used with nominal data, and those that are used with ordinal data. With nominal data, we use the inferential procedure called the *chi square procedure.*

## CHI SQUARE PROCEDURES

Chi square procedures are used when participants are measured using a nominal variable. With nominal variables we do not measure an amount, but rather we indicate the *category* that participants fall into, and then count the number—the *frequency*—of individuals in each category. Thus, we have nominal variables when counting how many individuals answer yes, no, or maybe to a question; how many claim to vote Republican, Democratic, or Socialist; how many say that they were or were not abused children; and so on.

The next step is to determine what the data represent. For example, we might find that out of 100 people, 40 say yes to a question and 60 say no. These numbers indicate how the *frequencies are distributed* across the categories of yes/no. As usual, we want to draw inferences about the population: Can we infer that if we asked the entire population this question, 40% of the population would say yes and 60% would say no? Or would the frequencies be distributed in a different manner? To make inferences about the frequencies in the population, we perform the chi square procedure (pronounced "kigh square"). The **chi square procedure** is the nonparametric inferential procedure for testing whether the frequencies in each category in sample data represent specified frequencies in the population. The symbol for the chi square statistic is $\chi^2$.

> ***REMEMBER*** Use the *chi square procedure* ($\chi^2$) when you measure the number of participants falling into different categories.

Theoretically, there is no limit to the number of categories—levels—you may have in a variable and no limit to the number of variables you may have. Therefore, we describe a chi square design in the same way we described ANOVAs: When a study has only one variable, use the *one-way chi square;* when a study has two variables, use the *two-way chi square.*

## ONE-WAY CHI SQUARE: THE GOODNESS OF FIT TEST

The **one-way chi square** is used when data consist of the frequencies with which participants belong to the different categories of *one* variable. Here, we examine the relationship between the different categories and the frequency with which participants fall into each. We ask, "As the categories change, do the frequencies in the categories also change?"

Here is an example. Being right-handed or left-handed is apparently related to brain organization, and many of history's great geniuses were left-handed. Therefore, using an IQ test, we select a sample of 50 geniuses. Then we ask them whether they are left- or right-handed (ambidextrous is not an option). The total numbers of left- and right-handers are the frequencies in the two categories. The results are shown here:

***Handedness***

| *Left-Handers* | *Right-Handers* |
|---|---|
| $f_o = 10$ | $f_o = 40$ |

$k = 2$
$N = \text{total } f_o = 50$

Each column contains the frequency with which participants are in that category. We call this value the **observed frequency,** symbolized by $f_o$. The sum of the $f_o$s from all categories equals *N,* the total number of participants in the study. Notice that *k* stands for the number of categories, or levels, and here $k = 2$.

In the above results, 10 of the 50 geniuses (20%) are left-handers, and 40 of them (80%) are right-handers. Therefore, we might argue that the same distribution of 20% left-handers and 80% right-handers would occur in the population of geniuses. But, there is the usual problem: sampling error. Maybe our sample is unrepresentative, so that in the population of all geniuses we would not find this distribution of right- and left-handers. Maybe our results poorly represent some *other* distribution. As usual, this is the null hypothesis, implying that we are being misled by sampling error.

### Hypotheses and Assumptions for the One-Way Chi Square

Usually, researchers test the $H_0$ that there is no difference among the frequencies in the categories in the population, meaning that there is no relationship in the population. In the handedness study, for the moment we'll ignore that there are generally more right-handers than left-handers in the world. Therefore, if there is no relationship in the population, then our $H_0$ is that the frequencies of left- and right-handed geniuses in the population are equal. There is no conventional way to write this in symbols, so simply write $H_0$: *all frequencies in the population are equal.* This implies that if the observed frequencies ($f_o$) in the sample are not equal, it's because of sampling error.

The alternative hypothesis always implies that the study did demonstrate the predicted relationship, so $H_a$: *not all frequencies in the population are equal.* For our handedness study, $H_a$ implies that the observed frequencies represent different frequencies of left- and right-handers in the population of geniuses.

We can test only whether the sample frequencies are different, so the one-way $\chi^2$ tests *only* two-tailed hypotheses.

The one-way $\chi^2$ has five assumptions:

*1.* Participants are categorized along one variable having two or more categories, and we count the frequency in each category.

*2.* Each participant can be in only one category (i.e., you cannot have repeated measures).

*3.* Category membership is independent: The fact that an individual is in one category does not influence the probability that another participant will be in any category.

*4.* We include the responses of all participants in the study (i.e., you would not count only the number of right-handers, or in a different study, you would count both those who agree and disagree with a statement).

*5.* The theoretical basis requires that our "expected frequencies" be at least 5 per category.

## Computing the One-Way $\chi^2$

The first step in computing $\chi^2$ is to translate $H_0$ into the expected frequency for each category. The **expected frequency** is the frequency we expect in a category if the sample data perfectly represent the distribution of frequencies in the population described by the null hypothesis. The symbol for an expected frequency is $f_e$. Our $H_0$ is that the frequencies of left- and right-handedness are equal. If the sample perfectly represents this, then out of our 50 participants, 25 should be right-handed and 25 should be left-handed. Thus, the expected frequency in each category is $f_e = 25$.

With an $H_0$ that the frequencies in the categories are equal, the $f_e$ will be the same in all categories, and there's a shortcut for computing it:

*THE FORMULA FOR EACH EXPECTED FREQUENCY WHEN TESTING AN $H_0$ OF NO DIFFERENCE IS*

$$f_e \text{ in each category} = \frac{N}{k}$$

Thus, in our study, with $N = 50$ and $k = 2$,

$$f_e \text{ in each category} = \frac{50}{2} = 25$$

(Sometimes $f_e$ may contain a decimal. For example, if we included a third category, ambidextrous, then $k = 3$, and each $f_e$ would be 16.67.)

The $\chi^2$ compares the difference between our observed frequencies and the expected frequencies. *Note:* The one-way chi square procedure is also called the **goodness of fit test:** It tests how "good" the "fit" is between our data and the expected distribution of frequencies in the population that is described by $H_0$.

We compute an obtained $\chi^2$, which we'll call $\chi^2_{obt}$.

*THE FORMULA FOR CHI SQUARE IS*

$$\chi^2_{obt} = \Sigma\left(\frac{(f_o - f_e)^2}{f_e}\right)$$

This says to find the difference between $f_o$ and $f_e$ in each category, square that difference, and then divide it by the $f_e$ for that category. After doing this for all categories, sum the quantities, and the answer is $\chi^2_{obt}$.

For the handedness study we have these frequencies:

| ***Handedness*** | |
|---|---|
| ***Left-Handers*** | ***Right-Handers*** |
| $f_o = 10$<br>$f_e = 25$ | $f_o = 40$<br>$f_e = 25$ |

**Step 1:** *Compute the* $f_e$ *for each category:* We computed our $f_e$ to be 25 per category.

**Step 2:** *Create the fraction* $\frac{(f_e - f_o)^2}{f_e}$ *for each category:* Thus, the formula becomes

$$\chi^2_{obt} = \Sigma\left(\frac{(f_o - f_e)^2}{f_e}\right) = \left(\frac{(10 - 25)^2}{25}\right) + \left(\frac{(40 - 25)^2}{25}\right)$$

**Step 3:** *Perform the subtraction in the numerator of each fraction:* After subtracting,

$$\chi^2_{obt} = \left(\frac{(-15)^2}{25}\right) + \left(\frac{(15)^2}{25}\right)$$

**Step 4:** *Square the numerator in each fraction:* This gives

$$\chi^2_{obt} = \left(\frac{225}{25}\right) + \left(\frac{225}{25}\right)$$

**Step 5:** *Perform the division in each fraction and then sum the results:*

$$\chi^2_{obt} = 9 + 9 = 18$$

so

$$\chi^2_{obt} = 18$$

**Step 6:** *Compare* $\chi^2_{obt}$ *to* $\chi^2_{crit}$*:* This is discussed below.

## Interpreting the One-Way $\chi^2$

We interpret $\chi^2_{obt}$ by determining its location on the sampling distribution of $\chi^2$. The **$\chi^2$ distribution** contains all possible values of $\chi^2$ that occur when $H_0$ is true (the observed frequencies represent the model described by $H_0$). Thus, for the handedness study the $\chi^2$-distribution is the distribution of all possible values of $\chi^2$ when the frequencies in the two categories in the population are equal. You can envision the $\chi^2$-distribution as shown in Figure 13.1.

Even though the $\chi^2$-distribution is not at all normal, it is used in the same way as previous sampling distributions. When the data perfectly represent the $H_0$ situation, so that each $f_o$ equals its $f_e$, then $\chi^2$ is zero. However, sometimes by chance the observed frequencies differ from the expected frequencies, producing a $\chi^2$ greater than zero. The larger the $\chi^2$, the larger the differences, and then the less likely they are to occur when $H_0$ is true.

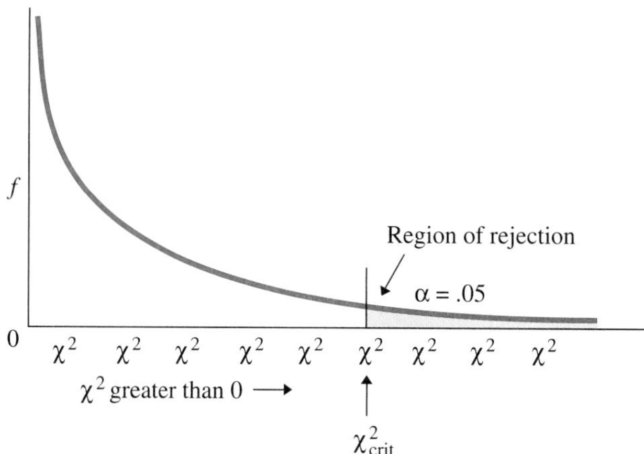


***FIGURE 13.1***
Sampling distribution of $\chi^2$ when $H_0$ is true

With chi square we again have two-tailed hypotheses but one region of rejection. If $\chi^2_{obt}$ is larger than the critical value, then it is in the region of rejection, and so $\chi^2$ is significant: The observed frequencies are unlikely to represent the distribution of frequencies in the population described by $H_0$.

Therefore, to determine if $\chi^2_{obt}$ is significant, compare it to the critical value, symbolized by $\chi^2_{crit}$. As with previous statistics, the $\chi^2$-distribution changes shape as the degrees of freedom change, so to find the appropriate value of $\chi^2_{crit}$, you must first determine the degrees of freedom.

*THE DEGREES OF FREEDOM IN A ONE-WAY CHI SQUARE EQUAL*

$$df = k - 1$$

where $k$ is the number of categories.

Find the critical value of $\chi^2$ in Table 6 in Appendix B, entitled "Critical Values of Chi Square." For the handedness study, $k = 2$ so $df = 1$, and with $\alpha = .05$, the $\chi^2_{crit} = 3.84$. Our $\chi^2_{obt}$ of 18 is larger than this $\chi^2_{crit}$, so the results are significant: We reject the $H_0$ that our categories are poorly representing a distribution of equal frequencies in the population (rejecting that we are poorly representing that geniuses are equally left- or right-handed).

When our $\chi^2_{obt}$ is significant, we accept the $H_a$ that the sample represents frequencies in the population that are not equal. In fact, as in our samples, we would expect to find about 20% left-handers and 80% right-handers in the population of geniuses. We conclude that we have evidence of a relationship between the categories of handedness and the frequency with which geniuses fall into each. Then, as usual, we interpret the relationship, here attempting to explain what aspects of being left-handed and being a genius are related.

Unlike ANOVA, a significant one-way chi square that involves more than two conditions is *not* followed by post hoc comparisons. A significant $\chi^2_{obt}$ indicates that, across all categories, the frequencies are significantly different. Then we use the observed frequency in each category to estimate the frequencies that would be found in the population. Also, there is no measure of effect size here.

If $\chi^2_{obt}$ had not been significant, we would not reject $H_0$ and would have no evidence—one way or the other—regarding how handedness is distributed among geniuses.

*Note:* This procedure can also be used to test an $H_0$ that the frequencies are distributed in some way other than equally across all categories. For example, only about 10% of the general population is left-handed, so we should test whether our geniuses fit this model. Now $H_0$ is that our geniuses are like the general population, being 10% left-handed and 90% right-handed. Our $H_a$ is that the data represent a population of geniuses that does not have this distribution. Each $f_e$ is again based on $H_0$, so left-handed geniuses should occur 10% of the time: 10% of our 50 geniuses is 5, so $f_e = 5$. Right-handed geniuses should occur 90% of the time: 90% of 50 is 45, so $f_e = 45$. We then compute $\chi^2_{obt}$, find $\chi^2_{crit}$, and interpret the results as we did previously.

## A QUICK REVIEW

- The one-way $\chi^2$ is used when counting the frequency of category membership along one variable.
- When $H_0$ is that the frequency of category membership is equal in the population, then $f_e = N/k$ for each category.

### More Examples

Below are the number of acts of graffiti that occur on one wall that is painted white, one that is painted dark blue, and one that is covered with chalkboard. $H_0$ is that there are no differences in the frequency of graffiti on the different coverings in the population.

| *White* | *Blue* | *Chalk* |
|---|---|---|
| $f_o = 8$<br>$f_e = 10$ | $f_o = 5$<br>$f_e = 10$ | $f_o = 17$<br>$f_e = 10$ |

1. $H_0$ says that the total of 30 acts should be evenly spread over the three conditions, so $f_e = N/k$ 30/3 = 10 for each category.
2. $\chi^2_{obt} = \Sigma\left(\frac{(f_e - f_o)^2}{f_e}\right) = \frac{(10-8)^2}{10} + \frac{(10-5)^2}{10} + \frac{(10-17)^2}{10}$
3. $\chi^2_{obt} = \frac{(2)^2}{10} + \frac{(5)^2}{10} + \frac{(-7)^2}{10}$
4. $\chi^2_{obt} = \frac{4}{10} + \frac{25}{10} + \frac{49}{10}$
5. $\chi^2_{obt} = .40 + 2.5 + 4.9 = 7.80$
6. With $df = k - 1 = 2$ and $\alpha = .05$, $\chi^2_{crit} = 5.99$. Therefore, different wall coverings produce a significant difference in the frequency of graffiti acts. In the population we expect about 27% (8/30) of graffiti on white walls, 17% (5/30) on blue walls, and 57% (17/30) on chalkboard walls.

### *For Practice:*

1. The one-way chi square is used when the study counts the ____ with which participants fall into different ____.
2. We find 21 participants in category A, and 39 participants in category B. $H_0$ is that the frequencies in the population are equal. The $f_e$ for category A is ____, and $f_e$ for category B is ____.
3. Compute $\chi^2_{obt}$ for question 2.
4. The $df$ is ____ so, at $\alpha = .05$, $\chi^2_{crit}$ is ____.
5. The $\chi^2_{obt}$ is ____, so in the population we expect membership is around ____% in A and around ____% in B.

**Answers**

1. frequency; categories
2. Each $f_e = 60/2 = 30$
3. $\chi^2_{obt} = \frac{(30-21)^2}{30} + \frac{(30-39)^2}{30} = 5.40$
4. 1; 3.84
5. significant; 35%; 65%

## THE TWO-WAY CHI SQUARE: THE TEST OF INDEPENDENCE

The **two-way chi square** is used when you count the frequency of category membership along *two* variables. (This is similar to the factorial ANOVA discussed in the previous chapter.) The procedure for computing $\chi^2$ is the same regardless of the number of categories in each variable. The assumptions of the two-way chi square are the same as for the one-way chi square.

### Logic of the Two-Way Chi Square

Here is a study that calls for a two-way chi square. At one time psychologists claimed that someone with a "Type A" personality tends to be very pressured and never seems to have enough time. The "Type B" personality, however, tends not to be so time pressured, and is more relaxed and mellow. A controversy developed over whether people with Type A personalities are less healthy, especially when it comes to having heart attacks. Therefore, say that we select a sample of 80 people and determine how many are Type A and how many are Type B. We then count the frequency of heart attacks in each type. We must also count how many in each type have *not* had heart attacks. Therefore, we have two categorical variables: personality type (A or B) and health (heart attack or no heart attack). Table 13.1 shows the layout of this study. Notice, with two rows and two columns, this is a 2 × 2 ("2 *by* 2") matrix, so we have a 2 × 2 design. With different variables, the design might be a 2 × 3, a 3 × 4, etc.

Although this looks like a two-way ANOVA, it is not analyzed like one. The two-way $\chi^2$ is also called the **test of independence** because it tests whether the frequency of participants falling into the categories of one variable is independent of the frequency of their falling into the categories of the other variable. Thus, our example study will test whether the frequencies of having or not having a heart attack are independent of the frequencies of being Type A or Type B. (Essentially, as in the two-way ANOVA, the two-way $\chi^2$ tests the *interaction,* testing whether the influence of one factor *depends on* the level of the other factor that is present. Thus, we'll ask, "Does the frequency of people having heart attacks depend on their frequency of being Type A or B?")

To understand "independence," in Table 13.2 the diagram on the left shows an example where category membership on our variables is perfectly independent. Here, the frequency of having or not having a heart attack does not depend on the frequency of being Type A or Type B. Another way to view the two-way $\chi^2$ is as a test of whether a *correlation* exists between the two variables. When variables are independent, there is no correlation, and using the categories from one variable is no help in predicting the

***TABLE 13.1***
A Two-Way Chi Square Design Comparing Participants' Personality Type and Health

| | | *Personality Type* | |
|---|---|---|---|
| | | *Type A* | *Type B* |
| *Health* | *Heart Attack* | $f_o$ | $f_o$ |
| | *No Heart Attack* | $f_o$ | $f_o$ |

**TABLE 13.2**

Examples of Independence and Dependence

*On the left, personality type and heart attacks are perfectly independent. On the right, personality type and heart attacks are perfectly dependent.*

| | | Personality Type | |
|---|---|---|---|
| | | Type A | Type B |
| Health | Heart Attack | $f_o = 20$ | $f_o = 20$ |
| | No Heart Attack | $f_o = 20$ | $f_o = 20$ |

| | | Personality Type | |
|---|---|---|---|
| | | Type A | Type B |
| Health | Heart Attack | $f_o = 40$ | $f_o = 0$ |
| | No Heart Attack | $f_o = 0$ | $f_o = 40$ |

frequencies for the other variable. Here, knowing if people are Type A or Type B does not help to predict if they do or do not have heart attacks (and the categories of heart attack and no heart attack do not help in predicting personality type).

However, the right-hand diagram in Table 13.2 shows one of the patterns we might see when the two variables are totally dependent. Here, the frequency of a heart attack or no heart attack *depends* on personality type. Likewise, a perfect correlation exists because whether people are Type A or Type B is a perfect predictor of whether or not they have had a heart attack (and vice versa).

Say that our actual data are shown in Table 13.3. There is a *degree* of dependence here because a heart attack tends to be the more frequent response for Type A personalities, while no heart attack is more frequent for Type B personalities. Therefore, there is some degree of correlation between the variables. On the one hand, we'd like to conclude that this relationship occurs in the population. On the other hand, perhaps there really is no correlation in the population, but by chance we obtained frequencies that poorly represent this. The above translate into our null and alternative hypotheses. In the two-way chi square,

*1.* $H_0$ is that category membership on one variable is independent of (not correlated with) category membership on the other variable. If the sample data look correlated, this is due to sampling error.

*2.* $H_a$ is that category membership on the two variables in the population is dependent (correlated).

**TABLE 13.3**

Observed Frequencies as a Function of Personality Type and Health

| | | Personality Type | |
|---|---|---|---|
| | | Type A | Type B |
| Health | Heart Attack | $f_o = 25$ | $f_o = 10$ |
| | No Heart Attack | $f_o = 5$ | $f_o = 40$ |

$N = 80$

### Computing the Two-Way Chi Square

Again the first step in computing $\chi^2$ is to compute the expected frequencies for each category. To do so, as shown in Table 13.4, first compute the total of the observed frequencies in each column and the total of the observed frequencies in each row. Also, note *N,* the total of all observed frequencies. Now compute the expected frequency in each *cell.* (A cell is a square in the diagram in Table 13.4 formed by a combination of personality type and heart attack/no heart attack.)

Each $f_e$ is based on the probability of a participant falling into the cell if the two variables are independent. For example, for the cell of Type A and heart attack, we'd determine the probability of someone in our study being Type A and the probability of someone in our study reporting a heart attack, when these variables are independent. The expected frequency in this cell then equals this probability multiplied times *N.* Luckily, the steps involved in this can be combined to produce this formula.

*THE FORMULA FOR COMPUTING THE EXPECTED FREQUENCY IN EACH CELL OF A TWO-WAY CHI SQUARE IS*

$$f_e = \frac{(\text{Cell's row total } f_o)(\text{Cell's column total } f_o)}{N}$$

This says that, for each cell, multiply the total observed frequencies for the row containing the cell times the total observed frequencies for the column containing the cell, and then divide by the *N* of the study.

Thus, to compute the two-way $\chi^2$:

**Step 1:** *Compute the* $f_e$ *for each cell:* Table 13.4 shows the completed $f_e$ for the example.

**Step 2:** *Compute* $\chi^2_{obt}$*:* Use the same formula used in the one-way design, which is

$$\chi^2_{\text{obt}} = \Sigma\left(\frac{(f_o - f_e)^2}{f_e}\right)$$

Here, the formula says to first form a fraction for each *cell:* In the numerator of each, square the difference between $f_e$ and $f_o$ for the cell. In the denominator is the $f_e$ for the cell. Thus, with the data in Table 13.4 we have

$$\chi^2_{\text{obt}} = \left(\frac{(25 - 13.125)^2}{13.125}\right) + \left(\frac{(10 - 21.875)^2}{21.875}\right) + \left(\frac{(5 - 16.875)^2}{16.875}\right) + \left(\frac{(40 - 28.125)^2}{28.125}\right)$$

**Step 3:** *Perform the subtraction in the numerator of each fraction:* After subtracting, we have

$$\chi^2_{\text{obt}} = \frac{(11.875)^2}{13.125} + \frac{(-11.875)^2}{21.875} + \frac{(-11.875)^2}{16.875} + \frac{(-11.875)^2}{28.125}$$

**Step 4:** *Square the numerator in each fraction:* This gives

$$\chi^2_{obt} = \frac{(141.016)}{13.125} + \frac{(141.016)}{21.875} + \frac{(141.016)}{16.875} + \frac{(141.016)}{28.125}$$

**Step 5:** *Perform the division in each fraction and then sum the results:*

$$\chi^2_{obt} = 10.74 + 6.45 + 8.36 + 5.01$$

so

$$\chi^2_{obt} = 30.56$$

**Step 6:** *Compare $\chi^2_{obt}$ to $\chi^2_{crit}$.* First, determine the degrees of freedom.

*THE DEGREES OF FREEDOM IN A TWO-WAY CHI SQUARE ARE*

$$df = (\text{Number of rows} - 1)(\text{Number of columns} - 1)$$

For our study, *df* is $(2 - 1)(2 - 1)$ which is 1. Find the critical value of $\chi^2$ in Table 6 in Appendix B. At $\alpha = .05$ and $df = 1$, the $\chi^2_{crit}$ is 3.84.

Our $\chi^2_{obt}$ of 30.56 is larger than $\chi^2_{crit}$, so the obtained $\chi^2$ is significant. Therefore, we reject $H_0$ that the variables are independent and accept the alternative hypothesis: We are confident that the sample represents frequencies from two variables that are dependent in the population. In other words, the correlation is significant such that the frequency of having or not having a heart attack depends on the frequency of being Type A or Type B (and vice versa).

If $\chi^2_{obt}$ is not larger than the critical value, do not reject $H_0$. Then we cannot say whether these variables are independent or not.

*REMEMBER* A significant *two-way* $\chi^2$ indicates that the sample data are likely to represent two variables that are dependent (correlated) in the population.

**TABLE 13.4**
Diagram Containing $f_o$ and $f_e$ for Each Cell
*Each $f_e$ equals the row total times the column total, divided by N.*

| | | ***Personality Type*** | | |
|---|---|---|---|---|
| | | ***Type A*** | ***Type B*** | |
| ***Health*** | ***Heart Attack*** | $f_o = 25$<br>$f_e = 13.125$<br>(35)(30)/80 | $f_o = 10$<br>$f_e = 21.875$<br>(35)(50)/80 | Row total = 35 |
| | ***No Heart Attack*** | $f_o = 5$<br>$f_e = 16.875$<br>(45)(30)/80 | $f_o = 40$<br>$f_e = 28.125$<br>(45)(50)/80 | Row total = 45 |
| | | Column total = 30 | Column total = 50 | $N = 80$ |

## A QUICK REVIEW

- The two-way $\chi^2$ is used when counting the frequency of category membership along two variables.
- The $H_0$ is that category membership for one variable is independent of category membership for the other variable.

### MORE EXAMPLES

We count the number of participants who indicate (1) that they like or dislike studying statistics and (2) their gender. The $H_0$ is that the frequency of liking/disliking statistics is independent of gender. The results are:

| | *Like* | *Dislike* | |
|---|---|---|---|
| *Male* | $f_o = 20$, $f_e = 15$ | $f_o = 10$, $f_e = 15$ | Total $f_o = 30$ |
| *Female* | $f_o = 5$, $f_e = 10$ | $f_o = 15$, $f_e = 10$ | Total $f_o = 20$ |
| | Total $f_o = 25$ | Total $f_o = 50$ | $N = 50$ |

1. Compute each $f_e$:
   For male–like, $f_e = (30)(25)/50 = 15$.
   For male–dislike, $f_e = (30)(25)/50 = 15$.
   For female–like, $f_e = (20)(25)/50 = 10$.
   For female–dislike, $f_e = (20)(25)/50 = 10$.
2. $\chi^2_{obt} = \frac{(20-15)^2}{15} + \frac{(10-15)^2}{15} + \frac{(5-10)^2}{10} + \frac{(15-10)^2}{10}$

3 and 4. $\chi^2_{obt} = 25/15 + 25/15 + 25/10 + 25/10$

5. $\chi^2_{obt} = 8.334$
6. $df = (2 - 1)(2 - 1) = 1$. With $\alpha = .05$, $\chi^2_{crit} = 3.84$, so the $\chi^2_{obt}$ is significant: The frequency of liking/disliking statistics *depends on*—is correlated with—whether participants are male or female.

### *For Practice:*

1. The two-way $\chi^2$ is used when we count the ____ with which participants fall into the ____ of two variables.
2. The $H_0$ in the two-way $\chi^2$ is that the frequencies in the categories of one variable are ____ of those of other variable.
3. Below are the frequencies for individuals who are satisfied/dissatisfied with their job and who must/must not work overtime. What is the $f_e$ in each cell?

| | *Overtime* | *No Overtime* |
|---|---|---|
| *Satisfied* | $f_o = 11$ | $f_o = 3$ |
| *Dissatisfied* | $f_o = 8$ | $f_o = 12$ |

4. Compute $\chi^2_{obt}$.
5. The $df =$ ____ and $\chi^2_{crit}$ is ____.
6. What do you conclude about these variables?

**Answers**

1. frequency; categories
2. independent
3. For satisfied–overtime, $f_e = (14)(19)/34 = 7.824$; for satisfied–no overtime, $f_e = (14)(15)/34 = 6.176$; for dissatisfied–overtime, $f_e = (20)(19)/34 = 11.176$; for dissatisfied–no overtime, $f_e = (20)(15)/34 = 8.824$.
4. $\chi^2_{obt} = \frac{(11-7.824)^2}{7.824} + \frac{(3-6.176)^2}{6.176} + \frac{(8-11.176)^2}{11.176} + \frac{(12-8.824)^2}{8.824} = 4.968$
5. 1; 3.84
6. $\chi^2_{obt}$ is significant: The frequency of job satisfaction/dissatisfaction depends on the frequency of overtime/no overtime.

## Describing the Relationship in a Two-Way Chi Square

A significant two-way chi square indicates a significant correlation between the two variables. To determine the size of this correlation, compute one of two new correlation coefficients, either the *phi coefficient,* or the *contingency coefficient.*

If you have performed a 2 × 2 chi square and it is significant, compute the **phi coefficient.** The symbol for the phi coefficient is $\phi$, and its value can be between 0 and 1. Think of phi as comparing your data to the ideal situations that were illustrated back in Table 13.2 when the variables are or are not dependent. A value of 0 indicates that the data are perfectly independent. The larger the value of phi, however, the closer the data come to being perfectly dependent.

*THE FORMULA FOR THE PHI COEFFICIENT IS*

$$\phi = \sqrt{\frac{\chi^2_{obt}}{N}}$$

The formula says to divide the $\chi^2_{obt}$ by $N$ (the total number of participants) and then find the square root.

For the heart attack study, $\chi^2_{obt}$ was 30.56 and $N$ was 80, so

$$\phi = \sqrt{\frac{\chi^2_{obt}}{N}} = \sqrt{\frac{30.56}{80}} = \sqrt{.382} = .62$$

Thus, on a scale of 0 to 1, where 1 indicates perfect dependence, the correlation is .62 between the frequency of heart attacks and the frequency of personality types. (Recall that by squaring a correlation coefficient we obtain the *proportion of variance accounted for,* the proportion of differences in one variable that is associated with the other variable. By not computing the square root in the formula above, we have $\phi^2$. For our study $\phi^2 = .38$. This is analogous to $r^2$, indicating that about 38% of the differences in whether people have heart attacks are associated with differences in their personality type—and vice versa.)

The other correlation coefficient is the **contingency coefficient,** symbolized by $C$. This is used to describe a significant two-way chi square that is *not* a 2 × 2 design (it's a 2 × 3, a 3 × 3, etc.).

*THE FORMULA FOR THE CONTINGENCY COEFFICIENT IS*

$$C = \sqrt{\frac{\chi^2_{obt}}{N + \chi^2_{obt}}}$$

This says to first add $N$ to the $\chi^2_{obt}$ in the denominator. Then divide that quantity into $\chi^2_{obt}$, and then find the square root. Interpret $C$ in the same way as $\phi$. (Likewise, $C^2$ is analogous to $\phi^2$.)

## STATISTICS IN THE RESEARCH LITERATURE: REPORTING $\chi^2$

A chi square is reported like previous results, except that in addition to *df,* we also include the *N.* For example, in our one-way design involving geniuses and handedness, we tested an *N* of 50, *df* was 1, and the significant $\chi^2_{obt}$ was 18. We report these results as $\chi^2\ (1, N = 50) = 18.00, p < .05$. We report a two-way $\chi^2$ using the same format.

As usual, a graph is useful for summarizing the data. For a one-way design, label the *Y* axis with frequency and the *X* axis with the categories, and then plot the $f_o$ in each category. With a nominal *X* variable, create a *bar graph.* The bar graph on the left in Figure 13.2 shows the results of our handedness study.

The right-hand graph in Figure 13.2 shows a bar graph for our heart attack study. To graph the data from a two-way design, place frequency on the *Y* axis and one of the nominal variables on the *X* axis. The levels of the other variable are indicated in the body of the graph. (This is similar to the way a two-way interaction was plotted in the previous chapter, except that here we create bar graphs.)

## A WORD ABOUT NONPARAMETRIC PROCEDURES FOR ORDINAL SCORES

We also have nonparametric procedures that are used with ordinal (rank-ordered) scores. You obtain ranked scores in a study for one of two reasons. First, sometimes you'll directly measure participants using ranked scores (directly assigning participants a score of 1st, 2nd, etc.). Second, sometimes you'll initially measure interval or ratio scores, but they violate the assumptions of parametric procedures by not being normally distributed or not having homogeneous variance. Then you transform these scores to ranks (the highest raw score is ranked 1, the next highest score is ranked 2, and so on). Either way, you then compute the same nonparametric inferential statistics.

> ***REMEMBER*** Perform *nonparametric procedures for ranked data* when the dependent variable is measured in, or transformed to, ordinal scores.

***FIGURE 13.2***

Frequencies of (a) left- and right-handed geniuses and (b) heart attacks and personality type

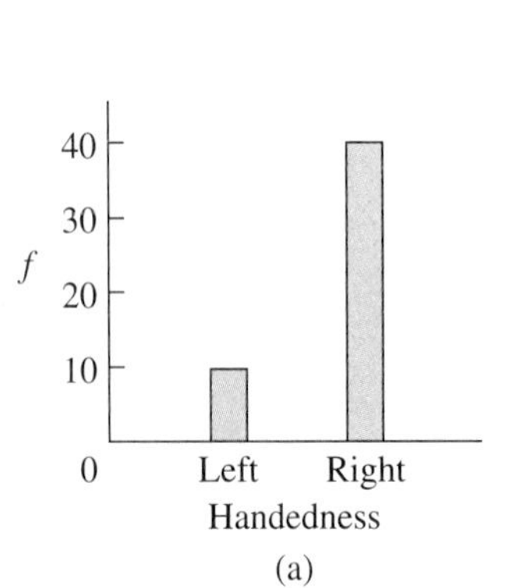


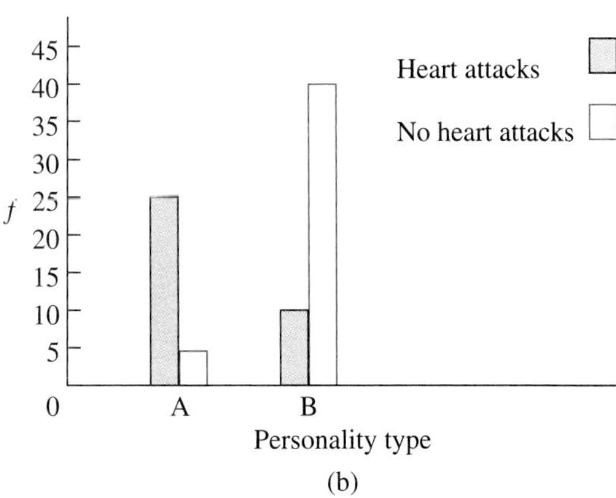

Although the computations for nonparametric procedures are different from those of parametric procedures, their logic and rules are the same. A relationship occurs here when the ordinal scores consistently change. For example, we might see the scores change from predominantly low ranks around 1st and 2nd in one group to predominantly higher ranks in another group, say around 6th or 7th. The null hypothesis says that if the sample shows this, it is because of sampling error, and the sample is poorly representing that no such relationship occurs in the population. The alternative hypothesis is that the pattern in the sample represents a similar relationship that would be found in the population. As usual, we test $H_0$ by computing an obtained statistic that describes our data. By comparing it to a critical value, we determine whether the sample relationship is significant. If it is, we conclude that the predicted relationship exists in the population (in nature). If the data are not significant, we retain $H_0$.

In the literature you will encounter a number of different nonparametric procedures. The computations for each are found in more advanced textbooks, but you should know with what type of design the most common procedures are used. As listed below, we have nonparametric procedures that are analogous to the Pearson correlation coefficient, to the independent- and related-samples *t*-tests, and to the one-way, between-subjects and one-way, within-subjects ANOVA.

*1.* The **Spearman rank-order correlation coefficient** is analogous to the Pearson correlation coefficient for ranked data. Its symbol is $r_s$. It produces a number between $\pm 1$ that describes the strength and type of linear relationship that is present when data consist of pairs of *X-Y* scores that are both ordinal scores. If significant, $r_s$ estimates the corresponding population coefficient.

*2.* The **Mann–Whitney *U* test** is analogous to the independent-samples *t*-test. It is performed when a study contains two independent samples of ordinal scores.

*3.* The **Wilcoxon *T* test** is analogous to the related-samples *t*-test. It is performed when a study has two related samples of ordinal scores. Recall that related samples occur either through *matching* pairs of participants or through *repeated measures* of the same participants.

*4.* The **Kruskal–Wallis *H* test** is analogous to a one-way, between-subjects ANOVA. It is performed when a study has one factor with at least three conditions, and each involves independent samples of ordinal scores.

*5.* The **Friedman $\chi^2$ test** is analogous to a one-way, within-subjects ANOVA. It is performed when a study has one factor with at least three levels, and each involves related samples of ordinal scores.

## CHAPTER SUMMARY

1. *Nonparametric procedures* are used when data do not meet the assumptions of parametric procedures. Nonparametric procedures are less powerful than parametric procedures.
2. *Chi square* ($\chi^2$) is used with one or more nominal (categorical) variables, and the data are the frequencies with which participants fall into each category.
3. The *one-way* $\chi^2$ compares the frequency of category membership along one variable. A significant $\chi^2_{obt}$ indicates that the observed frequencies are unlikely to represent the distribution of frequencies in the population as described by $H_0$.

4. The *two-way* $\chi^2$ tests whether the frequency of category membership on one variable is independent of the frequency of category membership on the other variable. A significant $\chi^2_{obt}$ indicates that the two variables are dependent, or correlated.
5. In a significant 2 × 2 chi square, the strength of the relationship is described by the *phi correlation coefficient* ($\phi$). In a significant two-way chi square that is not a 2 × 2, the strength of the relationship is described by the *contingency coefficient* (C). The larger these coefficients are, the closer the variables are to being perfectly dependent, or correlated. Squaring $\phi$ or $C$ gives the proportion of variance accounted for, the proportion of the differences in category membership on one variable that is associated with category membership on the other variable.
6. The correlation coefficient that describes the strength and type of linear relationship that is present between two ordinal variables is the *Spearman rank-order correlation coefficient* ($r_s$).
7. The *Mann–Whitney U test* is the nonparametric, independent-samples *t*-test for ordinal scores.
8. The *Wilcoxon* T *test* is the nonparametric, related-samples *t*-test for ranks.
9. The *Kruskal–Wallis* H *test* is the nonparametric, one-way, between-subjects ANOVA for ranks.
10. The *Friedman* $\chi^2$ *test* is the nonparametric, one-way, within-subjects ANOVA for ranks.

## KEY TERMS: Can You Define the Following?

$f_o$ *241*
$f_e$ *242*
$\chi^2_{obt}$ *242*
$\chi^2_{crit}$ *244*
$\phi$ *251*
$C$ *251*
$\chi^2$-distribution *243*
chi square procedure *240*
contingency coefficient *251*
expected frequency *242*
Friedman $\chi^2$ test *253*
goodness of fit test *242*
Kruskal–Wallis *H* test *253*
Mann–Whitney *U* test *253*
nonparametric statistics *240*
observed frequency *241*
one-way chi square *241*
phi coefficient *251*
$r_s$ *253*
Spearman rank-order correlation coefficient *253*
test of independence *246*
two-way chi square *246*
Wilcoxon *T* test *253*

## REVIEW QUESTIONS

(Answers for odd-numbered questions are in Appendix C.)

1. What do all nonparametric procedures have in common with all parametric procedures?
2. Which variable in an experiment determines whether to use parametric or nonparametric procedures?

*3.* (a) With which two scales of measurement do you use nonparametric procedures? (b) What two things can be "wrong" with interval/ratio scores that lead you to use nonparametric procedures for ranked data?

*4.* (a) Why, if possible, should a researcher design a study so that the data meet the assumptions of a parametric procedure? (b) Why shouldn't you use parametric procedures for data that clearly violate their assumptions?

*5.* (a) When do you use the chi square? (b) When do you use the one-way chi square? (c) When do you use the two-way chi square?

*6.* (a) What is the symbol for observed frequency? What does it mean? (b) What is the symbol for expected frequency? What does it mean?

*7.* What does a significant one-way chi square indicate?

*8.* What does a significant two-way chi square indicate?

*9.* (a) What is the phi coefficient, and when is it used? (b) What is the contingency coefficient, and when is it used?

*10.* What is the nonparametric version of each of the following? (a) the one-way, between-subjects ANOVA (b) the independent-samples *t*-test (c) the related-samples *t*-test (d) the Pearson correlation coefficient? (e) the one-way, within-subjects ANOVA?

## APPLICATION QUESTIONS

*11.* In the general population the distribution of political party affiliation is 30% Republican, 55% Democratic, and 15% other. To determine whether this distribution is also found among the elderly, in a sample of 100 senior citizens, we find 18 Republicans, 64 Democrats, and 18 other. (a) What are $H_0$ and $H_a$? (b) What is $f_e$ for each group? (c) Compute $\chi^2_{obt}$. (d) With $\alpha = .05$, what do you conclude about party affiliation in the population of senior citizens?

*12.* A survey finds that, given the choice, 34 females prefer males much taller than themselves, and 55 females prefer males only slightly taller than themselves. (a) What are $H_0$ and $H_a$? (b) With $\alpha = .05$, what would you conclude about the preference of females in the population? (c) Describe how you would graph these results.

*13.* Foofy counts the students who like Professor Demented and those who like Professor Randomsampler. She then performs a one-way $\chi^2$ to determine if there is a significant difference between the frequency with which students like each professor. (a) Why is this approach incorrect? (*Hint:* Check the assumptions of $\chi^2$.) (b) How should she analyze the data?

*14.* The following data reflect the frequency with which people voted in the last election and were satisfied with the officials elected:

| | | *Satisfied* | |
|---|---|---|---|
| | | *Yes* | *No* |
| *Voted* | *Yes* | 48 | 35 |
| | *No* | 33 | 52 |

(a) What are $H_0$ and $H_a$? (b) What is $f_e$ in each cell? (c) Compute $\chi^2_{obt}$. (d) With $\alpha = .05$, what do you conclude about these variables? (e) How consistent is this relationship?

15. A study determines the frequency of the different political party affiliations for male and female senior citizens. The following data are obtained:

| | | *Affiliation* | | |
|---|---|---|---|---|
| | | ***Republican*** | ***Democrat*** | ***Other*** |
| ***Gender*** | ***Male*** | 18 | 43 | 14 |
| | ***Female*** | 39 | 23 | 18 |

(a) What are $H_0$ and $H_a$? (b) What is $f_e$ in each cell? (c) Compute $\chi^2_{obt}$. (d) With $\alpha = .05$, what do you conclude about gender and party affiliation in the population of senior citizens? (e) How consistent is this relationship?

16. Select the statistical procedure to use in each of the following: (a) A study of the effects of a new pain reliever on rankings of the emotional content of words describing pain. A randomly selected group of people is tested before and after administration of the drug. (b) A study of the effects of eight different colors of spaghetti sauce on tastiness scores. A different random sample of people tastes each color of sauce, and then the tastiness scores are ranked. (c) A study of the effects of increasing amounts of alcohol consumption on reaction-time scores. The scores are ranked, and the same group of participants is tested after 1, 3, and 5 drinks. (d) In a study of family income, a wealthy and poor sample indicates the percentage of family income that was spent on clothing last year. Scores are then rank-ordered. (e) A study of marathon runners, to describe the relationship between their finishing position in Race A and their finishing position in Race B.

17. What is the basic logic of $H_0$ and $H_a$ in all nonparametric procedures for ranked data?

18. After testing 40 participants, our $\chi^2_{obt}$ was 13.31. With $\alpha = .05$, and $df = 2$, report this significant result.

19. A research article indicates that the Wilcoxon *T* test was significant ($p < .05$). (a) What does this test indicate about the design of the study? (b) What does it indicate about the nature of the scores? (c) What will you conclude about the relationship here?

20. A research article indicates that the Mann–Whitney *U* test was significant ($p < .01$). (a) What does this test indicate about the design of the study? (b) What docs it indicate about the scale of the dependent scores? (c) What will you conclude about the relationship?

21. If a researcher summarizes scores using the mode and computes a chi square, how has he or she measured the variable?

22. Thinking back on the previous chapters, what three aspects of your independent variable(s) and one aspect of your dependent variable determine the specific inferential procedure to perform in a particular experiment?

## SUMMARY OF FORMULAS

1. *The formula for chi square is*

$$\chi^2_{obt} = \Sigma\left(\frac{(f_o - f_e)^2}{f_e}\right)$$

*In a one-way chi square:*

$$f_e \text{ in each category} = \frac{N}{k}$$

$$df = k - 1$$

*In a two-way chi square:*

$$f_e = \frac{(\text{Cell's row total } f_o)(\text{Cell's column total } f_o)}{N}$$

$$df = (\text{Number of rows} - 1)(\text{Number of columns} - 1)$$

2. *The formula for the phi coefficient is*

$$\phi = \sqrt{\frac{\chi^2_{obt}}{N}}$$

3. *The formula for the contingency coefficient* (C) *is*

$$C = \sqrt{\frac{\chi^2_{obt}}{N + \chi^2_{obt}}}$$

# Additional Statistical Formulas

A.1: Confidence Intervals for the Two-Sample $t$-Test

A.2: Computing the Two-Way, Between-Subjects ANOVA

---

## A.1: CONFIDENCE INTERVALS FOR THE TWO-SAMPLE *t*-TEST

Two versions of a confidence interval can be used to describe the results from the two-sample $t$-test described in Chapter 9. For the independent-samples $t$-test we compute the *confidence interval for the difference between two* $\mu$*s;* for the related-samples $t$-test we compute the *confidence interval for* $\mu_D$.

### Confidence Interval for the Difference Between Two $\mu$s

The **confidence interval for the difference between two $\mu$s** describes a range of *differences* between two $\mu$s, any one of which is likely to be represented by the *difference* between our two sample means. This procedure is appropriate when the sample means are from *independent* samples. For example, in Chapter 9 we discussed the experiment that compared recall scores under the conditions of Hypnosis and No-hypnosis. We found a difference of +3 between the sample means $(\overline{X}_1 - \overline{X}_2)$, so if we could examine the corresponding $\mu_1$ and $\mu_2$, we'd expect that their difference, $(\mu_1 - \mu_2)$ would be *around* +3. The confidence interval contains the highest and lowest values of $\mu_1 - \mu_2$ around +3 that the difference between our sample means is likely to represent.

*THE FORMULA FOR THE CONFIDENCE INTERVAL FOR THE DIFFERENCE BETWEEN TWO $\mu$s IS*

$$(s_{\overline{X}_1-\overline{X}_2})(-t_{\text{crit}}) + (\overline{X}_1 - \overline{X}_2) \leq \mu_1 - \mu_2 \leq (s_{\overline{X}_1-\overline{X}_2})(+t_{\text{crit}}) + (\overline{X}_1 - \overline{X}_2)$$

Here, $\mu_1 - \mu_2$ stands for the unknown difference we are estimating. The $t_{\text{crit}}$ is the *two-tailed* value found for the appropriate $\alpha$ at $df = (n_1 - 1) + (n_2 - 1)$. The values of $s_{\overline{X}_1-\overline{X}_2}$ and $(\overline{X}_1 - \overline{X}_2)$ are computed in the independent-samples $t$-test.

In the hypnosis study the two-tailed $t_{\text{crit}}$ for $df = 30$ and $\alpha = .05$ is $\pm 2.042$, $s_{\overline{X}_1-\overline{X}_2}$ is 1.023, and $\overline{X}_1 - \overline{X}_2$ is +3. Filling in the formula gives

$$(1.023)(-2.042) + (+3) \leq \mu_1 - \mu_2 \leq (1.023)(+2.042) + (+3)$$

Multiplying 1.02 times $\pm 2.042$ gives

$$-2.089 + (+3) \leq \mu_1 - \mu_2 \leq +2.089 + (+3)$$

So finally,

$$.911 \leq \mu_1 - \mu_2 \leq 5.089$$

Because $\alpha = .05$, this is the 95% confidence interval: We are 95% confident that the interval between .911 and 5.089 contains the difference we'd find between the μs for no-hypnosis and hypnosis. In essence, if someone asked how big is the average difference between when the population recalls under hypnosis and when it recalls under no-hypnosis, we'd be 95% confident the difference is between .91 and 5.09.

> *REMEMBER* The *confidence interval for the difference between two μs* describes the difference between the population means represented by the difference between our sample means in the independent-samples *t*-test.

### *For Practice:*

1. In application problem 13 in Chapter 9, $\overline{X}_1 = 43$, $\overline{X}_2 = 39$, and $s_{\overline{X}_1 - \overline{X}_2} = 1.78$. At $\alpha = .05$ and $df = 28$, $t_{crit} = \pm 2.048$. What is the confidence interval for the difference between the μs?
2. In application problem 21 in Chapter 9, $\overline{X}_1 = 11.5$, $\overline{X}_2 = 14.1$, and $s_{\overline{X}_1 - \overline{X}_2} = 1.03$. At $\alpha = .05$ and $df = 18$, $t_{crit} = \pm 2.101$. What is the confidence interval for the difference between the μs?

**Answers:**

1. $(1.78)(-2.048) + 4 \leq \mu_1 - \mu_2 \leq (1.78)(+2.048) + 4 = .35 \leq \mu_1 - \mu_2 \leq 7.65$
2. $(1.03)(-2.101) + -2.6 \leq \mu_1 - \mu_2 \leq (1.03)(+2.101) + -2.6 = -4.76 \leq \mu_1 - \mu_2 \leq -.44$

## Computing the Confidence Interval for $\mu_D$

The other confidence interval is used with the related-samples *t*-test to describe the μ of the population of difference scores ($\mu_D$) that is represented by our sample of difference scores ($\overline{D}$.) The **confidence interval for $\mu_D$** describes a range of values of $\mu_D$, one of which our sample mean is likely to represent. The interval is defined by the highest and lowest values of $\mu_D$ that are not significantly different from $\overline{D}$.

*THE FORMULA FOR THE CONFIDENCE INTERVAL FOR $\mu_D$ IS*

$$(s_{\overline{D}})(-t_{crit}) + \overline{D} \leq \mu_D \leq (s_{\overline{D}})(+t_{crit}) + \overline{D}$$

This is the same formula used in the one-sample *t*-test in Chapter 8, except that the symbol $\overline{X}$ has been replaced by $\overline{D}$. The $t_{crit}$ is the *two-tailed* value for $df = N - 1$, where $N$ is the number of difference scores, $s_{\overline{D}}$ is the standard error of the mean difference computed in the *t*-test, and $\overline{D}$ is the mean of the difference scores.

For example, in Chapter 9 we discussed the related-samples experiment comparing the fear scores of participants who had or had not received our phobia therapy. We found the mean difference score in the sample was $\overline{D} = +3.6$, $s_{\overline{D}} = 1.25$, and with $\alpha = .05$ and $df = 4$, $t_{\text{crit}}$ is $\pm 2.776$. Filling in the formula gives

$$(1.25)(-2.776) + 3.6 \leq \mu_D \leq (1.25)(+2.776) + 3.6$$

which becomes

$$(-3.47) + 3.6 \leq \mu_D \leq (+3.47) + 3.6$$

and so

$$0.13 \leq \mu_D \leq 7.07$$

Thus, we are 95% confident that our sample mean of differences represents a population $\mu_D$ within this interval. In other words, if we performed this study on the entire population, we would expect the average difference in before- and after-therapy scores to be between 0.13 and 7.07.

### *For Practice:*

1. In application problem 17 in Chapter 9, $\overline{D} = +2.63$ and $s_{\overline{D}} = .75$. At $\alpha = .05$ and $df = 7$, $t_{\text{crit}} = \pm 2.365$. What is the confidence interval for $\mu_D$?
2. In application problem 19 in Chapter 9, $\overline{D} = 1.2$ and $s_{\overline{D}} = .359$. At $\alpha = .05$ and $df = 9$, $t_{\text{crit}} = \pm 2.262$. What is the confidence interval for the difference between the $\mu$s?

**Answers:**

1. $(.75)(-2.365) + 2.63 \leq \mu_D \leq (.75)(+2.365) + 2.63 = .86 \leq \mu_D \leq 4.40$
2. $(.359)(-2.262) + 1.2 \leq \mu_D \leq (.359)(+2.262) + 1.2 = .39 \leq \mu_D \leq 2.01$

## A.2: COMPUTING THE TWO-WAY, BETWEEN-SUBJECTS ANOVA

As discussed in Chapter 12, the following presents the formulas for computing the two-way, between subjects ANOVA, the Tukey *HSD* test for main effects and interactions, and $\eta^2$.

### Computing the ANOVA

Chapter 12 discusses a $3 \times 2$ design for the factors of volume of a message and participants' gender, and the dependent variable of persuasiveness. Organize the data as shown in Table A.1. The ANOVA involves five parts, computing (1) the sums and means, (2) the sums of squares, (3) the degrees of freedom, (4) the mean squares, and (5) the *F*s.

*TABLE A.1*

Summary of Data for 3 × 2 ANOVA

| Factor B: Gender | | Factor A: Volume — $A_1$: Soft | $A_2$: Medium | $A_3$: Loud | |
|---|---|---|---|---|---|
| | $B_1$: Male | 4<br>9<br>11<br>$\bar{X} = 8$<br>$\Sigma X = 24$<br>$\Sigma X^2 = 218$<br>$n = 3$ | 8<br>12<br>13<br>$\bar{X} = 11$<br>$\Sigma X = 33$<br>$\Sigma X^2 = 377$<br>$n = 3$ | 18<br>17<br>15<br>$\bar{X} = 16.67$<br>$\Sigma X = 50$<br>$\Sigma X^2 = 838$<br>$n = 3$ | $\bar{X}_{male} = 11.89$<br>$\Sigma X = 107$<br>$n = 9$ |
| | $B_2$: Female | 2<br>6<br>4<br>$\bar{X} = 4$<br>$\Sigma X = 12$<br>$\Sigma X^2 = 56$<br>$n = 3$ | 9<br>10<br>17<br>$\bar{X} = 12$<br>$\Sigma X = 36$<br>$\Sigma X^2 = 470$<br>$n = 3$ | 6<br>8<br>4<br>$\bar{X} = 6$<br>$\Sigma X = 18$<br>$\Sigma X^2 = 116$<br>$n = 3$ | $\bar{X}_{fem} = 7.33$<br>$\Sigma X = 66$<br>$n = 9$ |
| | | $\bar{X}_{soft} = 6$<br>$\Sigma X = 36$<br>$n = 6$ | $\bar{X}_{med} = 11.5$<br>$\Sigma X = 69$<br>$n = 6$ | $\bar{X}_{loud} = 11.33$<br>$\Sigma X = 68$<br>$n = 6$ | $\Sigma X_{tot} = 173$<br>$\Sigma X^2_{tot} = 2075$<br>$N = 18$ |

## Computing the Sums and Means

**Step 1:** *Compute* $\Sigma$X *and* $\Sigma$X$^2$ *in each cell:* Note the $n$ of the cell. For example, in the male–soft cell, $\Sigma X = 4 + 9 + 11 = 24$; $\Sigma X^2 = 4^2 + 9^2 + 11^2 = 218$; $n = 3$. Also, compute the mean in each cell (for the male–soft cell, $\bar{X} = 8$). These are the interaction means.

**Step 2:** *Compute* $\Sigma$X *vertically in each column of the study's diagram:* Add the $\Sigma X$s from the cells in a column (e.g., for soft, $\Sigma X = 24 + 12$). Note the $n$ in each column (here, $n = 6$) and compute the mean for each column (e.g., $\bar{X}_{soft} = 6$). These are the main effect means for factor A. (*Note:* Averaging the cell means in a column also gives the overall mean of the column.)

**Step 3:** *Compute* $\Sigma$X *horizontally in each row of the diagram:* Add the $\Sigma X$s from the cells in a row (for males, $\Sigma X = 24 + 33 + 50 = 107$). Note the $n$ in each row (here, $n = 9$). Compute the mean for each row (e.g., $\bar{X}_{male} = 11.89$). These are the main effect means for factor B. (Averaging the cell means in a row also gives the overall mean of the row.)

**Step 4:** *Compute* $\Sigma X_{tot}$*:* Add the $\Sigma X$ from the levels (columns) of factor A, so $\Sigma X_{tot} = 36 + 69 + 68 = 173$. (Or, add the $\Sigma X$ from the levels of factor B.)

**Step 5:** *Compute* $\Sigma X^2_{tot}$*:* Add the $\Sigma X^2$ from all cells, so $\Sigma X^2_{tot} = 218 + 377 + 838 + 56 + 470 + 116 = 2075$. Note $N$ (18).

### Computing the Sums of Squares

**Step 1:** *Compute the total sum of squares:*

*THE FORMULA FOR THE TOTAL SUM OF SQUARES IS*

$$SS_{tot} = \Sigma X^2_{tot} - \left(\frac{(\Sigma X_{tot})^2}{N}\right)$$

This says to divide $(\Sigma X_{tot})^2$ by $N$ and then subtract the answer from $\Sigma X^2_{tot}$.

From Table A.1, $\Sigma X_{tot} = 173$, $\Sigma X^2_{tot} = 2075$, and $N = 18$. Filling in the formula gives

$$SS_{tot} = 2075 - \left(\frac{(173)^2}{18}\right) = 2075 - 1662.72 = 412.28$$

*Note:* $(\Sigma X_{tot})^2/N$ above is also used later and is called the *correction* (here, the correction equals 1662.72).

**Step 2:** *Compute the sum of squares for factor A:* Always have factor A form your *columns.*

*THE FORMULA FOR THE SUM OF SQUARES BETWEEN GROUPS FOR COLUMN FACTOR A IS*

$$SS_A = \Sigma\left(\frac{(\Sigma X \text{ in the column})^2}{n \text{ of scores in the column}}\right) - \left(\frac{(\Sigma X_{tot})^2}{N}\right)$$

This says to square the $\Sigma X$ in each column of the study's diagram, divide by the $n$ in the column, add the answers together, and subtract the correction.

From Table A.1 the column sums are 36, 69, and 68, and $n$ was 6, so

$$SS_A = \left(\frac{(36)^2}{6} + \frac{(69)^2}{6} + \frac{(68)^2}{6}\right) - \left(\frac{(173)^2}{18}\right) = (216 + 793.5 + 770.67) - 1662.72$$

$$SS_A = 1780.17 - 1662.72 = 117.45$$

**Step 3:** *Compute the sum of squares between groups for factor B:* Factor B should form the *rows.*

*THE FORMULA FOR THE SUM OF SQUARES BETWEEN GROUPS FOR ROW FACTOR B IS*

$$SS_B = \Sigma\left(\frac{(\Sigma X \text{ in the row})^2}{n \text{ of scores in the row}}\right) - \left(\frac{(\Sigma X_{tot})^2}{N}\right)$$

This says to square the $\Sigma X$ for each row of the diagram and divide by the $n$ in the level. Then add the answers and subtract the correction.

In Table A.1 the row sums are 107 and 66, and $n$ was 9, so

$$SS_{\text{B}} = \left(\frac{(107)^2}{9} + \frac{(66)^2}{9}\right) - 1662.72 = 1756.11 - 1662.72 = 93.39$$

**Step 4:** *Compute the sum of squares between groups for the interaction:* First, compute the overall sum of squares between groups, $SS_{\text{bn}}$.

*THE FORMULA FOR THE OVERALL SUM OF SQUARES BETWEEN GROUPS IS*

$$SS_{\text{bn}} = \Sigma\left(\frac{(\Sigma X \text{ in the cell})^2}{n \text{ of scores in the cell}}\right) - \left(\frac{(\Sigma X_{\text{tot}})^2}{N}\right)$$

Find $(\Sigma X)^2$ for each cell and divide by the $n$ of the cell. Then add the answers together and subtract the correction.

From Table A.1

$$SS_{\text{bn}} = \left(\frac{(24)^2}{3} + \frac{(33)^2}{3} + \frac{(50)^2}{3} + \frac{(12)^2}{3} + \frac{(36)^2}{3} + \frac{(18)^2}{3}\right) - 1662.72$$

$$SS_{\text{bn}} = 1976.33 - 1662.72 = 313.61$$

To find $SS_{\text{A}\times\text{B}}$, subtract the sum of squares for both main effects (in Steps 2 and 3) from the overall $SS_{\text{bn}}$. Thus,

*THE FORMULA FOR THE SUM OF SQUARES BETWEEN GROUPS FOR THE INTERACTION IS*

$$SS_{\text{A}\times\text{B}} = SS_{\text{bn}} - SS_{\text{A}} - SS_{\text{B}}$$

In our example $SS_{\text{bn}} = 313.61$, $SS_{\text{A}} = 117.45$, and $SS_{\text{B}} = 93.39$, so

$$SS_{\text{A}\times\text{B}} = 313.61 - 117.45 - 93.39 = 102.77$$

**Step 5:** *Compute the sum of squares within groups:* Subtract the overall $SS_{\text{bn}}$ in Step 4 from the $SS_{\text{tot}}$ in Step 1 to obtain the $SS_{\text{wn}}$.

*THE FORMULA FOR THE SUM OF SQUARES WITHIN GROUPS IS*

$$SS_{\text{wn}} = SS_{\text{tot}} - SS_{\text{bn}}$$

Above, $SS_{\text{tot}} = 412.28$ and $SS_{\text{bn}} = 313.61$, so

$$SS_{\text{wn}} = 412.28 - 313.61 = 98.67$$

### Computing the Degrees of Freedom

**Step 1:** *The degrees of freedom between groups for factor A is* $k_A - 1$*, where* $k_A$ is the number of levels in factor A. (In our example, $k_A$ is the three levels of volume, so $df_A = 2$.)

**Step 2:** *The degrees of freedom between groups for factor B is* $k_B - 1$*, where* $k_B$ is the number of levels in factor B. (In our example $k_B$ is the two levels of gender, so $df_B = 1$.)

**Step 3:** *The degrees of freedom between groups for the interaction is the* df *for factor A multiplied times the* df *for factor B.* (In our example $df_A = 2$ and $df_B = 1$, so $df_{A \times B} = 2$.)

**Step 4:** *The degrees of freedom within groups equals* $N - k_{A \times B}$, where $N$ is the total $N$ of the study and $k_{A \times B}$ is the number of cells in the study. (In our example $N$ is 18 and we have six cells, so $df_{wn} = 18 - 6 = 12$.)

**Step 5:** *The degrees of freedom total equals* $N - 1$. Use this to check your previous calculations, because the sum of the above *df*s should equal $df_{tot}$. (In our example $df_{tot} = 17$.)

Place each *SS* and *df* in the ANOVA summary table as shown in Table A.2. Perform the remainder of the computations using this table.

### Computing the Mean Squares

**Step 1:** *Compute the mean square between groups for factor A:*

*THE FORMULA FOR THE MEAN SQUARE BETWEEN GROUPS FOR FACTOR A IS*

$$MS_A = \frac{SS_A}{df_A}$$

***TABLE A.2***

Summary Table of Two-Way ANOVA with *df* and Sums of Squares

| *Source* | *Sum of Squares* | df | *Mean Square* | F |
|---|---|---|---|---|
| Between | | | | |
| Factor A (volume) | 117.45 | 2 | $MS_A$ | $F_A$ |
| Factor B (gender) | 93.39 | 1 | $MS_B$ | $F_B$ |
| Interaction (vol × gen) | 102.77 | 2 | $MS_{A \times B}$ | $F_{A \times B}$ |
| Within | 98.67 | 12 | $MS_{wn}$ | |
| Total | 412.28 | 17 | | |

From Table A.2,

$$MS_{\text{A}} = \frac{117.45}{2} = 58.73$$

**Step 2:** *Compute the mean square between groups for factor B:*

*THE FORMULA FOR THE MEAN SQUARE BETWEEN GROUPS FOR FACTOR B IS*

$$MS_{\text{B}} = \frac{SS_{\text{B}}}{df_{\text{B}}}$$

In our example

$$MS_{\text{B}} = \frac{93.39}{1} = 93.39$$

**Step 3:** *Compute the mean square between groups for the interaction:*

*THE FORMULA FOR THE MEAN SQUARE BETWEEN GROUPS FOR THE INTERACTION IS*

$$MS_{\text{A}\times\text{B}} = \frac{SS_{\text{A}\times\text{B}}}{df_{\text{A}\times\text{B}}}$$

Thus, we have

$$MS_{\text{A}\times\text{B}} = \frac{102.77}{2} = 51.39$$

**Step 4:** *Compute the mean square within groups:*

*THE FORMULA FOR THE MEAN SQUARE WITHIN GROUPS IS*

$$MS_{\text{wn}} = \frac{SS_{\text{wn}}}{df_{\text{wn}}}$$

Thus, we have

$$MS_{\text{wn}} = \frac{98.67}{12} = 8.22$$

### Computing *F*

**Step 1:** *Compute the* $F_{obt}$ *for factor A:*

*THE FORMULA FOR THE MAIN EFFECT OF FACTOR A IS*

$$F_A = \frac{MS_A}{MS_{wn}}$$

In our example we have

$$F_A = \frac{58.73}{8.22} = 7.14$$

**Step 2:** *Compute the* $F_{obt}$ *for factor B:*

*THE FORMULA FOR THE MAIN EFFECT OF FACTOR B IS*

$$F_B = \frac{MS_B}{MS_{wn}}$$

Thus,

$$F_B = \frac{93.39}{8.22} = 11.36$$

**Step 3:** *Compute the* $F_{obt}$ *for the interaction:*

*THE FORMULA FOR THE INTERACTION EFFECT IS*

$$F_{A \times B} = \frac{MS_{A \times B}}{MS_{wn}}$$

Thus, we have

$$F_{A \times B} = \frac{51.39}{8.22} = 6.25$$

And now the finished summary table is in Table A.3.

**Interpreting Each *F*** Determine whether each $F_{obt}$ is significant by comparing it to the appropriate $F_{crit}$. To find each $F_{crit}$ in the $F$-tables (Table 4 in Appendix B), use the $df_{bn}$ and the $df_{wn}$ used in computing the corresponding $F_{obt}$.

***TABLE A.3***
Completed Summary Table of Two-Way ANOVA

| *Source* | *Sum of Squares* | df | *Mean Square* | F |
|---|---|---|---|---|
| Between | | | | |
| Factor A (volume) | 117.45 | 2 | 58.73 | 7.14 |
| Factor B (gender) | 93.39 | 1 | 93.39 | 11.36 |
| Interaction (vol × gen) | 102.77 | 2 | 51.39 | 6.25 |
| Within | 98.67 | 12 | 8.22 | |
| Total | 412.28 | 17 | | |

*1.* To find $F_{crit}$ for testing $F_A$, use $df_A$ as the *df* between groups and $df_{wn}$. In our example $df_A = 2$ and $df_{wn} = 12$. So for $\alpha = .05$, the $F_{crit}$ is 3.88.

*2.* To find $F_{crit}$ for testing $F_B$, use $df_B$ as the *df* between groups and $df_{wn}$. In our example $df_B = 1$ and $df_{wn} = 12$. So at $\alpha = .05$, the $F_{crit}$ is 4.75.

*3.* To find $F_{crit}$ for the interaction, use $df_{A \times B}$ as the *df* between groups and $df_{wn}$. In our example $df_{A \times B} = 2$ and $df_{wn} = 12$. Thus, at $\alpha = .05$, the $F_{crit}$ is 3.88.

Interpret each $F_{obt}$ as you have previously: If an $F_{obt}$ is larger than its $F_{crit}$, the corresponding main effect or interaction effect is significant. For the example all three effects are significant: $F_A$ (7.14) is larger than its $F_{crit}$ (3.88), $F_B$ (11.36) is larger than its $F_{crit}$ (4.75), and $F_{A \times B}$ (6.25) is larger than its $F_{crit}$ (3.88).

## Performing the Tukey *HSD* Test

Perform post hoc comparisons on any significant $F_{obt}$. If the *ns* in all levels are equal, perform Tukey's *HSD* procedure. However, the procedure is computed differently for an interaction than for a main effect.

**Performing Tukey's *HSD* Test on Main Effects** Perform the *HSD* on each main effect, using the procedure described in Chapter 11 for a one-way design. Recall that the formula for the *HSD* is

$$HSD = (q_k)\left(\sqrt{\frac{MS_{wn}}{n}}\right)$$

The $MS_{wn}$ is from the two-way ANOVA, and $q_k$ is found in Table 5 of Appendix B for $df_{wn}$ and *k* (where *k* is the number of levels in the factor). The *n* in the formula is the number of scores in a level. Be careful here: For each factor there may be a different value of *n* and *k.* In the example six scores went into each mean for a level of volume (each column), but nine scores went into each mean for a level of gender (each row.) The *n* is the *n* in each group that you are presently comparing! Also, because $q_k$ depends on *k,* when factors have a different *k,* they have different values of $q_k$.

After computing the *HSD* for a factor, find the difference between each pair of main effect means in the factor. Any difference that is larger than the *HSD* is a significant difference. In the example, for the volume factor, $n = 6$, $MS_{wn} = 8.22$, and with $\alpha = .05$, $k = 3$, and $df_{wn} = 12$ the $q_k$ is 3.77. Thus, the *HSD* for factor A is 4.41. The main effect mean for soft (6) differs from the means for medium (11.5) and loud (11.33) by more than 4.41, so these are significant differences. The means for medium and loud, however, differ by less than 4.41, so they do not differ significantly.

**Performing Tukey's *HSD* Test on Interaction Effects** The post hoc comparisons for a significant interaction involve the cell means. However, as discussed in Chapter 12, we perform only *unconfounded* comparisons, in which two cells differ along only one factor. Therefore, we find the differences only between the cell means within the same column or within the same row. Then we compare the differences to the *HSD.* However, when computing the *HSD* for an interaction, we find $q_k$ using a slightly different procedure.

Previously, we found $q_k$ in Table 5 using *k,* the number of means being compared. For an interaction first determine the *adjusted k.* This value "adjusts" for the actual number of unconfounded comparisons you will make. Obtain the *adjusted k* from Table A.4 (or at the beginning of Table 5 of Appendix B). In the left-hand column locate the design of your study. Do not be concerned about the order of the numbers. We called our persuasiveness study a 3 × 2 design, so look at the row labeled "2 × 3." Reading across that row, confirm that the middle column contains the number of cell means in the interaction (we have 6). In the right-hand column is the *adjusted k* (for our study it is 5).

The *adjusted k* is the value of *k* to use to obtain $q_k$ from Table 5. Thus, for the persuasiveness study with $\alpha = .05$, $df_{\text{wn}} = 12$, and in the column labeled $k = 5$, the $q_k$ is 4.51. Now compute the *HSD* using the same formula used previously. In each cell are 3 scores, so

$$HSD = (q_k)\left(\sqrt{\frac{MS_{\text{wn}}}{n}}\right) = (4.51)\left(\sqrt{\frac{8.22}{3}}\right) = 7.47$$

The *HSD* for the interaction is 7.47.

The differences between our cell means are shown in Table A.5. On the line connecting any two cells is the absolute difference between their means. Any difference between two means that is larger than the *HSD* is a significant difference. Only three differences are significant: (1) between the mean for females at the soft volume and the mean for females at the medium volume, (2) between the mean for males at the soft volume and the mean for males at the loud volume, and (3) between the mean for males at the loud volume and the mean for females at the loud volume.

## Computing $\eta^2$

In the two-way ANOVA we again compute *eta squared* ($\eta^2$) to describe effect size—the proportion of variance in dependent scores that is accounted for by a relationship.

**TABLE A.4**
Values of Adjusted *k*

| *Design of Study* | *Number of Cell Means in Study* | *Adjusted Value of* k |
|---|---|---|
| 2 × 2 | 4 | 3 |
| 2 × 3 | 6 | 5 |
| 2 × 4 | 8 | 6 |
| 3 × 3 | 9 | 7 |
| 3 × 4 | 12 | 8 |
| 4 × 4 | 16 | 10 |
| 4 × 5 | 20 | 12 |

**TABLE A.5**
Table of the Interaction Cells Showing the Differences Between Unconfounded Means

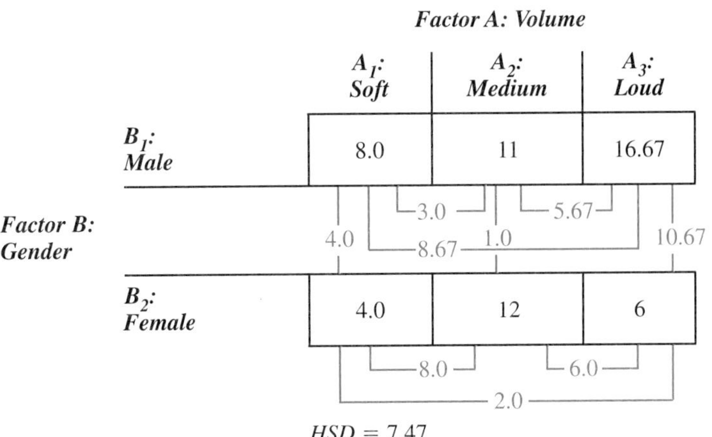

Factor A: Volume
$A_1$: Soft
$A_2$: Medium
$A_3$: Loud
Factor B: Gender
$B_1$: Male
$B_2$: Female
8.0
11
16.67
3.0
5.67
4.0
8.67
1.0
10.67
4.0
12
6
8.0
6.0
2.0
HSD = 7.47


Compute a separate $\eta^2$ for each significant main and interaction effect. Recall that the formula was

$$\eta^2 = \frac{SS_{\text{bn}}}{SS_{\text{tot}}}$$

Here, we divide the $SS_{\text{tot}}$ into the sum of squares between groups for each significant effect, either $SS_{\text{A}}$, $SS_{\text{B}}$, or $SS_{\text{A}\times\text{B}}$. For example, for our factor A (volume), $SS_{\text{A}}$ was 117.45 and $SS_{\text{tot}}$ was 412.28. Therefore, the $\eta^2$ is .28. Thus, the main effect of changing the volume of a message accounts for 28% of our differences in persuasiveness scores. For the gender factor, $SS_{\text{B}}$ is 93.39, so $\eta^2$ is .23: The conditions of male or female account for an additional 23% of the variance in scores. Finally, for the interaction, $SS_{\text{A}\times\text{B}}$ is 102.77, so $\eta^2 = .25$: The particular combination of gender and volume we created in our cells accounts for an additional 25% of the differences in persuasiveness scores.

### *For Practice:*

1. A study compared the performance of males and females tested by either a male or a female experimenter. Here are the data:

| | | Factor A: Participants | |
|---|---|---|---|
| | | *Level $A_1$: Males* | *Level $A_2$: Females* |
| *Factor B: Experimenter* | *Level $B_1$: Male Experimenter* | 6<br>11<br>9<br>10<br>9 | 8<br>14<br>17<br>16<br>19 |
| | *Level $B_2$: Female Experimenter* | 8<br>10<br>9<br>7<br>10 | 4<br>6<br>5<br>5<br>7 |

(a) Using $\alpha = .05$, perform an ANOVA and complete the summary table.

(b) Compute the main effect means and interaction means.

(c) Perform the appropriate post hoc comparisons.

(d) What do you conclude about the relationships that this study demonstrates?

(e) Compute the effect size where appropriate.

**Answers:**

1. (a)

| *Source* | *Sum of Squares* | **df** | *Mean Square* | **F** |
|---|---|---|---|---|
| Between groups | | | | |
| Factor A | 7.20 | 1 | 7.20 | 1.19 |
| Factor B | 115.20 | 1 | 115.20 | 19.04 |
| Interaction | 105.80 | 1 | 105.80 | 17.49 |
| Within groups | 96.80 | 16 | 6.05 | |
| Total | 325.00 | | | |

For each factor, $df = 1$ and 16, so $F_{crit} = 4.49$: Factor B and the interaction are significant, $p < .05$.

(b) For factor A, $\overline{X}_1 = 8.9$, $\overline{X}_2 = 10.1$; for factor B, $\overline{X}_1 = 11.9$, $\overline{X}_2 = 7.1$; for the interaction, $\overline{X}_{A_1B_1} = 9.0$, $\overline{X}_{A_1B_2} = 8.8$, $\overline{X}_{A_2B_1} = 14.8$, $\overline{X}_{A_2B_2} = 5.4$.

(c) Because factor A is not significant and factor B contains only two levels, such tests are unnecessary for them. For A × B, *adjusted* $k = 3$, so $q_k = 3.65$, $HSD = (3.65)(\sqrt{6.05/5}) = 4.02$; the only significant differences are between males and females tested by a male, and between females tested by a male and females tested by a female.

(d) Conclude that a relationship exists between gender and test scores when testing is done by a male, and that male versus female experimenters produce a relationship when testing females, $p < .05$.

(e) For B, $\eta^2 = 115.2/325 = .35$; for A × B, $\eta^2 = 105.8/325 = .33$.

# Statistical Tables

*TABLE 1*

Proportions of Area under the Standard Normal Curve: The *z*-Tables

Column (A) lists *z*-score values. Column (B) lists the proportion of the area between the mean and the *z*-score value. Column (C) lists the proportion of the area beyond the *z*-score in the tail of the distribution. (*Note:* Because the normal distribution is symmetrical, areas for negative *z*-scores are the same as those for positive *z*-scores.)

| (A) z | (B) Area Between Mean and z | (C) Area Beyond z in Tail | (A) z | (B) Area Between Mean and z | (C) Area Beyond z in Tail | (A) z | (B) Area Between Mean and z | (C) Area Beyond z in Tail |
|---|---|---|---|---|---|---|---|---|
| 0.00 | .0000 | .5000 | 0.30 | .1179 | .3821 | 0.60 | .2257 | .2743 |
| 0.01 | .0040 | .4960 | 0.31 | .1217 | .3783 | 0.61 | .2291 | .2709 |
| 0.02 | .0080 | .4920 | 0.32 | .1255 | .3745 | 0.62 | .2324 | .2676 |
| 0.03 | .0120 | .4880 | 0.33 | .1293 | .3707 | 0.63 | .2357 | .2643 |
| 0.04 | .0160 | .4840 | 0.34 | .1331 | .3669 | 0.64 | .2389 | .2611 |
| 0.05 | .0199 | .4801 | 0.35 | .1368 | .3632 | 0.65 | .2422 | .2578 |
| 0.06 | .0239 | .4761 | 0.36 | .1406 | .3594 | 0.66 | .2454 | .2546 |
| 0.07 | .0279 | .4721 | 0.37 | .1443 | .3557 | 0.67 | .2486 | .2514 |
| 0.08 | .0319 | .4681 | 0.38 | .1480 | .3520 | 0.68 | .2517 | .2483 |
| 0.09 | .0359 | .4641 | 0.39 | .1517 | .3483 | 0.69 | .2549 | .2451 |
| 0.10 | .0398 | .4602 | 0.40 | .1554 | .3446 | 0.70 | .2580 | .2420 |
| 0.11 | .0438 | .4562 | 0.41 | .1591 | .3409 | 0.71 | .2611 | .2389 |
| 0.12 | .0478 | .4522 | 0.42 | .1628 | .3372 | 0.72 | .2642 | .2358 |
| 0.13 | .0517 | .4483 | 0.43 | .1664 | .3336 | 0.73 | .2673 | .2327 |
| 0.14 | .0557 | .4443 | 0.44 | .1700 | .3300 | 0.74 | .2704 | .2296 |
| 0.15 | .0596 | .4404 | 0.45 | .1736 | .3264 | 0.75 | .2734 | .2266 |
| 0.16 | .0636 | .4364 | 0.46 | .1772 | .3228 | 0.76 | .2764 | .2236 |
| 0.17 | .0675 | .4325 | 0.47 | .1808 | .3192 | 0.77 | .2794 | .2206 |
| 0.18 | .0714 | .4286 | 0.48 | .1844 | .3156 | 0.78 | .2823 | .2177 |
| 0.19 | .0753 | .4247 | 0.49 | .1879 | .3121 | 0.79 | .2852 | .2148 |
| 0.20 | .0793 | .4207 | 0.50 | .1915 | .3085 | 0.80 | .2881 | .2119 |
| 0.21 | .0832 | .4168 | 0.51 | .1950 | .3050 | 0.81 | .2910 | .2090 |
| 0.22 | .0871 | .4129 | 0.52 | .1985 | .3015 | 0.82 | .2939 | .2061 |
| 0.23 | .0910 | .4090 | 0.53 | .2019 | .2981 | 0.83 | .2967 | .2033 |
| 0.24 | .0948 | .4052 | 0.54 | .2054 | .2946 | 0.84 | .2995 | .2005 |
| 0.25 | .0987 | .4013 | 0.55 | .2088 | .2912 | 0.85 | .3023 | .1977 |
| 0.26 | .1026 | .3974 | 0.56 | .2123 | .2877 | 0.86 | .3051 | .1949 |
| 0.27 | .1064 | .3936 | 0.57 | .2157 | .2843 | 0.87 | .3078 | .1922 |
| 0.28 | .1103 | .3897 | 0.58 | .2190 | .2810 | 0.88 | .3106 | .1894 |
| 0.29 | .1141 | .3859 | 0.59 | .2224 | .2776 | 0.89 | .3133 | .1867 |

**TABLE 1 (CONT.)**

Proportions of Area under the Standard Normal Curve: The z-Tables

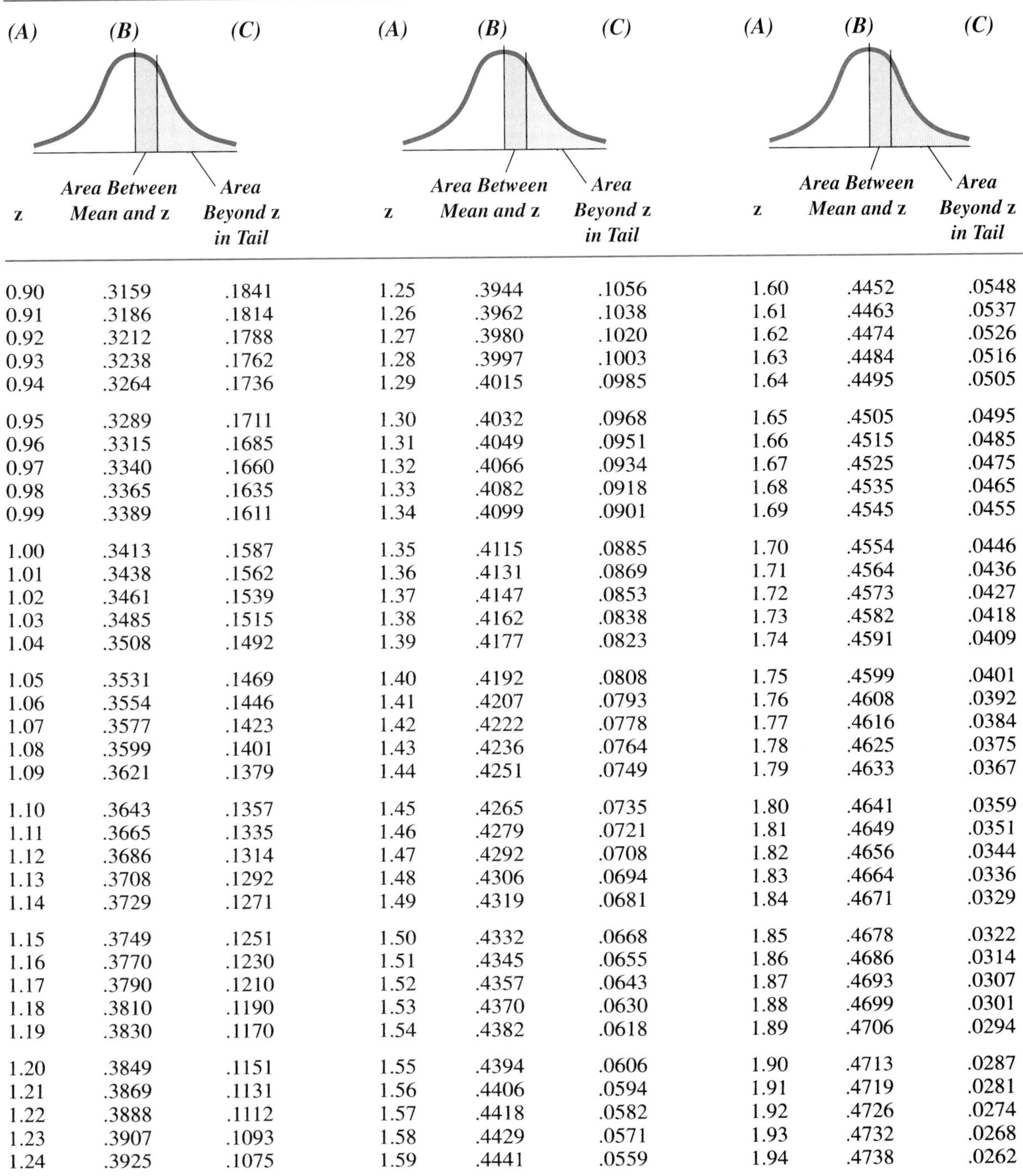

| (A) z | (B) Area Between Mean and z | (C) Area Beyond z in Tail | (A) z | (B) Area Between Mean and z | (C) Area Beyond z in Tail | (A) z | (B) Area Between Mean and z | (C) Area Beyond z in Tail |
|---|---|---|---|---|---|---|---|---|
| 0.90 | .3159 | .1841 | 1.25 | .3944 | .1056 | 1.60 | .4452 | .0548 |
| 0.91 | .3186 | .1814 | 1.26 | .3962 | .1038 | 1.61 | .4463 | .0537 |
| 0.92 | .3212 | .1788 | 1.27 | .3980 | .1020 | 1.62 | .4474 | .0526 |
| 0.93 | .3238 | .1762 | 1.28 | .3997 | .1003 | 1.63 | .4484 | .0516 |
| 0.94 | .3264 | .1736 | 1.29 | .4015 | .0985 | 1.64 | .4495 | .0505 |
| 0.95 | .3289 | .1711 | 1.30 | .4032 | .0968 | 1.65 | .4505 | .0495 |
| 0.96 | .3315 | .1685 | 1.31 | .4049 | .0951 | 1.66 | .4515 | .0485 |
| 0.97 | .3340 | .1660 | 1.32 | .4066 | .0934 | 1.67 | .4525 | .0475 |
| 0.98 | .3365 | .1635 | 1.33 | .4082 | .0918 | 1.68 | .4535 | .0465 |
| 0.99 | .3389 | .1611 | 1.34 | .4099 | .0901 | 1.69 | .4545 | .0455 |
| 1.00 | .3413 | .1587 | 1.35 | .4115 | .0885 | 1.70 | .4554 | .0446 |
| 1.01 | .3438 | .1562 | 1.36 | .4131 | .0869 | 1.71 | .4564 | .0436 |
| 1.02 | .3461 | .1539 | 1.37 | .4147 | .0853 | 1.72 | .4573 | .0427 |
| 1.03 | .3485 | .1515 | 1.38 | .4162 | .0838 | 1.73 | .4582 | .0418 |
| 1.04 | .3508 | .1492 | 1.39 | .4177 | .0823 | 1.74 | .4591 | .0409 |
| 1.05 | .3531 | .1469 | 1.40 | .4192 | .0808 | 1.75 | .4599 | .0401 |
| 1.06 | .3554 | .1446 | 1.41 | .4207 | .0793 | 1.76 | .4608 | .0392 |
| 1.07 | .3577 | .1423 | 1.42 | .4222 | .0778 | 1.77 | .4616 | .0384 |
| 1.08 | .3599 | .1401 | 1.43 | .4236 | .0764 | 1.78 | .4625 | .0375 |
| 1.09 | .3621 | .1379 | 1.44 | .4251 | .0749 | 1.79 | .4633 | .0367 |
| 1.10 | .3643 | .1357 | 1.45 | .4265 | .0735 | 1.80 | .4641 | .0359 |
| 1.11 | .3665 | .1335 | 1.46 | .4279 | .0721 | 1.81 | .4649 | .0351 |
| 1.12 | .3686 | .1314 | 1.47 | .4292 | .0708 | 1.82 | .4656 | .0344 |
| 1.13 | .3708 | .1292 | 1.48 | .4306 | .0694 | 1.83 | .4664 | .0336 |
| 1.14 | .3729 | .1271 | 1.49 | .4319 | .0681 | 1.84 | .4671 | .0329 |
| 1.15 | .3749 | .1251 | 1.50 | .4332 | .0668 | 1.85 | .4678 | .0322 |
| 1.16 | .3770 | .1230 | 1.51 | .4345 | .0655 | 1.86 | .4686 | .0314 |
| 1.17 | .3790 | .1210 | 1.52 | .4357 | .0643 | 1.87 | .4693 | .0307 |
| 1.18 | .3810 | .1190 | 1.53 | .4370 | .0630 | 1.88 | .4699 | .0301 |
| 1.19 | .3830 | .1170 | 1.54 | .4382 | .0618 | 1.89 | .4706 | .0294 |
| 1.20 | .3849 | .1151 | 1.55 | .4394 | .0606 | 1.90 | .4713 | .0287 |
| 1.21 | .3869 | .1131 | 1.56 | .4406 | .0594 | 1.91 | .4719 | .0281 |
| 1.22 | .3888 | .1112 | 1.57 | .4418 | .0582 | 1.92 | .4726 | .0274 |
| 1.23 | .3907 | .1093 | 1.58 | .4429 | .0571 | 1.93 | .4732 | .0268 |
| 1.24 | .3925 | .1075 | 1.59 | .4441 | .0559 | 1.94 | .4738 | .0262 |

**TABLE 1 (CONT.)**

Proportions of Area under the Standard Normal Curve: The z-Tables

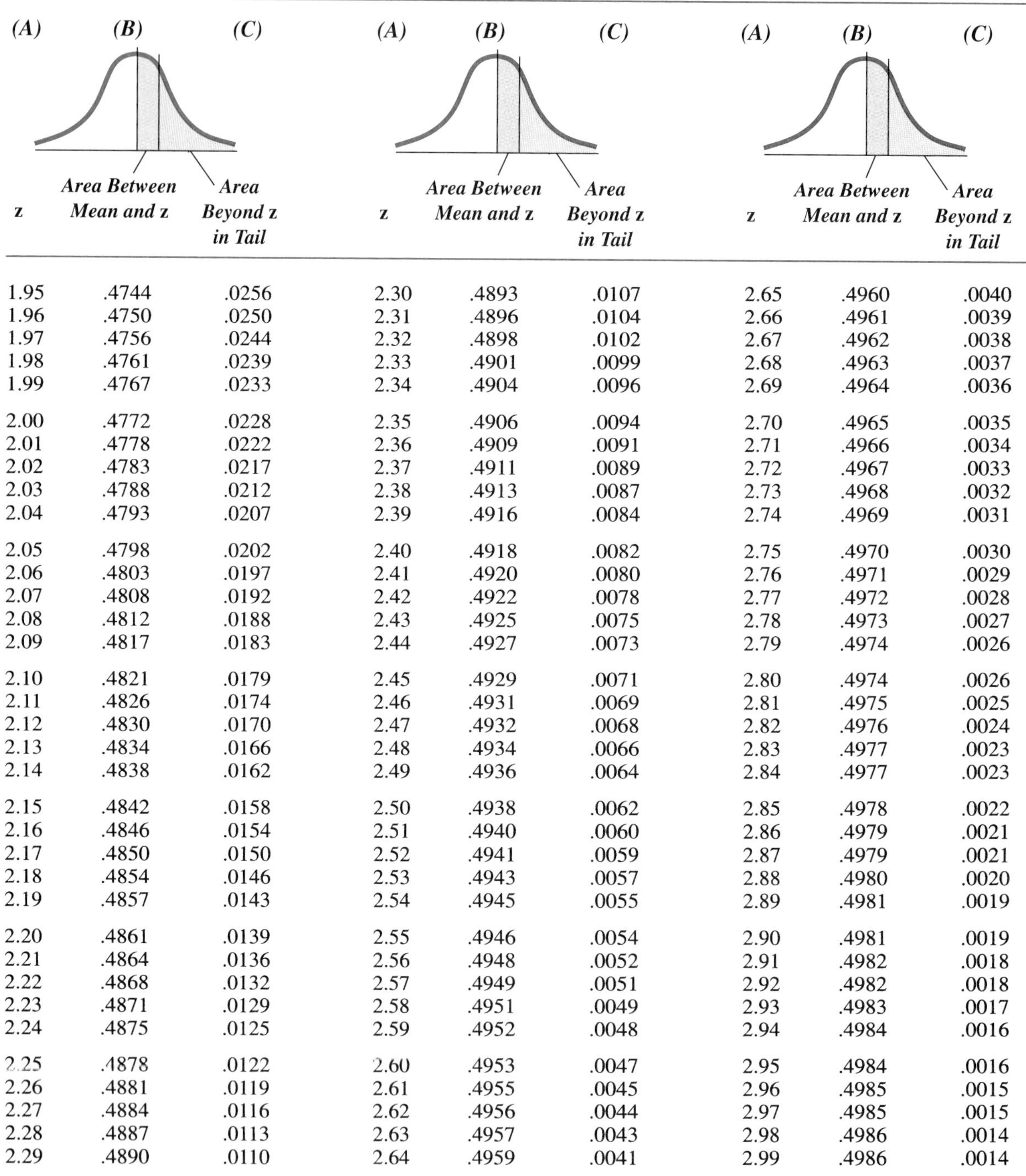

| (A) z | (B) Area Between Mean and z | (C) Area Beyond z in Tail | (A) z | (B) Area Between Mean and z | (C) Area Beyond z in Tail | (A) z | (B) Area Between Mean and z | (C) Area Beyond z in Tail |
|---|---|---|---|---|---|---|---|---|
| 1.95 | .4744 | .0256 | 2.30 | .4893 | .0107 | 2.65 | .4960 | .0040 |
| 1.96 | .4750 | .0250 | 2.31 | .4896 | .0104 | 2.66 | .4961 | .0039 |
| 1.97 | .4756 | .0244 | 2.32 | .4898 | .0102 | 2.67 | .4962 | .0038 |
| 1.98 | .4761 | .0239 | 2.33 | .4901 | .0099 | 2.68 | .4963 | .0037 |
| 1.99 | .4767 | .0233 | 2.34 | .4904 | .0096 | 2.69 | .4964 | .0036 |
| 2.00 | .4772 | .0228 | 2.35 | .4906 | .0094 | 2.70 | .4965 | .0035 |
| 2.01 | .4778 | .0222 | 2.36 | .4909 | .0091 | 2.71 | .4966 | .0034 |
| 2.02 | .4783 | .0217 | 2.37 | .4911 | .0089 | 2.72 | .4967 | .0033 |
| 2.03 | .4788 | .0212 | 2.38 | .4913 | .0087 | 2.73 | .4968 | .0032 |
| 2.04 | .4793 | .0207 | 2.39 | .4916 | .0084 | 2.74 | .4969 | .0031 |
| 2.05 | .4798 | .0202 | 2.40 | .4918 | .0082 | 2.75 | .4970 | .0030 |
| 2.06 | .4803 | .0197 | 2.41 | .4920 | .0080 | 2.76 | .4971 | .0029 |
| 2.07 | .4808 | .0192 | 2.42 | .4922 | .0078 | 2.77 | .4972 | .0028 |
| 2.08 | .4812 | .0188 | 2.43 | .4925 | .0075 | 2.78 | .4973 | .0027 |
| 2.09 | .4817 | .0183 | 2.44 | .4927 | .0073 | 2.79 | .4974 | .0026 |
| 2.10 | .4821 | .0179 | 2.45 | .4929 | .0071 | 2.80 | .4974 | .0026 |
| 2.11 | .4826 | .0174 | 2.46 | .4931 | .0069 | 2.81 | .4975 | .0025 |
| 2.12 | .4830 | .0170 | 2.47 | .4932 | .0068 | 2.82 | .4976 | .0024 |
| 2.13 | .4834 | .0166 | 2.48 | .4934 | .0066 | 2.83 | .4977 | .0023 |
| 2.14 | .4838 | .0162 | 2.49 | .4936 | .0064 | 2.84 | .4977 | .0023 |
| 2.15 | .4842 | .0158 | 2.50 | .4938 | .0062 | 2.85 | .4978 | .0022 |
| 2.16 | .4846 | .0154 | 2.51 | .4940 | .0060 | 2.86 | .4979 | .0021 |
| 2.17 | .4850 | .0150 | 2.52 | .4941 | .0059 | 2.87 | .4979 | .0021 |
| 2.18 | .4854 | .0146 | 2.53 | .4943 | .0057 | 2.88 | .4980 | .0020 |
| 2.19 | .4857 | .0143 | 2.54 | .4945 | .0055 | 2.89 | .4981 | .0019 |
| 2.20 | .4861 | .0139 | 2.55 | .4946 | .0054 | 2.90 | .4981 | .0019 |
| 2.21 | .4864 | .0136 | 2.56 | .4948 | .0052 | 2.91 | .4982 | .0018 |
| 2.22 | .4868 | .0132 | 2.57 | .4949 | .0051 | 2.92 | .4982 | .0018 |
| 2.23 | .4871 | .0129 | 2.58 | .4951 | .0049 | 2.93 | .4983 | .0017 |
| 2.24 | .4875 | .0125 | 2.59 | .4952 | .0048 | 2.94 | .4984 | .0016 |
| 2.25 | .4878 | .0122 | 2.60 | .4953 | .0047 | 2.95 | .4984 | .0016 |
| 2.26 | .4881 | .0119 | 2.61 | .4955 | .0045 | 2.96 | .4985 | .0015 |
| 2.27 | .4884 | .0116 | 2.62 | .4956 | .0044 | 2.97 | .4985 | .0015 |
| 2.28 | .4887 | .0113 | 2.63 | .4957 | .0043 | 2.98 | .4986 | .0014 |
| 2.29 | .4890 | .0110 | 2.64 | .4959 | .0041 | 2.99 | .4986 | .0014 |

**TABLE 1 (CONT.)**
Proportions of Area under the Standard Normal Curve: The z-Tables

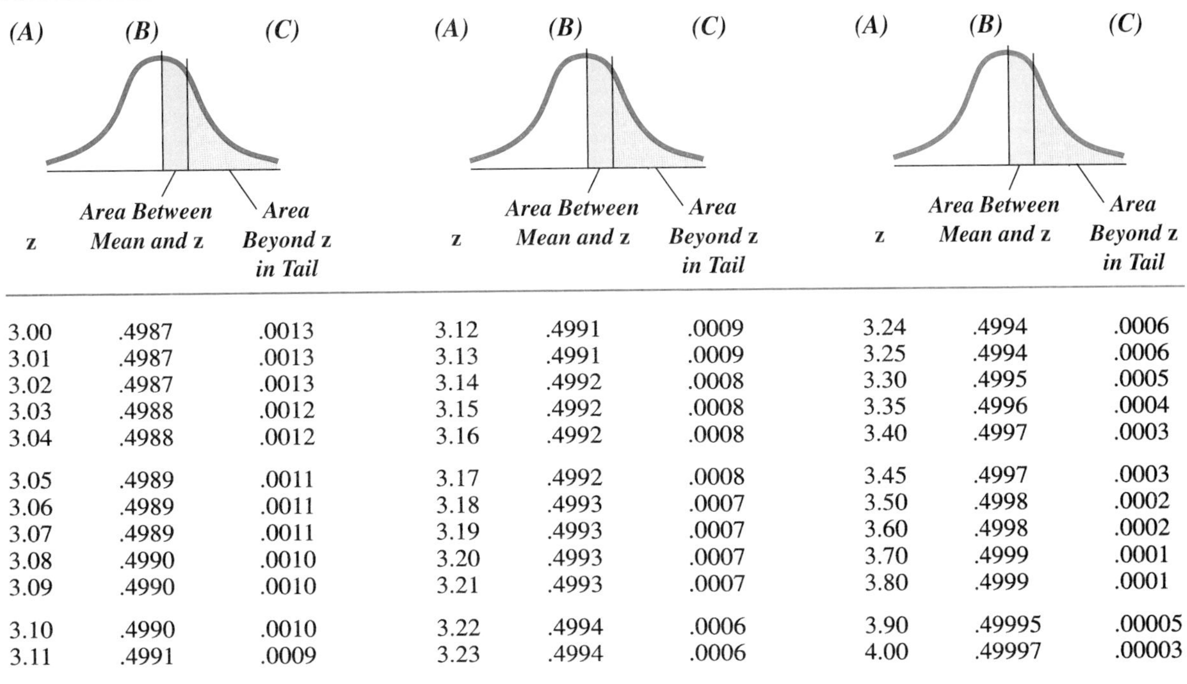

| (A) z | (B) Area Between Mean and z | (C) Area Beyond z in Tail | (A) z | (B) Area Between Mean and z | (C) Area Beyond z in Tail | (A) z | (B) Area Between Mean and z | (C) Area Beyond z in Tail |
|---|---|---|---|---|---|---|---|---|
| 3.00 | .4987 | .0013 | 3.12 | .4991 | .0009 | 3.24 | .4994 | .0006 |
| 3.01 | .4987 | .0013 | 3.13 | .4991 | .0009 | 3.25 | .4994 | .0006 |
| 3.02 | .4987 | .0013 | 3.14 | .4992 | .0008 | 3.30 | .4995 | .0005 |
| 3.03 | .4988 | .0012 | 3.15 | .4992 | .0008 | 3.35 | .4996 | .0004 |
| 3.04 | .4988 | .0012 | 3.16 | .4992 | .0008 | 3.40 | .4997 | .0003 |
| 3.05 | .4989 | .0011 | 3.17 | .4992 | .0008 | 3.45 | .4997 | .0003 |
| 3.06 | .4989 | .0011 | 3.18 | .4993 | .0007 | 3.50 | .4998 | .0002 |
| 3.07 | .4989 | .0011 | 3.19 | .4993 | .0007 | 3.60 | .4998 | .0002 |
| 3.08 | .4990 | .0010 | 3.20 | .4993 | .0007 | 3.70 | .4999 | .0001 |
| 3.09 | .4990 | .0010 | 3.21 | .4993 | .0007 | 3.80 | .4999 | .0001 |
| 3.10 | .4990 | .0010 | 3.22 | .4994 | .0006 | 3.90 | .49995 | .00005 |
| 3.11 | .4991 | .0009 | 3.23 | .4994 | .0006 | 4.00 | .49997 | .00003 |

*TABLE 2*

Critical Values of $t$: The $t$-Tables

(*Note:* Values of $-t_{crit}$ = values of $+t_{crit}$.)

***Two-Tailed Test***

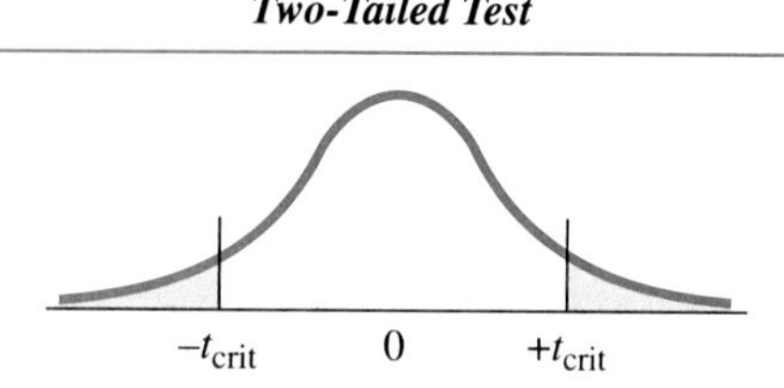


| | ***Alpha Level*** | |
|---|---|---|
| **df** | **α = *.05*** | **α = *.01*** |
| 1 | 12.706 | 63.657 |
| 2 | 4.303 | 9.925 |
| 3 | 3.182 | 5.841 |
| 4 | 2.776 | 4.604 |
| 5 | 2.571 | 4.032 |
| 6 | 2.447 | 3.707 |
| 7 | 2.365 | 3.499 |
| 8 | 2.306 | 3.355 |
| 9 | 2.262 | 3.250 |
| 10 | 2.228 | 3.169 |
| 11 | 2.201 | 3.106 |
| 12 | 2.179 | 3.055 |
| 13 | 2.160 | 3.012 |
| 14 | 2.145 | 2.977 |
| 15 | 2.131 | 2.947 |
| 16 | 2.120 | 2.921 |
| 17 | 2.110 | 2.898 |
| 18 | 2.101 | 2.878 |
| 19 | 2.093 | 2.861 |
| 20 | 2.086 | 2.845 |
| 21 | 2.080 | 2.831 |
| 22 | 2.074 | 2.819 |
| 23 | 2.069 | 2.807 |
| 24 | 2.064 | 2.797 |
| 25 | 2.060 | 2.787 |
| 26 | 2.056 | 2.779 |
| 27 | 2.052 | 2.771 |
| 28 | 2.048 | 2.763 |
| 29 | 2.045 | 2.756 |
| 30 | 2.042 | 2.750 |
| 40 | 2.021 | 2.704 |
| 60 | 2.000 | 2.660 |
| 120 | 1.980 | 2.617 |
| ∞ | 1.960 | 2.576 |

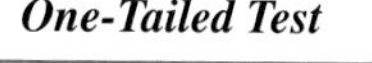

***One-Tailed Test***

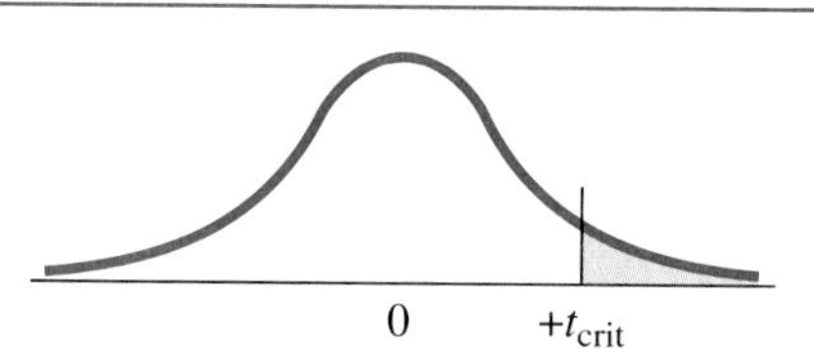


| | ***Alpha Level*** | |
|---|---|---|
| **df** | **α = *.05*** | **α = *.01*** |
| 1 | 6.314 | 31.821 |
| 2 | 2.920 | 6.965 |
| 3 | 2.353 | 4.541 |
| 4 | 2.132 | 3.747 |
| 5 | 2.015 | 3.365 |
| 6 | 1.943 | 3.143 |
| 7 | 1.895 | 2.998 |
| 8 | 1.860 | 2.896 |
| 9 | 1.833 | 2.821 |
| 10 | 1.812 | 2.764 |
| 11 | 1.796 | 2.718 |
| 12 | 1.782 | 2.681 |
| 13 | 1.771 | 2.650 |
| 14 | 1.761 | 2.624 |
| 15 | 1.753 | 2.602 |
| 16 | 1.746 | 2.583 |
| 17 | 1.740 | 2.567 |
| 18 | 1.734 | 2.552 |
| 19 | 1.729 | 2.539 |
| 20 | 1.725 | 2.528 |
| 21 | 1.721 | 2.518 |
| 22 | 1.717 | 2.508 |
| 23 | 1.714 | 2.500 |
| 24 | 1.711 | 2.492 |
| 25 | 1.708 | 2.485 |
| 26 | 1.706 | 2.479 |
| 27 | 1.703 | 2.473 |
| 28 | 1.701 | 2.467 |
| 29 | 1.699 | 2.462 |
| 30 | 1.697 | 2.457 |
| 40 | 1.684 | 2.423 |
| 60 | 1.671 | 2.390 |
| 120 | 1.658 | 2.358 |
| ∞ | 1.645 | 2.326 |

From Table 12 of E. Pearson and H. Hartley, *Biometrika Tables for Statisticians*, Vol. 1, 3rd ed. (Cambridge: Cambridge University Press, 1966.) Reprinted with the permission of the Biometrika Trustees.

**TABLE 3**

Critical Values of the Pearson Correlation Coefficient: The *r*-Tables

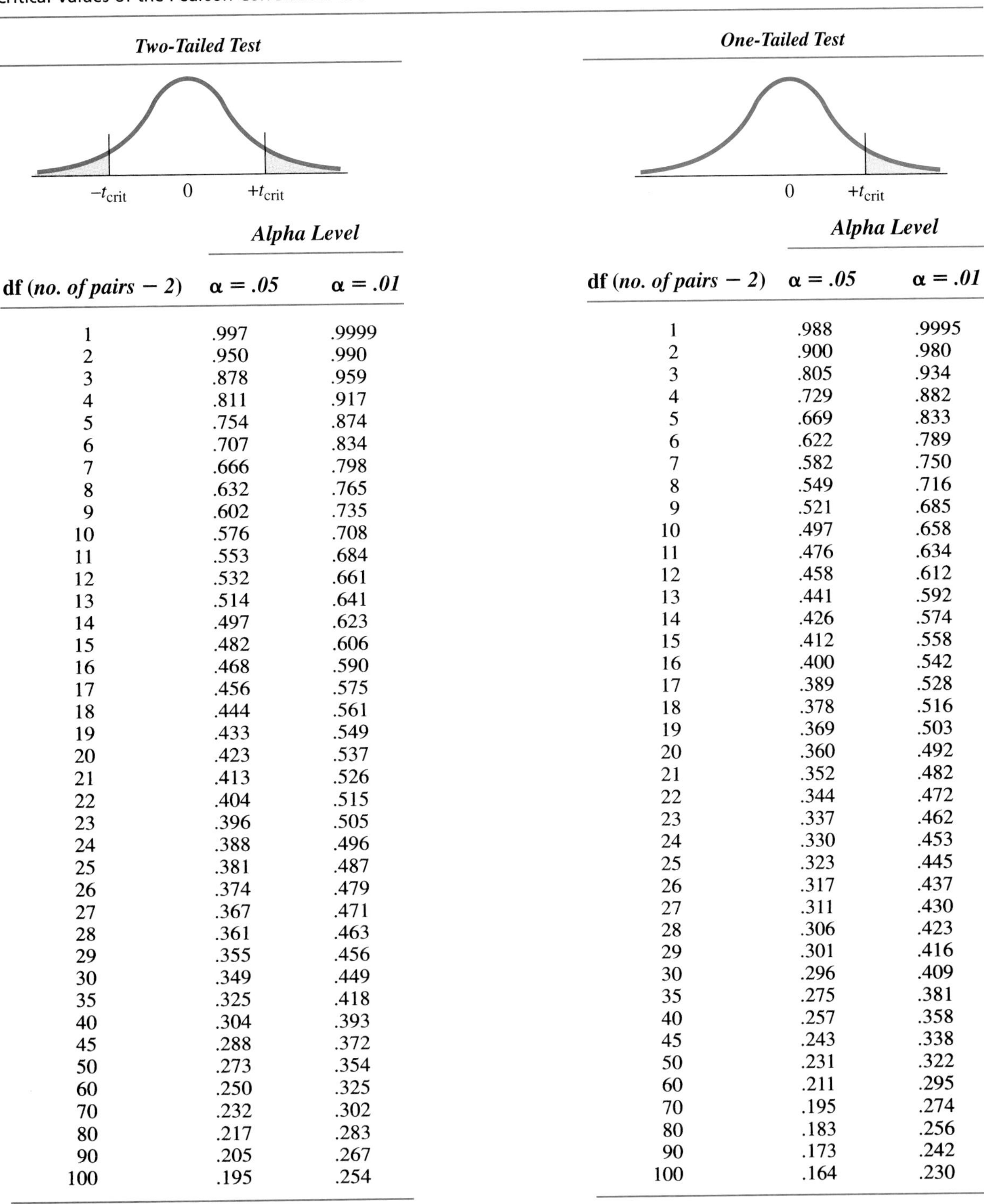


*Two-Tailed Test*

| df (*no. of pairs* − 2) | Alpha Level $\alpha = .05$ | $\alpha = .01$ |
|---|---|---|
| 1 | .997 | .9999 |
| 2 | .950 | .990 |
| 3 | .878 | .959 |
| 4 | .811 | .917 |
| 5 | .754 | .874 |
| 6 | .707 | .834 |
| 7 | .666 | .798 |
| 8 | .632 | .765 |
| 9 | .602 | .735 |
| 10 | .576 | .708 |
| 11 | .553 | .684 |
| 12 | .532 | .661 |
| 13 | .514 | .641 |
| 14 | .497 | .623 |
| 15 | .482 | .606 |
| 16 | .468 | .590 |
| 17 | .456 | .575 |
| 18 | .444 | .561 |
| 19 | .433 | .549 |
| 20 | .423 | .537 |
| 21 | .413 | .526 |
| 22 | .404 | .515 |
| 23 | .396 | .505 |
| 24 | .388 | .496 |
| 25 | .381 | .487 |
| 26 | .374 | .479 |
| 27 | .367 | .471 |
| 28 | .361 | .463 |
| 29 | .355 | .456 |
| 30 | .349 | .449 |
| 35 | .325 | .418 |
| 40 | .304 | .393 |
| 45 | .288 | .372 |
| 50 | .273 | .354 |
| 60 | .250 | .325 |
| 70 | .232 | .302 |
| 80 | .217 | .283 |
| 90 | .205 | .267 |
| 100 | .195 | .254 |

*One-Tailed Test*

| df (*no. of pairs* − 2) | Alpha Level $\alpha = .05$ | $\alpha = .01$ |
|---|---|---|
| 1 | .988 | .9995 |
| 2 | .900 | .980 |
| 3 | .805 | .934 |
| 4 | .729 | .882 |
| 5 | .669 | .833 |
| 6 | .622 | .789 |
| 7 | .582 | .750 |
| 8 | .549 | .716 |
| 9 | .521 | .685 |
| 10 | .497 | .658 |
| 11 | .476 | .634 |
| 12 | .458 | .612 |
| 13 | .441 | .592 |
| 14 | .426 | .574 |
| 15 | .412 | .558 |
| 16 | .400 | .542 |
| 17 | .389 | .528 |
| 18 | .378 | .516 |
| 19 | .369 | .503 |
| 20 | .360 | .492 |
| 21 | .352 | .482 |
| 22 | .344 | .472 |
| 23 | .337 | .462 |
| 24 | .330 | .453 |
| 25 | .323 | .445 |
| 26 | .317 | .437 |
| 27 | .311 | .430 |
| 28 | .306 | .423 |
| 29 | .301 | .416 |
| 30 | .296 | .409 |
| 35 | .275 | .381 |
| 40 | .257 | .358 |
| 45 | .243 | .338 |
| 50 | .231 | .322 |
| 60 | .211 | .295 |
| 70 | .195 | .274 |
| 80 | .183 | .256 |
| 90 | .173 | .242 |
| 100 | .164 | .230 |

*TABLE 4*

Critical Values of *F:* The *F*-Tables

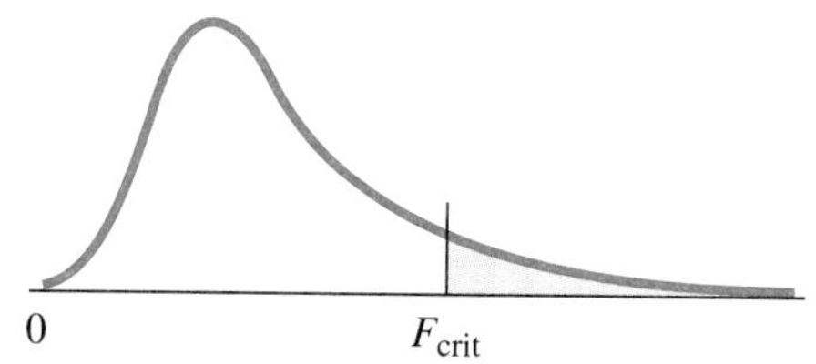


Critical values for α = .05 are in **dark numbers.**
Critical values for α = .01 are in light numbers.

| *Degrees of Freedom Within Groups (degrees of freedom in denominator of* F*-ratio)* | α | *Degrees of Freedom Between Groups (degrees of freedom in numerator of* F*-ratio)* | | | | | | | | | | | | | | |
|---|---|---|---|---|---|---|---|---|---|---|---|---|---|---|---|---|
| | | *1* | *2* | *3* | *4* | *5* | *6* | *7* | *8* | *9* | *10* | *11* | *12* | *14* | *16* | *20* |
| 1 | **.05** | **161** | **200** | **216** | **225** | **230** | **234** | **237** | **239** | **241** | **242** | **243** | **244** | **245** | **246** | **248** |
| | .01 | 4,052 | 4,999 | 5,403 | 5,625 | 5,764 | 5,859 | 5,928 | 5,981 | 6,022 | 6,056 | 6,082 | 6,106 | 6,142 | 6,169 | 6,208 |
| 2 | **.05** | **18.51** | **19.00** | **19.16** | **19.25** | **19.30** | **19.33** | **19.36** | **19.37** | **19.38** | **19.39** | **19.40** | **19.41** | **19.42** | **19.43** | **19.44** |
| | .01 | 98.49 | 99.00 | 99.17 | 99.25 | 99.30 | 99.33 | 99.34 | 99.36 | 99.38 | 99.40 | 99.41 | 99.42 | 99.43 | 99.44 | 99.45 |
| 3 | **.05** | **10.13** | **9.55** | **9.28** | **9.12** | **9.01** | **8.94** | **8.88** | **8.84** | **8.81** | **8.78** | **8.76** | **8.74** | **8.71** | **8.69** | **8.66** |
| | .01 | 34.12 | 30.82 | 29.46 | 28.71 | 28.24 | 27.91 | 27.67 | 27.49 | 27.34 | 27.23 | 27.13 | 27.05 | 26.92 | 26.83 | 26.69 |
| 4 | **.05** | **7.71** | **6.94** | **6.59** | **6.39** | **6.26** | **6.16** | **6.09** | **6.04** | **6.00** | **5.96** | **5.93** | **5.91** | **5.87** | **5.84** | **5.80** |
| | .01 | 21.20 | 18.00 | 16.69 | 15.98 | 15.52 | 15.21 | 14.98 | 14.80 | 14.66 | 14.54 | 14.45 | 14.37 | 14.24 | 14.15 | 14.02 |
| 5 | **.05** | **6.61** | **5.79** | **5.41** | **5.19** | **5.05** | **4.95** | **4.88** | **4.82** | **4.78** | **4.74** | **4.70** | **4.68** | **4.64** | **4.60** | **4.56** |
| | .01 | 16.26 | 13.27 | 12.06 | 11.39 | 10.97 | 10.67 | 10.45 | 10.27 | 10.15 | 10.05 | 9.96 | 9.89 | 9.77 | 9.68 | 9.55 |
| 6 | **.05** | **5.99** | **5.14** | **4.76** | **4.53** | **4.39** | **4.28** | **4.21** | **4.15** | **4.10** | **4.06** | **4.03** | **4.00** | **3.96** | **3.92** | **3.87** |
| | .01 | 13.74 | 10.92 | 9.78 | 9.15 | 8.75 | 8.47 | 8.26 | 8.10 | 7.98 | 7.87 | 7.79 | 7.72 | 7.60 | 7.52 | 7.39 |
| 7 | **.05** | **5.59** | **4.47** | **4.35** | **4.12** | **3.97** | **3.87** | **3.79** | **3.73** | **3.68** | **3.63** | **3.60** | **3.57** | **3.52** | **3.49** | **3.44** |
| | .01 | 12.25 | 9.55 | 8.45 | 7.85 | 7.46 | 7.19 | 7.00 | 6.84 | 6.71 | 6.62 | 6.54 | 6.47 | 6.35 | 6.27 | 6.15 |
| 8 | **.05** | **5.32** | **4.46** | **4.07** | **3.84** | **3.69** | **3.58** | **3.50** | **3.44** | **3.39** | **3.34** | **3.31** | **3.28** | **3.23** | **3.20** | **3.15** |
| | .01 | 11.26 | 8.65 | 7.59 | 7.01 | 6.63 | 6.37 | 6.19 | 6.03 | 5.91 | 5.82 | 5.74 | 5.67 | 5.56 | 5.48 | 5.36 |
| 9 | **.05** | **5.12** | **4.26** | **3.86** | **3.63** | **3.48** | **3.37** | **3.29** | **3.23** | **3.18** | **3.13** | **3.10** | **3.07** | **3.02** | **2.98** | **2.93** |
| | .01 | 10.56 | 8.02 | 6.99 | 6.42 | 6.06 | 5.80 | 5.62 | 5.47 | 5.35 | 5.26 | 5.18 | 5.11 | 5.00 | 4.92 | 4.80 |
| 10 | **.05** | **4.96** | **4.10** | **3.71** | **3.48** | **3.33** | **3.22** | **3.14** | **3.07** | **3.02** | **2.97** | **2.94** | **2.91** | **2.86** | **2.82** | **2.77** |
| | .01 | 10.04 | 7.56 | 6.55 | 5.99 | 5.64 | 5.39 | 5.21 | 5.06 | 4.95 | 4.85 | 4.78 | 4.71 | 4.60 | 4.52 | 4.41 |
| 11 | **.05** | **4.84** | **3.98** | **3.59** | **3.36** | **3.20** | **3.09** | **3.01** | **2.95** | **2.90** | **2.86** | **2.82** | **2.79** | **2.74** | **2.70** | **2.65** |
| | .01 | 9.65 | 7.20 | 6.22 | 5.67 | 5.32 | 5.07 | 4.88 | 4.74 | 4.63 | 4.54 | 4.46 | 4.40 | 4.29 | 4.21 | 4.10 |
| 12 | **.05** | **4.75** | **3.88** | **3.49** | **3.26** | **3.11** | **3.00** | **2.92** | **2.85** | **2.80** | **2.76** | **2.72** | **2.69** | **2.64** | **2.60** | **2.54** |
| | .01 | 9.33 | 6.93 | 5.95 | 5.41 | 5.06 | 4.82 | 4.65 | 4.50 | 4.39 | 4.30 | 4.22 | 4.16 | 4.05 | 3.98 | 3.86 |
| 13 | **.05** | **4.67** | **3.80** | **3.41** | **3.18** | **3.02** | **2.92** | **2.84** | **2.77** | **2.72** | **2.67** | **2.63** | **2.60** | **2.55** | **2.51** | **2.46** |
| | .01 | 9.07 | 6.70 | 5.74 | 5.20 | 4.86 | 4.62 | 4.44 | 4.30 | 4.19 | 4.10 | 4.02 | 3.96 | 3.85 | 3.78 | 3.67 |
| 14 | **.05** | **4.60** | **3.74** | **3.34** | **3.11** | **2.96** | **2.85** | **2.77** | **2.70** | **2.65** | **2.60** | **2.56** | **2.53** | **2.48** | **2.44** | **2.39** |
| | .01 | 8.86 | 6.51 | 5.56 | 5.03 | 4.69 | 4.46 | 4.28 | 4.14 | 4.03 | 3.94 | 3.86 | 3.80 | 3.70 | 3.62 | 3.51 |
| 15 | **.05** | **4.54** | **3.68** | **3.29** | **3.06** | **2.90** | **2.79** | **2.70** | **2.64** | **2.59** | **2.55** | **2.51** | **2.48** | **2.43** | **2.39** | **2.33** |
| | .01 | 8.68 | 6.36 | 5.42 | 4.89 | 4.56 | 4.32 | 4.14 | 4.00 | 3.89 | 3.80 | 3.73 | 3.67 | 3.56 | 3.48 | 3.36 |
| 16 | **.05** | **4.49** | **3.63** | **3.24** | **3.01** | **2.85** | **2.74** | **2.66** | **2.59** | **2.54** | **2.49** | **2.45** | **2.42** | **2.37** | **2.33** | **2.28** |
| | .01 | 8.53 | 6.23 | 5.29 | 4.77 | 4.44 | 4.20 | 4.03 | 3.89 | 3.78 | 3.69 | 3.61 | 3.55 | 3.45 | 3.37 | 3.25 |

**TABLE 4 (CONT.)**
Critical Values of *F*: The *F*-Tables

| *Degrees of Freedom Within Groups (degrees of freedom in denominator of F-ratio)* | α | *Degrees of Freedom Between Groups (degrees of freedom in numerator of F-ratio)* 1 | 2 | 3 | 4 | 5 | 6 | 7 | 8 | 9 | 10 | 11 | 12 | 14 | 16 | 20 |
|---|---|---|---|---|---|---|---|---|---|---|---|---|---|---|---|---|
| 17 | .05 | 4.45 | 3.59 | 3.20 | 2.96 | 2.81 | 2.70 | 2.62 | 2.55 | 2.50 | 2.45 | 2.41 | 2.38 | 2.33 | 2.29 | 2.23 |
| | .01 | 8.40 | 6.11 | 5.18 | 4.67 | 4.34 | 4.10 | 3.93 | 3.79 | 3.68 | 3.59 | 3.52 | 3.45 | 3.35 | 3.27 | 3.16 |
| 18 | .05 | 4.41 | 3.55 | 3.16 | 2.93 | 2.77 | 2.66 | 2.58 | 2.51 | 2.46 | 2.41 | 2.37 | 2.34 | 2.29 | 2.25 | 2.19 |
| | .01 | 8.28 | 6.01 | 5.09 | 4.58 | 4.25 | 4.01 | 3.85 | 3.71 | 3.60 | 3.51 | 3.44 | 3.37 | 3.27 | 3.19 | 3.07 |
| 19 | .05 | 4.38 | 3.52 | 3.13 | 2.90 | 2.74 | 2.63 | 2.55 | 2.48 | 2.43 | 2.38 | 2.34 | 2.31 | 2.26 | 2.21 | 2.15 |
| | .01 | 8.18 | 5.93 | 5.01 | 4.50 | 4.17 | 3.94 | 3.77 | 3.63 | 3.52 | 3.43 | 3.36 | 3.30 | 3.19 | 3.12 | 3.00 |
| 20 | .05 | 4.35 | 3.49 | 3.10 | 2.87 | 2.71 | 2.60 | 2.52 | 2.45 | 2.40 | 2.35 | 2.31 | 2.28 | 2.23 | 2.18 | 2.12 |
| | .01 | 8.10 | 5.85 | 4.94 | 4.43 | 4.10 | 3.87 | 3.71 | 3.56 | 3.45 | 3.37 | 3.30 | 3.23 | 3.13 | 3.05 | 2.94 |
| 21 | .05 | 4.32 | 3.47 | 3.07 | 2.84 | 2.68 | 2.57 | 2.49 | 2.42 | 2.37 | 2.32 | 2.28 | 2.25 | 2.20 | 2.15 | 2.09 |
| | .01 | 8.02 | 5.78 | 4.87 | 4.37 | 4.04 | 3.81 | 3.65 | 3.51 | 3.40 | 3.31 | 3.24 | 3.17 | 3.07 | 2.99 | 2.88 |
| 22 | .05 | 4.30 | 3.44 | 3.05 | 2.82 | 2.66 | 2.55 | 2.47 | 2.40 | 2.35 | 2.30 | 2.26 | 2.23 | 2.18 | 2.13 | 2.07 |
| | .01 | 7.94 | 5.72 | 4.82 | 4.31 | 3.99 | 3.76 | 3.59 | 3.45 | 3.35 | 3.26 | 3.18 | 3.12 | 3.02 | 2.94 | 2.83 |
| 23 | .05 | 4.28 | 3.42 | 3.03 | 2.80 | 2.64 | 2.53 | 2.45 | 2.38 | 2.32 | 2.28 | 2.24 | 2.20 | 2.14 | 2.10 | 2.04 |
| | .01 | 7.88 | 5.66 | 4.76 | 4.26 | 3.94 | 3.71 | 3.54 | 3.41 | 3.30 | 3.21 | 3.14 | 3.07 | 2.97 | 2.89 | 2.78 |
| 24 | .05 | 4.26 | 3.40 | 3.01 | 2.78 | 2.62 | 2.51 | 2.43 | 2.36 | 2.30 | 2.26 | 2.22 | 2.18 | 2.13 | 2.09 | 2.02 |
| | .01 | 7.82 | 5.61 | 4.72 | 4.22 | 3.90 | 3.67 | 3.50 | 3.36 | 3.25 | 3.17 | 3.09 | 3.03 | 2.93 | 2.85 | 2.74 |
| 25 | .05 | 4.24 | 3.38 | 2.99 | 2.76 | 2.60 | 2.49 | 2.41 | 2.34 | 2.28 | 2.24 | 2.20 | 2.16 | 2.11 | 2.06 | 2.00 |
| | .01 | 7.77 | 5.57 | 4.68 | 4.18 | 3.86 | 3.63 | 3.46 | 3.32 | 3.21 | 3.13 | 3.05 | 2.99 | 2.89 | 2.81 | 2.70 |
| 26 | .05 | 4.22 | 3.37 | 2.98 | 2.74 | 2.59 | 2.47 | 2.39 | 2.32 | 2.27 | 2.22 | 2.18 | 2.15 | 2.10 | 2.05 | 1.99 |
| | .01 | 7.72 | 5.53 | 4.64 | 4.14 | 3.82 | 3.59 | 3.42 | 3.29 | 3.17 | 3.09 | 3.02 | 2.96 | 2.86 | 2.77 | 2.66 |
| 27 | .05 | 4.21 | 3.35 | 2.96 | 2.73 | 2.57 | 2.46 | 2.37 | 2.30 | 2.25 | 2.20 | 2.16 | 2.13 | 2.08 | 2.03 | 1.97 |
| | .01 | 7.68 | 5.49 | 4.60 | 4.11 | 3.79 | 3.56 | 3.39 | 3.26 | 3.14 | 3.06 | 2.98 | 2.93 | 2.83 | 2.74 | 2.63 |
| 28 | .05 | 4.20 | 3.34 | 2.95 | 2.71 | 2.56 | 2.44 | 2.36 | 2.29 | 2.24 | 2.19 | 2.15 | 2.12 | 2.06 | 2.02 | 1.96 |
| | .01 | 7.64 | 5.45 | 4.57 | 4.07 | 3.76 | 3.53 | 3.36 | 3.23 | 3.11 | 3.03 | 2.95 | 2.90 | 2.80 | 2.71 | 2.60 |
| 29 | .05 | 4.18 | 3.33 | 2.93 | 2.70 | 2.54 | 2.43 | 2.35 | 2.28 | 2.22 | 2.18 | 2.14 | 2.10 | 2.05 | 2.00 | 1.94 |
| | .01 | 7.60 | 5.42 | 4.54 | 4.04 | 3.73 | 3.50 | 3.33 | 3.20 | 3.08 | 3.00 | 2.92 | 2.87 | 2.77 | 2.68 | 2.57 |
| 30 | .05 | 4.17 | 3.32 | 2.92 | 2.69 | 2.53 | 2.42 | 2.34 | 2.27 | 2.21 | 2.16 | 2.12 | 2.09 | 2.04 | 1.99 | 1.93 |
| | .01 | 7.56 | 5.39 | 4.51 | 4.02 | 3.70 | 3.47 | 3.30 | 3.17 | 3.06 | 2.98 | 2.90 | 2.84 | 2.74 | 2.66 | 2.55 |
| 32 | .05 | 4.15 | 3.30 | 2.90 | 2.67 | 2.51 | 2.40 | 2.32 | 2.25 | 2.19 | 2.14 | 2.10 | 2.07 | 2.02 | 1.97 | 1.91 |
| | .01 | 7.50 | 5.34 | 4.46 | 3.97 | 3.66 | 3.42 | 3.25 | 3.12 | 3.01 | 2.94 | 2.86 | 2.80 | 2.70 | 2.62 | 2.51 |
| 34 | .05 | 4.13 | 3.28 | 2.88 | 2.65 | 2.49 | 2.38 | 2.30 | 2.23 | 2.17 | 2.12 | 2.08 | 2.05 | 2.00 | 1.95 | 1.89 |
| | .01 | 7.44 | 5.29 | 4.42 | 3.93 | 3.61 | 3.38 | 3.21 | 3.08 | 2.97 | 2.89 | 2.82 | 2.76 | 2.66 | 2.58 | 2.47 |
| 36 | .05 | 4.11 | 3.26 | 2.86 | 2.63 | 2.48 | 2.36 | 2.28 | 2.21 | 2.15 | 2.10 | 2.06 | 2.03 | 1.98 | 1.93 | 1.87 |
| | .01 | 7.39 | 5.25 | 4.38 | 3.89 | 3.58 | 3.35 | 3.18 | 3.04 | 2.94 | 2.86 | 2.78 | 2.72 | 2.62 | 2.54 | 2.43 |
| 38 | .05 | 4.10 | 3.25 | 2.85 | 2.62 | 2.46 | 2.35 | 2.26 | 2.19 | 2.14 | 2.09 | 2.05 | 2.02 | 1.96 | 1.92 | 1.85 |
| | .01 | 7.35 | 5.21 | 4.34 | 3.86 | 3.54 | 3.32 | 3.15 | 3.02 | 2.91 | 2.82 | 2.75 | 2.69 | 2.59 | 2.51 | 2.40 |
| 40 | .05 | 4.08 | 3.23 | 2.84 | 2.61 | 2.45 | 2.34 | 2.25 | 2.18 | 2.12 | 2.07 | 2.04 | 2.00 | 1.95 | 1.90 | 1.84 |
| | .01 | 7.31 | 5.18 | 4.31 | 3.83 | 3.51 | 3.29 | 3.12 | 2.99 | 2.88 | 2.80 | 2.73 | 2.66 | 2.56 | 2.49 | 2.37 |
| 42 | .05 | 4.07 | 3.22 | 2.83 | 2.59 | 2.44 | 2.32 | 2.24 | 2.17 | 2.11 | 2.06 | 2.02 | 1.99 | 1.94 | 1.89 | 1.82 |
| | .01 | 7.27 | 5.15 | 4.29 | 3.80 | 3.49 | 3.26 | 3.10 | 2.96 | 2.86 | 2.77 | 2.70 | 2.64 | 2.54 | 2.46 | 2.35 |

**TABLE 4 (CONT.)**
Critical Values of *F*: The *F*-Tables

| *Degrees of Freedom Within Groups (degrees of freedom in denominator of* F*-ratio)* | α | *Degrees of Freedom Between Groups (degrees of freedom in numerator of* F*-ratio)* | | | | | | | | | | | | | | |
|---|---|---|---|---|---|---|---|---|---|---|---|---|---|---|---|---|
| | | *1* | *2* | *3* | *4* | *5* | *6* | *7* | *8* | *9* | *10* | *11* | *12* | *14* | *16* | *20* |
| 44 | **.05** | **4.06** | **3.21** | **2.82** | **2.58** | **2.43** | **2.31** | **2.23** | **2.16** | **2.10** | **2.05** | **2.01** | **1.98** | **1.92** | **1.88** | **1.81** |
| | .01 | 7.24 | 5.12 | 4.26 | 3.78 | 3.46 | 3.24 | 3.07 | 2.94 | 2.84 | 2.75 | 2.68 | 2.62 | 2.52 | 2.44 | 2.32 |
| 46 | **.05** | **4.05** | **3.20** | **2.81** | **2.57** | **2.42** | **2.30** | **2.22** | **2.14** | **2.09** | **2.04** | **2.00** | **1.97** | **1.91** | **1.87** | **1.80** |
| | .01 | 7.21 | 5.10 | 4.24 | 3.76 | 3.44 | 3.22 | 3.05 | 2.92 | 2.82 | 2.73 | 2.66 | 2.60 | 2.50 | 2.42 | 2.30 |
| 48 | **.05** | **4.04** | **3.19** | **2.80** | **2.56** | **2.41** | **2.30** | **2.21** | **2.14** | **2.08** | **2.03** | **1.99** | **1.96** | **1.90** | **1.86** | **1.79** |
| | .01 | 7.19 | 5.08 | 4.22 | 3.74 | 3.42 | 3.20 | 3.04 | 2.90 | 2.80 | 2.71 | 2.64 | 2.58 | 2.48 | 2.40 | 2.28 |
| 50 | **.05** | **4.03** | **3.18** | **2.79** | **2.56** | **2.40** | **2.29** | **2.20** | **2.13** | **2.07** | **2.02** | **1.98** | **1.95** | **1.90** | **1.85** | **1.78** |
| | .01 | 7.17 | 5.06 | 4.20 | 3.72 | 3.41 | 3.18 | 3.02 | 2.88 | 2.78 | 2.70 | 2.62 | 2.56 | 2.46 | 2.39 | 2.26 |
| 55 | **.05** | **4.02** | **3.17** | **2.78** | **2.54** | **2.38** | **2.27** | **2.18** | **2.11** | **2.05** | **2.00** | **1.97** | **1.93** | **1.88** | **1.83** | **1.76** |
| | .01 | 7.12 | 5.01 | 4.16 | 3.68 | 3.37 | 3.15 | 2.98 | 2.85 | 2.75 | 2.66 | 2.59 | 2.53 | 2.43 | 2.35 | 2.23 |
| 60 | **.05** | **4.00** | **3.15** | **2.76** | **2.52** | **2.37** | **2.25** | **2.17** | **2.10** | **2.04** | **1.99** | **1.95** | **1.92** | **1.86** | **1.81** | **1.75** |
| | .01 | 7.08 | 4.98 | 4.13 | 3.65 | 3.34 | 3.12 | 2.95 | 2.82 | 2.72 | 2.63 | 2.56 | 2.50 | 2.40 | 2.32 | 2.20 |
| 65 | **.05** | **3.99** | **3.14** | **2.75** | **2.51** | **2.36** | **2.24** | **2.15** | **2.08** | **2.02** | **1.98** | **1.94** | **1.90** | **1.85** | **1.80** | **1.73** |
| | .01 | 7.04 | 4.95 | 4.10 | 3.62 | 3.31 | 3.09 | 2.93 | 2.79 | 2.70 | 2.61 | 2.54 | 2.47 | 2.37 | 2.30 | 2.18 |
| 70 | **.05** | **3.98** | **3.13** | **2.74** | **2.50** | **2.35** | **2.23** | **2.14** | **2.07** | **2.01** | **1.97** | **1.93** | **1.89** | **1.84** | **1.79** | **1.72** |
| | .01 | 7.01 | 4.92 | 4.08 | 3.60 | 3.29 | 3.07 | 2.91 | 2.77 | 2.67 | 2.59 | 2.51 | 2.45 | 2.35 | 2.28 | 2.15 |
| 80 | **.05** | **3.96** | **3.11** | **2.72** | **2.48** | **2.33** | **2.21** | **2.12** | **2.05** | **1.99** | **1.95** | **1.91** | **1.88** | **1.82** | **1.77** | **1.70** |
| | .01 | 6.96 | 4.88 | 4.04 | 3.56 | 3.25 | 3.04 | 2.87 | 2.74 | 2.64 | 2.55 | 2.48 | 2.41 | 2.32 | 2.24 | 2.11 |
| 100 | **.05** | **3.94** | **3.09** | **2.70** | **2.46** | **2.30** | **2.19** | **2.10** | **2.03** | **1.97** | **1.92** | **1.88** | **1.85** | **1.79** | **1.75** | **1.68** |
| | .01 | 6.90 | 4.82 | 3.98 | 3.51 | 3.20 | 2.99 | 2.82 | 2.69 | 2.59 | 2.51 | 2.43 | 2.36 | 2.26 | 2.19 | 2.06 |
| 125 | **.05** | **3.92** | **3.07** | **2.68** | **2.44** | **2.29** | **2.17** | **2.08** | **2.01** | **1.95** | **1.90** | **1.86** | **1.83** | **1.77** | **1.72** | **1.65** |
| | .01 | 6.84 | 4.78 | 3.94 | 3.47 | 3.17 | 2.95 | 2.79 | 2.65 | 2.56 | 2.47 | 2.40 | 2.33 | 2.23 | 2.15 | 2.03 |
| 150 | **.05** | **3.91** | **3.06** | **2.67** | **2.43** | **2.27** | **2.16** | **2.07** | **2.00** | **1.94** | **1.89** | **1.85** | **1.82** | **1.76** | **1.71** | **1.64** |
| | .01 | 6.81 | 4.75 | 3.91 | 3.44 | 3.14 | 2.92 | 2.76 | 2.62 | 2.53 | 2.44 | 2.37 | 2.30 | 2.20 | 2.12 | 2.00 |
| 200 | **.05** | **3.89** | **3.04** | **2.65** | **2.41** | **2.26** | **2.14** | **2.05** | **1.98** | **1.92** | **1.87** | **1.83** | **1.80** | **1.74** | **1.69** | **1.62** |
| | .01 | 6.76 | 4.71 | 3.88 | 3.41 | 3.11 | 2.90 | 2.73 | 2.60 | 2.50 | 2.41 | 2.34 | 2.28 | 2.17 | 2.09 | 1.97 |
| 400 | **.05** | **3.86** | **3.02** | **2.62** | **2.39** | **2.23** | **2.12** | **2.03** | **1.96** | **1.90** | **1.85** | **1.81** | **1.78** | **1.72** | **1.67** | **1.60** |
| | .01 | 6.70 | 4.66 | 3.83 | 3.36 | 3.06 | 2.85 | 2.69 | 2.55 | 2.46 | 2.37 | 2.29 | 2.23 | 2.12 | 2.04 | 1.92 |
| 1000 | **.05** | **3.85** | **3.00** | **2.61** | **2.38** | **2.22** | **2.10** | **2.02** | **1.95** | **1.89** | **1.84** | **1.80** | **1.76** | **1.70** | **1.65** | **1.58** |
| | .01 | 6.66 | 4.62 | 3.80 | 3.34 | 3.04 | 2.82 | 2.66 | 2.53 | 2.43 | 2.34 | 2.26 | 2.20 | 2.09 | 2.01 | 1.89 |
| ∞ | **.05** | **3.84** | **2.99** | **2.60** | **2.37** | **2.21** | **2.09** | **2.01** | **1.94** | **1.88** | **1.83** | **1.79** | **1.75** | **1.69** | **1.64** | **1.57** |
| | .01 | 6.64 | 4.60 | 3.78 | 3.32 | 3.02 | 2.80 | 2.64 | 2.51 | 2.41 | 2.32 | 2.24 | 2.18 | 2.07 | 1.99 | 1.87 |

**TABLE 5**

Values of Studentized Range Statistic, $q_k$

For a one-way ANOVA, or a comparison of the means from a main effect, the value of $k$ is the number of means in the factor.

To compare the means from an interaction, find the appropriate design (or number of cell means) in the table below and obtain the adjusted value of $k$. Then use adjusted $k$ as $k$ to find the value of $q_k$.

Values of Adjusted $k$

| *Design of Study* | *Number of Cell Means in Study* | *Adjusted Value of* k |
|---|---|---|
| 2 × 2 | 4 | 3 |
| 2 × 3 | 6 | 5 |
| 2 × 4 | 8 | 6 |
| 3 × 3 | 9 | 7 |
| 3 × 4 | 12 | 8 |
| 4 × 4 | 16 | 10 |
| 4 × 5 | 20 | 12 |

Values of $q_k$ for $\alpha = .05$ are **dark numbers** and for $\alpha = .01$ are light numbers.

| *Degrees of Freedom Within Groups (degrees of freedom in denominator of F-ratio)* | α | k = *Number of Means Being Compared* 2 | 3 | 4 | 5 | 6 | 7 | 8 | 9 | 10 | 11 | 12 |
|---|---|---|---|---|---|---|---|---|---|---|---|---|
| 1 | **.05** | **18.00** | **27.00** | **32.80** | **37.10** | **40.40** | **43.10** | **45.40** | **47.40** | **49.10** | **50.60** | **52.00** |
| | .01 | 90.00 | 135.00 | 164.00 | 186.00 | 202.00 | 216.00 | 227.00 | 237.00 | 246.00 | 253.00 | 260.00 |
| 2 | **.05** | **6.09** | **8.30** | **9.80** | **10.90** | **11.70** | **12.40** | **13.00** | **13.50** | **14.00** | **14.40** | **14.70** |
| | .01 | 14.00 | 19.00 | 22.30 | 24.70 | 26.60 | 28.20 | 29.50 | 30.70 | 31.70 | 32.60 | 33.40 |
| 3 | **.05** | **4.50** | **5.91** | **6.82** | **7.50** | **8.04** | **8.48** | **8.85** | **9.18** | **9.46** | **9.72** | **9.95** |
| | .01 | 8.26 | 10.60 | 12.20 | 13.30 | 14.20 | 15.00 | 15.60 | 16.20 | 16.70 | 17.10 | 17.50 |
| 4 | **.05** | **3.93** | **5.04** | **5.76** | **6.29** | **6.71** | **7.05** | **7.35** | **7.60** | **7.83** | **8.03** | **8.21** |
| | .01 | 6.51 | 8.12 | 9.17 | 9.96 | 10.60 | 11.10 | 11.50 | 11.90 | 12.30 | 12.60 | 12.80 |
| 5 | **.05** | **3.64** | **4.60** | **5.22** | **5.67** | **6.03** | **6.33** | **6.58** | **6.80** | **6.99** | **7.17** | **7.32** |
| | .01 | 5.70 | 6.97 | 7.80 | 8.42 | 8.91 | 9.32 | 9.67 | 9.97 | 10.20 | 10.50 | 10.70 |
| 6 | **.05** | **3.46** | **4.34** | **4.90** | **5.31** | **5.63** | **5.89** | **6.12** | **6.32** | **6.49** | **6.65** | **6.79** |
| | .01 | 5.24 | 6.33 | 7.03 | 7.56 | 7.97 | 8.32 | 8.61 | 8.87 | 9.10 | 9.30 | 9.49 |
| 7 | **.05** | **3.34** | **4.16** | **4.69** | **5.06** | **5.36** | **5.61** | **5.82** | **6.00** | **6.16** | **6.30** | **6.43** |
| | .01 | 4.95 | 5.92 | 6.54 | 7.01 | 7.37 | 7.68 | 7.94 | 8.17 | 8.37 | 8.55 | 8.71 |
| 8 | **.05** | **3.26** | **4.04** | **4.53** | **4.89** | **5.17** | **5.40** | **5.60** | **5.77** | **5.92** | **6.05** | **6.18** |
| | .01 | 4.74 | 5.63 | 6.20 | 6.63 | 6.96 | 7.24 | 7.47 | 7.68 | 7.87 | 8.03 | 8.18 |
| 9 | **.05** | **3.20** | **3.95** | **4.42** | **4.76** | **5.02** | **5.24** | **5.43** | **5.60** | **5.74** | **5.87** | **5.98** |
| | .01 | 4.60 | 5.43 | 5.96 | 6.35 | 6.66 | 6.91 | 7.13 | 7.32 | 7.49 | 7.65 | 7.78 |

***TABLE 5 (CONT.)***

Values of Studentized Range Statistic, $q_k$

| *Degrees of Freedom Within Groups (degrees of freedom in denominator of F-ratio)* | α | k = *Number of Means Being Compared* | | | | | | | | | | |
|---|---|---|---|---|---|---|---|---|---|---|---|---|
| | | *2* | *3* | *4* | *5* | *6* | *7* | *8* | *9* | *10* | *11* | *12* |
| 10 | **.05** | **3.15** | **3.88** | **4.33** | **4.65** | **4.91** | **5.12** | **5.30** | **5.46** | **5.60** | **5.72** | **5.83** |
| | .01 | 4.48 | 5.27 | 5.77 | 6.14 | 6.43 | 6.67 | 6.87 | 7.05 | 7.21 | 7.36 | 7.48 |
| 11 | **.05** | **3.11** | **3.82** | **4.26** | **4.57** | **4.82** | **5.03** | **5.20** | **5.35** | **5.49** | **5.61** | **5.71** |
| | .01 | 4.39 | 5.14 | 5.62 | 5.97 | 6.25 | 6.48 | 6.67 | 6.84 | 6.99 | 7.13 | 7.26 |
| 12 | **.05** | **3.08** | **3.77** | **4.20** | **4.51** | **4.75** | **4.95** | **5.12** | **5.27** | **5.40** | **5.51** | **5.62** |
| | .01 | 4.32 | 5.04 | 5.50 | 5.84 | 6.10 | 6.32 | 6.51 | 6.67 | 6.81 | 6.94 | 7.06 |
| 13 | **.05** | **3.06** | **3.73** | **4.15** | **4.45** | **4.69** | **4.88** | **5.05** | **5.19** | **5.32** | **5.43** | **5.53** |
| | .01 | 4.26 | 4.96 | 5.40 | 5.73 | 5.98 | 6.19 | 6.37 | 6.53 | 6.67 | 6.79 | 6.90 |
| 14 | **.05** | **3.03** | **3.70** | **4.11** | **4.41** | **4.64** | **4.83** | **4.99** | **5.13** | **5.25** | **5.36** | **5.46** |
| | .01 | 4.21 | 4.89 | 5.32 | 5.63 | 5.88 | 6.08 | 6.26 | 6.41 | 6.54 | 6.66 | 6.77 |
| 16 | **.05** | **3.00** | **3.65** | **4.05** | **4.33** | **4.56** | **4.74** | **4.90** | **5.03** | **5.15** | **5.26** | **5.35** |
| | .01 | 4.13 | 4.78 | 5.19 | 5.49 | 5.72 | 5.92 | 6.08 | 6.22 | 6.35 | 6.46 | 6.56 |
| 18 | **.05** | **2.97** | **3.61** | **4.00** | **4.28** | **4.49** | **4.67** | **4.82** | **4.96** | **5.07** | **5.17** | **5.27** |
| | .01 | 4.07 | 4.70 | 5.09 | 5.38 | 5.60 | 5.79 | 5.94 | 6.08 | 6.20 | 6.31 | 6.41 |
| 20 | **.05** | **2.95** | **3.58** | **3.96** | **4.23** | **4.45** | **4.62** | **4.77** | **4.90** | **5.01** | **5.11** | **5.20** |
| | .01 | 4.02 | 4.64 | 5.02 | 5.29 | 5.51 | 5.69 | 5.84 | 5.97 | 6.09 | 6.19 | 6.29 |
| 24 | **.05** | **2.92** | **3.53** | **3.90** | **4.17** | **4.37** | **4.54** | **4.68** | **4.81** | **4.92** | **5.01** | **5.10** |
| | .01 | 3.96 | 4.54 | 4.91 | 5.17 | 5.37 | 5.54 | 5.69 | 5.81 | 5.92 | 6.02 | 6.11 |
| 30 | **.05** | **2.89** | **3.49** | **3.84** | **4.10** | **4.30** | **4.46** | **4.60** | **4.72** | **4.83** | **4.92** | **5.00** |
| | .01 | 3.89 | 4.45 | 4.80 | 5.05 | 5.24 | 5.40 | 5.54 | 5.56 | 5.76 | 5.85 | 5.93 |
| 40 | **.05** | **2.86** | **3.44** | **3.79** | **4.04** | **4.23** | **4.39** | **4.52** | **4.63** | **4.74** | **4.82** | **4.91** |
| | .01 | 3.82 | 4.37 | 4.70 | 4.93 | 5.11 | 5.27 | 5.39 | 5.50 | 5.60 | 5.69 | 5.77 |
| 60 | **.05** | **2.83** | **3.40** | **3.74** | **3.98** | **4.16** | **4.31** | **4.44** | **4.55** | **4.65** | **4.73** | **4.81** |
| | .01 | 3.76 | 4.28 | 4.60 | 4.82 | 4.99 | 5.13 | 5.25 | 5.36 | 5.45 | 5.53 | 5.60 |
| 120 | **.05** | **2.80** | **3.36** | **3.69** | **3.92** | **4.10** | **4.24** | **4.36** | **4.48** | **4.56** | **4.64** | **4.72** |
| | .01 | 3.70 | 4.20 | 4.50 | 4.71 | 4.87 | 5.01 | 5.12 | 5.21 | 5.30 | 5.38 | 5.44 |
| ∞ | **.05** | **2.77** | **3.31** | **3.63** | **3.86** | **4.03** | **4.17** | **4.29** | **4.39** | **4.47** | **4.55** | **4.62** |
| | .01 | 3.64 | 4.12 | 4.40 | 4.60 | 4.76 | 4.88 | 4.99 | 5.08 | 5.16 | 5.23 | 5.29 |

**TABLE 6**
Critical Values of Chi Square: The $\chi^2$-Tables

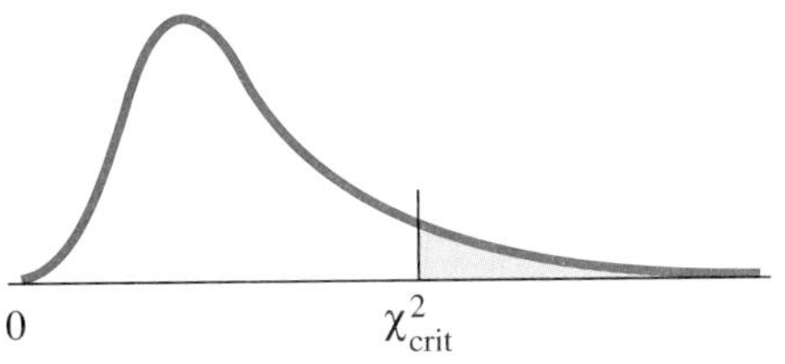


| df | Alpha Level $\alpha = .05$ | $\alpha = .01$ |
|---|---|---|
| 1 | 3.84 | 6.64 |
| 2 | 5.99 | 9.21 |
| 3 | 7.81 | 11.34 |
| 4 | 9.49 | 13.28 |
| 5 | 11.07 | 15.09 |
| 6 | 12.59 | 16.81 |
| 7 | 14.07 | 18.48 |
| 8 | 15.51 | 20.09 |
| 9 | 16.92 | 21.67 |
| 10 | 18.31 | 23.21 |
| 11 | 19.68 | 24.72 |
| 12 | 21.03 | 26.22 |
| 13 | 22.36 | 27.69 |
| 14 | 23.68 | 29.14 |
| 15 | 25.00 | 30.58 |
| 16 | 26.30 | 32.00 |
| 17 | 27.59 | 33.41 |
| 18 | 28.87 | 34.80 |
| 19 | 30.14 | 36.19 |
| 20 | 31.41 | 37.57 |
| 21 | 32.67 | 38.93 |
| 22 | 33.92 | 40.29 |
| 23 | 35.17 | 41.64 |
| 24 | 36.42 | 42.98 |
| 25 | 37.65 | 44.31 |
| 26 | 38.88 | 45.64 |
| 27 | 40.11 | 46.96 |
| 28 | 41.34 | 48.28 |
| 29 | 42.56 | 49.59 |
| 30 | 43.77 | 50.89 |
| 40 | 55.76 | 63.69 |
| 50 | 67.50 | 76.15 |
| 60 | 79.08 | 88.38 |
| 70 | 90.53 | 100.42 |



STATISTICAL TABLES

# Answers to Odd-Numbered Questions

## Chapter 1

1. So that they understand the language and procedures used in research.
3. A relationship exists when certain scores on one variable are associated with certain scores on the other variable so as the scores on one variable change, the scores on the other variable change in a consistent fashion.
5. The design of the study and the scale of measurement used.
7. The independent variable is the overall variable the researcher is interested in; the conditions are the specific amounts or categories of the independent variable under which participants are tested.
9. They are used to organize, summarize, and describe the characteristics of a sample of scores.
11. (a) A statistic describes a characteristic of a sample of scores. A parameter describes a characteristic of a population of scores. (b) Statistics use letters from the English alphabet. Parameters use letters from the Greek alphabet.
13. Poindexter's is an experiment because he manipulated alcohol consumption; Foofy's is a correlational study because she merely measured participants on both variables.
15. (a) Each score on $X$ is matched with one and only one $Y$ score. (b) A different batch of $Y$ scores is paired with each $X$ score. (c) Virtually the same batch of $Y$ scores occurs with every $X$ score.
17. Samples A ($Y$ scores increase) and D ($Y$ scores increase then decrease).
19.

| *Variable* | *Qualitative or Quantitative* | *Continuous or Discrete* | *Type of Measurement Scale* |
|---|---|---|---|
| Gender | qualitative | discrete | nominal |
| Academic major | qualitative | discrete | nominal |
| Number of minutes before and after an event | quantitative | continuous | interval |
| Restaurant ratings (best, next best, etc.) | quantitative | discrete | ordinal |
| Speed | quantitative | continuous | ratio |
| Number of dollars in your pocket | quantitative | discrete | ratio |
| Position in line | quantitative | discrete | ordinal |
| Change in weight | quantitative | continuous | interval |

## Chapter 2

1. $N$ is the number of scores in a sample; $f$ is frequency, the number of times a score occurs.
3. (a) In a bar graph adjacent bars do not touch; in a histogram they do. (b) Bar graphs are used with nominal or ordinal scores; histograms are used with interval or ratio scores. (c) A histogram has a bar above each score; a polygon has datapoints above the scores that are connected by straight lines. (d) Histograms are used with a few different interval or ratio scores; polygons are used with a wide range of interval/ratio scores.
5. A data point
7. A positively skewed distribution has only one tail at the extreme high scores; a negatively skewed distribution has only one tail at the extreme low scores.
9. Scores in the left-hand tail are *low* scores; in the right-hand tail are *high* scores.
11. (a) The middle IQ score has the highest frequency in a symmetrical distribution; the higher and lower scores

have lower frequencies, and the highest and lowest scores have a relatively very low frequency. (b) The agility scores form a symmetrical distribution containing two distinct "humps" where there are two scores that occur more frequently than the surrounding scores. (c) The memory scores form an asymmetrical distribution in which there are some very infrequent, extremely low scores, but there are not correspondingly infrequent high scores.

13. It indicates that the test was difficult for the class, because most often the scores are low or middle scores, and seldom are there high scores.
15. (a) bar graph (b) polygon (c) bar graph (d) histogram
17. (a) 35% of the sample scored below your score. (b) The score occurred 40% of the time. (c) It is one of the highest and least frequent scores. (d) It is one of the lowest and least frequent scores. (e) 60% of the area under the curve and thus 60% of the distribution is to the left of (below) your score.
19. (a) 70, 72, 60, 85, 45; (b) 10th percentile; (c) .50; (d) .50 − .10 = .40; (e) A total of .50 + .35 = .85 of the curve is to the left of 80 so it is at the 85th percentile.
21.

| *Score* | f | *Relative Frequency* |
|---|---|---|
| 53 | 1 | .06 |
| 52 | 3 | .17 |
| 51 | 2 | .11 |
| 50 | 5 | .28 |
| 49 | 4 | .22 |
| 48 | 0 | .00 |
| 47 | 3 | .17 |

23.

| *Score* | f | *Relative Frequency* |
|---|---|---|
| 16 | 5 | .33 |
| 15 | 1 | .07 |
| 14 | 0 | .00 |
| 13 | 2 | .13 |
| 12 | 3 | .20 |
| 11 | 4 | .27 |

## *Chapter 3*

1. It indicates where on a variable most scores tend to be located.
3. The mode is a most frequently occurring score, used with nominal scores.
5. The mean is the average score—the mathematical center of a distribution, used with symmetrical distributions of interval or ratio scores.
7. Because here the mean is not near most of the scores.
9. $\mu$ is the symbol for a population mean, estimated from a sample mean.
11. (a) $X - \bar{X}$; (b) $\Sigma(X - \bar{X})$; (c) The total distance scores are above the mean equals the total distance scores are below the mean.
13. (a) Mean; (b) Median (these ratio scores are skewed); (c) Mode (this is a nominal variable); (d) Median (this is an ordinal variable)
15. (a) $\Sigma X = 8$, $N = 4$, $\bar{X} = 2.00$; Mdn = 2; Mode = 2; (b) $\Sigma X = 31$, $N = 6$, $\bar{X} = 5.1666 = 5.17$; Mdn = 5; Mode = 5; (c) $\Sigma X = 40$, $N = 5$, $\bar{X} = 8.00$; Mdn = 8; Mode = 8; (d) $\Sigma X = 59$, $N = 6$, $\bar{X} = 9.833 = 9.83$; Mdn = 10; Mode = 10 and 11
17. Mean errors do not change until there has been 5 hours of sleep deprivation. Mean errors then increase as a function of increasing sleep deprivation.
19. (a) Line graph; income on $Y$ axis, age on $X$ axis; find median income per age group (income is skewed); (b) Bar graph; positive votes on $Y$ axis, presence or absence of a wildlife refuge on $X$ axis; find mean number of votes if normally distributed; (c) Line graph; running speed on $Y$ axis, amount of carbohydrates consumed on $X$ axis; find mean running speed if normally distributed; (d) Bar graph; alcohol abuse on $Y$ axis, ethnic group on $X$ axis; find mean rate of alcohol abuse per group if normally distributed.
21. (a) The means for Conditions 1, 2, and 3 are 15, 12, and 9, respectively.

(b)

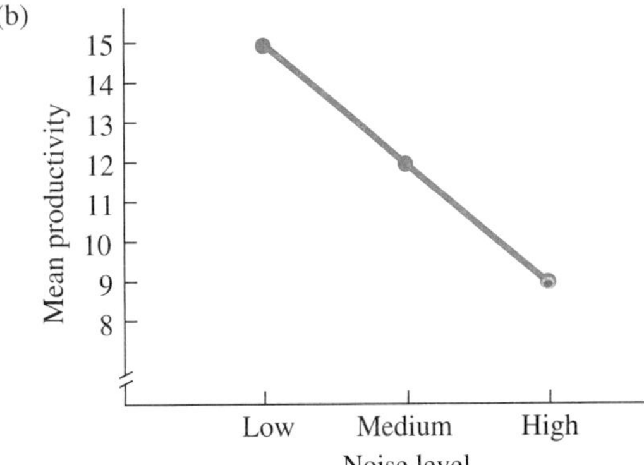


(c)

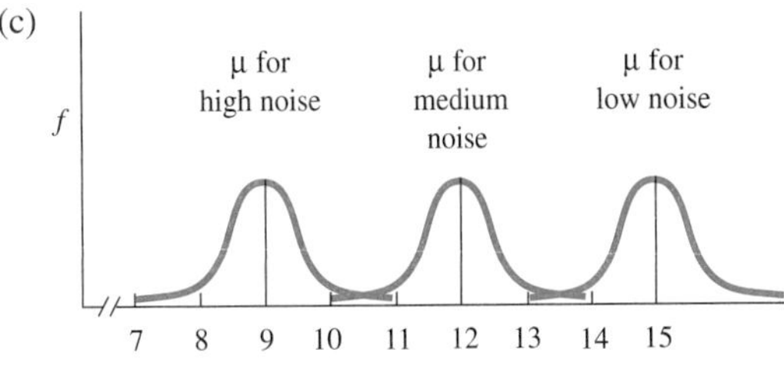

(d) In nature, as noise level increases, the typical productivity score decreases from around 15 to around 12 to around 9.

## Chapter 4

*1.* (a) To know how spread out scores are and how accurately the mean summarizes them; (b) The distribution's shape, its central tendency, and its variability.

*3.* (a) The range is the distance between the highest and lowest scores in a distribution; (b) Because it includes only the most extreme and often least-frequent scores, so it does not summarize most of the differences in a distribution; (c) With nominal or ordinal scores or with interval/ratio scores that cannot be accurately described by other measures.

*5.* (a) Variance is the average of the squared deviations around the mean; (b) Variance equals the squared standard deviation, and the standard deviation equals the square root of the variance.

*7.* Because the unbiased estimates divide by the quantity $N - 1$, resulting in a slightly larger estimate.

*9.* (a) Range $= 8 - 0 = 8$, so the scores span 8 different scores. (b) $\Sigma X = 41$, $\Sigma X^2 = 231$, $N = 10$, so $S_X^2 = (231 - 168.1)/10 = 6.29$: the average squared deviation of creativity scores from the mean is 6.29. (c) $S_X = \sqrt{6.29} = 2.51$: the "average deviation" of creativity scores from the mean is 2.51.

*11.* About 160 people. $\overline{X} = 4.10$ so $X = 1.59$ is the score one $S_X$ below the mean $(4.10 - 2.51 = 1.59)$. About 16% of the scores are below this $X$, and 16% of 1000 is 160.

*13.* (a) Because the sample tends to be normally distributed, the population should be normal too. (b) Because $\overline{X} = 1297/17 = 76.29$, we would estimate the $\mu$ to be 76.29. (c) The estimated population variance is $(99{,}223 - 98{,}953.47)/16 = 16.85$. (d) The estimated standard deviation is $\sqrt{16.85} = 4.10$. (e) Between 72.19 $(76.29 - 4.10)$ and 80.39 $(76.29 + 4.10)$.

*15.* (a) Guchi: his standard deviation is larger, his scores are spread out around the mean, so he tends to be a more inconsistent student. (b) Pluto: his scores are closer to the mean so it more accurately describes all of his scores. (c) Pluto, because we predict each will score at his mean score, and Pluto's scores are closer to his mean than Guchi's are to his mean. (d) Guchi, because his scores vary more widely above and below 60.

*17.* (a) Compute the mean and sample standard deviation in each condition. (b) Changing conditions A, B, C changes dependent scores from around 11.00 to 32.75 to 48.00, respectively. (c) The $S_X$ for the three conditions are .71, 1.09, and .71, respectively. Participants scored rather consistently in each condition.

*19.* (a) The scores in distribution A are less spread out than in B. (b) Find the scores at $\pm 1S_X$ from the mean: 68% of the scores are between 35 and 45 in A; between 30 and 50 in B.

*21.* (a) For conditions 1, 2, and 3, we'd expect $\mu$s of about 13.33, 8.33, and 5.67, respectively. (b) Somewhat inconsistently: based on $s_X$ we'd expect a $\sigma_X$ of 4.51, 2.52, and 3.06, respectively.

## Chapter 5

*1.* (a) A $z$-score indicates the distance, measured in standard deviation units, that a score is above or below the mean. (b) $z$-scores can be used to interpret scores from any normal distribution of interval or ratio scores.

*3.* It is the distribution after transforming a distribution of raw scores into $z$-scores.

*5.* Because $z$-scores standardize or equate different distributions so that they can be compared.

*7.* (a) It is our model of the perfect normal $z$-distribution. (b) It is a model of any normal distribution of raw scores after being transformed to $z$-scores. (c) The raw scores should be approximately normally distributed and the sample should be relatively large.

*9.* (a) That it is normally distributed, that its $\mu$ equals the $\mu$ of the raw score population, and that its standard deviation (the standard error of the mean) equals the raw score population's standard deviation divided by the square root of $N$. (b) Because it indicates the characteristics of any sampling distribution, without our having to actually measure all possible sample means.

*11.* (a) He should consider the size of each class' standard deviation. (b) Small. This will give him a large positive $z$-score, placing him at the top of his class. (c) Large. Then he will have a small negative $z$ and be close to the mean.

*13.* $\Sigma X = 103$, $\Sigma X^2 = 931$, and $N = 12$, so $S_X = 1.98$ and $\overline{X} = 8.58$.
(a) For $X = 10$, $z = (10 - 8.58)/1.98 = +.72$.
(b) For $X = 6$, $z = (6 - 8.58)/1.98 = -1.30$.

*15.* (a) $z = +1.0$ (b) $z = -2.8$
(c) $z = -.70$ (d) $z = -2.0$

*17.* (a) .4706 (b) .0107 (c) $.3944 + .4970 = .8914$
(d) $.0250 + .0250 = .05$

*19.* From the $z$-table the 25th percentile is at approximately $z = -.67$. The cutoff score is then $X = (-.67)(10) + 75 = 68.3$.

*21.* For City A her salary has a $z$ of $(27{,}000 - 50{,}000)/15{,}000 = -1.53$. For City B her salary has a $z$ of $(12{,}000 - 14{,}000)/1000 = -2.0$. City A is the better offer, because her income will be closer to the average cost of living in that city.

## Chapter 6

1. (a) The likelihood of, or our confidence in, the event. (b) The relative frequency of the event in the population.
3. It is selecting a sample so that all elements or individuals have the same chance of selection.
5. Because of chance, the members of a sample are unrepresentative of the population, so that $\overline{X}$ is different from $\mu$, or the sample represents some other population.
7. It indicates whether or not the sample's $z$-score (and the sample $\overline{X}$) lies in the region of rejection.
9. No. The probability of a boy is still .5.
11. The $p$ of a hurricane is 160/200 = .80. The uncle is looking at an unrepresentative sample over the past 13 years. Poindexter fails to realize that $p$ is based on the long run, and so in the next few years there may not be a hurricane.
13. She may have obtained an unrepresentative sample, so that the population does not actually prefer sauerkraut juice.
15. No. With a $z = (24 - 18)/2.19 = +2.74$, this mean falls beyond the critical value of 1.96. It is unlikely to represent this population.
17. (a) The $\overline{X} = 321/9 = 35.67$; $\sigma_{\overline{X}} = 5/\sqrt{9}, = 1.67$. Then $z = (35.67 - 30)/1.67 = +3.40$. With a critical value of $\pm 1.96$, conclude that the football players do not represent this population. (b) Football players, as represented by your sample, form a population different from nonfootball players, having a $\mu$ of about 35.67.
19. (a) Chance should not produce a sample that is very unlikely to come from the population, so we reject that it does. (b) Samples from the population are likely to occur, so we accept that the sample represents this population.
21. (a) For Fred's sample, $\mu = 26$, and for Ethel's, $\mu = 18$. (b) The population with $\mu = 26$ is most likely to produce a sample with $\overline{X} = 26$, and the population with $\mu = 18$ is most likely to produce a sample with $\overline{X} = 18$.

## Chapter 7

1. Because a sample may (1) poorly represent one population so there is not really a relationship, or (2) represent some other population and there is a relationship.
3. $\alpha$ stands for the criterion probability; it determines the size of the region of rejection, and it is the theoretical probability of a Type I error.
5. They describe the predicted relationship that may or may not be demonstrated in an experiment.
7. Use a two-tailed test when predicting a relationship but not the direction that scores will change. Use a one-tailed test when predicting the direction the scores will change.
9. (a) Power is the probability of not making a Type II error. (b) So we do not miss relationships when they exist. (c) When results are not significant, we worry if we missed a real relationship.
11. (a) Changing the independent variable from a week other than finals week to finals week increases the dependent variable of amount of pizza consumed; the experiment will not demonstrate an increase. (b) Changing the independent variable from not performing breathing exercises to performing them changes the dependent variable of blood pressure; the experiment will not demonstrate a change. (c) Changing the independent variable by increasing hormone levels changes the dependent variable of pain sensitivity; the experiment will not demonstrate a change. (d) Changing the independent variable by increasing amount of light will decrease the dependent variable of frequency of dreams; the experiment will not demonstrate a decrease.
13. (a) A two-tailed test: we do not predict the direction that scores will change. (b) $H_0$: $\mu = 50$, $H_a$: $\mu \neq 50$ (c) $\sigma_{\overline{X}} = 12/\sqrt{49} = 1.714$; $z_{obt} = (54.63 - 50)/1.714 = +2.70$ (d) $z_{crit} = \pm 1.96$ (e) Yes, because $z_{obt}$ is beyond $z_{crit}$, the results are significant: Changing from the condition of no music to the condition of music results in test scores' changing from a $\mu$ of 50 to a $\mu$ around 54.63.
15. (a) The probability of a Type I error is $p < .05$. The error would be concluding that music influences scores when really it does not. (b) By rejecting $H_0$, there is no chance of making a Type II error. It would be concluding that music does not influence scores when really it does.
17. (a) She is incorrect. In both studies the researchers decided the results were unlikely to reflect sampling error from the $H_0$ population; they merely defined "unlikely" differently. (b) The probability of a Type I error is less in Study B.
19. This study seeks to prove the null hypothesis, seeking to reject $H_a$ and accept $H_0$ (which cannot be done.) At best, both hypotheses will be retained.
21. (a) The researcher decided that the difference between the scores for Brand X and other brands is too large to have resulted by chance. (b) The $p < .44$ indicates the probability is .44 that the researcher made a Type I error. This $p$ is far too large for us to accept the conclusion.

## Chapter 8

1. (a) The $t$-test and the $z$-test. (b) Compute $z$ if the standard deviation of the population ($\sigma_X$) is known; compute $t$ if $\sigma_X$ is estimated by $s_X$.

3. (a) $s_{\bar{X}}$ is the estimated standard error of the mean; $\sigma_{\bar{X}}$ is the true standard error of the mean. (b) Both are used as a standard deviation to locate a sample mean on the sampling distribution of means.
5. (a) Degrees of freedom. (b) Because the appropriate $t_{crit}$ depends on the *df*. (c) $df = N - 1$
7. To describe the relationship and interpret it.
9. It describes a range of values of $\mu$, one of which our $\bar{X}$ is likely to represent.
11. (a) $H_0$: $\mu = 68.5$; $H_a$: $\mu \neq 68.5$ (b) $s_{\bar{X}} = \sqrt{130.42/10} = 3.611$; $t_{obt} = (78.5 - 68.5)/3.61 = +2.77$ (c) With $df = 9$, $t_{crit} = \pm 2.262$. (d) The technique produces a significant improvement in scores: $t_{obt}(9) = 2.77$, $p < .05$. (e) $(3.61)(-2.262) + 78.5 \leq \mu \leq (3.61)(+2.262) + 78.5 = 70.33 \leq \mu \leq 86.67$
13. (a) $H_0$: $\mu = 50$; $H_a$: $\mu \neq 50$ (b) $s_{\bar{X}} = \sqrt{569.869/8} = 8.44$; $t_{obt} = (53.25 - 50)/8.44 = +.39$ (c) For $df = 7$, $t_{crit} = \pm 2.365$ (d) $t(7) = +.39$, $p > .05$ (e) The results are not significant, so do not compute the confidence interval. (f) She has no evidence that strong arguments change people's attitudes toward this issue.
15. (a) $H_0$: $\mu = 12$; $H_a$: $\mu \neq 12$. $\bar{X} = 8.667$, $s^2_X = 4.67$; $s_{\bar{X}} = \sqrt{4.67/6} = .882$; $t_{obt} = (8.667 - 12)/.882 = -3.78$. $df = 7$, $t_{crit} = \pm 2.571$. The results are significant, so there is evidence of a relationship: Without computers $\mu = 12$; with computers $\mu$ is around 8.67. (b) The 95% confidence interval for $\mu$ is $(.882)(-2.571) + 8.67 \leq \mu \leq (.882)(+2.571) + 8.67$, so $\mu$ is between 6.40 and 10.94.
17. (a) No; the closest *df* is 30, with $t_{crit} = +1.697$, and the results are not beyond it. (b) Yes; the $t_{obt}$ is beyond 1.697.
19. (a) $t(42) = +6.72$, $p < .01$ (b) $t(5) = -1.72$, $p > .05$

## Chapter 9

1. (a) The independent-samples *t*-test and the related-samples *t*-test. (b) Whether the scientist created independent samples or related samples.
3. By using a matched-samples or repeated-measures design.
5. By testing the same participants under all conditions.
7. Homogeneity of variance is when the variances in the populations are equal.
9. (a) $s_{\bar{X}_1 - \bar{X}_2}$ is the standard error of the difference—the standard deviation of the sampling distribution of differences between means from independent samples. (b) $s_{\bar{D}}$ is the standard error of the mean difference, the standard deviation of the sampling distribution of $\bar{D}$ from related samples.
11. $t(40) = +4.55$, $p < .05$.
13. (a) $H_0$: $\mu_1 - \mu_2 = 0$; $H_a$: $\mu_1 - \mu_2 \neq 0$. (b) $s^2_{pool} = 23.695$; $s_{\bar{X}_1 - \bar{X}_2} = 1.78$; $t_{obt} = (43 - 39)/1.78 = +2.25$ (c) With $df = (15 - 1) + (15 - 1) = 28$, $t_{crit} = +2.048$. (d) The results are significant: In the population, hot baths (with $\mu$ about 43) produce different relaxation scores from those produced by cold baths (with $\mu$ about 39). (e) $r^2_{pb} = (2.25)^2/[(2.25)^2 + 28] = .15$. (f) No, changing bath temperature accounts for only .15 of the differences in relaxation scores, so it does not have a large effect.
15. (a) She should retain $H_0$, because in her one-tailed test the signs of $t_{obt}$ and $t_{crit}$ are different. (b) She probably did not subtract her sample means in the same way that she subtracted the $\mu$s in her hypotheses.
17. (a) $H_0$: $\mu_D = 0$; $H_a$: $\mu_D \neq 0$. (b) $\bar{D} = 2.625$, $s^2_D = 4.554$, $t_{obt} = (2.625 - 0)/.754 = +3.48$ (c) Low and High sunshine exposure result in a significant difference in well-being. (d) $t(7) = +3.48$, $p < .05$. (e) For Low predict the $\bar{X}$ of 15.5. For High predict the $\bar{X}$ of 18.13. (f) $r^2_{pb} = 3.48^2/[(3.48)^2 + 7] = .64$
19. (a) $H_0$: $\mu_D \leq 0$; $H_a$: $\mu_D > 0$. (b) $\bar{D} = 1.2$, $s^2_D = 1.289$, $s_{\bar{D}} = .359$; $t_{obt} = (1.2 - 0)/.359 = +3.34$. (c) With $df = 9$, $t_{crit} = +1.833$. (d) The results are significant. Children exhibit more aggressive acts after watching the show (with $\mu$ about 3.9) than they do before the show (with $\mu$ about 2.7). (e) $r^2_{pb} = (3.34)^2/[(3.34)^2 + 9] = .55$; so violence is an important variable here.
21. (a) Two-tailed. (b) $H_0$: $\mu_1 - \mu_2 = 0$, $H_a$: $\mu_1 - \mu_2 \neq 0$. (c) $\bar{X}_1 = 11.5$, $s^2_1 = 4.72$; $\bar{X}_2 = 14.1$, $s^2_2 = 5.86$, $s_{\bar{X}_1 - \bar{X}_2} = 1.03$, $t_{obt} = (11.5 - 14.1)/1.03 = -2.52$. With $df = 18$, $t_{crit} = \pm 2.101$, so $t_{obt}$ is significant. (d) Police who've taken this course are more successful at solving disputes than police who have not taken it. The $\mu$ for the police with the course is around 14.1, and the $\mu$ for police without the course is around 11.5. (e) $r^2_{pb} = .26$; taking the course is somewhat important.

## Chapter 10

1. (a) In experiments we manipulate one variable and measure participants on another variable; in correlational studies we measure participants on two variables. (b) In experiments we compute the mean of the dependent ($Y$) scores for each condition (each $X$); in correlational studies we examine the relationship over all $X$-$Y$ pairs by computing a correlation coefficient.
3. (a) A scatterplot is a graph of the individual data points from a set of $X$-$Y$ pairs. (b) A regression line is the summary straight line through the center of a scatterplot.
5. (a) As the $X$ scores increase, the $Y$ scores tend to increase. (b) As the $X$ scores increase, the $Y$ scores tend to decrease. (c) As the $X$ scores increase, the $Y$ scores do not only increase or only decrease.

7. (a) ρ stands for the Pearson correlation coefficient in the population. (b) ρ is estimated from an $r$ calculated on a sample.
9. Compute $r_{obt}$, create the two- or one-tailed $H_0$ and $H_a$, set up the sampling distribution and, using $df = N - 1$, find $r_{crit}$; compare $r_{obt}$ to $r_{crit}$.
11. (a) It is the proportion of all of the differences in $Y$ scores that are associated with changes in the $X$ variable. (b) Compute $r^2$. (c) The larger the $r^2$, the more useful and important the relationship is.
13. (a) He forgot the inferential test of $r$. (b) $H_0$: $\rho = 0$; $H_a$: $\rho \neq 0$. (c) With $df = 18$, the two-tailed $r_{crit} = \pm.444$. (d) $r(18) = +.21$, $p > .05$; $r$ is not significant, so there is no evidence of a relationship. (e) None.
15. (a) $\Sigma X = 38$, $\Sigma X^2 = 212$, $\Sigma Y = 68$, $\Sigma Y^2 = 552$, $\Sigma XY = 317$, $N = 9$; $r = (2853 - 2584)/\sqrt{(464)(344)} = +.67$. (b) $H_0$: $\rho \leq 0$; $H_a$: $\rho > 0$. (c) With $df = 7$, the one-tailed $r_{crit} = +.582$. (d) $r(7) = +.67$, $p < .05$; this $r$ is significantly different from zero, so there is a strong relationship here. (e) In the population of nurses, we'd expect a ρ of around +.67. (f) $r^2 = (.67)^2 = .45$; this is useful, because 45% of differences in absenteeism are related to differences in burnout level.
17. (a) $H_0$: $\rho = 0$; $H_a$: $\rho \neq 0$. (b) With $df = 70$, the two-tailed $r_{crit} = \pm.232$. (c) $r(70) = +.38$, $p < .05$. (d) The $r$ is significantly different from zero, indicating a moderate relationship; in the population we expect ρ is around +.38. (e) $r^2$ and linear regression.
19. (a) Because we cannot compare correlations this way. (b) Computing $r^2$, $+.40^2 = .16$, and $+.80^2 = .64$. The study time variable is four times as important as the speed variable in these relationships.

## Chapter 11

1. (a) Analysis of variance. (b) A study that contains one independent variable. (c) An independent variable. (d) A condition of the independent variable. (e) Another name for a level. (f) All samples are independent. (g) All samples are related.
3. (a) It is the probability of making a Type I error after comparing all means in an experiment. (b) Multiple $t$-tests result in an experiment-wise error rate larger than alpha, but performing ANOVA and then post hoc tests keeps the experiment-wise error rate equal to alpha.
5. (a) When $F_{obt}$ is significant and $k$ is greater than 2. Because the $F_{obt}$ indicates only that two or more level means differ; post hoc tests determine which levels differ significantly. (b) When $F_{obt}$ is not significant or when $k = 2$.
7. It compares the $MS_{bn}$ to the $MS_{wn}$.
9. It indicates the effect size as the proportion of variance in dependent scores accounted for by changing the levels of the independent variable.
11. (a) $H_0$: $\mu_1 = \mu_2 = \mu_3 = \mu_4$. (b) $H_a$: not all μs are equal. (c) $H_0$ is that a relationship is not represented; $H_a$ is that one is represented.
13. (a) The $MS_{bn}$ is less than the $MS_{wn}$ and $H_0$ is assumed to be true. (b) He made a computational error—$F_{obt}$ cannot be a negative number.
15. (a) For a relationship to be potentially important, we must first believe that it's a real relationship. (b) Significant indicates the sample relationship is unlikely to occur if there is not a real relationship in the population. (c) A significant relationship is unimportant if it accounts for little of the variance.
17. This is a related-samples design, probably comparing the weights of one group before and after they dieted. (b) The one-way within-subjects ANOVA.
19. (a)

| *Source* | *Sum of Squares* | df | *Mean Square* | F |
|---|---|---|---|---|
| Between | 134.80 | 3 | 44.93 | 17.08 |
| Within | 42.00 | 16 | 2.63 | |
| Total | 176.80 | 19 | | |

(b) With $df = 3$ and 16, $F_{crit} = 3.24$, so $F_{obt}$ is significant, $p < .05$. (c) For $k = 4$ and $df_{wn} = 16$, $q_k = 4.05$, so $HSD = (4.05)(\sqrt{2.63/5}) = 2.94$: $\bar{X}_4 = 4.4$, $\bar{X}_6 = 10.8$, $\bar{X}_8 = 9.40$, $\bar{X}_{10} = 5.8$. Only ages 4 versus 10 and ages 6 versus 8 do not differ significantly. (d) $\eta^2 = 134.8/176.8 = .76$, this relationship accounts for 76% of the variance, so it's very important.
21. (a) $df_{bn} = 2$, $df_{wn} = 12$, $df_{tot} = 14$, $MS_{bn} = 326.08$, $MS_{wn} = 51.063$, $F_{obt} = 6.39$. (b) For $df_{bn} = 2$ and $df_{wn} = 12$, $F_{crit} = 3.88$. (c) $F(2,12) = 6.39$, $p < .05$. (d) With $k = 3$ and $df_{wn} = 12$, $q_k = 3.77$. $HSD = 3.77(\sqrt{51.063/5}) = 11.92$. Low versus high, and medium versus high differ significantly. (e) Increasing volume significantly decreases accuracy when volume is increased from low to high or from medium to high. (f) $\eta^2 = 652.16/1264.92 = .52$; changing volume accounts for .52 of the variance in scores, which is a substantial amount, so this is an important variable.

## Chapter 12

1. (a) She can use a $t$-test or a one-way ANOVA. (b) A two-way, between-subjects ANOVA; a two-way, within-subjects ANOVA; or a two-way, mixed-design ANOVA.

(c) Whether both factors are tested using independent samples, both factors are tested using related samples, or one factor involves related samples and the other involves independent samples.

*3.* A main effect mean is based on scores in a level of one factor after collapsing across the other factor. A cell mean is the mean of scores from a particular combination of a level of factor A with a level of factor B.

*5.* (a) A confounded comparison involves two cells that differ along more than one factor. It occurs with cells diagonally positioned in a study's diagram. (b) An unconfounded comparison involves two cells that differ along only one factor. It occurs with means within the same column or within the same row of a diagram. (c) Because we cannot determine which factor produced the difference.

*7.* (a) $H_0$ is that the $\mu$s represented by the main effect means from factor A are all equal; $H_a$ is that not all $\mu$s are equal. (b) $H_0$ is that the $\mu$s represented by the main effect means from factor B are all equal; $H_a$ is that they are not all equal. (c) $H_0$ is that the $\mu$s represented by the cell means do not form an interaction; $H_a$ is that they do form an interaction.

*9.* (a) That changing a factor produced at least two main effect means that differ significantly. (b) That the relationship between one factor and the dependent scores changes depending on which level of the other factor is present.

*11.* *Study 1:* For A, means are 7 and 9; for B, means are 3 and 13. Apparently there are effects for A and B but not for A × B. *Study 2:* For A, means are 7.5 and 7.5; for B, means are 7.5 and 7.5. There is no effect for A or B, but there is an effect for A × B. *Study 3:* For A, means are 8 and 8; for B, means are 11 and 5. There is no effect for A, but there are effects for B and A × B.

*13.* Perform Tukey's post hoc comparisons on each main effect and the interaction, graph each main effect and interaction, and compute each $\eta^2$.

*15.* Only the main effect for difficulty level is significant.

*17.* (a) For low reward $\overline{X} = 8$; for medium $\overline{X} = 10$; and for high $\overline{X} = 12$. It appears that as reward increases, performance increases. (b) For low practice $\overline{X} = 7$; for medium $\overline{X} = 8$; for high $\overline{X} = 15$. It appears that increasing practice increases performance. (c) Yes: How the scores change with increasing reward depends on the level of practice, and vice versa. (d) By comparing the three means within each column and the three means within each row.

*19.* (a) $\overline{X}_{\text{males}} = 8.9$, $\overline{X}_{\text{females}} = 10.1$; that changing from males to females raises scores from around 8.9 to around 10.1. (b) $\overline{X}_{\text{male}} = 11.9$, $\overline{X}_{\text{female}} = 7.1$; that changing from a male to a female experimenter lowers scores from around 11.9 to around 7.1. (c) For males with a male, $\overline{X} = 9.0$; for females with a male, $\overline{X} = 14.8$; for males with a female, $\overline{X} = 8.8$; for females with a female, $\overline{X} = 5.4$. Changing from male to female subjects with a male experimenter increases scores from around 9.0 to around 14.8. Changing from male to female subjects with a female experimenter decreases scores from around 8.8 to around 5.4.

### Chapter 13

*1.* They all test whether, due to sampling error, the data poorly represent the absence of the predicted relationship in the population.

*3.* (a) Either nominal or ordinal scores. (b) They may form very nonnormal distributions, or their populations may not have homogeneous variance, so they are transformed to ranks.

*5.* (a) When the data consist of the frequency that participants fall into each category of one or more variables. (b) When categorizing participants using one variable. (c) When simultaneously categorizing participants using two variables.

*7.* That the sample frequencies are unlikely to represent the distribution of frequencies in the population that are described by $H_0$.

*9.* (a) It is the correlation coefficient between the two variables used in a significant 2 × 2 chi square design. (b) $C$ is the correlation coefficient between the two variables used in a significant two-way chi square that is not a 2 × 2 design.

*11.* (a) $H_0$: The elderly population is 30% Republican, 55% Democrat, and 15% other; $H_a$: Affiliations in the elderly population are not distributed this way. (b) For Republicans, $f_e = (.30)(100) = 30$; for Democrats, $f_e = (.55)(100) = 55$; and for others, $f_e = (.15)(100) = 15$. (c) $\chi^2_{\text{obt}} = 4.80 + 1.47 + .60 = 6.87$ (d) For $df = 2$, $\chi^2_{\text{crit}} = 5.99$, so the results are significant: Party membership in the population of senior citizens is different from party membership in the general population, and it is distributed as in our samples, $p < .05$.

*13.* (a) The frequency with which students *dislike* each professor also must be included. (b) She can perform a separate one-way $\chi^2$ on the data for each professor to test for a difference between the frequency for "like" and "dislike," or she can perform a two-way $\chi^2$ to determine if liking or disliking one professor is correlated with liking or disliking the other professor.

*15.* (a) $H_0$: Gender and political party affiliation are independent in the population; $H_a$: Gender and political party affiliation are dependent in the population. (b) For males, Republican $f_e$ = (75)(57)/155 = 27.58, Democrat $f_e$ = (75)(66)/155 = 31.94, and other $f_e$ = (75)(32)/155 = 15.48. For females, Republican $f_e$ = (80)(57)/155 = 29.42, Democrat $f_e$ = (80)(66)/155 = 34.06, and other $f_e$ = (80)(32)/155 = 16.52. (c) $\chi^2_{obt} = 3.33 + 3.83 + .14 + 3.12 + 3.59 + .133 = 14.14$ (d) With $df = 2$, $\chi^2_{crit} = 5.99$, so the results are significant: In the population, frequency of political party affiliation depends on gender, $p < .05$. (e) $C = \sqrt{14.14/(155 + 14.14)} = .29$, indicating a somewhat consistent relationship.

17. $H_0$ is that the relationship in the ordinal scores in the sample poorly represent that no relationship exists in the population. $H_a$ is that the sample data accurately represent the relationship in the population.
19. (a) The design involved a within-subjects factor with two conditions. (b) The scores were ordinal scores. (c) That the rank scores in one group were significantly higher or lower than those in the other group.
21. By counting the frequency that participants fall into different categories of a nominal variable.

# GLOSSARY

**Alpha** The Greek letter $\alpha$, which symbolizes the criterion, the size of the region of rejection of a sampling distribution, and the theoretical probability of making a Type I error

**Alternative hypothesis** The statistical hypothesis describing the population parameters that the sample data represent if the predicted relationship does exist; symbolized by $H_a$

**Analysis of variance** The parametric procedure for determining whether significant differences exist in an experiment containing two or more sample means; abbreviated ANOVA

**ANOVA** Abbreviation of analysis of variance

**Bar graph** A graph in which a free-standing vertical bar is centered over each score on the *X* axis; used with nominal or ordinal scores

**Between-subjects ANOVA** The type of ANOVA that is performed when a study involves between-subjects factors

**Between-subjects factor** An independent variable that is studied using independent samples in all conditions

**Biased estimator** The formula for the variance or standard deviation involving a final division by *N*, used to describe a sample, but which tends to underestimate the population variability.

**Bimodal distribution** A symmetrical frequency polygon with two distinct humps where there are relatively high-frequency scores and with center scores that have the same frequency

**Cell** In a two-way ANOVA, the combination of one level of one factor with one level of the other factor

**Cell mean** The mean of the scores from one cell in a two-way design.

**Central limit theorem** A statistical principle that defines the mean, standard deviation, and shape of a theoretical sampling distribution

**$\chi^2$-distribution** The sampling distribution of all possible values of $\chi^2$ that occur when the samples represent the distribution of frequencies described by the null hypothesis

**Chi square procedure** The nonparametric inferential procedure for testing whether the frequencies of category membership in the sample represent the predicted frequencies in the population

**Collapsing** In a two-way ANOVA, averaging together all scores from all levels of one factor in order to calculate the main effect means for the other factor

**Complete factorial design** A two-way ANOVA design in which all levels of one factor are combined with all levels of the other factor

**Condition** An amount or category of the independent variable that creates the specific situation under which subjects' scores on the dependent variable are measured

**Confidence interval for $\mu$** A range of values of $\mu$, one of which is likely to be represented by the sample mean

**Confounded comparison** In a two-way ANOVA, a comparison of two cells that differ along more than one factor

**Contingency coefficient** The statistic that describes the strength of the relationship in a two-way chi square when there are more than two categories for either variable; symbolized by *C*

**Continuous scale** A measurement scale that allows for fractional amounts of the variable being measured

**Correlation coefficient** A number that describes the type and the strength of the relationship present in a set of data

**Correlational study** A procedure in which subjects' scores on two variables are measured, without manipulation of either variable, to determine whether they form a relationship

**Criterion** The probability that defines whether a sample is unlikely to have occurred by chance and thus is unrepresentative of a particular population

**Critical value** The value of the sample statistic that marks the edge of the region of rejection in a sampling distribution; values that fall beyond it lie in the region of rejection

**Curvilinear relationship** See *Nonlinear relationship*

**Data point** A dot plotted on a graph to represent a pair of *X* and *Y* scores

**Degrees of freedom** The number of scores in a sample that are free to vary, and thus the number that is used to calculate an estimate of the population variability; symbolized by *df*

**Dependent variable** In an experiment, the variable that is measured under each condition of the independent variable

**Descriptive statistics** Procedures for organizing and summarizing data so that the important characteristics can be described and communicated

**Design** The way in which a study is laid out so as to demonstrate a relationship

**Deviation** The distance that separates a score from the mean and thus indicates how much the score differs from the mean

**Discrete scale** A measurement scale that allows for measurement only in whole-number amounts

**Effect size** An indicator of the amount of influence that changing the conditions of the independent variable had on dependent scores.

**Estimated population standard deviation** The unbiased estimate of the population standard deviation calculated from sample data using degrees of freedom ($N - 1$); symbolized by $s_X$

**Estimated population variance** The unbiased estimate of the population variance calculated from sample data using degrees of freedom ($N - 1$); symbolized by $s_X^2$

**Estimated standard error of the mean** An estimate of the standard deviation of the sampling distribution of means, used in calculating the one-sample *t*-test; symbolized by $s_{\bar{X}}$

**Eta squared** The proportion of variance in the dependent variable that is accounted for by changing the levels of a factor, and thus the measurement of effect size; symbolized by $\eta^2$

**Expected frequency** In chi square, the frequency expected in a category if the sample data perfectly represent the distribution of frequencies in the population as described by the null hypothesis; symbolized by $f_e$

**Experiment** A research procedure in which one variable is actively changed or manipulated, the scores on another variable are measured to determine whether there is a relationship

**Experimental hypotheses** Two statements made before a study is begun, describing the predicted relationship that may or may not be demonstrated by the study

**Experiment-wise error rate** The probability of making a Type I error when comparing all means in an experiment

**Factor** In ANOVA, an independent variable

***F*-distribution** The sampling distribution of all possible values of *F* that occur when the null hypothesis is true and all conditions represent one population $\mu$

***F*-ratio** In ANOVA, the ratio of the mean square between groups to the mean square within groups

**Frequency** The number of times each score occurs within a set of data; also called simple frequency; symbolized by *f*

**Frequency distribution** A distribution of scores, organized to show the number of times each score occurs in a set of data

**Frequency polygon** A graph that shows interval or ratio scores (*X* axis) and their frequencies (*Y* axis), using data points connected by straight lines

**Friedman $\chi^2$ test** The nonparametric version of the one-way, within-subjects ANOVA for ranked scores

***F* statistic** In ANOVA, the statistic used to compare all sample means for a factor to determine whether two or more sample means represent different population means; equal to the *F*-ratio

**Goodness of fit test** A name for the one-way chi square, because it tests how "good" the "fit" is between the data and $H_0$

**Histogram** A graph similar to a bar graph but with adjacent bars touching, used to plot the frequency distribution of a small range of interval or ratio scores

**Homogeneity of variance** A characteristic of data describing populations represented by samples in a study that have the same variance

**Incomplete factorial design** A two-way ANOVA design in which not all levels of the two factors are combined

**Independent samples** Samples created by selecting each participant for one sample, without regard to the participants selected for any other sample

**independent-samples *t*-test** The parametric procedure used for significance testing of sample means from two independent samples

**Independent variable** In an experiment, a variable that is changed or manipulated by the experimenter; a variable hypothesized to cause a change in the dependent variable

**Inferential statistics** Procedures for determining whether sample data represent a particular relationship in the population

**Interval estimation** A way to estimate a population parameter by describing an interval within which the population parameter is expected to fall

**Interval scale** A measurement scale in which each score indicates an actual amount and there is an equal unit of measurement between consecutive scores, but in which zero is simply another point on the scale (not zero amount)

**Kruskal–Wallis *H* test** The nonparametric version of the one-way, between-subjects ANOVA for ranked scores

**Level** In ANOVA, each condition of the factor (independent variable); also called treatment

**Linear regression** The procedure used to predict Y scores based on correlated X scores

**Linear regression line** The straight line that summarizes the scatterplot of a linear relationship by, on average, passing through the center of all *Y* scores

**Linear relationship** A relationship in which the *Y* scores tend to change in only one direction as the *X* scores increase, forming a slanted straight regression line on a scatterplot

**Line graph** A graph of an experiment when the independent variable is an interval or ratio variable; plotted by connecting the data points with straight lines

**Main effect** In a two-way ANOVA, the effect on the dependent scores of changing the levels of one factor; found by collapsing over the other factor

**Main effect mean** The mean of the level of one factor after collapsing across the levels of the other factor.

**Mann–Whitney *U* test** The nonparametric version of the independent-samples *t*-test for ranked scores when *n* is less than or equal to 20

**Matched-samples design** An experiment in which each participant in one sample is matched on an extraneous variable with a participant in the other sample

**Mean** The score located at the mathematical center of a distribution

**Mean square** In ANOVA, an estimated population variance, symbolized by *MS*

**Mean square between groups** In ANOVA, the variability in scores that occurs between the levels in a factor or the cells in an interaction

**Mean square within groups** In ANOVA, the variability in scores that occurs in the conditions, or cells

**Measures of central tendency** Statistics that summarize the location of a distribution on a variable by indicating where the center of the distribution tends to be located

**Measures of variability** Statistics that summarize the extent to which scores in a distribution differ from one another

**Median** The score located at the 50th percentile; symbolized by Mdn

**Mode** The most frequently occurring score in a sample

**Negative linear relationship** A linear relationship in which the *Y* scores tend to decrease as the *X* scores increase

**Negatively skewed distribution** A frequency polygon with low-frequency, extreme low scores but without corresponding low-frequency, extreme high ones, so that its only pronounced tail is in the direction of the lower scores

**Nominal scale** A measurement scale in which each score is used simply for identification and does not indicate an amount

**Nonlinear relationship** A relationship in which the *Y* scores change their direction of change as the *X* scores change; also called a curvilinear relationship

**Nonparametric statistics** Inferential procedures that do not require stringent assumptions about the raw score population represented by the sample data

**Nonsignificant** Describes results that are considered likely to result from chance sampling error when the predicted relationship does not exist; it indicates failure to reject the null hypothesis

**Normal curve** The symmetrical, bell-shaped curve produced by graphing a normal distribution

**Normal distribution** A set of scores in which the middle score has the highest frequency and, proceeding toward higher or lower scores, the frequencies at first decrease slightly, but then decrease drastically, with the highest and lowest scores having very low frequency

**Null hypothesis** The statistical hypothesis describing the population parameters that the sample data represent if the predicted relationship does not exist; symbolized by $H_0$

**Observed frequency** In chi square, the frequency with which participants fall into a category of a variable; symbolized by $f_o$

**One-sample *t*-test** The parametric procedure used to test the null hypothesis for a one-sample experiment when the standard deviation of the raw score population must be estimated

**One-tailed test** The test used to evaluate a statistical hypothesis that predicts that scores will only increase or only decrease

**One-way ANOVA** The analysis of variance performed when an experiment has only one independent variable

**One-way chi square** The chi square procedure for testing whether the sample frequencies of category membership on one variable represent the predicted distribution of frequencies in the population

**Ordinal scale** A measurement scale in which scores indicate rank order

**Parameter** A number that describes a characteristic of a population of scores, symbolized by a letter from the Greek alphabet

**Parametric statistics** Inferential procedures that require certain assumptions about the raw score population represented by the sample data; usually used with scores most appropriately described by the mean

**Participants** The individuals who are measured in a sample

**Pearson correlation coefficient** The correlation coefficient that describes the linear relationship between two interval or ratio variables; symbolized by *r*

**Percentile** The percentage of all scores in the sample that are below a particular score

**Phi coefficient** The statistic that describes the strength of the relationship in a two-way chi square when there are only two categories for each variable; symbolized by $\phi$

**point-biserial correlation coefficient** A statistic for describing a relationship which, when squared, indicates the proportion of variance in dependent scores that is accounted for by the independent variable in a two-sample experiment

**Point estimation** A way to estimate a population parameter by describing a point on the variable at which the population parameter is expected to fall

**Pooled variance** The weighted average of the sample variances in a two-sample experiment; symbolized by $s^2_{\text{pool}}$

**Population** The large group of all possible scores that would be obtained if the behavior of every individual of interest in a particular situation could be measured

**Population standard deviation** The square root of the population variance, or the square root of the average squared deviation of scores around the population mean; symbolized by $\sigma_X$

**Population variance** The average squared deviation of scores around the population mean; symbolized by $\sigma^2_X$

**Positive linear relationship** A linear relationship in which the *Y* scores tend to increase as the *X* scores increase

**Positively skewed distribution** A frequency polygon with low-frequency, extreme high scores but without corresponding low-frequency, extreme low ones, so that its only pronounced tail is in the direction of the higher scores

**Post hoc comparisons** In ANOVA, statistical procedures used to compare all possible pairs of sample means in a significant effect, to determine which means differ significantly from each other

**Power** The probability that a statistical test will detect a true relationship and allow the rejection of a false null hypothesis; the probability of avoiding a Type II error

**Predicted *Y* score** In linear regression, the best prediction of the *Y* scores at a particular *X*, based on the linear relationship summarized by the regression line; symbolized by $Y'$

**Probability** A mathematical statement indicating the likelihood that an event will occur when a particular population is randomly sampled; symbolized by $p$

**Probability distribution** The probability of every possible event in a population, derived from the relative frequency of every possible event in that population

**Proportion of the area under the curve** The proportion of the total area beneath the normal curve at certain scores, which represents the relative frequency of those scores

**Proportion of variance accounted for** The proportion of the differences in scores that is associated with changes in the *X* variable

**Random sampling** A method of selecting samples so that all members of the population have the same chance of being selected for a sample

**Range** The distance between the highest and lowest scores in a set of data

**Ratio scale** A measurement scale in which each score indicates an actual amount, there is an equal unit of measurement, and there is a true zero

**Raw scores** The scores initially measured in a study

**Region of rejection** That portion of a sampling distribution containing values considered too unlikely to occur by chance, found in the tail or tails of the distribution

**Regression line** The line drawn through the long dimension of a scatterplot that best fits the center of the scatterplot, thereby visually summarizing the scatterplot and indicating the type of relationship that is present

**Related samples** Samples created by matching each participant in one sample with a participant in the other sample or by repeatedly measuring the same participant under all conditions

**related-samples *t*-test** The parametric procedure used for significance testing of sample means from two related samples

**Relationship** A correlation between two variables whereby a change in one variable is accompanied by a consistent change in the other

**Relative frequency** The proportion of time a score occurs in a distribution, which is equal to the proportion of the total number of scores that the score's simple frequency represents

**Relative standing** A description of a particular score derived from a systematic evaluation of the score using the characteristics of the sample or population in which it occurs

**Repeated-measures design** A related-samples design in which the same subjects are measured repeatedly under all conditions of an independent variable

**Representative sample** A sample whose characteristics accurately reflect those of the population

**Sample** A relatively small subset of a population, intended to represent the population; a subset of the complete group of scores found in any particular situation

**Sample standard deviation** The square root of the sample variance or the square root of the average squared deviation of sample scores around the sample mean; symbolized by $S_X$

**Sample variance** The average squared deviation of a sample of scores around the sample mean; symbolized by $S^2_X$

**Sampling distribution of *r*** A frequency distribution showing all possible values of the coefficient that occur when samples of a particular size are drawn from a population whose correlation coefficient is zero

**Sampling distribution of differences between means** A frequency distribution showing all possible differences between two means that occur when two independent samples of a particular size are drawn from the population of scores described by the null hypothesis

**Sampling distribution of mean differences** A frequency distribution showing all possible mean differences that occur when the difference scores from two related samples of a particular size are drawn from the population of difference scores described by the null hypothesis

**Sampling distribution of means** A frequency distribution showing all possible sample means that occur when samples of a particular size are drawn from a population

**Sampling error** The difference, due to random chance, between a sample statistic and the population parameter it represents

**Scatterplot** A graph of the individual data points from a set of *X*-*Y* pairs

**Significant** Describes results that are too unlikely to accept as resulting from chance, sampling error when the predicted relationship does not exist; it indicates rejection of the null hypothesis

**Spearman rank-order correlation coefficient** The correlation coefficient that describes the linear relationship between pairs of ranked scores; symbolized by $r_s$

**Squared sum of *X*** A result calculated by adding all scores and then squaring their sum; symbolized by $(\Sigma X)^2$

**Standard error of the difference** The estimated standard deviation of the sampling distribution of differences between the means of independent samples in a two-sample experiment; symbolized by $s_{\bar{X}_1-\bar{X}_2}$

**Standard error of the mean** The standard deviation of the sampling distribution of means; used in the *z*-test (symbolized by $\sigma_{\bar{X}}$) and estimated in the one-sample *t*-test (symbolized by $s_{\bar{X}}$)

**Standard error of the mean difference** The standard deviation of the sampling distribution of mean differences between related samples in a two-sample experiment; symbolized by $s_{\bar{D}}$

**Standard normal curve** A theoretical perfect normal curve, which serves as a model of the perfect normal *z*-distribution

**Standard scores** See *z-score*

**Statistic** A number that describes a characteristic of a sample of scores, symbolized by a letter from the English alphabet

**Statistical hypotheses** Two statements ($H_0$ and $H_a$) that describe the population parameters the sample statistics will represent if the predicted relationship exists or does not exist

**Strength of a relationship** The extent to which one value of *Y* within a relationship is consistently associated with one and only one value of *X;* also called the degree of association

**Subjects** See *Participants*

**Sum of squares** The sum of the squared deviations of a set of scores around a statistic

**Sum of the deviations around the mean** The sum of all differences between the scores and the mean; symbolized as $\Sigma(X - \bar{X})$

**Sum of the squared *X*s** A result calculated by squaring each score in a sample and adding the squared scores; symbolized by $\Sigma X^2$

**Sum of *X*** The sum of the scores in a sample; symbolized by $\Sigma X$

**Tail (of a distribution)** The far-left or far-right portion of a frequency polygon, containing the relatively low-frequency, extreme scores

***t*-distribution** The sampling distribution of all possible values of *t* that occur when samples of a particular size are selected from the raw score population described by the null hypothesis

**Test of independence** A name for the two-way chi square, because it tests whether the frequencies in the categories of one variable are independent of the categories of the other variable

**Treatments** The conditions of the independent variable; also called levels

**Treatment effect** The result of changing the conditions of an independent variable so that different populations of scores having different $\mu$s are produced

**Tukey's *HSD* multiple comparisons test** The post hoc procedure performed with ANOVA to compare means from a factor in which all levels have equal *n*

**Two-tailed test** The test used to evaluate a statistical hypothesis that predicts a relationship but not whether scores will increase or decrease

**Two-way ANOVA** The parametric inferential procedure performed when an experiment contains two independent variables

**Two-way, between-subjects ANOVA** The parametric inferential procedure performed when both factors are between-subjects factors

**Two-way chi square** The chi square procedure for testing whether, in the population, frequency of category membership on one variable is independent of frequency of category membership on the other variable

**Two-way interaction effect** In a two-way ANOVA, the effect in which the relationship between one factor and the dependent scores depends on the level of the other factor that is present

**Two-way, mixed-design ANOVA** The parametric inferential procedure performed when the design involves one within-subjects factor and one between-subjects factor

**Two-way, within-subjects ANOVA** The parametric inferential procedure performed when both factors are within-subjects factors

**Type I error** A statistical decision-making error in which a large amount of sampling error causes rejection of the null hypothesis when the null hypothesis is true (that is, when the predicted relationship does not exist)

**Type II error** A statistical decision-making error in which the closeness of the sample statistic to the population parameter described by the null hypothesis causes the null hypothesis to be retained when it is false (that is, when the predicted relationship does exist)

**Type of relationship** The overall direction in which the $Y$ scores change as the $X$ scores change in a relationship

**Unbiased estimator** The formula for the variance or standard deviation involving a final division by $N - 1$, calculated using sample data to estimate the population variability

**Unconfounded comparisons** In a two-way ANOVA, a comparison of two cells that differ along only one factor

**Unimodal** A distribution whose frequency polygon has only one hump and thus has only one score qualifying as the mode

**Variable** Anything that, when measured, can produce two or more different scores

**Wilcoxon *T* test** The nonparametric version of the related-samples $t$-test for ranked scores

**Within-subjects ANOVA** The type of ANOVA performed when a study involves within-subjects factors

**Within-subjects factor** The type of factor created when an independent variable is studied using related samples in all conditions because subjects are either matched or repeatedly measured

***z*-distribution** The distribution of $z$-scores produced by transforming all raw scores in a distribution into $z$-scores

***z*-score** The statistic that describes the location of a raw score in terms of its distance from the mean when measured in standard deviation units; symbolized by $z$; also known as a standard score because it allows comparison of scores on different kinds of variables by equating, or standardizing, the distributions

***z*-test** The parametric procedure used to test the null hypothesis for a single-sample experiment when the true standard deviation of the raw score population is known

# INDEX